THE GREEKS AND US

THE GREEKS
AND US

ESSAYS IN HONOR OF
ARTHUR W. H. ADKINS

EDITED BY

ROBERT B. LOUDEN
PAUL SCHOLLMEIER

THE UNIVERSITY OF CHICAGO PRESS
CHICAGO & LONDON

ROBERT B. LOUDEN is associate professor of philosophy at the University of Southern Maine. PAUL SCHOLLMEIER is associate professor of philosophy at the University of Nevada, Las Vegas.

The University of Chicago Press, Chicago 60637
The University of Chicago Press, Ltd., London
© 1996 by The University of Chicago
All rights reserved. Published 1996
Printed in the United States of America
05 04 03 02 01 00 99 98 97 96   1 2 3 4 5
ISBN 0-226-49394-6 (cloth)
0-226-49395-4 (paper)

Chapter 4, "Plato's *Crito:* The Authority of Law and Philosophy," is reprinted from James Boyd White, *Acts of Hope: Creating Authority in Literature, Law, and Politics* (University of Chicago Press), © 1994 by The University of Chicago. All rights reserved.

Library of Congress Cataloging-in-Publication Data

The Greeks and us : essays in honor of Arthur W. H. Adkins / edited
by Robert B. Louden and Paul Schollmeier.
p.   cm.
Essays from a conference held Apr. 8–9, 1994, at the University of Chicago.
"The published works of Arthur W. H. Adkins": p.
Includes bibliographical references and index.
ISBN 0-226-49394-6 (cloth : alk. paper). — ISBN 0-226-49395-4 (pbk. : alk. paper)
1. Ethics, Ancient—Congresses.   2. Philosophy, Ancient—Congresses.   3. Greek
literature—History and criticism—Congresses.   4. Greece—Civilization—Con-
gresses.   I. Adkins, A. W. H. (Arthur W. H.)   II. Louden, Robert B., 1953—
III. Schollmeier, Paul.
BJ161.G74   1996
170—dc20   96-16375
CIP

CONTENTS

MEMORIAL NOTE

THE EDITORS NOTE with deep regret and great sadness that Arthur Adkins died while this volume was being prepared for publication. Professor Adkins was a true inspiration to all those who contributed to this volume and to his colleagues and his many students. His loss is deeply felt by all.

ACKNOWLEDGMENTS

THE EDITORS WOULD LIKE to express their thanks to the following individuals and organizations for their support.

First, to the many individuals and groups within the University of Chicago who helped to organize and bring about the symposium in honor of the sixty-fifth birthday of Arthur W. H. Adkins. The symposium took place on April 8–9, 1994, on the University campus, and the essays in this volume grew out of it. Braxton Ross, Elizabeth Asmis, and Christopher Bobonich undertook to act as a local planning committee. Professor Ross, formerly chair of the Classics Department at Chicago, put a great deal of effort into the conference before his untimely death. We are very grateful for his services as chief liaison for participants outside of the University and as a unifying force for the many campus groups involved as well. Cosponsors for the symposium include the Chicago Humanities Institute, the Visiting Committee to the Division of the Humanities, the Classics Department, the Committee on the Ancient Mediterranean World, the Philosophy Department, the Divinity School, and the Law School, all of the University of Chicago. Margot Browning, assistant director of the Chicago Humanities Institute; Patricia McIntosh, secretary of the Classics Department; and David Rehm (formerly a philosophy graduate student, now assistant professor of philosophy at Mount St. Mary's College) also provided valuable aid before and during the symposium.

Second, to the many helpful and efficient staff members at the University of Chicago Press who assisted in the preparation of the manuscript. Special thanks are extended here to T. David Brent, senior editor; Matt Howard, editorial associate; Margaret Mahan, managing editor; Elmer Borklund, who copyedited the manuscript; and Martin White, who prepared the index.

Third, to the Faculty Professional Development Committee of the University of Southern Maine and to the Department of Philosophy at the University of Nevada, Las Vegas, for providing financial support for the editors.

And, finally, a very special thanks to Elizabeth Adkins for her valuable behind-the-scenes support and for her assistance with the editing of the contribution by Professor Adkins and of his bibliography.

INTRODUCTION

Robert B. Louden

THE PAPERS IN THIS VOLUME were originally presented at a symposium in honor of Arthur W. H. Adkins's sixty-fifth birthday, held at the University of Chicago in April of 1994.[1] Beginning with his first book, *Merit and Responsibility: A Study in Greek Values* (1960), Adkins has stimulated continuing debate among a wide range of scholars concerning the overall characterization of ancient Greek ethics, the connections between the various periods and sources of ancient Greek moral thought, and the extent, nature, and causes of the differences between ancient and modern moral values. His work has also provoked predictable methodological skirmishes among specialists about the best way to approach the study of ancient Greek values. Building on the perspectives of earlier scholars such as his teacher E. R. Dodds[2] and Bruno Snell,[3] Adkins has persistently defended his position in such later works as *From the Many to the One: A Study of Personality and Views of Human Nature in the Context of Ancient Greek Society, Values, and Beliefs* (1970) and *Moral Values and Political Behavior in Ancient Greece: From Homer to the End of the Fifth Century* (1972) as well as in an impressive series of articles and critical reviews. He has also written an important book on Greek poetry, *Poetic Craft in the Early Greek Elegists* (1985). Readers will find a bibliography of his major writings at the end of this volume.

Although known as a classicist, Adkins has always revealed a strong concern for the kinds of conceptual issues regarding the uses of language and shifts in word meanings that have engrossed ordinary language philosophers in the twentieth century. Moreover, he has always insisted that moral conceptual schemes can be correctly understood only if one possesses solid empirical knowledge of the larger worldviews that create them. These broader, interdisciplinary concerns have helped to win him a wide readership, one that includes not only classicists and philosophers but also

1

historically oriented social scientists pursuing cross-cultural comparisons, scholars of comparative religion, legal systems, and intellectual history, and indeed all who share a serious interest in ancient Greek values.

Adkins came to the University of Chicago in 1974 and since 1977 has been the Edward Olson Professor of Greek and Professor of Philosophy and Early Christian Literature. He served as Chair of the Classics Department at Chicago (1975–80) and was also founding Chair of the Committee on the Ancient Mediterranean World (1979–92). While at Chicago he also directed two different National Endowment for the Humanities (NEH) Summer Seminars for College Teachers: "Greek Values, Greek Society and the Interpretation of Greek Texts" (1978) and "Ancient Greek Values and Modern Values" (1985). Educated at the University of Oxford, he has had a distinguished career, having held earlier positions at the University of Glasgow (1954–56); Bedford College, University of London (1956–61); Exeter College, Oxford (1961–65); and the University of Reading (1966–74), where he held the Chair in Classics. Adkins was also a Senior Visiting Fellow of the Society for the Humanities at Cornell University in 1969–70.

The eminent contributors to this volume include classicists, philosophers, law professors (one of whom also serves as Chief Judge for the United States Court of Appeals for the Seventh Circuit), historians, and scholars of comparative religion. Several of them also hold joint appointments in disciplines such as English and Comparative Literature as well as in interdisciplinary programs such as South Asian Languages and Civilizations, Social Thought, and the Ancient Mediterranean World. While this diversity of representation testifies to the extremely broad influence of Adkins's work, it also means that the scope of the essays presented here, as well as the assumptions, concerns, and styles of their authors, is wider than is often the case with contemporary scholarly anthologies. As a means of orienting the reader, in the following sections I highlight some of the major connecting themes among the contributions, articulating both the different perspectives represented by the contributors and, where appropriate, their further connections to Adkins's own work and to the scholarly debate that it has generated. My aim here is not (as is often the case with editors' introductions) simply to summarize the contents of each individual contribution but rather to bring some of their underlying connections to light: to show the thematic unity behind the diversity of outlook and style.

PHILOSOPHY AND LITERATURE

Relations between philosophy and literature got off to a bad start when Plato, in one of the least-loved sections of the *Republic,* has Socrates announce that we are justified in banishing poets from the well-governed *polis* (605 b). Yet the strongest point of contact among the following contributions concerns the number of different ways in which the relationship between philosophy and literature arises. Because Adkins's work has always focused on ancient Greek values (particularly *moral* values, though, as we will see below, the contestability of 'moral' is also an issue explored in several of the contributions), the specific arena in which this issue is played out is the sphere of moral values.

Philosophy Versus Literature. Several contributors argue that literature alone can show us what is at stake morally. Lee Yearley, for instance, in his exploration of Herman Melville's account of heroic virtue in *Billy Budd,* writes: "Melville believes only . . . literary techniques and uses of mythic materials can make present what actually happens and is at stake. They alone can focus our attention both on the ambiguity of concrete events and the more important general meanings they may carry. The need to focus our attention is perhaps most pronounced when issues about heroic virtue are the subject; that is, when Melville deals with the highest and lowest reaches of human life, with the heroic in its finest and most twisted forms." Literature was Melville's chosen form, Yearley claims, "in significant part because he thought that literature alone could adequately present ideas and ideals like this one [the ideal of heroic virtue], at least to people in his culture." On this view, the techniques of theory and philosophy are too coarse-grained to catch the relevant moral details; too flat-footed to react properly to the necessary nuances.[4]

In his essay on Sophocles' much under-discussed play, *The Women of Trachis,* Bernard Williams also explores two ways in which fiction can serve as a corrective to "the defective consciousness of moral philosophy." The more familiar way involves "dense fictions," typified above all by realistic novels that provide "a depth of characterization and social background which gives substance to the moral situation and brings it nearer to everyday experience." The second way, championed by Williams himself in his essay and at greater length in his recent book, *Shame and Necessity* (1993), is the way of "stark fictions." The paradigm of stark fictions is found in the tragedies of Sophocles, and they serve to correct the illusions of moral philosophy both by drawing readers' attention to the horrors and undeserved evils of life as well as by eliciting from us appropriate attitudes toward these horrors, attitudes the achievements of which, though "necessarily obscure," do offer "a necessary supplement and a suitable limitation to" the tireless optimism of moral philosophy.

Philosophy as Literature. A different way of viewing philosophy's relationship to literature—particularly in the area of ethics—is found in

James Boyd White's contribution on Plato's *Crito*. Rejecting the often-assumed opposition between the two genres, White announces that his goal is to read

> this "philosophic" text not as a string of propositions but as "literature," that is, with an eye to possibilities of meaning richer and more complex than the propositional; but we would do this in part in the hope of being instructed in the falseness of the way we habitually distinguish between these two forms of thought and expression. It may be that great philosophy is literary in many of its deepest commitments, great literature philosophic, and that what is called for is a way of reading both that attempts to recognize their full dimensions of meaning.[5]

This attempt to read philosophy as literature, White adds, is particularly appropriate in cases where the text in question is a dialogue whose aim is to engage readers' reflective capacities about the conditions under which they must live their lives. Needless to say, the *Crito* fits this criterion perfectly.

Philosophy with Literature. Robert B. Louden, in his Response to Williams, advocates yet another view concerning the relationship between philosophy and literature in the context of ethics. His strategy is not to dissolve the distinction between the two genres but rather to articulate complementary roles for each of them in the larger project of achieving ethical understanding. The concrete imagery and expressive power of literature give it an advantage over abstractions of theory and philosophy at the "initial moment of impact" when we are confronted with a moral problem, but fiction must also turn to moral philosophy when we begin to reflect on the meaning of specific moral examples and their relationship to our own lives. According to this model, there is thus "no need to view the matter as a turf battle which only one side can win."[6]

On the other hand, several other respondents strongly resist all such strategies of reconciliation, on the ground that they mask important differences. Richard Posner, responding to Martha Nussbaum, writes: "I know that rhetoric buffs like to merge the syllogism with the metaphor and everything in between, but I think there are useful distinctions between science and poetry." And Charles Gray, in his Response to White, rejects the easy dichotomy between propositional and performative uses of language in an attempt to articulate more clearly the complex argumentative aims of Plato's *Crito*. The famous speech of the Nomoi (which on White's reading consists merely of a "series of conclusory declarations, with very little argument to support them, and that mostly, though not entirely, of low quality") does, Gray agrees, exhibit "the looseness and multifarious resources" of a forensic speech. But, he adds, this does not mean "that the Nomoi fail to state clearly the best available arguments for the conclusion they want."

From Particulars to Universals: Via Theory or Myth? In the remarks made by several of the contributors about myth we find yet another position concerning the relationship between philosophy and literature. The debate between philosophy and literature within ethics often comes down to the issue of whether pride of place should be granted to particulars or to universals. In their desire to stand back and see how things do (or do not) hang together, philosophers and theorists generally stress universals—wide-ranging conceptual nets intended to explain and justify particular goings-on. Defenders of literature recoil from such flights of abstraction and prefer to embrace the specificity and concreteness of narrative descriptions.

But an important exception to this latter generalization occurs when we examine the role of myths in literature. Precisely because they are stories involving "larger-than-life" characters which occur in a timeless past, myths also involve a move from particulars to universals. As Lévi-Strauss remarks: "Myth is language, functioning on an especially high level where meaning succeeds practically at 'taking off' from the linguistic ground on which it keeps rolling."[8]

Two different examples of this move from particulars to universals by means of myth are explored in the following essays. Yearley initiates his investigation of Melville's moves by remarking that "Melville treasures the concrete but sees it, first, as a locus of ambiguity and, second, as a carrier of larger meanings." The mythic dimensions of *Billy Budd* are then amplified by Respondent Wendy Doniger, who herself has written extensively on Hindu mythology.[9] The seemingly disconnected final chapters of Melville's story (in which varied responses to Billy Budd's life and death are presented) are, she argues, tools of the trade for writers who employ myths. This intended multivalence allows the myth to become "a prism through which all moral views can be refracted." Similarly, Stephanie Nelson, in her exploration of justice and farming in Hesiod's *Works and Days,* argues that abstractions, while "not part of the world of the poem," are "part of the world of the poet" in the sense that the various vignettes of farming found in Hesiod's poem are designed always to inform readers of the will of Zeus. Hesiod's vignettes "are not place holders for abstract philosophical concepts." The snail's trip (a signal to men to begin harvesting) "is not emblematic of the will of Zeus" but rather "the snail's trip *is* the will of Zeus." Respondent David Grene elaborates on Nelson's claim when he concludes that the *Works and Days* is Hesiod's image of "the mythological moment," a moment that exists "when past and present are united, not as in the narrative of history, but in already repeated acts.

Not . . . to control the outcome by repeating the original act, but to participate in an unknowable certainty."

•

Before moving on, a few brief words about how the philosophy-literature relationship problem surfaces in Adkins's own writings are also in order. While none of the above skirmishes features prominently in his work, his writings have generated several more specific methodological debates concerning the relationship between ancient Greek literature and moral philosophy. In his attempts to track the development of ancient Greek values, Adkins has always worked with a variety of both literary and philosophical materials. Part of the explanation here is chronological: his explorations typically begin with the Homeric World, an oral culture in which philosophical texts in the modern sense were simply not produced. He then moves into the more abstract terrains of Plato and Aristotle, carrying the value judgments of Homer's characters along with him. But in proceeding in this manner, Adkins also makes a crucial assumption concerning the relationship between literature and philosophy in the ancient world. The value judgments found in the *Iliad* and *Odyssey* form, he holds, "part of the data of ethics" for Plato and Aristotle, data which the philosophers never sufficiently challenge and analyze, since it is so deeply etched in their own culture.[10] On this score he has been challenged on several fronts. Are we moving more easily than we should from unsystematic Greek popular morality to systematic Greek moral philosophy?[11] To what extent are we even entitled to assume that the value judgments found in Homer's epics correspond to historical reality—refer, that is, to actual moral communities?[12] Can we gain an accurate understanding of ancient Greek moral schemes by focusing exclusively on how a core group of value terms are allegedly used in literary and philosophical texts, or is such a narrowly "lexical approach" guaranteed only to mislead?[13] But despite these and other criticisms of his position on the relationship between ancient Greek literature and philosophy, even his sternest opponents concede that "Adkins has helped to stimulate the currently burgeoning interest in the relationship between Greek literature and moral philosophy."[14]

Moral Versus Nonmoral Values

A second theme which is addressed in several of the contributions concerns the distinction between moral and nonmoral values and the place of this distinction in ancient Greek culture. In a symposium honoring Arthur Adkins, the appearance of this topic is probably inevitable, for the most controversial aspect of his writings has always been his conviction that ancient Greek ethics is radically different from modern understandings of morality.

One way (call it the generic way) to define 'morality' is to use the term to refer to whatever standards of praise and blame intended to influence human conduct and ways of life prevail in a society at a given time. According to this minimal definition, all human societies will have a morality of some sort, if for no other reason than that the activities of praising and blaming one another and of trying to influence each other's behavior and life styles would appear to form an inescapable part of who we are. But sometimes judgments concerning what is 'morally right' or 'morally good' are construed more narrowly to refer exclusively to motives not based on self-interest. On this second view, not all praising and blaming is to be construed as *moral* praising and blaming. We might praise a man for his professional accomplishments, but not be inclined to call him a morally good person if (as is sometimes the case with those who attain a high level of professional achievement) we find out that personal ambition was the driving force in his life, and that this ambition leads him always to put his own interests before the interests of others.

On Adkins's view, the early Greeks possessed morality in the first sense but not in the second. The Greeks of Homeric society praised and blamed one another for things that they did (and did not) do, but the issue of withholding moral judgment until a proper assessment of the agent's motives could be made was not a part of their moral scheme. Rather, they espoused an ethics of success[15] and of self-interest, a value scheme in which the 'competitive' virtues of military prowess and wealth consistently trumped the 'co-operative' or 'quiet' virtues of justice and fairness. And in such an ethics results are clearly what count most: "Success is so imperative that only results have any value: intentions are unimportant."[16]

For those who have read their Nietzsche,[17] such pronouncements concerning ancient Greek morality should come as no surprise. And yet they still have a tendency to shock. Among the many criticisms leveled against Adkins's account of ancient Greek ethics, the following questions deserve pride of place: First, is Adkins fair to the Greeks? He holds that even "the gods as portrayed generally in the Homeric poems are far from just,"[18] but this claim flies in the face of the fact that the Greek word *dikē* (usually translated as 'justice') "connotes a universal order that the gods maintain: this order, though it is by no means moral in the sense in which Christianity believes in a moral order, cannot be said to be without a moral element."[19] Second, can Adkins's frequently deployed distinction between competitive and cooperative virtues really do the work it was designed to do? For instance, if cooperation is (as seems to be the case) often necessary for success, then won't "the majority of actions which might ordinarily be called 'co-operative' . . . prove also to belong to the competitive category,

as Adkins defines it"?[20] And might not some of the virtues deemed by
Adkins to be co-operative or quiet turn out in many instances to be highly
competitive? For instance, *sōphrosunē*, prudence or good sense, "which
might seem to be, and is treated by Adkins as, a 'quiet' virtue, . . . is often
directed to the pursuit of one's own interest with very little regard to anything that could be called co-operation."[21] Third, has Adkins exaggerated
the alleged moral differences between the Greeks and us? Perhaps it is "not
true that there has been as big a shift in underlying [moral] conceptions"
as he supposes, and that there even exist "some unacknowledged similarities between Greek conceptions and our own."[22]

The moral-nonmoral distinction features prominently in two of the
following discussions. In "Justice and Farming in the *Works and Days*,"
Nelson denies that Hesiod makes any kind of modern distinction between
the moral and the practical or useful. "What is in accordance with the will
of Zeus is, for Hesiod, what works in the world as Hesiod knows it." In
arguing that the morally right and pragmatically efficient "are, for Hesiod,
ipso facto, the same" she is in effect reaffirming the presence of Adkins's
ethics of success[23] in early Greek ethics. And she finds this pragmatic ethics
not so much on the human as on the divine plane—precisely where critics
such as Lloyd-Jones claim it does not exist.

Paul Schollmeier's contribution, "Kantian Imperatives and Greek Values," is concerned primarily with Plato and Aristotle and thus examines a
later period of Greek ethics in which (on Adkins's view) the role of intentions and the rightful place of the cooperative virtues are slowly beginning
to make their presence felt. In defending a wider sense of intrinsically valuable activity found in both Plato and Aristotle (one that encompasses a
variety of different practical as well as theoretical endeavors) over Kant's
narrower commitment to autonomous moral choice, Schollmeier takes
exception to Adkins's frequently quoted remark that "we are all Kantians
now."[24] And in intentionally siding with the Greeks over Kant, he endorses Williams's recent claim that "the basic ethical ideas possessed by
the Greeks were different from ours, and also in better condition."[25]

Candace Vogler, in her Response to Schollmeier, overcomes her own
unease with Kantianism to present a more sympathetic account of Kantian self-legislation. Though supportive of Schollmeier's project of focusing on ancient Greek views about "ordinary doings" and noninstrumental
practical attitudes, she remains unconvinced that the Kantian distinction
between hypothetical and categorical imperatives represents the most ef-
ficacious approach to the topic.

Finally, Adkins's own contribution to this volume, "The 'Speech of
Lysias' in Plato's *Phaedrus*," explores some additional differences between ancient Greek and modern conceptions of morality. Building on his

earlier investigations into the important Greek notion of *philia*[26] (usually rendered as 'friendship,' though on Adkins's view this is too narrow, "since 'friendship' in English is usually restricted to relationships in which there is some emotional warmth, whereas *philia* in Greek encompasses all co-operative relationships"), he argues that modern interpreters of Plato's *Phaedrus* have systematically misunderstood the opening speech in the dialogue, assuming (among other things) that Plato's own criticism of the speech "must be made on moral grounds, in some sense of 'moral' instantly comprehensible to the modern reader." Instead, Adkins suggests, the position advocated in the opening speech makes much more sense when interpreted within the context of ancient Greek views concerning the central importance of *philia*-relationships: the need to form dependable alliances of mutual assistance. In maintaining that a youth should form a relationship with a nonlover rather than a lover, Lysias is merely advocating that a sexualized friendship is preferable to an exploitative sexual relationship, at least in the sense that it is "more likely to endure as a stable relationship after sexual desire has cooled." Plato's criticism of Lysias' position is then reinterpreted by Adkins as an attempt to offer "a new account of *eros*," one which escapes the alleged dangers of the old one (in part by pinning the alleged dangers on "an alien who could not appreciate the behavior of Athenians").

THE GREEKS AND US

Adkins has always stressed the otherness of the Greeks[27] in his writings, and in recent years he has also recognized that comparisons between 'us' and 'them' ought not to proceed from overly simplistic accounts of who 'we' are.[28] He announces in the opening sentence of *Merit and Responsibility* that his research "was originally undertaken in the hope that it might make clear to me why I could not understand the moral philosophy of Plato and Aristotle,"[29] and one need scratch only slightly below his proper philological surface to find an amazed anthropologist confronting a foreign culture.

In this last section I wish to discuss not the vexed issue of *how* different the ancient Greeks are from us (a popular and perhaps overworked theme among Adkins and his critics) but rather to illustrate briefly the various ways in which several contributors to this volume use such differences to tell us things about ourselves.

In earlier works such as *The Fragility of Goodness* and *Love's Knowledge,* Martha Nussbaum has raised a variety of new questions about ancient Greek texts for new audiences. Here she explores the relevance of ancient Greek norms to modern sexual controversies in her contribution,

"Platonic Love and Colorado Law." Building on earlier scholarship in this area by such writers as Kenneth Dover, David Halperin, and John J. Winkler,[30] as well as on her personal experience as an expert witness[31] invited to give testimony at a trial in Denver, Colorado, concerning the constitutionality of Amendment 2 (which, until it was declared unconstitutional, barred all local ordinances protecting homosexuals and lesbians from discrimination), Nussbaum argues that ancient Greek texts relating to sexuality "have the potential to make a valuable contribution to our contemporary legal and moral thought, and this in four ways." First, they force us to confront the possibility that what we regard as natural and nearly universal in this area of our conduct is in fact merely conventional and local. Second, they permit us to test empirically whether certain contemporary assumptions made in this area actually hold, namely, that toleration of same-sex acts and relationships leads to a destruction of family life and of the social fabric. Third, we find valuable concrete arguments in ancient Greek texts that same-sex relationships can and do promote important human goals. "They may communicate love, friendship, and joy; they may advance shared political, intellectual, and artistic ends." And fourth, there exists the hope that the empathetic descriptions of such relationships found in Greek literature and philosophy may help contemporary readers of them to view same-sex lovers as fellow human beings rather than as "altogether alien and weird."

Richard Posner, in his Response to Nussbaum, draws attention to two fundamental differences between contemporary American and ancient Greek sexual attitudes—differences which, he believes, render attempts to find contributions to contemporary moral and legal thought in ancient Greek texts much more problematic. The first concerns the fact that the standard form of Greek homosexuality consisted, at least at the onset of the relationship, of relationships between adult men and adolescent boys. But "it is about as difficult to get Americans to view pederasty with anything but horror as it would be to get them to approve of infanticide." (Infanticide was also practiced and approved of by the Greeks.) The second difference is that the situation of homosexuals in societies (such as ancient Greece) of noncompanionate marriage is much easier than it is in societies (such as contemporary America) of companionate marriage. In the former, husband and wife are not expected to be close companions who associate continuously in child rearing and household management, and the husband-wife relationship is not viewed as one of approximate equals, based on mutual respect and affection. In such situations so little "is demanded of the husband that it is easy for homosexuals to have stable marriages and pursue erotic satisfaction on the side." But a society in which companionate marriage is the norm will tend to force out homosexuals, "making them for the first time deviant in a socially significant sense, forcing them into their own subculture, making them strange and even threatening." [32]

A different strategy for using Greek texts to tell us things about ourselves is evident in Bernard Williams's discussion of *The Women of Trachis*. In appealing to the "stark fictions" of Sophoclean tragedy as "a necessary supplement and a suitable limitation to the tireless aim of moral philosophy to make the world safe for well-disposed people," Williams is deploying Greek texts to cut through what he believes to be the mist of Cartesian- and Kantian-inspired modern delusions concerning the soul, freedom, and autonomous choice. It is for this reason that he finds ancient Greek ethical conceptions to be "in better condition" than ours: when properly approached, "they can denounce the falsity or the partiality or the limitations of our images of ourselves." [33]

Finally, a more ambiguous deployment of ancient Greek ethical conceptions is explored by Lee Yearley in "Heroic Virtue in America: Aristotle, Aquinas, and Melville's *Billy Budd*." While emphasizing that the heroic is a basic category for all three thinkers, Yearley also stresses Melville's recognition "that for many modern people heroism is a suspect or discredited notion because it often generates activities or people that are problematic at best." Melville, unlike Aristotle and Aquinas, "stresses the deficiencies that must accompany modern heroism," the "slim confidence that aspiring modern heroes will have," and "the immense difficulties that even decent people will have in approaching a heroic standard." In other words, Melville is intentionally placing ancient Greek moral categories into a context where they do not fit seamlessly as a means of forcing his readers to confront the changed moral situation of modern Americans.

The reader will doubtless find many more points of contact among the papers in this volume than those surveyed above, as well as many points of agreement and disagreement that are not intimated in what I have said. It is as an aid to such discoveries that I have introduced these signposts.

•

The days when a dramatist would have a character in one of his plays earnestly proclaim that "nobody can say a word against Greek: it stamps a man at once as an educated gentleman" are clearly over. [34] Many people today (including at least one of the contributors to this volume) are convinced that our former infatuation with Greece will shrink drastically in the near future. Posner, for instance, in resisting Nussbaum's pleas on behalf of the contributions that ancient Greek texts can supposedly bring to contemporary moral and legal thought, notes that "there may be other judges and public officials besides myself in whose mental world Plato and Aristotle figure largely, but if so I don't know any. Between computer-style modernity and multiculturalism, I believe the role of classical civilization in American thinking is going to shrink rather than expand in the coming years." Still, perhaps we should be more cautious in making predictions concerning what future generations will or will not respond to in ancient Greek culture. Many of the themes that feature prominently in the following discussions would not even have been mentioned in a scholarly book on the Greeks published only a short while ago. Somehow, part of the process by which modernity takes in other traditions and continually readjusts its self-image seems at some point always to include a reexamination of the Greeks. Regardless of whether one views the Greeks as an exotic race whose mores shock and bewilder modern sensibilities, or as not so terribly different from us in their fundamental standards of praise and blame and in their moral ideals, or as somewhere (but where, precisely?) in between, the sense that one cannot ignore them is still hard to shake off.

NOTES

1. Adkins's own contribution, "The 'Speech of Lysias' in Plato's *Phaedrus*," is presented here for the first time.

2. See especially *The Greeks and the Irrational* (Berkeley: University of California Press, 1951). The dedication page on Adkins's second book, *From the Many to the One*, reads: "Eric Robertson Dodds—in whose steps must follow all who wish to understand the ancient Greeks."

3. *Die Entdeckung des Geistes* (Hamburg: Claassen und Goverts, 1948), translated by T. G. Rosenmeyer as *The Discovery of the Mind: The Greek Origins of European Thought* (Cambridge: Harvard University Press, 1953). In the preface to *Merit and Responsibility* (Oxford: Clarendon Press, 1960), Adkins notes that his own "manner of treatment owes much to Professor Snell's *Endeckung des Geistes*" (vi). Many of Snell's key assumptions concerning Homer's characters are criticized by contributor Bernard Williams in his *Shame and Necessity* (Berkeley: University of California Press, 1993). See especially 21–26, 28, 29, 33, 178, n. 21, 180, n. 32, 182, n. 44, and 193, n. 5.

4. Martha Nussbaum, another contributor to this volume, has also defended the superiority of literature over philosophy in developing ethical understanding in many of her writings. In the introduction to *Love's Knowledge: Essays on Philosophy and Literature* (New York: Oxford University Press, 1990), she states that "certain truths about human life can only be fittingly and accurately stated in the language and forms characteristic of the narrative artist. With respect to certain elements of human life, the terms of the novelist's art are alert winged creatures, perceiving where the blunt terms of ordinary speech, or of abstract theoretical discourse, are blind, acute where they are obtuse, winged where they are dull and heavy" (5).

5. The attempt to break down the assumed dichotomy between philosophy and literature is a pervasive theme in many of White's writings. See, for example, *When*

Words Lose Their Meaning: Constitutions and Reconstitutions of Language, Character, and Community (Chicago: University of Chicago Press, 1984), chapter 4; *Heracles' Bow: Essays on the Rhetoric and Poetics of the Law* (Madison: University of Wisconsin Press, 1985), xi–xii, 127–28; and *Justice as Translation: An Essay in Cultural and Legal Criticism* (Chicago: University of Chicago Press, 1990), xi–xii, 29–31, 250–51. Nussbaum (in less adversarial moments) also raises "the idea of a philosophical style that is the ally of literature, one that is not identical to the styles of the literary works, but directs the reader's attention to the salient features of those works, setting their insights in a perspicuous relation to other alternatives, other texts" (*Love's Knowledge*, 49).

6. I pursue this theme at greater length in *Morality and Moral Theory: A Reappraisal and Reaffirmation* (New York: Oxford University Press, 1992), 152–58.

7. Generally but not always. Antitheorists (many of whom are philosophers) hold that the generalizing strategies of theory are misguided enterprises, particularly when applied in the fields of ethics and literature. See, for example, *Against Theory: Literary Studies and the New Pragmatism*, edited by W. J. T. Mitchell (Chicago: University of Chicago Press, 1985); and *Anti-Theory in Ethics and Moral Conservatism*, edited by Stanley G. Clarke and Evan Simpson (Albany: State University of New York Press, 1989).

8. Claude Lévi-Strauss, *Structural Anthropology*, translated by Claire Jacobson and Brooke Grundfest Schoepf (Garden City: Anchor Books), 206.

9. See, for example, *Other Peoples' Myths: The Cave of Echoes* (New York: Macmillan, 1988); *Tales of Sex and Violence: Folklore, Sacrifice, and Danger in the Jaiminiya Brahmans* (Chicago: University of Chicago Press, 1985); *Women, Androgynes, and Other Mythical Beasts* (Chicago: University of Chicago Press, 1980); *The Origins of Evil in Hindu Mythology* (Berkeley: University of California Press, 1976); and *Asceticism and Eroticism in the Mythology of Siva* (New York: Oxford University Press, 1973).

10. *Merit and Responsibility*, 9.

11. K. J. Dover, *Greek Popular Morality In the Time of Plato and Aristotle* (Oxford: Basil Blackwell, 1974; reprint ed., Indianapolis: Hackett Publishing Company, 1994), especially 1–5. See also Adkins's critical review "Problems in Greek Popular Morality," *Classical Philology* 73 (1978): 143–58.

12. A. A. Long, "Morals and Values in Homer," *Journal of Hellenic Studies* 90 (1970): 121–139. See also Adkins's reply, "Homeric Values and Homeric Society," *Journal of Hellenic Studies* 91 (1971): 1–14.

13. Compare Richard Robinson, review of *Merit and Responsibility*, *Philosophy* 32 (1962), 279; Hugh Lloyd-Jones, *The Justice of Zeus* (Berkeley: University of California Press, 1971), 2–3; Dover, *Greek Popular Morality*, 46–50; "The Portrayal of Moral Emotions in Greek Poetry," *Journal of Hellenic Studies* 103 (1983): 35–48; and Adkins, "Problems in Greek Popular Morality," 153.

14. Mary Whitlock Blundell, *Helping Friends and Harming Enemies: A Study in Sophocles and Greek Ethics* (Cambridge: Cambridge University Press, 1989), 5. Blundell briefly surveys and endorses a number of criticisms of Adkins's approach on 4–5.

15. It should be emphasized that Adkins was not the first to characterize Homeric morality in this manner. Bruno Snell, for instance, in analyzing the value

judgments found in the *Iliad* and *Odyssey,* writes: "The formula: 'it seemed better to him' means literally: 'it seemed more profitable, more remunerative to him.' The decision is made on the grounds that one alternative is recognized as the more advantageous procedure" (*The Discovery of the Mind,* 103). See n. 3 above.

16. Adkins, *Merit and Responsibility,* 35. This is not to say to Homer's characters lack intentions or are represented by him as not making decisions. This is not part of Adkins's view, although critics such as Williams have attributed it to him (see, for example, *Shame and Necessity,* 50–52, 63–64). But it is to say that on Adkins's view assessments of intentions are unimportant in the moral value judgments made by Homer's characters and that assessments concerning results are paramount. Homeric ethics, on Adkins's view, thus can be seen as a particular application of Machiavelli's famous consequentialist pronouncement that "in the actions of all men, and especially of princes, where there is no impartial arbiter, one must consider the final result." (*The Prince,* translated by Peter Bondanella and Mark Musa [New York: Oxford University Press, 1984], 60).

17. Nietzsche writes that "the judgment 'good' did *not* originate with those to whom 'goodness' was shown! Rather it was 'the good' themselves, that is to say, the noble, powerful, high-stationed and high-minded, who felt and established themselves and their actions as good, that is, of the first rank, in contradistinction to all the low, low-minded, common and plebian." (*On the Genealogy of Morals,* First Essay, section two; translated by Walter Kaufmann [New York: Random House, 1967]). Oddly enough, Hugh Lloyd-Jones, a persistent critic of Adkins's failure to grasp the role of justice in ancient Greek ethics (see note 19 below), claims that Nietzsche "is not an immoralist, except in the sense that he criticises modern notions about morals" (*Blood for the Ghosts: Classical Influences in the Nineteenth and Twentieth Centuries* [Baltimore: Johns Hopkins University Press, 1982], 167). Nietzsche and Lloyd-Jones would seem to have radically different understandings of ancient Greek ethics.

18. Adkins, *Merit and Responsibility,* 62. In a similar vein Adkins's teacher E. R. Dodds writes: "I find no indication in the narrative of the *Iliad* that Zeus is concerned with justice as such" (*The Greeks and the Irrational* [Berkeley: University of California Press, 1957], 32).

19. Hugh Lloyd-Jones, "A Note on Homeric Morality," *Classical Philology* 82 (1987), 310. (Lloyd-Jones argues for this claim at much greater length in *The Justice of Zeus.*)

20. A. A. Long, "Morals and Values in Homer," *Journal of Hellenic Studies* 90 (1970), 123. See also Adkins's reply in "Homeric Values and Homeric Society," *Journal of Hellenic Studies* 91 (1971), 3ff.

21. J. L. Creed, "Moral Values in the Age of Thucydides," *Classical Quarterly* 23 (1973), 215. Adkins does include *sōphrosunē* as one of the quiet virtues in *Merit and Responsibility,* 37, 61. However, on 247 he also acknowledges that the term refers to "prudence in one's own interests." Adkins replies at length to Creed's criticisms in "Merit, Responsibility, and Thucydides," *Classical Quarterly* 25 (1975): 209–220. Creed, in "Is it Wrong to Call Plato a Utilitarian?" *Classical Quarterly* 28 (1978): 352–65, acknowledges that "Adkins rightly takes me to task . . . for appearing to suggest that he did not appreciate the importance of the

co-operative element in competitive virtue, or of the prudential element in *sōphro-sunē*" (360, n. 53).

22. Bernard Williams, *Shame and Necessity,* 7, 2.

23. Albeit a kind of success in which "knowledge and skills different from those of the fighting man are needed" (*Merit and Responsibility,* 72).

24. *Merit and Responsibility,* 2, compare 253. Schollmeier is not the first critic to take exception to Adkins's generalization. Dover, for instance, writes: "Unless I am seriously deceiving myself, I and most of the people I know well find the Greeks of the Classical period easier to understand than Kantians" (*Greek Popular Morality,* 3, n. 3).

25. Bernard Williams, *Shame and Necessity,* 4.

26. Arthur W. H. Adkins, "'Friendship' and 'Self-Sufficiency' in Homer and Aristotle," *Classical Quarterly* 13 (1963): 30–45. Martha Nussbaum also comments briefly on the speech of Lysias in her contribution to this volume.

27. In this respect too he follows Snell, who cautions readers on the first page of his introduction that "we are quick to forget how radically the experience of Homer differs from our own" (*The Discovery of the Mind,* v).

28. In "The 'Morality' of Homer," for instance, Adkins notes that "it seems appropriate to inquire what characteristics 'our morality' has. No simple answer can be given. At the present time, there are four major types of moral philosophers, distinguished by the prominence that they give to duties, rights, ends, and virtues. Virtue-ethics, nearly extinct for many years, has recently returned to the scene. Each of the four camps disagrees with the other three. Many would disagree with the other three. No virtue-ethicist would accept as virtues only characteristics that *cannot* benefit their possessors" (*Classical Philology* 82 [1987], 313). This passage differs radically in tone from that of the "We're all Kantians now" opening of *Merit and Responsibility.*

29. *Merit and Responsibility,* 1.

30. K. J. Dover, *Greek Homosexuality* (Cambridge: Harvard University Press, 1978); David M. Halperin, *One Hundred Years of Homosexuality: and Other Essays on Greek Love* (London: Routledge, 1990); and John J. Winkler, *The Constraints of Desire: The Anthropology of Sex and Gender in Ancient Greece* (London: Routledge, 1990).

31. For a brief account of Nussbaum's testimony (and her exchange with fellow expert witness John Finnis), see *The New Republic,* 15 November 1993, 12–13.

32. Both of these issues are pursued by Posner at much greater length in *Sex and Reason* (Cambridge: Harvard University Press, 1992). See especially 41–44. For a somewhat different account of same-sex relationships in ancient Greece than that found in either Nussbaum or Posner, see Adkins's contribution, "The 'Speech of Lysias' in Plato's *Phaedrus.*" Posner's second point concerning companionate marriage has an obvious heterosexual assumption behind it, and it would seem that the concept of companionate marriage is detachable from this assumption. In a society where companionate marriage (of either a heterosexual or same-sex variety) is the norm, greater demands are placed on marriage partners, and those who wish to pursue erotic satisfactions on the side in such a society will indeed be

"deviant in a socially significant sense." But in such a society it will not necessarily be only homosexuals who are the "deviants."

33. Bernard Williams, *Shame and Necessity*, 4, 20. See also 26, n. 15, 41–42 nn., and 43–44 for examples of alleged Cartesian and Kantian assumptions in modern interpretations of the Greeks.

34. Bernard Shaw, *Major Barbara*, in *Bernard Shaw: Complete Plays with Prefaces*, vol. 1 (New York: Dodd, Mead & Company, 1963), 344. The speaker is Lady Britomart, who is referring to her future son-in-law, Adolphus Cusins, professor of Greek. According to one critic, "it is a well-known fact that Shaw based Adolphus Cusins, his professor of Greek, on Gilbert Murray, but it is less well known that he based Lady Britomart on Murray's real-life mother-in-law, Lady Rosalind Howard, Countess of Carlisle. (Shaw jokingly told Murray in a letter that he was at work on a play to be called 'Murray's Mother-in-law')" (Louis Crompton, *Shaw the Dramatist* [Lincoln: University of Nebraska Press, 1969], 105). In a note which immediately precedes the play, Shaw also hints that it "stands indebted to him [Murray] in more ways than one" (*Complete Plays*, vol. 1, 340). Murray held the Regis Chair of Greek at Oxford University from 1909 to 1936 and was an extremely influential teacher, translator, and scholar in his day. See, for example, Lloyd-Jones's tribute on 195–214 of *Blood for the Ghosts*. For a valuable discussion of Victorian England's infatuation with the Greeks, see Richard Jenkyns, *The Victorians and Ancient Greece* (Cambridge: Harvard University Press, 1980). Jenkyns notes, for instance, that for the Victorians, even "more than Latin, Greek was the stamp that authenticated culture and class" (63); and that from "Coleridge to Kingsley, from Sydney to Wilde, writers loved to declare that the very language of Greece was an enchantment, and far superior even to the Latin tongue" (155).

1

JUSTICE AND FARMING IN THE WORKS AND DAYS

Stephanie Nelson

HE *WORKS AND DAYS* IS NOT A POEM ABOUT JUSTICE AND FARM-
ING.[1] It is a poem about human life. Or at least so one might judge
from the number and variety of aspects of life that it deals with.
The poem presents its various topics in sections. After the Proem, Hesiod
uses the two Erides (and war and farming and begging and pottery) to
introduce us to Perses and the court case. This introduction is followed by
a section of myths, and a fable, which provide the theological background
to the poem. The myths are followed by the section on *dikē*, "justice,"
which is followed by what West calls a "free-wheeling" section, which
contains advice on honesty, hard work, and social relations.[2] The next
section is on farming, followed by its complement, sailing.[3] Then another
"free-wheeling" section, on social relations and religious taboos, and finally the "Days." Farming and justice are only two sections out of nine.
They neither begin the poem nor end it, nor, in any simple count, either of
lines or of sections, are they particularly central.

Nonetheless, as Aristotle says, following Hesiod, "No talk dies out
altogether which many people give voice to" (*WD* 763–64; *Ethics*
1153b27). The poem is not, as it is sometimes made out to be, a farmer's
handbook appended to the exhortations of an Old Testament prophet.[4]
But a persistent feeling remains that the *Works and Days is* concerned, in
some particular way, with justice and farming.

The *Theogony*, like the *Works and Days,* can seem a hodgepodge. But
once its central idea, the rise of Zeus and the emergence of his order, is
grasped, the unity of the poem becomes clear.[5] The *Works and Days* has
two such ideas—justice and farming. If we picture the *Theogony* as a
circle, we should picture the *Works and Days* as an ellipse, defined by
these two focal points. The geometrical analogy is interesting because it is
not either focal point of an ellipse, in itself, which defines the figure, but
the relation between the two. If the analogy holds one cannot examine the

Works and Days like the man who learned Chinese metaphysics by first studying Chinese, and then studying metaphysics. Even given that the *Works and Days* is about farming and justice, we cannot understand it by examining justice, or farming, in isolation. In order to grasp the theme and unity of the poem we must try to see how justice and farming are related.

FARMING

I will start, in the reverse order from Hesiod, with farming. I do so because there is something pleasantly definite about farming, while an examination of the archaic concept of *dikē* seems, occasionally, like the event held in State Fairs in Maine, where a gang of children attempts to capture a greased pig. We have, incidentally, no reason to believe that Hesiod felt this way. Hesiod no more explains to his audience what *dikē* is than he explains what farming is. Men must have farms, and they must have courts. Hesiod assumes for the one, as he assumes for the other, what they are. What he is interested in is what they *mean*. This, I believe, he conveys as much in the way in which he presents farming, or justice, as in what he says about them.

Although it is always fun to do, there is really no need to demonstrate that not only is the *Works and Days* not a farming manual, but neither is its farming section.[6] Neither Perses, nor the kings, nor Hesiod's wider audience needed to be taught how to farm. Those who farmed already knew; those who did not did not need to learn. Consequently Hesiod does not teach farming. It is, I think, true that a number of aphorisms in the *Works and Days* stem from traditional farmers' proverbs, and these are intended, in some sense, to be instructive. Most of these occur in the thirty lines preceding the opening of the farmer's year, the farmer's year itself being one of the least aphoristic sections of the poem.[7] Proverbs like them are no less common today than they were in Hesiod's time. To quote two of my favorites: "Be not the first by whom the new is tried,/ Nor yet the last to lay the old aside" and (a very Hesiodic one, if Hesiod had been a Christian) "Live as if to die tomorrow; farm as if to live forever." There is a great deal of truth in these proverbs. They do not, however, teach you how to farm.

What Hesiod's section on farming accomplishes is not instruction, but description. What it describes is what it feels like to farm. It does so by describing the farmer's year.[8] The year is not merely an organizing principle for the section. It is the hero of the piece, alive, in its bustle and *longeurs*, its intensity and relaxation, its heat and cold, its frustrations, anxieties, and comforts. For each season Hesiod creates a little picture, a vignette.[9] The detail he evokes is not only precise—the relief that comes with the autumn rains, the shrill, continual whine of the crickets in summer, the howl of the North wind in the forests in January, the strain on the yoke-straps as the oxen begin to plow—it is, most often, sensory. We are invited not merely to *see*, but to *feel*, each picture, and so each season. Details such as the chirp of the crickets, the flight of the wild beasts before the North wind, the feel of a gentle West wind on one's face in the summer heat do not teach us how to farm. They are not even really describing farming. What they are describing is the *experience* of farming.

Each of Hesiod's individual vignettes is in itself a snapshot. But when these snapshots are taken together, the section is transformed from a collection of static scenes into a dynamic whole. The real force of Hesiod's description appears not in the picture of any single season, but in their sequence—the drama of Hesiod's year. We can see this best by taking a quick trip through it.

The year begins in early fall, after the harvest and threshing are over, before the time for the fall plowing and sowing. In the following section on sailing Hesiod points out that this is the time for sailing, since there is nothing really critical to be done on the farm. Here he suggests cutting wood and getting tools ready. It is a relaxed time. Hesiod takes over thirty lines (*WD* 414–47), more than three times the space that he allots to the harvest (*WD* 571–81), to describe it.

What Hesiod has been gradually leading us up to, with his making of a wagon and plows and his discussion of the best age for oxen and plowmen, is the fall plowing and sowing. Here Hesiod increases the tempo. We are given three short vignettes rather than one long one. We listen to the voice of the crane who "bites at the heart of an oxenless man" (*WD* 451). We are reminded of the fallow we may or may not have adequately broken the spring before. And finally we see the archetypical moment, the moment when, with a prayer to Zeus and Demeter, you grasp the plow-stilt in your hand, the oxen strain against the straps, and the little slave boy follows behind with his mattock, "making work for the birds" (*WD* 470). Hesiod captures the tension of the moment by jumping ahead, to a picture of a good harvest, one of a disastrous harvest, and one of a harvest rescued at the last moment. One can never know.

Winter is next. It lasts a long time. The wild beasts in the forests, the cattle and the goats, the old man "running like a wheel" (*WD* 518), all shrink before the North wind. Even the octopus, "in his fireless home and miserable haunts" (*WD* 525), seems to feel it. Only the sheep, with their woolly coats, and the young girl taking a nap inside, "not yet knowing the works of golden Aphrodite" (*WD* 521), stay warm. But, after sixty lines, spring comes, and in barely twenty lines Hesiod jumps us ahead three months, to the spring harvest. We are hardly prepared. Hesiod tells us to hurry.

And then it is summer. Fifteen lines describing the leisure of a summer picnic lead into the last details of the year: finishing the threshing, storing the grain, arranging about the servants, getting a dog to watch the stores. Finally we rest. But then it is time for the vintage and that hardly is finished when, in mid-line, the Pleiades appear once more, and it is time, before we were quite aware of it, to start the sowing again. The year has, as (I think) Hesiod says, come full circle (WD 617). Everything done in its season has returned unto itself again.

Hesiod's description of the farmer's year is carefully crafted. What it reveals, above all, is a feeling for the balance of nature. There is first the balance inherent in the regular cycle of the seasons, of winter against summer, heat against cold, rainy season against dry. There is also the balance that the farmer feels, a balance which Hesiod brings out in two sequences of anticipation, hurry, and rest, first in the leisurely wood cutting of early fall, the rush of the later fall plowing, and the long cold wait of winter, and second, in the early spring pruning, the urgent spring harvest, and the relaxation of a summer picnic outside in the heat.[10] And as the spring is balanced against the fall, so also the cold winter anticipation of the harvest is balanced against the summer certainty, good or bad, of the harvest itself. Then there is preparing the oxen in the fall, the half-rations of the oxen in the winter, and the rest of the oxen in summertime. There is the spring pruning of the vines, just before harvesting, and the fall gathering in of the grapes, just before sowing. This is what the drama of Hesiod's account adds, the balance not only of nature, but also of the way the farmer must live with nature, suiting his rhythms to hers.

Hesiod's description of farming leaves us with a sense of balance, but it also leaves us with a sense of the complexity of that balance. The complexity occurs first in the number of elements it contains. Hesiod is describing the seasons, but a season is not a thing; it is rather a conjunction of events. In making us feel the farmer's experience of farming, Hesiod continually draws our attention outward, toward the constellations, the winds, the wild creatures, and all the elements that partly are, and partly are not, of the farm. Hesiod's third harvest is rescued:

> When the cuckoo calls cuckoo from the leaves of the oak
> At first, and brings joy to men over the boundless earth,
> Then, if Zeus should rain on the third day and not cease
> Neither over nor under-filling the hoof-mark of the ox,
> Thus the late-plower might rival the man who plowed early.
>
> WD 486–90

And there is a time for spring sailing:

> When at first, as much as a crow, going forward
> Makes its track, so much a man sees the leaves
> Sprout on the top of the fig-tree, then the sea is passable.
>
> WD 679–81

These passages are particularly vivid examples of an overall tendency. Hesiod composes his vignettes out of the multiplicity of his world. They are also examples of the second complexity that Hesiod introduces into the balance—the sense of risk. The "right season" for any task is always somewhat equivocal. Spring sailing is, as Hesiod says, "snatched" (WD 684), as we would say, from the jaws of disaster.[11] Yet, driven by need, men sail even in the spring. Harvests are sometimes saved at the last moment, and sometimes not. As Hesiod says: "One way at one time and another at another is the mind of Zeus who holds the aegis./ It is a hard thing for mortal men to understand" (WD 483–84). To farm is to live by the rhythm Zeus has established in the seasons. But Zeus does not always make the seasons work the same way.

Hesiod creates a drama in our experience of farming by making us experience the variables of the farmer's world. We sow not by rule, on the fifteenth of November, but when the crane flies overhead. We prune our vines with the swallow and harvest with the snail. Despite the usual feeling that Hesiod is a dour old curmudgeon whose only concern is that we should see that life means work, work, and more work, there is very little feeling of the harshness of labor in the farming section itself.[12] What there is instead is a deep sense of the balance of the seasons, and of the nearly infinite number of factors, heat and cold, rain and sun, deer, snails and swallows, stars and winds, which make up each one of what we call a season. This balance is not one Hesiod invented. The balance is that of the order of Zeus, as it is expressed in the Seasons, Zeus' daughters. It is the balance of Genesis, of "seedtime and harvest, and cold and heat, and summer and winter, and day and night" (Genesis 8:22). It is for Hesiod, as it is for Genesis, the order of god. It is also, for Hesiod, perilous.

JUSTICE, THE UNIVERSAL BALANCE

Justice is, in many ways, similar to the Seasons. She too is a daughter of Zeus. In fact, at the end of the *Theogony,* she, along with Peace and Good Order, *are* the Seasons, in an identification apparently original to Hesiod. The passage implies that Hesiod associates justice and farming, which depends upon the seasons. It does not tell us *how* he associates them. To discover that we need to turn to the *Works and Days,* where, perversely, Hesiod never make the identification.[13]

Justice, as we all know, is a balance. Even today she holds her scales, although blindfolded, which would have surprised Hesiod. In the *Oresteia* justice is the balance that demands that a man suffer as he has done (*Choephoroi,* 62–67, 306–12). With an agricultural twist, which no doubt created the identification, the Scholiast on the Ethics quotes Hesiod: "If a man sows evil, he will reap an evil profit;/ If he suffers as he has done, justice will be straight" (Fragment 286).[14] Nor is it idiosyncratic of Aristotle, in Book Five of the *Ethics,* to discuss justice in terms of proportion (1132b20–1134a15). As Aristotle implies, the Greek word *isos,* meaning both "equal" and "fair," almost demands that justice be discussed in terms of a balance. I remember Professor Adkins once pointing out that we should not attribute a belief in a clockwork destiny to people who did not have clocks. We should also recall that when Hesiod, or Aristotle, speaks of a fair exchange, or, in our expression, of "paying someone back," he is not thinking of digital scales. A balance is the tool that Hesiod, or Aristotle, would have used to measure what was fair and just.[15]

Justice, through the idea of the balance, is related to a complex of ideas, of measure (*metron*), proportion (*kairos*), and season (*hōra*), as important as any in Greek thought.[16] Largely because of this set of associations the Greek word *dikē* has a range much larger than our word "justice" or than the Latin *justitia.* We need only recall Zeus' scales in the *Iliad,* Heraclitus' fragment ("It is necessary to know that war is common, that dikē is strife, and that all things come to be according to strife and necessity") or Anaximander's ("for things give *dikē* and retribution to each other for *adikia* according to the assessment of time") to see how far this complex can extend. Its range can be little less than cosmic. Hence for Jane Harrison "Dikē . . . is the way of life of each natural thing, each plant, each animal, each man. It is also the way, the usage, the regular course of that great animal the Universe, the way that is made manifest in the Seasons, in the life and death of vegetation; and when it comes to be seen that these depend on the heavenly bodies, Dikē is manifest in the changes of the rising and setting of constellations, in the waxing and waning of the moon and in the daily and yearly courses of the sun."[17]

HESIOD'S "THIS *DIKĒ* HERE"

With the pronouncement of the Cambridge school our work appears to be complete. *Dikē* is the way of nature, and as farming is clearly dependent upon nature, the relation of justice and farming seems self-evident. Nor are the notions of measure, proportion, and season, upon which the cosmic implications of *dikē* depend, absent in the *Works and Days.* The

Works and Days uses key words to link together Hesiod's otherwise separate sections.[18] These are, as it were, the threads which run throughout the various segments of the fabric, and unite them into one overall design. Prominent among them are "measure" (*metron*), "proportion" (*kairos*), and "season" (*hōra*)—"seasonableness" is, in fact, the single dominant theme of the sections on farming and sailing.[19] Only the smallest of steps is still required to link Hesiod's idea of justice to the way of "that great animal, the Universe."

Hesiod never takes that step. He does not use the key words *metron*, *kairos*, and *hōra* in the section on *dikē*, and he does not bring up *dikē* when he is using these key words. Far from seeing *dikē* as "the way of Nature," Hesiod does his best to deny just this, telling Perses that animals eat one another, while to man, apparently exclusively, Zeus gave *dikē* (*WD* 276–80). "Justice" in the *Works and Days* is pragmatic and concrete. As Michael Gagarin points out, there is barely a single use of the word *dikē* in the *Works and Days* which does not refer simply to the assembly where the "gift-gobbling" kings render their decisions.[20] When Hesiod speaks of kings, he means *these* kings, the ones who like to judge "this *dikē* here" (*WD* 38–39, 268–69); when Hesiod says *dikē*, he tends to mean the same, not a universal concept but "this justice right here"—the case between himself and Perses.

For reasons I mostly will not go into here, I do not believe that the conclusion which Gagarin draws, that *dikē* in the *Works and Days* has only a judicial but not a moral sense, is tenable. Hesiod sees all the usual moral offenses, such as maltreatment of suppliants, guest-friends, or parents, as offenses against *dikē*. That he does so is clear from the passage in the *Works and Days* which declares that Zeus sees the snatching of wealth as equivalent to these offenses and upon all such "unjust deeds" brings a harsh return (*WD* 32–34). Moreover, that Hesiod understands there to be some standard for dikē higher than the courts is clear from the whole argument of the poem, which is that the kind of *dikē* that Perses and the kings deal in is not good enough. There is a "moral" as well as a merely "legal" sense to the word *dikē*. Alongside the *dikē* of the law court is *Dikē*, the daughter of Zeus, who should be manifested in it. When she is not, when men "drive her out and judge her not straightly" (*WD* 224), they pay for it.

But, for all this, the difficulty that Gagarin raises remains. Hesiod discusses *dikē* only in the judicial sense of the word. Of twenty-five uses of the word in the *Works and Days,* twenty-one occur in the section of the poem which is specifically about the courts. Of *all* the uses of *dikē* in the poem, only one, *WD* 712, occurs outside of any judicial context whatsoever.[21]

The obvious reason for this is the one that Hesiod points to: Perses.

This is how, at the very beginning of the poem, the subject of *dikē* is introduced, and this is the kind of *dikē* that Hesiod sticks to. The purpose of the poem is not to prove to Perses and the kings that they cannot pervert the "way of nature" or the "way of life." It is to prove to Perses that he cannot get away with perjury, and to the kings that they cannot get away with taking bribes. Consequently, Hesiod's section on *dikē* makes one and one point only: neither perjurers (read Perses) nor crooked judges (read, of Thespiae) can avoid the punishment that Zeus sends down on such behavior.

THE EPIC PARTICULAR

Justice, to Hesiod, is the concrete and specific fact that men have courts. This, at first, seems to separate it from farming. To the extent that we are thereby barred from statements about the all-pervasive balance of the cosmos, it does. But from another point of view, Hesiod's way of dealing with justice is very like his way of dealing with farming. If Hesiod does not treat *dikē* as man's participation in the universal balance of the cosmos, neither does he treat farming as man's relation to nature. Hesiod never uses the word "nature" (*phusis*). He likes specifics. Even when his promises sound universal (for example, "But even so I will speak the mind of Zeus who holds the aegis / For the Muses have taught me to sing unfathomable song" *WD* 661–62), his advice is rather less cosmic. The mind of Zeus determines that fifty days after the solstice is the best time to sail. Hesiod's description of farming does not describe God's relation to nature and to man. It describes how the snail climbs up a plant to escape the Pleiades just about harvest time.

Dikē and farming are not the only two topics which Hesiod discusses as particulars rather than as abstract concepts. Almost all of Hesiod's topics, with the exception of the myths, are particular. Hesiod treats not the relation of man and man, but how to deal with a wife, a child, a brother, a servant, a neighbor, or a friend. Once we realize this, the section of the poem which has always seemed the most problematic, the lucky and unlucky days, appears far less peculiar.[22] What Hesiod does here is simply to treat each day as a particular and individual unit, with its own nature, regardless of what happened yesterday, or might happen tomorrow. He sees a "day," in other words, just as he sees a person, not as an indifferent example of a universal type but as a specific particular. A person is a child or a brother, a servant or a wife. A day is the fifth, or the seventh, the ninth or the twentieth. As each of the former has its own nature and must be dealt with accordingly, so does each of the latter.

The fact that Hesiod speaks in specifics rather than abstractions does not mean that Hesiod is uninterested in the overall will of Zeus. It means only that the general inclination of epic, toward the specific rather than the general, and toward the concrete rather than the abstract, is as strong in Hesiod as it is in Homer. Achilles tells Odysseus not that man is mortal but that cattle and tripods and horses may be lost or won, but the life of man, once it has passed the barrier of his teeth, cannot be retaken (*Iliad* 9. 405–409). Nor does Hesiod tell us about the relation of man and nature as determined by the will of Zeus. He tells us about the snail.

Concrete, specific examples are, of course, more dramatic than philosophic abstractions, and so more suitable to epic poetry. That epic poetry tends to avoid abstractions does not necessarily imply that the poets who composed it never thought abstractly.[23] But whether abstractions are or are not part of the world of the poet, they do not play a critical role in the world of the poem. Hesiod's specifics, his vignettes of farming, his particular court case, or his lucky and unlucky days, are not placeholders for abstract philosophical concepts. The snail's trip is not emblematic of the will of Zeus, as it works through nature to man as farmer. Within the world of the *Works and Days* the snail's trip *is* the will of Zeus. And so, within the world of the poem, Hesiod's case with Perses is *dikē*.

Hesiod describes *dikē* concretely, just as he describes farming. The effect in both cases is the same. As Hesiod's description of the farmer's year makes us feel what it is like to farm, his account of Perses and the kings makes us feel all the indignation of a man cheated in just the place where he should have found redress. Hesiod sets the situation up for us at the very beginning of the poem. By the time we get to the section on justice we require only occasional reminders. We do not view Hesiod's account of the fall of mighty judges dispassionately, nor are we supposed to. We view them as Hesiod meant us to view them, with the satisfaction that comes from seeing the villain get his just deserts. When, in the introduction to the farming section, it is revealed that Perses, having squandered his ill-gotten goods, has been begging from Hesiod, our reaction is, as it is meant to be, shock.[24] Our shock is meant to turn to indignation. When Hesiod responds with a decided no: "I will give you no more,/ No further measure." (*WD* 396–97) my own reaction is "damn right." Hesiod, in short, uses the specifics of his poetry just as Homer does. as we participate in the scene our own emotional response brings the scene to life and validates, for us, the poet's vision.

JUSTICE AND FARMING

Whether there was or was not a "Boeotian" school of epic and whether Hesiod did or did not understand himself to be writing "wisdom literature," the *Works and Days* is the only Greek poem of its kind that we have. Whatever it was historically, the poem is, for us, *sui generis*. This makes it much harder to evaluate. Homer, like Hesiod, employs epic diction, and inclines to the specific rather than to the abstract. But the "specifics" of Homeric poetry are Achilles and Hector, Odysseus and Penelope, people whose stories have the unity and universal interest that the stories of all human beings have. Hesiod's "characters" are justice and seasons, strife and lucky days. Their story has no plot. The unity of his poem, and its universal interest, had to be of a different kind. He found them in the context of the poem.

Hesiod creates a context for the *Works and Days* by introducing the poem with myth. This introduction tells us that Zeus wants human life to be hard, that to try and escape his will is futile, and that *dikē* is part of Zeus' will. This theme is maintained throughout the *Works and Days* by the poem's key ideas, of which proportion, measure, and due season are paramount. To these we should add the need for intelligence, which is the way men are able to *perceive* measure, season, and proportion. Having added this we can see why these key words continue the context of the myths.

Zeus has made life hard for us by making work intrinsic to human life. He has also made it hard in a subtler way. He has made life difficult by making it equivocal. Thus, in the Pandora myth, Zeus introduces hardship into human life by creating an evil that looks like good, so that men rush to embrace it. This same theme appears in the Erides, the good and evil sisters who reveal the double nature of strife. It appears again in the doubleness of hope, or of *aidōs* (*WD* 317–19, 500–501).[25] In each of these cases good and evil are twins. It is hard for men to tell them apart. Giving, sparing, trusting, marrying, having children and friends, talking, and dining out all have their good and bad sides in the *Works and Days*. It is because of this that men need intelligence. We have to see how much, when, and for how long. As Hesiod says: "Watch the right measure, proportion in all things is best" (*WD* 694). The proverb is not meant academically. The context is the chance of breaking the axle of the wagon and spoiling your goods—or of overloading the boat, and dying at sea. Human life is hard. This is why balance and measure are its central requirements.

The fact that Zeus wants human life to be hard connects justice and farming immediately. What Perses and the kings have attempted to do is to get something for nothing. This is the whole point of injustice as Hesiod presents it—to get things without having to work for them. Hesiod knows that Zeus does not allow men to get away with this. He knows this partly through the traditions he repeats in his section *dikē* and partly through his own observation. Hesiod is a farmer. He has lived the fact that the gods have placed sweat before human *aretē*—and not figuratively (*WD*

289–90). The evidence that this is Zeus' will is precisely the fact that the earth will not produce food on its own. It would be a surprising thing if the gods went to all this trouble, and then forgot that men can also get rich, without labor, simply by flattering the gift-gobbling kings.[26]

Hesiod focuses the *Works and Days* on the courts and on Perses out of more than mere revenge. When Hesiod draws our attention to Perses, *these* gift-gobbling kings, and judicial decisions on property, he is centering his poem on the kind of justice that Aristotle also focuses on, economic justice.[27] Hesiod feels the connection between *bios* "life" and *bios* "livelihood" very deeply. "Goods," he tells us, "are life-breath for wretched mortals" (*WD* 686). This is the significance of Hesiod's "economic" concept of *dikē*. Economics, as our livelihood, is our life. As the fulcrum of human life this is also the place where Zeus has, paradigmatically, made life hard. By keeping *dikē* in the courts, Hesiod extended rather than restricted its range. He also gave it a necessary connection to farming.

THE POSITIVE SIDE OF JUSTICE

There is, however, one problem with connecting Hesiod's sections on justice and farming in this way. Hesiod's section on justice is not really about justice. It is about injustice. It tells us, specifically, that men cannot commit perjury or give crooked decisions with impunity. At its most universal it tells us that men cannot get goods they have not paid for. It does not tell us what men *should* do in order to be just. This is not unusual. In the case of a virtue like courage or wisdom we have a fairly good idea of what a courageous act, or a wise statement, might be. In the case of justice it is hard to say anything except that a just act or statement is one that is not unjust.

What is unusual about Hesiod's section on *dikē* is not that it is negative, but that it is succeeded by two sections that really are about justice, in a positive sense. These are the sections that West calls "free-wheeling," that surround the section on farming and sailing, and connect it to the courts on the one hand, and to the Days on the other.[28] Both sections are dazzling, not to say bewildering, in their multiplicity. They deal with wives and children, work and neighbors, trust, shame, gossip, lending and borrowing, when to open a jar, and how to cross a river. What Hesiod tells us, in each case, is how men ought to behave. What he is describing, in other words, is *dikē*.

Hesiod's sense of *dikē* is simple. As he says in this section: "Property is not for snatching; what is god-given is much better" (*WD* 320). "God-given" wealth is wealth won under the conditions that Zeus has intended for man: justice (or rather, avoiding injustice) and toil.[29] This is the negative connection of justice and farming. But there is also a positive connection. Hesiod's multiplicity is not merely a hodgepodge. It has an underlying theme, that a man can get only what he pays for. Here, however, by introducing the key ideas of measure, proportion, and season, Hesiod makes of this theme another kind of balance. The underlying principle of Hesiod's "free-wheeling" section is a simple one—reciprocity:

> Take fair measure from your neighbor, and pay him back fairly
> In the same measure, and even better, if you are able
> So when in need, even afterwards, you may find him sufficient
>
> WD 349–51

> Be friends with a friend; go to one who goes to you,
> And give to a man that gives, not to one who does not.
> To a giver any man gives, to a nongiver, no one does.
>
> WD 353–55

> The best treasure among men is a tongue that is sparing,
> The greatest boon when a man speaks in measure.
> Speak evil, and soon you will hear worse spoken of yourself.
>
> WD 719–21

The simple fact that men give to those who give, not to those who do not, means that human relations are founded on reciprocity. This notion is contained in the very word *philia*. *Ton phileonta philein* ("Be friends with a friend") would, actually, be better translated: "maintain a relationship of reciprocity with one who maintains a relationship of reciprocity with you," which is harder to put into meter.[30] It is here that we see, most clearly, the relation of friendship to justice.

Aristotle, in Book Eight of the *Ethics*, treats *philia* in terms of balance, measure, and reciprocity, just the terms in which, in Book Five, he treated *dikē*. He is explicit about the link between the two, telling us that where men have *philia* there is no need for them to have *dikē* as well.[31] The same link exists for Hesiod. With neighbors, with friends, in trade, and even in gossip we pay with equal measure, whether of good for good or (and here Polemarchus' definition of justice enters in) of evil for evil:

> Make not a comrade the equal of a brother.
> If you do, be not the first to do evil;
> Do not lie for the pleasure of talk. But if he begins
> Either saying a word that is hateful, or doing a deed,
> Remember, and pay him back double. If then again
> He would have friendship, and wishes to offer you *dikē*
> Accept it.
>
> WD 707–13

The *dikē* here is not justice as determined by a judge in court.[32] It is simply amends which compensate for an injury, and so restore the balance of friendship.

This is the one nonjudicial use of the word *dikē* in the *Works and Days*. It also explains why Hesiod can be so certain that punishment follows injustice. As he declared in the section on *dikē*. "For himself a man prepares evil, preparing evil for another./ An evil plan is worst for the planner" (*WD* 265–67). Punishment is simply the other side of reciprocity. If punishment did not follow injustice the balance of reciprocity, the balance that underlies all human relations, would be undone.

Hesiod does see *dikē* as a universal balance, but it comes up not in the section on the courts but in the section on dealing with other people. The balance is no more academic in human relations than it is in overloading a ship. It is embedded in the world and in our own emotional response to it, in our goodwill toward those who do good to us (*charis*), and in our indignation at those who do evil. They are responses triggered by particulars. Few men get angry at abstract injustice, or find the idea of the Good particularly heartwarming. Our response to Perses is different. It is enough to assure us that men do in fact, desire good for those who give, and evil for those who take too much.

The human instinct to give good for good, and evil for evil, is a balance, like the balance of seedtime and harvest. Like that balance it is made up of a nearly infinite number of factors. And, like the balance of seedtime and harvest, it is equivocal. The sections which surround the farming and sailing section are the two which most directly focus on balance and reciprocity in human affairs. They are also the two which point out the double nature of wives and children and neighbors, of trust and generosity, of shame, and of giving and sparing. Men live by reciprocity; they give to those that give, not to those that do not. But one should not give too much: things are better at home, things out of doors come to harm (*WD* 365). Trust is important: let the wages to a friend be fixed (*WD* 370). But not too much: with your brother smile, and get a witness (*WD* 371). Trust and distrust alike destroy a man (*WD* 372). Giving, sparing, trusting, marrying, having children and friends, talking, and dining out all have their good and their bad sides. As in farming so also in life altogether, there is no simple rule to determine the right time or the right measure. There is only a sensitivity to all the factors involved, and an awareness of the importance of the judgment. Justice is a balance. It is not one easily determined.

Hesiod's description of farming in the *Works and Days* has often been taken as the practical complement to Hesiod's moral advice.[33] Such an interpretation completely mistakes Hesiod's purpose. Modern scholars tend to distinguish justice, as a moral question, from farming, which they perceive as a merely practical one. Hesiod does not divide the moral from the practical.[34] Hesiod's gods are immanent rather than transcendent, manifested in the day-to-day world in which Hesiod lives.[35] It is not by consulting either a sacred or a philosophic text that Hesiod discovers what is in accordance with the will of Zeus. What is in accordance with the will of Zeus is, for Hesiod, what works in the world as Hesiod knows it. Hesiod's ordinary life thus both manifests Zeus' will and his only evidence as to what Zeus' will is. What succeeds in this world succeeds because it is the will of Zeus that it should do so. As it succeeds it is, pragmatically, the right course. As it is in accordance with the will of Zeus it is, as we would say, morally right. The two are, for Hesiod, *ipso facto,* the same.[36]

As Hesiod declares quite explicitly, he is just because it pays.[37] If justice did not pay, he would not be just (*WD* 270–73). To a culture nourished on Christianity and Kant this is naive moral thinking, a confusion of the moral and the pragmatic. For Hesiod it is precisely the fact that injustice cannot pay that proves that Zeus will not allow it. And, as *dikē* is not, for Hesiod, a moral rather than a practical question, neither is farming a practical rather than a moral one. It is not merely a way of making money; it is, like justice, a *nomos* ("way") which Zeus has established for man. Hesiod chooses farming from among the various ways a man could grow wealthy because he, like so many other peasant farmers, sees farming as the particular livelihood and way of life that God has ordained for man.[38] It is, as such, inherently linked to justice.

The logical connection of justice and farming in the *Works and Days* is that both express, as two sides of one coin, the fundamental will of Zeus, that men cannot have goods without hardship. The deeper connection of justice and farming we see in the way in which Hesiod presents the two topics. Justice is the balance that determines human life, just as the seasons are the balance that determines farming. The balance is both profound and complex. To know and live with the balance of the seasons is to feel their infinite complexity. To know the right measure to give to neighbors or friends, in the family or in court, is to deal with the infinite complexity of human relations. For Hesiod, Zeus has determined that human life shall be a balance, and a difficult balance, of good and evil. This is the thread which runs through and unites the multiplicity of the world, as it unites the various topics of the *Works and Days.*

Hesiod's refusal to give Perses any further measure and the slow trip of the snail up into the shade of the plant are each of them concrete particulars. They are related only in one way, that both manifest the will of Zeus. This is the true focus of the *Works and Days,* just as it is of the *Theogony.* What Hesiod is concerned with is the will of Zeus. As much for Hesiod as for Heraclitus, *this dikē,* the will of Zeus, is *eris*—the principle which Zeus has established in the roots of the earth. As much for

Hesiod as for Anaxagoras, it is a principle of universal balance and exchange. As much for Hesiod as for Jane Harrison, it is the "way of that great animal, the Universe."

NOTES

1. I refer to *dikē* as "justice" in this paper when my focus is on elements that the two concepts have in common, as "*dikē*" when my focus is on elements particular to the Greek concept. In both cases I mean it to be understood that I see *dikē* neither as completely separate from "justice" nor as identical to it.

2. M. L. West, *Hesiod: "Works and Days"* (Oxford: Clarendon Press, 1978), 45. The Greek text used throughout this paper is West's. Translations are my own.

3. See West, 313. Paul Mazon, "Hésiode: La Composition des *Travaux et des Jours.*" *Revue des Études Anciennes* 14 (1912): 351; and Peter Walcot, "The Composition of the *Works and Days*" *Revue des Études Grecques* 74 (1971): 11. They fail to notice that Hesiod's seasons for sailing are precisely the times when the farmer can afford to be away from the farm. Hesiod's sailor spends his winter plowing (*WD* 623).

4. For the *Works and Days* as a poem in two halves, one on justice and one on farming see, for example: Edward Kennard Rand, "Horatian Urbanity in Hesiod's *Works and Days*," *American Journal of Philology* 32 (1911), 148; Malcolm Heath, "Hesiod's Didactic Poetry," *Classical Quarterly* ns 35 (1983), 245; Bernard Knox, "Work and Justice in Archaic Greece: Hesiod's *Works and Days*," in *Essays: Ancient and Modern* (Baltimore: The Johns Hopkins University Press, 1989), 21. For a thematic unitarianism see Arthur W. H. Adkins, "Cosmogony and Order in Ancient Greece," in *Cosmogony and Ethical Order: New Studies in Comparative Ethics,* edited by Robin W. Lovin and Frank E. Reynolds (Chicago: University of Chicago Press, 1985), 62.

5. Peter Walcot, *Hesiod and the Near East* (Cardiff: 1966), 33: "Hesiod's poem is not just the story of the beginnings of the universe and the history of the gods: it is even more a resounding hymn of praise in honor of Zeus." Eric A. Havelock, *The Great Concept of Justice from its Shadow in Homer to its Substance in Plato* (Cambridge: Harvard University Press, 1978), 209, sees this as equally true of the *Works and Days*: "The entire *Works and Days* can be viewed as a "Zeus-poem" insofar as it continually presents the lives and deeds of mankind as taking place under his superintendency and subject to his superior purpose." Friedrich Solmsen, *Hesiod and Aeschylus* (Ithaca: Cornell University Press, 1949), 21ff., refers to Hesiod's two layers of reality, the mythic and the immediate, and at 78 states that "the two phases of reality have in common, however, the central figure of Zeus. For the Zeus of the heroic epos was in every respect qualified, nay almost destined, to become the symbol and exponent of the world order which embraces all features of Hesiod's experience."

6. Peter Walcot, "Hesiod and the Law," *Symbolae Osloenses* 38 (1963), 6, points out: "To call the poem a handbook on farming or a farmer's calendar is to consider only a small part of the complete text. Such a description applies to verses 383–614 alone, a mere 235 out of more than 740 lines, and even from these we

must deduct the poet's digressions and particularly his sketches of winter (verses 504–63) and the height of summer (verses 582–96)." Nicholas F. Jones, "Perses, Work 'In Season,' and the Purpose of the *Works and Days*," *Classical Journal* 79 (1984): 307–23, notes that Perses' problem is not ignorance but procrastination. Thalia Phillips Howe, "Linear B and Hesiod's Breadwinners," *Transactions of the American Philological Association* 89 (1958): 45–65, commenting that Hesiod's advice is so painfully obvious that his audience must have been composed either of total idiots or of the totality inexperienced, argues that agriculture is being newly introduced. For a refutation see Peter Walcot, *Greek Peasants Ancient and Modern: A Comparison of Social and Moral Values* (Manchester: Manchester University Press, 1970), 20–23.

7. For Hesiod's use of traditional material in the *Works and Days*, see Charles Rowan Beye, "The Rhythm of Hesiod's *Works and Days*," *Harvard Studies in Classical Philology* 76 (1972): 23–43; A. Hoekstra, "Hésiode, *Les Travaux et les Jours*, 405–407, 317–319, 21–24; L'Élément proverbial et son adaptation." *Mnemosyne* 4th ser. 3 (1950): 89–114.

8. This has been often noted, but not, I think, really taken in. See West, 52: "we are taken methodically through the year to the time of the next ploughing" and Mazon, 347. In contrast Svein Østerud "The Individuality of Hesiod," *Hermes* 104 (1976), 16.

9. Hesiod uses this technique often, for example, in the Five Ages, or the just and unjust cities (Rand, 138). For the impressionistic tone of Hesiod's account of farming see B. A. van Groningen, *La Composition littéraire archaïque grecque* (Amsterdam: Verhandelingen der Konnklijke Nederlandse Akademie van Weten-schappen, 1958), 291. West, 252, comments: "A pictorial quality invests even his most technical precepts: by the end, while we may not be much better equipped to run a farm than before, we have a real sense of how it looked and felt at different stages of the year," without, as usual, considering the possibility that this might be deliberate.

10. Hesiod brings out the parallel of sowing and harvest by employing parallel techniques. In both he introduces an extraneous activity, first wood-cutting, then vine-pruning, finally the vintage, to distract us and in both he moves from farmer commanding slaves, to farmer and slaves together, to the farmer himself. Hence Hesiod's contradictory accounts of who does the plowing; West, 273; Friedrich Solmsen, review of *Hesiod: "Works and Days,"* by M. L. West, in *Gnomon* 52 (1980), 217.

11. Harpraktos is a resonant word in the *Works and Days;* see, for example, *WD* 38, 320, 356.

12. Pierre Waltz, *Hésiode et son poème moral* (Bibliòtheque des Universites du Midi, Fascicule no. 12. Bordeaux: Feret & Fils, 1906), 63: "Mais ce n'est pas tout que être laborieux: il faut encore savoir déployer à propos son activité, avant tout faire chaque chose en temps."

13. For *hōra* as simply a "season" see *WD* 409, 450, 460, 494, 575, 584, 664; *Th.* 58, 754. The only other appearance the Horae make in Hesiod, as goddesses, is to crown Pandora with spring flowers (*WD* 75), the traditional task of the natural seasons, and, given the nature of Pandora: "And then in her breast the guide, the slayer of Argos/ Fashioned lies and slippery words and a thievish

way" (*WD* 77–79), a task singularly inappropriate to Peace, Justice, and Good Order.

14. *Hesiod* (Oxford: Clarendon Press, 1970), edited by Friedrich Solmsen; fragments edited by R. Merkelbach and M. L. West.

15. See also the Homeric Hymn *To Hermes*, 324. As Martin P. Nilsson, *Greek Piety*, translated by Herbert Jennings Rose (New York: W. W. Norton and Co., 1969), 35, puts it: "For the Greeks justice was the retribution which counters wrong-doing." See also John Ferguson, *Moral Values in the Ancient World* (London: 1958), 28; J. Walter Jones, *The Law and Legal Theory of the Greeks: An Introduction* (Oxford: Clarendon Press, 1956), 27–28. Hesiod describes justice as the accomplishment of a "turning back" that balances and negates the harm done (*Th* 89) and as a "harsh return in exchange for unjust deeds" (*WD* 334). "*Dikē*," as the measure which restores the balance, is the punishment, as well as the decision (*WD* 238–39); Jean-Pierre Vernant, *Myth and Thought Among the Greeks*, (London: Routledge and Kegan Paul, 1983), 107.

16. See, for example, Hesiod's use of *parakairia rezōn* ("acting outside the proportion" *WD* 329) to describe an *adikon ergon*. See also West, 240; Theognis, 199; Pindar, *O.* 8.24; Solon 13.11; and L. R. Palmer, "The Indo-European Origins of Greek Justice," *Transactions of the Philological Society* (1950), 153ff. for numerous other examples. Palmer argues for an etymological connection of *dikē* as a "boundary word," to *metron, kairos,* and *moros* and, at 162ff. for a further connection to *aisa* and *moira* pointing to Hesiod's identification of *Dikē* as one of the Horae (168, n. 1).

17. Jane Ellen Harrison *Themis: A Study of the Social Origins of Greek Religion*, 2nd ed. (Cambridge: Cambridge University Press, 1912), 517. See G. S. Kirk, J. E. Raven, and M. Schofield, *The Presocratic Philosophers*, 2nd edition, (Cambridge: Cambridge University Press, 1983), 193, for Heraclitus, 107 for Anaximander.

18. For Hesiod's use of "key words" for emphasis, and to point out themes and connections, see W. J. Verdenius, "Aufbau und Absicht der Erga," in *Hésiode et son influence*, (Entretiens sur l'antiquité classique vii. Geneva: Fondation Hardt, 1962) 111–59 and "L'Association des idées comme principe de composition dans Homère, Hésiode, Théognis," *Revue des Études Grecques* 73 (1960): 345–61.

19. "*Dikē*" also serves, although to a lesser extent, as a key word in the poem, primarily continuing the thread of Hesiod's case against Perses.

20. Michael Gagarin, "*Dikē* in the *Works and Days*," *Classical Philology* 68 (1975), 87: "every use of *dikē* in Hesiod belongs to the second area of meaning, 'settlement, legal process.'" For other visions of the concrete nature of archaic Greek justice, see Lionel Pearson, *Popular Ethics in Ancient Greece* (Stanford: Stanford University Press, 1962), 43–48, 234, n. 13; Kurt Latte, "Der Rechtsgedanke in archaischen Griechentum" *Antike u. Abendland* 2 (1946), 65; Havelock, 213, 216–217. Matthew Dickie, "*Dikē* as a Moral Term in Hesiod and Homer," *Classical Philology* 73 (1978), 100, argues, I believe correctly, that *dikē can* mean justice or righteousness in Hesiod or Homer although "it is more commonly used to mean 'custom' or 'judgment.'" See Dickie, 91–92, and W. J. Verdenius, *A Commentary on Hesiod: Works and Days, vv. 1–382*, Mnemosyne Supplement 86 (Leiden: E. J. Brill, 1985), 10, for a summary.

21. WD 9 asks Zeus to straighten the judicial *themistes* with *dikē*. WD 239 and 256 describe Zeus' punishment of unjust judges. WD 192 describes perjury in the iron age. WD 280, on perjury, makes it clear that it is judicial justice to which Hesiod is referring. WD 36, 39, 124, 213, 217, 219, 220, 221, 225, 249, 250, 254, 262, 264, 269, 275, 283 describe the courts directly. The adjective *dikaios* is used of the courts at WD 190, 217, 226, and 280; of gaining "greater *dikē*," presumably "settlement" at 270 and 271; and nonjudicially of the heroes at WD 158. The adjective *adikos* is used in a judicial context at WD 260 and 272 and in a nonjudicial context at 334.

22. Friedrich Solmsen rejects this section in "The 'Days' of the *Works and Days*," *Transactions of the American Philological Association* 94 (1963): 293–330, largely on the grounds of superstition. But as there are far fewer objections to the need to avoid placing the ladle on the jar, or to washing in woman's bath water, if you are a man, superstition cannot be the only problem. See West, 346ff., for a refutation and, for the unity of "Days" and year David Grene, "Hesiod: Religion and Poetry in the *Works and Days*," in *Radical Pluralism and Truth: David Tracy and the Hermeneutics of Religion*, edited by Werner G. Jeanrond and Jennifer L. Rike (New York: Crossroads, 1991), 147. On the topic more generally, see Pierre Bordieu, "The Attitude of the Algerian Peasant towards Time," in *Mediterranean Countrymen: Essays in the Social Anthropology of the Mediterranean*, edited by Julian Pitt-Rivers (Paris: Mouton and Co., 1963), 69.

23. That epic poetry *tends* to avoid generalizations does not mean, of course, that it never employs them, particularly as proverbs. At 694, for example, Hesiod declares "proportion in all things is best" and at 218 that "a fool learns by suffering."

24. Precisely this shock has led many modern commentators to believe that Perses must be fictional, as no real person could be so inconsistent. See Mark Griffith, "Personality in Hesiod," *Classical Antiquity* 2 (1983), 57: "the character and behavior of Perses vary according to the rhetorical point that Hesiod wishes to make"; West, 33–40; and Ulrich von Wilamowitz-Moellendorff, *Hesiodos' "Erga"* (Berlin: Weidmannsche Buchhandlung, 1928), 133–35. In fact, if the section is not teaching farming, neither is Perses "jerked back from the edge of the grave, back through his life as an established farmer, to be instructed in the first principles of farming" (West, 51–52), and most of the inconsistency felt in Hesiod's picture of Perses disappears. For Perses' consistency see also Heath, 245f.

25. "Ever since the Prometheus fraud instituted the first sacrificial meal, everything in human life has had its dark shadow and its wrong side.... There can no longer be happiness without unhappiness, birth without death, abundance without toil, knowledge without ignorance, man without woman, Prometheus without Epimetheus" (Jean-Pierre Vernant, "Sacrifice in Greek Myths," in *Mythologies*, edited by Yves Bonnefoy, translated under the direction of Wendy Doniger [Chicago: University of Chicago Press, 1991] vol. 1, 423–24). For Hesiod's particular sense of ambiguity see also Vernant, *Thought*, 239–41.

26. For the usual connection of justice and work, as two benefits, see Joseph Fontenrose, "Work, Justice, and Hesiod's Five Ages," *Classical Philology* 69 (1974), 7. The connection also works the other way: no one without some guarantee of property would sow a field in fall for someone else to reap in spring.

27. See Aristotle's distinction between justice as complete virtue, or the "lawful," and justice as a specific, primarily economic virtue, not taking more than one's due (*Nicomachean Ethics* 1129a25ff.). Aristotle points out that it is the being done for "profit" (1130a24ff.) that characterizes the latter. Heber Michel Hays, "Notes on the Works and Days of Hesiod" (Ph.D. diss., University of Chicago, 1918), 58–62, also sees "two strata of ethical sentiment" (60) in Hesiod, one traditional, and one centered on property rights.

28. For the parallelism of the two latter sections Walcot, 8, 12; Richard Hamilton, *The Architecture of Hesiodic Poetry*, AJP Monographs in Classical Philology, edited by Diskin Clay (Baltimore: Johns Hopkins University Press, 1989), 73.

29. See Verdenius, WD, 161: "'god-given' is equivalent to 'lawfully acquired,'" WD 379–80. "Easily might Zeus provide limitless wealth to more./ [Since] More hands mean more work, and more increase." As Pandora evidences, Hesiod does not see the "gifts" of Zeus as an unmixed blessing. For Homeric man's responsibility for the interventions and gifts of the gods, see Arthur W. H. Adkins, *Merit and Responsibility* (Oxford: Oxford University Press, 1960; repr., Chicago: University of Chicago Press, 1975), 16.

30. See Arthur W. H. Adkins, "'Friendship' and 'Self-Sufficiency' in Homer and Aristotle," *Classical Quarterly*, n.s., 13 (1963): 36–39.

31. "Where men are friends there is no need for justice, but men who are just need friendship as well" (1155a27). For the reciprocity of *philia* see 1158b30ff., 1162a35ff. and the summary which begins Book Nine, 1163b30ff.

32. West, 216, 331, glosses as "atonement," Paul Mazon, *Les Travaux et jours* (Paris: Librairie Hachette et Cie, 1914), 143, as "une satisfaction." See also *Odyssey* 2.74–79 for the justice of paying oneself back.

33. Beginning with Aristophanes' *Frogs*: 1030–36. See also Griffith, 89: "From 286 onward, Hesiod's instruction is concerned more with work and farming than with litigation or larger issues of justice or morality. He is now speaking as technical expert." See Mazon, 346: "A ces leçons de haute morale succèdent des conseils plus pratiques." West, 59: "If Hesiod began the written version without envisaging the further prospects which appear after line 380, the inference is that moral sermon and technical instruction on agriculture had hitherto been separate items in his repertoire."

34. As evidenced also by Hesiod's myths, his social advice, religious taboos, or lucky and unlucky days, none of which can be classed as "moral" or "practical." Hence Hesiod tells us to pay back what we have borrowed (WD 349–50) and follows this "moral" advice with the "practical" reason: so you can borrow again (WD 351). See Nilsson, 50–51, and Harrison, 96, for this unity of the moral, practical, and religious.

35. See Walter F. Otto, *The Homeric Gods: The Spiritual Significance of Greek Religion*, translated by Moses Hadas (New York: Thames and Hudson, 1954), 6, 169–73; Walter Burkert, *Greek Religion*, translated by John Raffan (Cambridge: Harvard University Press, 1985), 125–70; 271–72.

36. A results or "shame" culture, which focuses on success rather than moral intention, will tend to make this association. See E. R. Dodds, *The Greeks and the Irrational* (Berkeley: University of California Press, 1951), especially 28–50; Ad-

kins, *Merit*, especially 46–57, 153–68; Hugh Lloyd-Jones, *The Justice of Zeus,*
2nd ed. (Berkeley: University of California Press, 1983), 25–26. For this equation
among modern peasants, see Edward C. Banfield, with the assistance of Laura
Fasano Banfield, *The Moral Basis of a Backward Society* (Chicago: The Free
Press/Research Center in Economic Development and Cultural Change, The University of Chicago, 1958), 140–43.

37. West, 47, summarizes Hesiod's argument: "*Dikē* is good because the gods
reward it. Hybris is bad because the gods punish it. Work is good because it brings
prosperity, independence, and hence social status. Idleness is bad because it brings
want and forces you to beg or turn to crime. Work and righteousness, in short, are
what succeed in the world, or in other words, they are what the gods have prescribed for men." See also Adkins, "Cosmogony," 54.

38. As Grene, 147, puts it, Hesiod "is inducting this pupil—or perhaps a hypothetical pupil as well as Perses—into farming as itself the imaginative clue to
the universe." See also Marcel Detienne, *Crise agraire et attitude religieuse chez
Hésiode* (Collection Latomus, Revue des Études Latines, no. 68. Brussels: Ber-
chem, 1963), 33 and passim for a good study of Hesiod as a peasant, with peasant
views on both justice and work. The omnipresence of farming in the *Works and
Days* cannot be explained by reference to the economic conditions of the times.
No other Greek author allots any similar position to farming, although agriculture
remained the predominant livelihood of Greece throughout the Classical period.

RESPONSE

David Grene

This is a hard paper to respond to, partly because there were so very many
important points raised in it, and partly because they were so well woven
into a complex whole that it is difficult to pick some of them apart without
falsifying what is being said, which lies in the entire paper. However, I am
going to take certain of what seemed to me especially interesting ideas
and, I hope, complement them by certain of the contexts in which they are
embedded in the *Works and Days* which Ms. Nelson did not directly include—nearly always because it would have blurred the clarity and drive
of her presentation by an excess of detail. Finally I would like briefly to
engage on my own account on a very ambitious if not foolish task, which
I would describe as an attempt to present the mind of Hesiod as I see it in
the *Works and Days,* and to include some observations on the quality of
the poetry.

The first comment I have to make on Ms. Nelson's paper is on a point
which goes to the very heart of the poem. She says that the poem is about
what it *feels* like to farm. I am glad that Ms. Nelson abandoned any long
discussion of the negative proposition—that clearly this work could not
consciously teach anyone how to farm. This has been done ad nauseam; I

am afraid that I have argued in this vein myself at times. But Ms. Nelson's continuation of this proposition is very telling indeed. The poem deals with the farmer's year because, though each of the scenes is in the nature of an individual snapshot, it is the sequence that achieves most of the effect. This sequence, when resolved into its opposite elements, hot and cold, energy and comparative idleness, and success and failure, lives supremely in the farmer's year. It is true that the flash-back and flash-forward in the Hesiodic rendering makes sometimes for difficult reading. For example, at 458–60, when we are right at the beginning of the ploughing, which is to be followed directly by sowing for the harvest, we have

> But the moment that sign of the ploughing appears
> then drive yourself on and your servants, all of you,
> and plough, wet and dry, as the ploughing season dictates;
> WD 458–60 (all translations mine)

We find at 462

> The ploughland you must work first in spring; if you
> plough it again in the summer the land will not play you false.

What this is concerned with is what you should have done with the land you are just about to plough to make it fit to plough then and there in fall. One may not see right away that the references to the spring and summer ploughings are indeed preliminary and not the operation which you are now witnessing. Undoubtedly, however, the treatment of the farmer's year as a sequence of the vignettes is one very important aspect of the poem's extraordinary vividness, in the dramatic exhibition of the unity of the impressions which constitute the *feeling* of what farming is like. It is from her personal and clear understanding of what farming *is* like that Ms. Nelson elaborates her great discussion of balance, in farming and justice, and wisdom as the understanding of that balance.

The next aspect of the paper that impressed me so much was Ms. Nelson's emphasis on Hesiod's substitution of concrete detail for any direct engagement with abstraction either in farming or justice. This is brilliantly summed up in her sentence "the snail's trip is not emblematic of the will of Zeus, as it works through nature and to man as farmer. . . . The snail's trip *is* the will of Zeus." This leads directly to her remarkable treatment of *dikē*. Ms. Nelson takes notice of the critics who have shown that there is an overwhelming numerical superiority of references to *dikē* in a strictly legal setting. Yes, of course this fits with the specificity of Hesiod's charge against Perses and the lawsuit which started the whole dissension between them. But Ms. Nelson is surely right that the passage from 320 to 334 equating wrong to suppliants, to orphan children, to the practice of incest, to the injury to old parents as all *adikia* which is punished by Zeus makes certain that the much more general sense, of *dikē* as a kind of morality, is correct. I believe that Hesiod would certainly back her definition of injustice as getting something for nothing" in the economic sphere. So *dikē* comes out as being the righting of a somewhat tremulous and disturbed balance.

I would like to relate these two points to certain aspects of the poem that powerfully support them, material mostly drawn from the two myths. Hesiod's is a mind much preoccupied with the hardness of the world in which God deals with mankind. He uses "the gods" or "Zeus" almost indiscriminately. The gods, we are told, made man's livelihood difficult. The land could always be more fertile than it is—and this is because the fertility depends on Zeus, as the weather. Furthermore, at the beginning in the Golden Age there was no need of agriculture at all; the land yielded crops of itself. The process of making man's task as a farmer a real task, and difficult, was apparently caused from the beginning by Zeus' wrath against Prometheus for cheating him. (I assume that this refers to the earlier episode of the sacrifice mentioned in the *Theogony*.) At this point he—that is Zeus—hid fire, but Prometheus stole it and gave it back to man. (This of course is a different version from what we get in Aeschylus' *Prometheus*.) So Zeus now sends to mankind, as a direct punishment for the theft of fire by Prometheus, Pandora. So far everything seems clear and unequivocal.

But there are several curious things about Zeus' vengeance on man by the creation of Pandora. At 95, when Pandora took the lid off the jar all sorts of ills are launched wandering over the earth, but especially diseases. Hope, only, remained shut up in the jar, because before it could escape, Pandora clapped the lid of the jar shut. The very next line reads "through designs of Zeus the Cloud Gatherer." Admittedly the question of the jar and the ills in it is very vexed—not least because the diseases are spread through the world by getting *out* of the jar—that is, their effectiveness depends on getting out. But Hope's value is exactly that she stayed *in* the jar. There is some inconsistency here, but I don't want to wrestle with this. But West refuses to acknowledge that the line on Zeus' designs in connection with the retention of Hope is spurious; it is seemingly already there in the first and best medieval manuscripts. West thinks, and I certainly agree, that Zeus wanted man to live with Hope. There is nothing to be gained as far as I can see in arguing as to whether *elpis* ("hope," but also simply "expectation") is mostly illusory. It is well to remember that in Aeschylus' *Prometheus* Prometheus gave man "blind hopes" when he took from them foreknowing the day of their death (*Prometheus Bound* 248) which is probably the right way to render *moros* here. The Chorus says, "That is a great gift you gave to mortals" (*Prometheus Bound* 251).

So that, in Aeschylus' sense, anyway, whether hope is what we call hope or expectation, it gave man the chance to go forward blindly, clear of the oppression of the certainty of destruction. Now of course in the Aeschylean play all that is good for man is championed by Prometheus, and what is destructive by Zeus. But what about Hesiod? Does not the retention of Hope as part of man's lot in life in the *Works and Days*, taken in conjunction with the use made of hope in Aeschylus, suggest very strongly that this Hope or Expectation was, surprisingly, part of Zeus' design for something good for man or at any rate something that makes his punishments more bearable? It seems as if Zeus' punishment of mankind is somehow ambiguous; in part it undoubtedly is punishment, but with the punishment there is to be mingled something that is *not* punishment, something that significantly tilts the balance slightly the other way. I think this goes together with the paper's emphasis on the constant combination of opposites in the sequence of the seasons in farming and how one perceives them and on the doubles that Ms. Nelson discusses where all sorts of social relations, from feasting and making friends on, are such a mixture of good and bad that one is constantly driven to make decisions as to the exact balance to strike. So it is maybe worth noting that in the initial punishment of man by the creation and character of Pandora, Zeus himself sets the terms on which man faces his punishment, diseases and so forth, but also with the addition of hope to keep him from the certainty of despair.

The second myth so gently offered the audience or readers

> There is another story—if you like I will tell you its substance,
> well, and skillfully; and you lay it up in your heart.
> It tells how the gods and mortal men spring from the same
> beginnings. WD 106–108

concentrates on some kind of common origin of men and gods—or common background, which is just a possible rendering of the Greek words (*WD* 108). This general description of the material proves important. There are three of the five Ages which show how the human and divine can intersect, that is, that they are not the entirely separable beings, in origin anyway, that appears to be the case in the first myth. The Golden Age men live a life almost entirely of free of mankind's sorrows and threats and after death become *daimones* who have responsibility in the world for the guardianship of justice at Zeus' orders. The Silver Age men are encumbered with a hundred-year childhood and a short adulthood and a kind of life that Zeus apparently finds unsatisfactory; they fought one another and failed in their duties to the gods and are sent off to the Underworld. Still, though of second rank, they are a kind of gods in the Underworld and obtain honor as such. Again in the Age of the Heroes (I am for a moment skipping the intervening Bronze Age men) some of the Greats of that period attained the Islands of the Blessed though the most of them died at Thebes and Troy. I submit that in no one of these three ages is Justice seriously relevant. The Golden Age men did not need it, the Silver Agers are incapable of it; it is quite true that the Age of the Heroes as seen in Homer certainly is concerned with questions of Justice and balance and fairness in the Hesiodic sense. But there is an air of slight remoteness in the way Hesiod refers to them. I suspect that what is implied is that they were not human, in the ordinary sense of Hesiod's contemporary world—that they were not human in vulnerability nor in their concerns with a living, and that they were perhaps altogether too grand for what Hesiod wanted to describe. If this is so, one is left with two Ages only where Justice might play a significant role. In one of them, the Bronze Men, it certainly failed to do so. Linking them with the time when Bronze was still used exclusively and Iron was not yet, they are more or less historically dated—just as the Heroic Age is historically described as that which directly precedes Hesiod's own. But wanting agriculture (they ate no bread) and spending their time in civil war and hunting, their life-style is in Hesiodic terms not human. If all of this is right, Justice is the fragment of protection that Zeus gave to man in the Iron Age—certainly in its penultimate form. (I will discuss shortly whether the Iron Age as described involves a last phase which is not yet.)

It is true, of course, that in each of the first three Ages it is explicitly said that they are Ages of Man. But it is exactly there, I think, that the special emphasis of the Other Logos (*heteros logos*) comes into play. Yes, these are all men, but these three all show that it is possible for such men to become at least a kind of God. The Bronze Age is dismissed in very pejorative terms. In spite of all their terribleness black Death got hold of them, and they go to the Underworld without names.

This leaves us with the Iron Age.

It is possible that Hesiod means us to think that the Iron Age has not yet reached its final stage. Having spoken of the ills of mankind, he says at 179 that there is still good mixed with the ills *and* that Zeus will destroy this breed of moral men, too, *when* their temples are grey even at birth and so on. Aidos and Nemesis are shown as leaving men for the Tribes of the Immortals; what will be left for man is sorrowful pain and there *will be* no defence against evil. What follows is, first, the address to the kings in the shape of the tale of the hawk and the songbird, and then a long address to Perses on the avoidance of Hybris and the rewards of those who administer Justice properly and the punishments of those who do the opposite. We then recur to the kings who are warned of the vengeful surveillance of their doings by Zeus and his thirty thousand appointed guardians who will punish them. We are told that the eye of Zeus sees all and notices all and *if he will* he sees clearly what sort of justice is this justice which a city keeps within it. What follows is very enigmatic and had better be quoted exactly:

> Were that not so, I would not be just myself nor would I have my
>   son so—for it is a bad thing to be just if the unjust should get
>   more justice than the just man;
> but I do not believe that yet Zeus of Counsel will make such an
>   ending.   WD 270–73

The two difficulties are in the words *nun dē* in 270 and in the final line: *alla ta g' ou pō eolpa telein dia mētioenta.*

If the first line means "as things are now," and it certainly looks like that, the whole passage means that Hesiod would not choose Justice here and now, to be so badly treated as he had been in Perses' lawsuit—where the unjust man got more of a share of justice than the just, that is, got a better decision of the case than himself, but he does not expect that Zeus will *yet* fulfill that. Perhaps this means that although the judgment has gone against Hesiod, Zeus may still exact punishment against Perses. Or conceivably the last line means "I do not expect that yet Zeus will abandon man altogether and give over justice." Personally I prefer the first meaning, but it is surely a very hard matter to be certain of. Whichever of these is right, there is no doubt that in this, the hardest to bear of the Ages, Zeus' justice is the only obstacle against final ruin for the good.

In each of the Ages Zeus established men who, apparently through their inward drift of character, find the destined end. But he has also set up Justice and its protectors as a palliative of the almost inevitable downward trend—the only exception being the Age of Heroes. He has given his famous ruling at 275–78:

> For this is the Rule for men that the Son of Cronos has given—
> for the fish and the beasts and the winged birds,
> that they should devour one another, for they have no Justice
>   among them—
> but to man he has given Justice and she proves to be far the best
>   WD 276–81

It is in the Iron Age that the tension between the evil which is almost at its greatest is still challenged by the palliative which Zeus has also created for them—if they choose to avail of it.

It is often said, and justly, that Hesiod's temperament is pessimistic. It is indeed a very correct version of the farmer's pessimism. There are signs of when and how you can do everything in your year, and you do them, and *usually* you will be better off, for the signs are the signs for you of the balance of the elements in the seasons. But not absolutely always will you be better off, since the mind of Zeus cannot be read completely and from our point of view is often inconsistent. And in Justice you have clear indications that it is favored by Zeus against Injustice; yet is it safe to infer that Zeus will always do so? "I do not expect that *yet* Zeus of Counsel will make such an ending," that is, the evil outcome that might conceivably be anticipated.

What is remarkable is that out of such pessimism, or at least incertitude of the good outcome, the impression of Hesiod's poetry is one of exuberance; the power of the words, the rhythm of the phrase keep bursting through the cracks of the formulas especially when Hesiod is watching a scene—the straining oxen with the goad coming down on their backs, the little boy with his mattock making work for the birds, the watchfulness of the ploughbeam lest it be worm-eaten. It is the impression of a fiercely happy Hesiod. It is a poetry of vision and rich in physical details; these are the details that pertain to the evolved presence of the object in view, not to the rhetorical or ornamental effect. That is why it is the poetry that in the *Works and Days* is essential to the understanding of what farming is and finally the understanding of the world of reality, which it expressed for him, totally.

I have said sometimes that the *Works and Days* is Hesiod's image of the mythological moment. The mythological moment exists when past and present are united, not as in the narrative of history, but in already repeated acts. Not, as Eliade has it, to *control* the outcome by repeating the original act, but to participate in an unknowable certainty. The landscape includes everything from the warning cry of the cranes, which signal the beginning of ploughing, to the struggle naked in the toil of harvest, to the picnic later. All in the context of Hesiod's warning about the value of Justice, but also in the context of the doubtfulness of whether this Justice will bring you happiness, because any formulation that man makes of Zeus' true designs is lamentably unsure. Zeus could have made farming easy, he could have made life easy. He made both difficult.

The image that Hesiod creates expresses his religious sense. But it is a religion that disavows the strength of doctrine or even belief and removes itself to a poetry of vision and hearing, in physical detail. Thus, paradoxically, the *dikē* of farming, that is the *dikē* that expresses in farming the *dikē* of the world of men in general, is not true doctrine or even belief so much as it is the myth of the conjunction of time and event.

2

THE WOMEN OF TRACHIS:
FICTIONS, PESSIMISM, ETHICS

Bernard Williams

> You see the great indifference of the gods
> to these things that have happened,
> who begat us and are called our fathers
> and look on such sufferings.
> What is to come no one can see,
> but what is here now is pitiable for us
> and shameful for them,
> but of all men hardest for him
> on whom this disaster has fallen.
> Maiden, do not stay in this house:
> you have seen death and many agonies,
> fresh and strange,
> and there is nothing here that is not Zeus.
>
> (Sophocles, *Trachiniae* 1266–78)

PHILOSOPHY, AND IN PARTICULAR MORAL PHILOSOPHY, is still deeply attached to giving good news. It is no longer attached (and in the case of Anglo-American philosophy, rarely ever was) to telling redemptive world-historical stories, and its good news no longer takes the forms familiar from such stories. It is not a matter of Leibniz's cosmic cost-benefit analysis, for instance, under which the balance of good over bad is optimal, and—roughly—nothing could have been locally improved without making the whole total worse. Leibniz's story, nevertheless, is worth a moment's attention, before we come back to things that we now can take more seriously.

This statement of Leibniz's view is indeed rough, because Leibniz requires us to accept two ideas which may seem incompatible though in fact they are not, and a proper formulation has to allow for this. The first idea is that we can understand what would count as a local improvement. We must understand this at some level, since Leibniz's theory is offered as a theodicy, that is to say, as a justification offered to people who reasonably see certain local happenings, such as those recounted in *Candide,* as disasters, and ask why those things rather than less disastrous things have to happen.

The second idea is that we cannot really understand what would count as a local improvement. This is because the idea of an improvement gets a grip on us, and in particular prompts a demand for a justification, only if it is understood as possible. We have many mere wishes that go against possibility, to change the past, for instance, or (as a friend of mine once said) to be monogamously married to each of four people at once, but they do not support any serious conception of an improvement and are no focus for a grievance. But on Leibniz's view, there cannot, strictly speaking, be any improvements, since no room for improvement is left by the Law of Sufficient Reason (in its strong form, in which it claims that this is the best of all possible worlds because it combines the maximum of variety with the maximum of simplicity). Nevertheless, it is still true that at a certain, very superficial, level we do understand the idea of a local improvement. For instance, we know that if it were in our power simply to affect the local environment, without consideration for wider regularities, these are the kinds of things we should try to prevent. So the two ideas are not after all incompatible. We think we have a grievance, but when we properly understand the situation, we see that we do not. So, Leibniz told us, there is a theodicy.

Whether this would really be enough for a theodicy raises further questions. For instance, it might be thought a reproach to God that the Law of Sufficient Reason should take the form it does: it suggests a heartless modernist preference on his part for intellectual elegance over a detailed concern for his creatures' interests. If it is then replied that it is fatuous to reproach God for his choice of a creative plan, this seems to be abandoning theodicy rather than contributing to it: that reply could have been given before Leibniz started, as indeed God had already given it to Job.

The context of theodicy of course radically shapes the discussion of what might count as good or bad news. The idea of an *improvement,* in this connection, implies something both better and possible, and the reason why the notion of possibility came into it was that the argument was shaped in order to offer a justification. It was trying to answer a grievance, by showing that the grievance was based on a misunderstanding, an excessively narrow view of things. If we move away from the world in which Leibniz, on God's behalf, dealt with a grievance—a world that now seems immeasurably remote from us—it is less clear how ideas of necessity and possibility shape our reactions to hideous events. If we are not sending complaints, then there seems less reason why our discontents can be lightened by the understanding that what happened was necessary. Perhaps a mere wish, so long as it is not too fantastic, can sustain them. Once the idea of a grievance goes away, with its restriction to the possible—a restriction which itself seems be grounded in the rather strange idea of being fair to God—then perhaps the room for discontent can expand. We can be relatively discontented even with the necessary.

Alternatively, perhaps the room for discontent should contract. Have we got a focus for discontent at all, when there is no longer anyone to receive and possibly answer a complaint? Discontent makes sense, surely, only if there can be at least some expectation of something better; without that, we are merely unhappy. So should we not say that once we lose the structure of theodicy, the very idea of good news or bad news on a cosmic scale falls away? There is simply the good or bad news that comes to us on the scale of local misfortune, such as is brought about by human action, successful or unsuccessful, helpful or malign. There is no larger question. So philosophical good news, like philosophical bad news, becomes an oxymoron—unless it means the good news, or more often the bad news, about philosophy.

This must be to go too fast. Our "discontents" can surely reach beyond local unhappiness and can be directed to an object which is more than local: directed, for instance, to what we can understand of human history, of human achievements and their costs. This unhappiness perhaps does presuppose the defeated expectation of something better, but not as a focus of complaint: what has failed is not justification but hope. This is illustrated by another redemptive story which has also departed, Hegel's. We can leave aside some of its wider cosmic aspirations: the relevant point here is that the story was meant to provide a focus for the thought that despite the horrors which underlie every human achievement, artistic, ethical or political, the enterprise will have been worthwhile.

As with Leibniz, the thought must be that the horrors were necessary—without that, we simply have another focus for regret. But in Hegel, necessity is supposed to exercise a different kind of leverage on our thoughts. On Leibniz's account, the structure of the necessity is itself part of what makes the totality worthwhile, since it is based on God's choice of the most elegantly complex universe. For Hegel, the necessity need not in itself contribute part of the value, though perhaps it could do so. The complex working of the Geist to turn suffering into historical achievement is not itself the supreme achievement. Moreover, the value of the achievement does not have to transcend a human understanding of that value, as it does with Leibniz. Other considerations laid aside, it is merely that we can reflect "without *this, that* could not be, and the value of *that* means that *this,* after all, was worthwhile."

No doubt we do not understand exactly what this reflection might mean. However, we do understand it well enough to recognize at least two different ways of rejecting it. Someone may think that the comparisons involved come out wrong: no achievement could be worth *this*. At the limit, this objection could take the form of thinking that the comparisons were absurd, because there was no sensible way of laying such things alongside one another. The achievement and the suffering are incommensurable, and the supposed justification, which outweighs the one with the other, comes to no more than an affirmation. Even in this form, however, this line of objection is different from that other rejection of such thoughts, which sees the very idea of such a comparison as indecent, a moral outrage. This rejection says rather, in the spirit of Kant, that no *achievement* could be worth this. No good or bad news can be found in history or the actual balance of things at all. That seems to rise above all such questions, and set at least the most important values, moral values, beyond history. However, the Kantian story means more than this formulation reveals. For if no ultimately good or bad news can be found in history, it follows in particular that no ultimately bad news can be found in it, and this of course carries its own kind of good news, a point we shall come back to.

Hegel's own construction had a further feature, that the historical expression of necessity was, in its larger features, total. What had happened was all coherently necessary for the valued aspects of the outcome. We shall want to reject this strongly teleological dimension itself, but it is important that merely in rejecting this, we do not necessarily reject everything that Hegel conveyed. Schopenhauer certainly rejected the triumphalist teleology, but his declaration that life, even if it is incurably a painful and shapeless mess, is redeemed by art, conveyed what he could hardly deny was in some sense good news. At the same time, his view of the world apart from this was likely to give rise only to resignation.[1]

Nietzsche at first accepted Schopenhauer's expression of tragic pessimism, but he later tried to overcome the limitations of that outlook, and I take it that it was as part of this attempt that he was drawn to the model of willing the eternal recurrence. We have to ask: What it is that we need the affirmation of the eternal recurrence to overcome? What bad feeling is it—what discontent, as we put it earlier—that the horribleness of the world is supposed to inspire? This question repeatedly opens up. It opened up in the wake of Leibniz, when we asked what one's discontent is supposed to be if there is no place for a grievance. Similarly, the failure of every possible answer to Hegel's question may leave us with the conviction that there is no such question, and if there is no question, there will be, once again, no possible focus for anything like discontent on a more than local scale. To insist that one must be left with some focus for one's discontents, even after Leibniz's and Hegel's questions have gone, may seem no better than finding some reason for being unhappy on a large scale— or, perhaps, finding some large scale on which to be unhappy. Something like this indeed seems to have been the situation of Wittgenstein. He insisted that there was no ultimate or metaphysical question about one's discontent with the world, and this left him with a problem of find-ing a more than personal object for his unhappiness, a problem that he seems to have tried to solve, in part, by directing his unhappiness on to philosophy.

For Nietzsche, there was no metaphysical question raised by the hor-rors that underlay every human achievement. Yet something was left, something that had to be met, not, certainly, by an answer, but by an affirmation. I take it that what the world's horrors presented him with was the prospect of being crushed by them.

Certainly he did not deny the necessity of the horrors to the achieve-ments. Going beyond Hegel in this as in other respects, he thought that the good not only required the bad but incorporated it: one of the meta-physicians' most basic illusions is their "belief in opposite values." [2] So if there is no honest and affirmative way of acknowledging the horrors, the only way of managing them will be to do what healthy people do all the time, and forget them. But Nietzsche seems to have thought, even if only sometimes, that such a Pyrrhonian reaction would represent weariness and a lack of vitality—a vitality taken, at this point at least, as implying truthfulness. So if there is to be truthfulness about the horrors, and no belief about their being worthwhile under some Leibnizian or Hegelian calculation, there will be only a fully conscious refusal to be crushed, and we shall need a conception, necessarily very schematic, of a life that might adequately express that refusal. The idea of the horrors having been "worth it" is operationalized, as one might quaintly put it, into the thought experiment of being prepared to will everything, with every hor-ror and every hideous triviality, to happen endlessly over again.

It is a good question what this model could possibly achieve. The af-firmation is supposed to be immensely costly, an achievement commen-surate with the dreadfulness of what it wills. Yet its content, and so, in-escapably, the affirmation itself, occurs in the gravity-free space of the imagination. Can the "greatest weight," as Nietzsche calls it,[3] really weigh anything, when it consists in willing an entirely contrary-to-fact recur-rence? Can it be more than a Styrofoam rock on a film set of cosmic hero-ism? The more familiar alternatives to willing the eternal recurrence are better defined in their effects: lying about the horrors, or forgetting about them—where that means *really* forgetting about them, except on the local scale, and getting on with one's life in a suitably unreflective way.

There is no opposition, obviously enough, between unreflective for-getting and working in philosophy. However, there are areas of philoso-phy which might be supposed to have a special commitment to not forget-ting or lying about the horrors, among them moral philosophy. No one with sense asks it to think about them all the time, but, in addressing what it claims to be our most serious concerns, it would do better if it did not make them disappear. Yet this is what in almost all its modern forms moral philosophy effectively does. This is above all because it tries to withdraw our ethical interest from both chance and necessity, except inasmuch as the necessary sets the parameters of effective action. Kantianism and consequentialism, despite their other differences (about free will, for instance), resemble each other, as Iris Murdoch has insisted, in sharing a concern with the practical. The direction of their attention in time is not in all respects the same, consequentialism being more concerned than Kantianism is with what we can now effect, and less interested in what a given agent in the past could have done at the moment of action. Nevertheless, the situation of the rational agent intending to change the world preoccupies them both, and the very plain fact that everything that an agent most cares about typically comes from, and can be ruined by, uncontrollable necessity and chance is no part of their concerns.

When in addition morality itself is disconnected historically and psychologically from the rest of life, as it often is by moral philosophy, and is left as a supposedly self-contained and self-explanatory realm of value, then necessity and chance and the bad news they bring with them are deliberately excluded. This itself, I suggested, counts as an affirmation of good news, and it is more effective as such than any theodicy. This good news, that only the moral really or seriously or ultimately matters, is shown and not said, and one is invited to accept it without even the disturbance of mentioning the matter.

The most important question here, obviously, concern how we should best think about such things. There are also some questions of how, if at all, moral philosophy within its own limits can conduct itself less evasively. Here I want to take up only a question narrower than either of these, about ways in which the defective consciousness of moral philosophy can be extended by appeal to fiction.

The most familiar appeal in ethics to fiction relies on the idea that fictional worlds can provide thought experiments for ethics. I take it that this is a version of the traditional idea that fiction can yield salutary *exempla* of virtue and vice. The idea has been significantly transmuted from an earlier world of clear statements and plain *exempla* to one in which fictions display ambiguities, moral conflicts that are imperfectly resolvable, multiple ethical interpretations and so forth, and this alteration reveals not merely changes in ethical consciousness but a changed relation of fiction both to ethical life and to moral philosophy. In a world in which there are clear moral statements and plain *exempla,* the relation between the two will tend to be something like that of text to illustration, and the role of the fiction will be that of an efficient aid. Once a certain degree of ambiguity is reached, however, the fiction will come to do things that direct statement cannot do, and working through the fiction will itself represent an extension of ethical thought, and conceivably of ethical experience. How much we can really effect by these means has been a much-discussed question; equally, to present any great fiction just in this light must be to take a limited view of it. However, in this area there is an intelligible and recognized association of fiction and ethical thought, and even of fiction and moral philosophy.

We can ask both what kinds of fiction can significantly help moral philosophy, and what styles of moral philosophy can be helped by fiction. (It could be a test of realism in a style of ethical thinking that it can learn from compelling fictions.) It is not surprising that the fiction that most easily responds to these needs, particularly when ethical thought is directed to traits of character, is (as I shall put it) "dense" fiction, above all the realistic novel, which provides a depth of characterization and social background which gives substance to the moral situation and brings it nearer to everyday experience. It may well be worth considering, for instance, how we would now describe and assess the way in which Mr. Jarndyce, in *Bleak House,* arranges for Esther Summerson's future life without consulting her, and what we can make of the approval of him that Dickens seems to expect from the reader.

The features of dense fictions that lend themselves to these thoughts also have dangers, which recent criticism has helped us to identify. Precisely because the impression of deep characterization and of social reality in such fiction is an artful construct, we can be misled into thinking that our ethical judgments are being extended, that we are gaining moral insight into a situation, when in fact our moral outlook has already done some of the work in constructing that situation. The sense of something hidden and waiting to be interpreted can be an artifact merely of fictional indeterminacy. Equally, the notorious deceptions of narrative closure can impose an ethical significance which would not be available in reality— unless, as often happens, reality itself is interpreted in terms of such deceptions.

Among their other effects, dense fictions can create the impression of necessity, but they do not typically do so in the spirit that will best compensate for the limitations of moral philosophy that have been the concern of this paper. There are, certainly, exceptions: outside the novel, *The Wild Duck* is one. But some of the most sharply delineated reminders of bad news in fiction are presented when necessity comes to the characters in the form of unmanageable chance, and the attempt to deploy this in the context of dense fiction runs the danger of coming too close to the territory that such notions equally supply to comedy and farce. (Some of Hardy illustrates this, including—as it seems to me—the climactic disaster in *Jude the Obscure.*)

There is another kind of fiction, which serves purposes in relation to moral philosophy different from the more familiar ones that are served by dense fictions. I shall call it "stark fiction," and a paradigm of it is offered by the tragedies of Sophocles. It is not merely that its style and structure avoids the anecdotal and the incidental, but that these resources are typically directed in a concentrated way to displaying the operations of chance and necessity. The phrase "a necessary chance," *anangkaia tuchē*, is to be found, twice, in the *Ajax*, and I have said something elsewhere about the ways in which this combination of ideas operates in Sophocles and about ways in which we can use it, although we do not accept all the assumptions of Sophocles' world.[4] We should not suppose, however, that the operations of stark fiction are always the same. One of several disservices that Aristotle rendered to the understanding of Greek tragedy was that of generating the idea that there is some one specific effect that makes tragedy ethically significant. Even among the surviving plays of Sophocles, to say nothing of other writers, each deals with the ethical—and reproves the limitations of our ethical ideas—in a significantly different way.

The play that is perhaps the least familiar among them, *The Women of Trachis,* is particularly relevant to the present discussion because its display of undeserved and uncompensated suffering is so entirely unrelieved. In a sense, it is very simple, compared for instance with the intricacies of the *Oedipus Tyrannus,* which it resembles to the extent of being a play of successive revelations; or compared to the *Philoctetes,* which it resembles in its display of hideous and destructive physical agony, but which deploys complex motives that have no part in this play.

The extreme starkness of the outcome and the simplicity of the effect are, needless to say, achieved by some complex adjustments. The character of Deianeira has often been seen as peculiarly sweet in a domestic style, a less active and formidable figure than most major Sophoclean women: like Chrysothemis, rather, or Ismene, but, unlike them, the initiator of the action, if a diffident one. She speaks in a way that can make her marriage seem a familiar type of story, as when she says (31 *et seq.*) that they have children now, whom Heracles "sees at times, like a farmer working in an outlying field, who sees it only when he sows and when he reaps." But it would be a mistake to think the aim is a touching naturalism; twenty lines before this, at the very beginning of the play, she had been telling us how she was wooed by a river, which presented itself first as a bull, then as a serpent, and then as a half-human creature from whose beard a waterfall fell. The aim is not naturalism, but an impression, above all, of vulnerability. It is significant, too, that the poison she prepares is, relative to the tradition, underdescribed. The story was that it was made from the centaur's semen, but this element has disappeared from the play. It is tempting to think that this was too sexually assertive an image to suit Deianeira's use of the substance in order to cancel, as she supposes, Heracles' erotic diversion and to regain him as her husband.

It is remarkable, as Nicole Loraux has pointed out,[5] that she kills herself with a sword, a male method of death. This weapon, the same as Ajax used in his suicide, stands in a gendered opposition to the noose, for instance, which Jocasta used. But the effect is certainly not that she is another Ajax, that there has been a transgressive reversal of roles. The image is rather that of passivity, of a brutal thing having been done to her. The nurse's narration of her death does not present us with the act itself: at one moment of that narration, Deianeira is undoing her gown, and the next moment she is dead. It is as though she had been killed rather than killed herself. The message conveyed by the weapon is not that she has killed herself as a male might do, but that she has been killed by males. In just three lines (933–35) we are told that her son had forced her to this act, and that she has without knowing it done the will of Nessus.

Heracles' death, equally, is unsuitable, and the story has again been adjusted, in this case in order to remove any hint of glory from it, to leave it as nothing but unredeemed and hideous suffering. Traditionally, when Heracles died and his body burned, he was deified, and that version is deployed by Sophocles at the end of the *Philoctetes;* but not here, where Heracles' last words only call on his "tough soul to put a steel bit in his mouth and hold back the screams, so that an end can be made of this unwanted, welcome, task"—welcome only because it will mean the end of the pain.

All the force of the play is directed to leaving in the starkest relief its extreme, undeserved, and uncompensated suffering, and this is what is registered in the famous and strange words with which it ends, quoted at the beginning of this paper. "There is nothing here that is not Zeus" is not a comforting or explanatory remark: it registers only inexplicable necessity, a necessity which may indeed be ascribed to the activities of the gods, but if so, to gods who do not explain themselves or take any notice of the suffering that they bring about. *Agnōmosunē* is what is ascribed to the gods, a negative thing, non-understanding, as contrasted with the *sungnōmosunē* of the line before, the shared understanding that Hyllus finds in his companions. Most remarkable, perhaps, is the idea that what has happened, pitiable for us, is "shameful for them"—and "them" can only be the gods. This doubly underscores the thought that there is no justification. What the gods do will be shameful because there is nothing they could say to excuse it. Moreover, their deeds can be understood as shameful only in the eyes of human beings, and that this can be so, that it even makes sense, shows that they have no authority in their power. They cannot give even the answer that Job received, an answer which offers no justification but which should at least silence the demand for one.

There is, of course, the old question, Aristotle's question, of how pleasure or profit could be got from watching such an enactment, but this is not the question here. It is essential that there is pleasure, and that something is achieved by such a play, and that it does not serve simply as an unwelcome reminder of cosmic awfulness. This is connected with what it achieves as a work of art, and, as Nietzsche already said in *The Birth of Tragedy,* this must lie, in part, in its enabling us to contemplate such things in honesty without being crushed by them. When later he said that we have art so that we do not perish from the truth,[6] he did not mean that we use art in order to escape from the truth: he meant that we have art so that we can both grasp the truth and not perish from it.

It is certainly not that the play's existence as a work of art in some sense *makes up* for the horrors, and to the extent that this is what the early Nietzsche meant by the idea that life is metaphysically redeemed through art, he was wrong, as he indeed came to think. The point of tragedy—or at least of those tragedies that are stark fictions—must lie rather in the fact that it lays its fictional horrors before us in a way that elicits attitudes we cannot take towards real horrors. With real horrors, we are sometimes practically engaged in them; sometimes, we have some particular reason to be upset by them; most of the time we are necessarily, and (as Nietzsche occasionally brought himself to say) healthily, inattentive to them. What we cannot possibly, or at least decently, adopt towards them is the range of attitudes appropriate to fictional horrors presented in art. Yet such a fiction can carry some understanding of the real horrors. One might say that it reveals their metaphysical structure, their relation, or lack of it, to the universe; except that any such formula follows Aristotle's bad example in trying to give a general account of "the tragic effect," and indeed does worse than Aristotle in hinting, as neither his account nor Nietzsche's does, that some suitably profound philosophical formulation might take the place of the tragedy itself.

It is a mistake to look for one aim even of stark fictions, and the immensely general ideas that I have glanced at here could at best offer a kind of pattern within which the effects of different works might be variously construed. Moreover, most of the things that can be achieved by stark fictions, and through the attitudes appropriate to them, are necessarily obscure. One of their more obvious achievements, however, if not the most basic or important, is to offer a necessary supplement and a suitable limitation to the tireless aim of moral philosophy to make the world safe for well-disposed people.

NOTES

1. See Nietzsche, "Attempt at a Self-Criticism," added to the 1886 edition of *The Birth of Tragedy.* One of the personal qualities that Nietzsche saluted in Scho-

penhauer was, notably, his cheerfulness. See "Schopenhauer as Educator," translated by William Arrowsmith in *Unmodern Observations* (New Haven: Yale University Press, 1990), 162.

2. Nietzsche's phase is "der Glaube an die Gegensätze der Werte." See *Beyond Good and Evil*, sec. 2.

3. Nietzsche's phrase is "das grösste Schwergewicht." See *The Gay Science*, sec. 351.

4. Lines 485, 803. I discuss Sophocles' significance for us (and, more generally, that of tragedy and the epic) in *Shame and Necessity* (Berkeley and Los Angeles: University of California Press, 1993). For the phrase from the *Ajax* see 104, 123–24.

5. In *Façons tragiques de tuer une femme* (Paris, 1985), translated by Anthony Forster as *Tragic Ways of Killing a Woman* (Cambridge, Mass.: Harvard University Press, 1987).

6. "Wir haben die *Kunst,* damit wir *nicht an der Wahrheit zugrunde gehn.*" This is from the *Nachlass* of the 1880's. See *Werke in 3 Bänden,* edited by Karl Schlechte (Munich, 1966), vol. 3, 832.

RESPONSE

Robert B. Louden

BAD NEWS ABOUT GOOD NEWS

I would like to start by asking whether moral philosophy "is still deeply attached to giving good news." While Bernard Williams acknowledges that moral philosophy is "no longer attached . . . to telling redemptive world-historical stories" à la Leibniz or Hegel, he nevertheless remains convinced that moral philosophy "in almost all its modern forms" aims tirelessly at making "the world safe for well-disposed people."

Suppose we start by saying that *one* thing (not the only thing) that moral philosophers typically try to do is to present an account and a justification of morally right action. Writing in 1930, and introducing a usage of terminology which was to influence fatefully subsequent moral philosophy, C. D. Broad states:

> I would first divide ethical theories into two classes, which I will respectively *deontological* and *teleological*.
>
> Deontological theories hold that there are ethical propositions of the form: "Such and such a kind of action would always be right (or wrong) in such and such circumstances, no matter what the consequences might be." [1]

"[N]o matter what the consequences might be." Where is the deep attachment to good news in an ethical theory that takes the deontological path?

If what one wants is a moral philosophy that "does not forget or lie about the horrors," then a normative perspective that advocates doing justice "though the heavens may fall" and which views the duty of honesty as "a sacred and unconditionally commanding law of reason that admits of no expediency whatsoever" (that is to say: no matter what tragedy may befall) would seem to be the most direct route.[2] Or, as Deianeira herself puts it, in *The Women of Trachis:* "do not cheat me of the truth! . . . Tell me the whole truth [*pan talēthes*]. To gain the reputation of a liar is utter dishonor for a free man [*eleutheros*]" (*Trachiniae* 437, 453–54).[3]

Now the other half of Broad's infamous dichotomy concerns teleological theories of ethics. "Teleological theories," he writes, "hold that the rightness . . . of an action is always determined by its tendency to produce certain consequences which are intrinsically good."[4] While most moral teleologies are not nearly as 'triumphalist' as the cosmic world histories to which Williams draws our attention, I do think that teleological ethical theories are likely suspects to question in the search for good-news mongers. For the most influential ones have been utilitarian, and their reductionist definitions of 'right' in terms of 'good' (when taken together with their concomitant injunction to *maximize* the good) do seem to imply an optimism that plenty of good can always be had and that tragedy can always be avoided—at least by those consequentialists in the know.

However, even here—in the midst of the good tidings of consequentialism—there appears to be theoretical space for a kind of *negative* consequentialism which might not lie about the horrors. This type of moral theory would say (to put it somewhat crudely): "Look, the world's a dark place, and there's unfortunately not a lot of good to be found in it. Still, on our view, what makes an act morally right is that it helps bring about better consequences than any other alternative. But here 'better' (in our dark circumstances) means 'less bad': one ought to choose those acts which lead to the fewest catastrophic consequences. 'Minimize catastrophes' (and not, as our optimistic brethren would have it, 'Maximize preference-satisfactions') shall be our motto."[5] Whether this method of practical decision-making would have helped Tekmessa in her confrontations with *anangkaia tuchē*—the "necessary chance" or "doom" toward which the "stark fictions" of Sophocles frequently direct us, fictions which Williams urges on us as a "necessary supplement and a suitable limitation" to the tireless good-news peddling of moral philosophy—is doubtful. "There is no greater evil for human beings than *anangkaia tuchē*," Tekmessa tells Ajax. She was born rich and free, but "Now I'm a slave. So it was decided by the gods, perhaps, and above all by your hand" (*Ajax* 485–90).[6] Such things "just happen," and here (as elsewhere) consequentialism demands of human beings that they know things which they cannot possibly know. Still, while I myself am no fan of consequentialism, it does seem to me that a negative consequentialism of the sort sketched above will get us in closer proximity to the tragic than will its rosier relative.

I have argued thus far that not all moral philosophies ignore tragedy. Deontologies face it squarely, and even negative consequentialisms will not run away from it. Within the history of modern ethics, Kant's ethical theory has always been the favorite paradigm of deontology. Yet Kant's moral philosophy also does not escape from the broad brush of Williams's good news criticism. Kantian morality, he tells us, "is disconnected historically and psychologically from the rest of life, and is left as a supposedly self-contained and self-explanatory realm of value, necessity and chance and the bad news they bring with them are deliberately excluded, and . . . this counts as an affirmation of good news." Here, as in previous writings,[7] Williams is objecting to Kant's effort to ground ethics in a conception of pure agency—a conception in which the determining grounds of the moral will are sharply distinguished not only from "gifts of nature" (*Naturgaben*) such as intelligence and wit and "gifts of fortune" (*Glücksgaben*) such as power and wealth (*Gr* 4: 393), but indeed, in which its free choices require "an independence of determination by *all* antecedent causes in the phenomenal world."[8] Ever since 1786, when Hermann Andreas Pistorius, in one of the first published reviews of Kant's *Groundwork*, confessed that "this double character of man, these two I's in the single subject, are for me, in spite of all the explanations which Kant and his students have given of it, . . . the most obscure and incomprehensible [*das Dunkelste und Unbegreiflichste*] in the entire critical philosophy,"[9] critics have wrestled with what Williams elsewhere calls "the more extravagant metaphysical luggage of the noumenal self."[10]

I cannot begin to untie such obscurities here, but I do wish to establish three quick points. First, the sense of self-righteousness which Williams attributes to the Kantian deontologist (feeling smug in the security of knowing that one has done the right thing from the purest of motives, whatever the consequences) simply does not ring true.[11] For Kant is profoundly skeptical as to whether anyone can ever know whether he or she has succeeded in doing the right thing for the right reason. As he writes in the *Groundwork*:

> In fact it is absolutely impossible [*schlecterdings unmöglich*] through experience to establish with complete certainty a single case in which the maxim of an action in other respects right has rested solely on moral grounds and on the thought of one's duty. . . . [W]e can never, even by the most strenuous self-examination, get to the bottom of our secret incentives [*Triebfedern*] (*Gr* 4: 407).

The very separation of noumenal and phenomenal causes which Williams disdains (when combined with the impossibility of our knowing the former) means that Kantian moral agents can never know for sure whether any of their motives are completely pure morally and immune to luck. Since the real morality of our conduct "remains entirely hidden [*gänzlich verborgen*] from us" (*Critique of Pure Reason* A551/B 579 n.), we are never in a position to know with certainty whether we have succeeded in doing the right thing for the right reason. Any attitude of moral self-righteousness or smugness (which, again, on Williams's view "counts as an affirmation of good news" in so far as the moral self is allegedly disconnected from the potentially bad news of necessity and chance) is thus entirely unwarranted on Kant's view.

Second, despite Kant's strong separation of the determining grounds of moral character from all *Natur-* and *Glücksgaben* in the *Groundwork,* he elsewhere clearly acknowledges that our moral lives are not totally up to us. Early in the *Lectures on Pedagogy,* for instance, he announces that "the human being can only become human through education. He is nothing [*Er ist nichts*] except what education makes of him" (9: 443). As one recent critic has observed, "because getting a good education is (at least partly) a matter of luck, Kant, too, would have to admit some influence of luck to morality.[12] More generally: Kant's commitment to transcendental freedom does not entail that moral agents are completely divorced from nature and history. Rather, they are to use nature and history to further moral ends, according to the requirements of pure practical reason. Interaction between the phenomenal and noumenal worlds is necessary if we are to make sense of human morality, for the latter requires that freely chosen purposes be actualized in the world of sense. As Kant states in his essay "Perpetual Peace," "the mechanism of nature" is itself to be "used by reason as a means to prepare the way for its own end, the rule of right" (8: 366–67).[13] Similarly, in the Introduction to the third *Critique,* he explicitly states that the realm of the concept of freedom "is *meant* to have an influence upon [the realm of the concept of nature] . . . that is to say, the concept of freedom is meant to actualize in the world of sense the purpose proposed by its laws" (5: 176).[14]

Third, if one insists (as Williams does) on interpreting Kant's doctrine of transcendental freedom in the heavy-handed "two-world" manner, one must at least grant that insofar as his philosophy is committed to giving good news by trying to isolate moral agents from the bad news of history and nature, it is not the deontology in his normative ethics that is the source of this commitment but rather his metaphysics of pure agency. It is no secret that few if any contemporary "Kantians" in ethics can swallow in anything close to unadulterated form Kant's theory of transcendental freedom. Although Kant himself was convinced that "to argue freedom away [*die Freiheit wegzuvernünfteln*] is as impossible for the most abstruse philosophy as it is for the most ordinary human reason" (*Gr* 4: 456;

cf. 5: 7, 3), growing numbers of contemporary philosophers appear determined to argue it away.[15]

Let me return again briefly to the larger issue of moral philosophy and
good news. A final reason for skepticism regarding Williams's claim that
moral philosophy "in almost all its modern forms" is deeply attached to
giving good news stems from the fact that Broad's overworked distinction
between deontological and teleological theories is not an exhaustive classification of the options in normative ethics. Some styles of ethical thinking, as Williams himself notes later in his paper, are primarily concerned
with traits of character rather than with the question "Which *acts* are
morally obligatory and why?" Philosophers who hold that character traits
such as courage and practical wisdom are fundamental to our ethical condition and who seek to better understand and justify them will also not be
committed only to giving good news. For courage and practical wisdom
only make sense as virtues against a background of at least occasional
bad news.

In sum, there is nothing inherent in moral philosophy per se that commits it to giving good news or to cultivating a defective consciousness.
Insofar as certain moral philosophies are deeply attached to giving good
news, the reasons why they are so attached often stem not from their normative ethics but from other sources. For some, the good news giving
stems from an underlying Panglossian commitment that (appearances to
the contrary) our world is "the best of all possible worlds" and that "all is
for the best."[16] For others, it can be traced to a conviction that "the history of the world is the progress of the consciousness of Freedom."[17] Williams holds (and I agree) that we today, like Sophocles' original audience,
"know that the world was not made for us, or we for the world, that our
history tells no purposive story, and that there is no position outside the
world or outside history from which we might hope to authenticate our
activities."[18] But nothing prevents moral philosophy from telling it like it
is, and, as part of its telling, from offering and defending strategies for
coping with how it is.

FICTION TO THE RESCUE?

Although I have argued thus far that moral philosophy per se is not, as
Williams holds, necessarily attached to giving good news, I do not wish to
claim that moral philosophy never needs help or that it can always heal
itself in cases where it does need help. On the contrary, I believe that moral
philosophy needs all the help it can get, and that it therefore continually
needs to turn not only to *all* of the various arts and humanities but to the
social and natural sciences as well in its attempt to portray accurately and
(where possible) justify our ethical condition. However, since Williams's

paper focuses specifically on *two* "ways in which the defective conscious-ness of moral philosophy can be extended by appeal to *fiction*" (emphasis mine), in what follows I shall restrict myself primarily to some remarks concerning moral philosophy's relation to certain kinds of fiction.

The first of Williams's two ways is what he calls "dense fictions"—typified above all by the realistic novel of a Dickens or an Austen "which provides a depth of characterization and social background which gives substance to the moral situation and brings it nearer to everyday experi-ence." The kinds of help that dense fictions are typically alleged to offer ethics include a heightened awareness of morally relevant particulars, a strengthened capacity for judgment, a sharper awareness of conflicting obligations and of the incommensurability of values, and a recognition of the moral significance of the emotions.[19]

The second way, which Williams himself champions in the present essay as well as in his book *Shame and Necessity* (1993), is the way of "stark" fictions, the paradigm of which "is offered by the tragedies of Sophocles." The primary purpose of stark fictions, as Kant might have put it, is to "wake us from our dogmatic slumbers"—that is, to lay before us the horrors and undeserved evils of life, horrors caused by the brute fact that our lives are not always ours and that there are things beyond our control. Equally important to the presentation of bad news made by stark fictions are their suggestions of the appropriate attitude to take toward the horrors—an attitude of understanding untouched by any hope of justifi-cation which enables us "to contemplate such things in honesty without being crushed by them."[20]

I applaud Williams's focus on stark fictions. I think he has succeeded admirably in both drawing our attention to a different kind of purpose that fiction can serve in relation to moral philosophy and in illuminating some crucial ways in which Sophocles' under-appreciated play, *The Women of Trachis,* eerily addresses our own ethical condition. But in keeping with a respondent's duty, in the remainder of my reply I wish to raise a few skeptical questions about stark fictions.

Several of my concerns perhaps come down to different ways of ask-ing for a clearer definition of "stark fiction." To begin with, there is a posited near-identity between dense fictions and novels on the one hand, and stark fictions and tragedies on the other, which does not seem to hold up. Clearly not all novels are dense, nor all tragedies stark. Counterex-amples in the first category would include the direct, terse, almost mini-malist style of Hemingway's novels and what are often tagged "metaphysi-cal" novels, such as Kafka's *The Castle.*[21] Examples of dense tragedies are admittedly harder to come up with (perhaps for the simple reason that plays are generally shorter than novels—playwrights thus can't go in for the depth of characterization and social background at which novelists often aim). But Williams himself mentions Ibsen's *The Wild Duck* (1884) in this context, and perhaps earlier plays such as *Pillars of Society* (1877) or *A Doll's House* (1879) would serve even better.

A second, related point: from what exactly does (what appears to us as) the unmistakably stark quality of Sophocles' tragedies stem? My hunch is that what strikes *us* as their starkness may be due partly to extraliterary factors which are foreign to our own artistic culture, such as the convention of the chorus, the masks worn by the actors (which means no facial expressions), the use of well-known stories (which meant that the audience already knew, to a great extent, what was coming)[22]—not to mention the strong influence of supernatural conceptions of necessity which Williams discusses at length in *Shame and Necessity*. If this is true, then starkness may be partly epiphenomenal rather than a deep-seated feature of fiction.

I suspect also that the medium of fiction per se has no monopoly on starkness. If the bottom line of stark fictions is that they force us to confront bad news and to adopt an attitude of understanding that does not seek justification, it would seem that other art forms could perform the task equally well. For example, aren't paintings such as Edvard Munch's *The Scream* and Goya's *Third of May, 1808* also stark in Williams's sense?

A further problem: how serviceable in practice is the dense-stark distinction when one approaches works of fiction with it? I tried earlier to demarcate them clearly from one another, and I *do* think there is something to the distinction. But let me quickly register three small doubts: First, are there important works of fiction which cut across the dense-stark dichotomy in ways which force us to question the very value of the distinction? Consider, for example, Melville's *Billy Budd,* as interpreted by Lee Yearley in his essay for this symposium. Is the mythical figure of Billy Budd stark or dense? Second, other critics (Nussbaum, for example) who also urge moral philosophers to study Greek tragedies do so on the grounds that they alert us to "the experiences of complex characters" who teach us about the "mutability of our circumstances and our passions, [and] conflicts among our commitments"[23]—that is, for precisely those reasons Williams associates with dense fictions rather than stark ones! (Williams, in referring to these same remarks of Nussbaum's in *Shame and Necessity*, complains that "not many of her reasons are specific to tragedy; some of them . . . seem to apply more to the novel than to tragedy."[24] And third, the basis of my second doubt may lie deeper than the usual interpretive battles over what texts mean. Williams himself, in earlier writings, has put much weight on notions such as conflicting obligations,[25] luck, and vulnerability[26]—ideas which were soon taken up in earnest by dense-fiction aficionados such as Nussbaum.[27] His concept of choice at present comes from Sophocles' odd phrase[28] *anangkaia tuchē*—"necessary chance" or "impending doom"—something stronger than mere luck (*tuchē*). But when does *tuchē* stop being merely bad and become necessary? At any rate, it does seem to me that Williams himself is partially responsible for occasional classificatory blurrings between density and starkness and that he needs to differentiate them more clearly from one another in order to make his own Sophoclean points stick.[29]

At one point in his essay Williams alludes to some "dangers" of dense fictions "that recent criticism has helped us to identify." This leads me to my next worry: might not stark fictions also contain their own inherent dangers, dangers to which criticism should alert us? One possible danger is that our ethical judgments, rather than being extended, will simply be extinguished by the weight of so much bad news. When Hyllus, at the end of *The Women of Trachis,* says "there is nothing here that is not Zeus [1278],"[30] the "here" refers to a string of disasters not mentioned in Williams's paper. Hyllus has promised to burn his father alive (1187–90), he has also promised to marry his father's lover Iole—the very same woman whom he believes to be the underlying cause of both of his parents' deaths (1216–1229), and he also has to live with the knowledge that his own falsely grounded rage made his mother kill herself (740, 930–32). What Williams wants from such fictions is an attitude of understanding which accepts that not everything can be justified. But at what point does such an attitude sink into a total despair from which there is no coming back?

Also, is it not likely that some of the admitted "dangers" of dense fictions will also be shared by stark fictions, since both are, after all, fictions? At one point Williams refers to the "artful constructs" of dense fictions which may only fool us into thinking that we are "gaining moral insight into a situation," and yet, as he reminds us later, the extreme starkness of the outcome of *The Women of Trachis* is also achieved only by means of "some complex adjustments." But might not artful constructs also be at work here, constructs which may be only fooling us into thinking that we have gained moral insight into a situation?

As a final note, I wish to underscore the simple point that the dichotomy of dense and stark fictions certainly does not exhaust the ways in which "the defective consciousness of moral philosophy" can be helped by fiction. Here, if anywhere, the scholar's urge to classify needs to be restrained. The ways in which fiction can help moral philosophy are infinite, for which moral philosophers (and others) should be grateful.[31]

My own favorite among the infinite types of aid that fiction brings to ethics (a type which itself admits of endless variations) is imagination. Shelley, in his *Defense of Poetry,* writes: "the great instrument of moral good is the imagination; and poetry administers to the effect by acting on the cause." [32] Dewey adds: "Hence it is that art is more moral than moralities. For the latter either are, or tend to become, consecrations of the *status quo,* reflections of custom, reinforcements of the established order." [33] Admittedly, romantics sometimes display a tendency simply to equate morality with imagination, and no morality exists without (among other things) strong constraints. But imagination is needed even in dealing with constraints, for we must always determine which moral precept is most relevant to the case at hand and then judge how exactly it is to be applied to the situation before us.

Ultimately, what creates the possibility for each of fiction's ways of helping moral philosophy is still best captured by Aristotle's well-known observation that poetry "is more philosophical [*philosophōteron*] and more important [*spoudaioteron*] than history; for poetry refers more to the universal [*ta katholou*], history the particular [*ta kath' hekaston*]." [34] Great art—even when it is a product of a radically different time and place from what we are accustomed to—tells us about ourselves. Art does express universal truths (truths which may constitute good news, bad news, or still other kinds of news) about our condition, but it embodies its claims concretely in individuals. As Heracles reminds us at the conclusion of the *Philoctetes:* "All this must be *your* suffering too" (1422, emphasis mine). This concretization strategy of art gives it an advantage over the abstractions of theory and philosophy at what might be called the initial "moment of impact." But we are then forced to reflect and to try to understand (if not, alas, to justify). "*What* does this tell me about *my* suffering? *What* attitude is called for here?" And at this point fiction needs reflection, that is, moral philosophy. But because they thus complement one another and help one another in striving toward the common goal of a clearer elucidation (and, where possible, justification) of our ethical condition, there is no need to view the matter as a turf battle which only one side can win.

Allow me to end on a lighter note. Granted, accurate reporting about our ethical condition requires us to present not only the good news but the bad news too. But morality is also more than just a pastiche of good news combined with bad news. In his "Attempt at a Self-Criticism," [35] Nietzsche attempts to get beyond what Williams refers to as the "limitations" of Schopenhauer's pessimism. Nietzsche advises: "you ought to learn to laugh, my young friends, if you are hell-bent on remaining pessimists. . . . Raise up your hearts, my brothers, high, higher! And don't forget your legs! Raise up your legs, too, good dancers; and still better: stand on your heads!" [36] In addition to the stark fictions of Sophocles, our "defective moral consciousness" also needs occasional exposure to the comic strategies of Aristophanes. Which the Greeks of course knew.

NOTES

1. C. D. Broad, *Five Types of Ethical Theory* (London: Routledge and Kegan Paul, 1930), 206. For more on Broad's terminological usage and the development of deontological ethics, see my "Toward a Genealogy of 'Deontology'" (forthcoming, *The Journal of the History of Philosophy*).

2. The infamous precept "Let justice be done though the heavens fall (*Fiat justitia et ruant coeli*)" comes from William Watson, *A Decacordon of Ten Quodlibetical Questions Concerning Religion and State* (1602). For a brief discussion and defense of the claim that "you are to do what you ought, no matter what tragedy may befall," see Alan Donagan, *The Theory of Morality* (Chicago: University of Chicago Press, 1977), 206–09. The remark about honesty is of course Kant's, from his essay "On a Supposed Right to Lie Because of Philanthropic Concerns," in *Kants gesammelte Schriften,* edited by the Deutsche (formerly Königliche Preussische) Akademie der Wissenschaft, vol. 8 (Berlin: Walter de Gruyter [and predecessors], 1902–), 427. Apart from the *Critique of Pure Reason* all references to Kant are to the volume and page numbers of this edition. References to the *Critique of Pure Reason* are to the standard A and B pagination of the first and second editions.

3. Electra, however, adopts a somewhat different attitude toward truth and justice:

Electra: Do I not seem to you to speak with justice [*sun dikē*]?

Chorus: Yet there are places where justice brings harm [*blabē*].

Electra: Under such laws [*nomoi*] I do not wish to live (*Electra* 1041–43).

In translating Sophocles, I have relied on the translations found in *The Complete Greek Tragedies,* edited by David Grene and Richmond Lattimore (Chicago: The University of Chicago Press, 1957). However, I have occasionally made minor modifications in these translations.

4. Broad, *Five Types of Ethical Theory,* 206–07.

5. Karl Popper, in vol. 1 of *The Open Society and its Enemies* (London: Routledge & Kegan Paul, 1945), toys briefly with this idea when he suggests that the utilitarian formula "Maximize happiness" be replaced with "Minimize suffering" (65, n. 6). See also J. J. C. Smart's discussion, "Negative Utilitarianism," in J. J. C. Smart and Bernard Williams, *Utilitarianism: For and Against* (London: Cambridge University Press, 1973), 28–30.

6. Williams's translation. See his discussion of this passage in *Shame and Necessity* (Berkeley: University of California Press, 1993), 104–05. Here he states: "the work of this poet [Sophocles] is central to many of the ideas I discuss [in this book]."

7. See, for example, his criticisms of pure agency in "Moral Luck," reprinted in *Moral Luck: Philosophical Papers 1973–80* (New York: Cambridge University Press, 1981), 29–30; and his attack on "the purity of morality" in *Ethics and the Limits of Philosophy* (Cambridge: Harvard University Press, 1985), 195–96.

8. Henry E. Allison, *Kant's Theory of Freedom* (New York: Cambridge University Press, 1990), 1 (emphasis mine). See also Allison's reply to Williams's objections to Kant's ethics, 191–98.

9. Hermann Andreas Pistorius, "Rezension der *Grundlegen der Metaphysik der Sitten*" (1786), reprinted in *Materialien zu Kants "Kritik der Praktischen Vernunft,"* edited by Rüdiger Bittner and Konrad Cramer (Frankfurt: Suhrkamp, 1975), 175. On 29, n. 1 of Kant's *Theory of Freedom* Allison incorrectly cites this as a review of Kant's *Kritik der Praktischen Vernunft*. For further discussion see Frederick C. Beiser, "The Good Pastorius," in *The Fate of Reason: German Philosophy from Kant to Fichte* (Cambridge: Harvard University Press, 1987), 189–92.

10. Williams, *Ethics and the Limits of Philosophy*, 65.

11. However, for some moralists it is indeed a problem. Dewey writes: "There are others who take seriously the idea of morals separated from the ordinary actualities of humanity and who attempt to live up to it. Some become engrossed in spiritual egotism. They are preoccupied with the state of their character, concerned for the purity of their motives and the goodness of their souls. The exaltation of conceit which sometimes accompanies this absorption can produce a corrosive inhumanity which exceeds the possibilities of any other known form of selfishness." (*Human Nature and Conduct: An Introduction to Social Psychology* [New York: Henry Holt and Company, 1922], 7). For discussion, see Edmund L. Pincoffs, *Quandaries and Virtues: Against Reductivism in Ethics* (Lawrence: University Press of Kansas, 1986, 112–14) and my *Morality and Moral Theory: A Reappraisal and Reaffirmation* (New York: Oxford University Press, 1992), 16–19.

12. *Moral Luck*, edited by Daniel Statman (Albany: State University of New York Press, 1993), 26, n. 3. This anthology contains recent replies to Williams's and Thomas Nagel's earlier essays on moral luck. I have recently prepared a new English translation of Kant's *Über Pädagogik*, to appear in vol. 7 of *The Cambridge Edition of the Works of Immanuel Kant*.

13. Compare Christine Korsgaard: "To the extent, or in the sense, that Kant believes that virtue can be taught, or made to flower by a good constitution, he must believe that it can be caused" ("Creating the Kingdom of Ends: Reciprocity and Responsibility," *Philosophical Perspectives* 6 [1992], 322). See also John R. Silber's discussion of "The Problem of the Two Standpoints," in "The Ethical Significance of Kant's *Religion*," in Immanuel Kant, *Religion Within the Limits of Reason Alone*, translated by Theodore M. Greene and Hoyt H. Hudson (New York: Harper & Row, 1960).

14. For further discussion of this point, see John H. Zammito, "The Ethical Turn in Kant's *Critique of Judgment*," in *The Genesis of Kant's Critique of Judgment* (Chicago: University of Chicago Press, 1992), 263–68.

15. For one recent example, see Hud Hudson, *Kant's Compatibilism* (Ithaca: Cornell University Press, 1994).

16. Voltaire, *Candide*, in *Candide, Zadig, and Selected Stories*, translated by Donald Frame (New York: New American Library), 16.

17. G. W. F. Hegel, *Vorlesungen über die Philosophie der Geschichte*, in *Werke: Theorie Werkausgabe* (Frankfurt: Suhrkamp, 1970), 12:32.

18. Williams, *Shame and Necessity*, 166.

19. These are all prominent themes in Martha C. Nussbaum's influential work in this area. See, for example, *Love's Knowledge* (New York: Oxford University

Press, 1990), especially chapters 1 and 5. See also n. 27 below concerning the relationship of Nussbaum's project to Williams's.

20. Compare Williams's earlier rejection of ethical theory's strong justificatory urge in *Ethics and the Limits of Philosophy*, 112–14, 199. Fiction, on this view, is superior to moral philosophy because it does not seek justification where no justification can be found. For criticism, see my *Morality and Moral Theory*, 150–52.

21. Williams does at one point refer specifically to the *realistic* novel in describing dense fictions. But even if literary typologists could agree on the exact scope of "realistic" novels (and I don't think they can), I doubt whether all members of the set could be accurately described as "dense."

22. See Bernard M. Knox's discussion of these and other related issues in his introduction to *Oedipus the King* (New York: Washington Square Press, 1970), xviii–xxix.

23. Martha C. Nussbaum, *The Fragility of Goodness: Luck and Ethics in Greek Tragedy and Philosophy* (New York: Cambridge University Press, 1986), 13.

24. Williams, *Shame and Necessity*, 173, n. 22.

25. For example, "Ethical Consistency," in *Problems of the Self: Philosophical Papers 1956–72* (New York: Cambridge University Press, 1973).

26. For example, "Moral luck," reprinted in *Moral Luck*.

27. In the acknowledgments to *The Fragility of Goodness*, Nussbaum writes: "The entire project . . . first took on concrete form as a possibility in a seminar on Moral Luck given by Bernard Williams at Harvard in 1972–73."

28. *Anangkaia tuchē* is not easy to translate into English. Williams's choice of "necessary chance" is quite literal, but sounds (intentionally?) odd. As he notes, the phrase occurs twice in the *Ajax* at lines 485 and 803. F. Storr, in his Loeb Classical Library translation (Cambridge: Harvard University Press, 1913), renders it first as "the coils of fate" and then as "impending doom" (45, 69). John Moore, in vol. 2 of The University of Chicago Press edition of *The Complete Greek Tragedies* (1957), translates it as "compelling fortune" and "doom" (231, 243).

29. At one point in *Shame and Necessity*, Williams translates *anangkaia tuchē* as "bad luck," when he observes that the Greeks "regarded being a slave as a paradigm of bad luck: *anangkaia tuchē*, the bad luck of being in a condition imposed and sustained by force" (123–24). But I still think (as his last phrase suggests?) that Sophoclean *anangkaia tuchē* would have to be an extremely severe form of bad luck—one "imposed and sustained by force" (*anangkē*).

30. The attribution of the closing lines is confused in the various manuscripts of the *Trachiniae*. See Charles Segal, *Tragedy and Civilization: An Interpretation of Sophocles* (Cambridge: Harvard University Press, 1981), 432, n. 143, for discussion and references. I agree with his judgment that there is "little doubt that they do belong to Hyllus."

31. One critic, for instance, after carefully excavating fifteen different types of novels and providing specific examples of each type, in effect gives up by noting: "Although the classification of novels is helpful in indicating the breadth and diversity of the form, the great novel transcends such categorization, existing as a

complete, many-faceted world in itself" (*The New Columbia Encyclopedia*, s.v. "Novel").

32. Percy Bysshe Shelley, *A Defense of Poetry*, edited by Albert S. Cook (Boston: Ginn & Co., 1890), 14.

33. John Dewey, *Art as Experience* (New York: Capricorn Books, 1958), 348. I discuss this issue at greater lengths in *Morality and Moral Theory*, 152–58. See also Mark Johnson, *Moral Imagination: Implications of Cognitive Science for Ethics* (Chicago: University of Chicago Press, 1993), especially chapter 8.

34. Aristotle, *Poetics* 1451b5–7. I do, however, agree with Richard Eldridge's observation that "this remark seriously undervalues history, which is not mere chronicle but itself involves the construction of narratives" (*On Moral Personhood: Philosophy, Literature, Criticism, and Self-Understanding* [Chicago: University of Chicago Press, 1989], 12). Similarly, one ought not to over-read Aristotle's claim by falling into the "progressivist" error of assuming that Greek tragedy "replaced" history (only to then be replaced by philosophy). See Bruno Snell, *The Discovery of the Mind: The Greek Origins of European Thought*, translated by T. G. Rosenmeyer (Cambridge: Harvard University Press, 1953), chapter 5, especially 90, 112. For appropriate criticism, see Williams, *Shame and Necessity*, 14–15, especially n. 23.

35. In his "Attempt at a Self-Criticism" (1886), Nietzsche clearly regrets that in the earlier *The Birth of Tragedy out of the Spirit of Music* (1872) he held on to Schopenhauerian formulations while also trying to "get beyond all this resignationism [*dieser ganze Resignationismus*]." However, I do believe (unlike Williams) that Nietzsche continued throughout his career to hold onto the Schopenhauerian idea that art can trump life: "*art* approaches as a saving sorceress, expert at healing (*als rettende, heilkundige Zauberin*). She alone knows how to turn these nauseous thoughts about the horror or absurdity of existence into notions with which one can live" (*BT* 7). For discussion of Nietzsche's relationship to Schopenhauer (with particular reference to their views about the transfigurative power of art), see Richard Schacht, "Nietzsche on Art in *The Birth of Tragedy*," in *Aesthetics: A Critical Anthology*, 2nd edition, edited by George Dickie, Richard Sclafani, and Ronald Roblin (New York: St. Martin's Press, 1989), especially 490–92.

36. Nietzsche, "Attempt at a Self-Criticism," 7. Compare *Thus Spoke Zarathustra* IV, 17–20.

3

HEROIC VIRTUE IN AMERICA: ARISTOTLE, AQUINAS, AND MELVILLE'S *BILLY BUDD*

Lee H. Yearley

THE PLOT LINE FOR THIS STORY about a story is simple. Aristotle presents an almost breathtaking picture, at one point, of how easily those who manifest heroic virtue will sacrifice themselves. Aquinas argues that Aristotle's portrait is correct but requires more explanation of why that can happen than Aristotle gives. A modern, Herman Melville, has doubts about almost all aspects of this traditional story. Yet the last work he writes, *Billy Budd,* deals not only with this story but reaffirms key parts of it. That work remains deeply ambiguous, and the ambiguity says something significant about two subjects: the differences between literary and theoretical pursuits and, most important here, the modern fate of the traditional story and the ideas of heroic virtue it contains.

HEROIC VIRTUE IN ARISTOTLE, AQUINAS, AND MELVILLE

Among the more influential passages in Aristotle is one that occurs in his treatment of friendship in the *Nicomachean Ethics*. Faced with the question of self-love's relationship to friendship, of whether people should most love themselves or someone else, Aristotle's treatment is striking. It contains, for example, one of his more dramatic analyses of how ordinary understandings of life, in this case ordinary understandings of self-love, can be mistaken.

The analysis rests on distinguishing among kinds of self-love. The good form of self-love leads to awarding oneself what is finest. Therefore a true understanding of self-love is not only compatible with, or actually demands, friendship but also leads to virtuous activity. Indeed, a true understanding even leads to possible sacrifice of oneself. This is encapsulated in the following remarkable and famous passage. "The excellent person labours for his friends and for his native country, and will die for them if he must; he will sacrifice . . . [to achieve] what is fine for himself. For he

66

will choose intense pleasure for a short time over mild pleasure for a long time, a year of living finely over many years of undistinguished life; and a single fine and great action over many small actions" (1169a18–25).[1]

Much can be said about this passage, not least about how many separable claims seem to be connected together in the last sentence quoted. Let us move forward, however, about a millennium and a half to Thomas Aquinas and his commentary on the *Nicomachean Ethics*. In this commentary Aquinas usually either simply explicates what he believes Aristotle is saying or even paraphrases him, but his additions can be noteworthy. For example, in commenting on the quoted passage he says that dying for a friend shows that one "choose[s] to delight for a short time in a brilliant work of virtue rather than for a long time in a quiet existence, i.e., indifferently in mediocre works of virtue."[2]

Elsewhere in the commentary Aquinas develops rationales for the judgments he sees contained in Aristotle. Some of these rationales appear when he expands the notion of martyrdom. He declares, for example, that any pursuit of a good which leads to one's death can be properly called an instance of martyrdom, a surrender of self to the genuine worship of God. Other rationales appear when he develops the ideas of self-love and friendship in his treatment of charity. The focal definition of charity is friendship with God, and he unabashedly notes that charity is characterized by all the marks of friendship and by all the reasons for self-sacrifice Aristotle identified. These and other treatments make clear that Aquinas thinks only an account of the good which has a secure objective base can properly warrant the kind of self-sacrifice Aristotle describes. And it is not, I hasten to add, an objective base that has anything to do with rewards people may receive after they die.[3]

Later commentators on Aquinas (some of whom, such as Bernard Lonergan, were also significant theologians in their own right) have argued that Aristotle's account can make sense only if it receives a basis like the one Aquinas gives it. Often they also argue that Aquinas himself did not recognize how his account differed from Aristotle's because he presumed Aristotle's views were closer to his own than in fact they were. Put in simple, and obviously contestable, terms, they argue that the sort of heroic virtue which finds expression in self-sacrifice can be intelligible and commendable only if the good or the "fine" has more objective reality than, in their view, Aristotle gives it.[4]

The issue in question here is surely one on which more than one paper or even book could be written. I want, nevertheless, to turn to another topic. The differences between Aristotle and Aquinas on the subject of heroic virtue are important but the similarities are even more striking, and one is particularly worthy of note here. Both believe not just that there are good reasons for self-sacrifice but that a good person also will see and easily act on those reasons. They do not, of course, think everyone will understand virtue's true character and therefore act in a heroic way. Aristotle's criticisms of erroneous ideas of self-love and Aquinas's treatment of topics like sin's hold on people and the dangers of false martyrdom make that clear.

Nevertheless, the ideal of heroic virtue is an intelligible one for them, and spontaneously actualizing it is seen as a real human possibility. Moreover, the whole topic can and should be discussed in a theoretical fashion. That is, a significant group in the community should have the requisite talents, training, and inclinations to benefit from the analysis such a discussion produces. Both Aristotle and Aquinas assume, then, that the notion of heroic virtue makes basic sense and that it can and should be discussed in a theoretical way. Indeed, I would argue that their viewpoint was shared by many people for much of what we call the Western tradition.

Herman Melville was neither a philosopher nor a theologian. And he was not a student of either Aristotle or Aquinas. He was, however, a man who grasped the significance of heroic virtue. Moreover, he believed Americans had not only recognized its importance, often in the guise of civic virtue, but also had manifested it, especially in the country's earlier history. As he and the country grew older, however, he saw the ideal—and all it represented—become frayed at best and unintelligible at worst. Melville's last novel, *The Confidence Man,* for example, was a tortuous trip through various permutations of the question of what anyone had a right to be confident about; that is, of what could generate and sustain the trust that must underlie heroic virtue.

Melville thought, then, that one could not presume that the ideal of heroic virtue made sense to people. Moreover, one surely could not believe the ideal made the kind of sense that allowed for the luxury of a theoretical analysis of its subtleties. In fact, literature was Melville's chosen form in significant part because he thought that literature alone could adequately present ideas and ideals like this one, at least to people in his culture. As he said, "For in this world of lies, Truth is forced to fly like a scared white doe in the woodlands, and only by cunning glimpses will she reveal herself as in Shakespeare and other masters of the great Art of Telling the Truth—even though it be covertly, and by snatches." [5]

I will focus here on Melville's last work, *Billy Budd,* a work that I will treat as a meditation on the possibility of heroic virtue in America. Before turning to that, however, allow me to say something about what I take to be at the core of the idea of heroic virtue.

HEROIC VIRTUE

Classical accounts of virtue in many traditions declare that virtuous behavior can arise from expressive motives. Many Aristotelian, Confucian, or Platonic accounts, for example, contain forms of the following argument: People choose a virtuous action not only because it contributes to goods they want to acquire but also because it expresses their conception of the good. This expressive component is at the core of what I mean by heroic virtue.[6]

An essential feature of this expressive, heroic idea is the answer it gives to one basic question: Why might or even should people act, especially act in dangerous ways, if they have severe doubts that their action will have the kind of effects on themselves and in the world that they hope it will? The answer is that the best kind of life simply demands such activity, and therefore no further questions about its contributions to the agent's or anyone else's happiness need to be raised. This does not mean such choices are made recklessly; indeed they must be well-considered if they are to be fully expressive. Nevertheless, it is not the good benefits received or given but the good expressed that is the crucial motivating force. Cautious pursuers of virtue will always doubt the sanity of those lovers of virtue who aim to express virtue. That is, the cautious will correctly see this love and its apparent imprudence as a crucial defining mark of the heroic, and therefore they will question the validity of the heroic ideal.[7]

Melville, like Aristotle or Aquinas, is the kind of person who believes ideas about virtue are inevitably linked with ideas about the heroic. This means the heroic is a fundamental category in any effort to sound the deeper characteristics of human goodness. All three also recognize, however, that ideas about the heroic often travel in disreputable, even noxious, company. This is especially true when the central trope for the heroic is military action.

Melville's grasp of the seriousness of this problem probably exceeds that found in Aristotle and Aquinas. His Civil War poetry returns to this problem over and over again, and once, when treating an earlier American war, he described the country as representing a kind of heroism gone astray. America is, he says, "intrepid, unprincipled, reckless, predatory, with boundless ambition, civilized in externals but a savage at heart."[8]

Melville's views on this matter reflect many distinctive modern motifs, motifs that sit uneasily with any idea of the heroic. For example, like many moderns he is suspicious of the ideal of aristocratic valor and he affirms notions which undergird such a suspicion, notions like the affirmation that everyday life is of great value and that even the most ordinary person is significant. Melville understands, then, that for many modern people heroism is a suspect or discredited notion because it often generates activities or people that are problematic at best.

Nevertheless, Melville continues to focus on the heroic. He does so, I think, for reasons that resemble those found in a near-contemporary, William James, who was well aware that notions of heroism are liable to sentimental excess as well as raw corruption. James also believed, however, that "each of us in his own person feels that a high-hearted indifference to life would expiate all his shortcomings." Indeed, James defends remarks like this by saying that "I am leaning only upon mankind's common instinct for reality, which in point of fact has always held the world to be essentially a theatre for heroism. In heroism, we feel, life's supreme mystery is hidden."[9]

This last statement is, I believe, a "dark saying" and leads in several directions. For now, however, let me just note my judgment that Melville, like James and some tragedians, believes that heroes and heroism disclose to us realities understandable in no other way. Heroes disclose such things because they stand between the mysterious gods and the manifest but limited truths of normal life. The heroic, then, both uncovers features of higher realities and illuminates the pedestrian character of ordinary activity.

MELVILLE'S *BILLY BUDD*: AN INTRODUCTION

Given this summary treatment, let us turn to Melville's *Billy Budd*. The story is familiar enough, I assume, so that a brief account will suffice. Although surely about America and probably about the modern world, the work occurs during the Napoleonic Wars, at the time of the great mutinies in the British navy. A British ship has as its captain a thoughtful and apparently just man, Captain Vere. The Master at Arms, Claggart, is a very intelligent man who plays a harsh but necessary role on the ship. He also manifests a pure malice (which the narrator says we will find difficult to envision) that is directed toward Billy Budd. Billy Budd, a wondrously innocent (or naive) sailor of great ability, has brought harmony to a troubled crew. He is, however, falsely incriminated by Claggart—accused of fomenting mutiny—largely because of Claggart's envy. Vere brings Budd and Claggart together when he hears the accusation. When confronted with the charge, Budd, a stutterer, is unable to reply and kills Claggart with a blow. After a manipulated trial on board the ship, held against naval regulations, Budd is hanged by Vere. Budd's last words are "God bless Captain Vere!" The book ends with Vere's death in battle and several reports about Billy's life and death.

In my view there are five major interpretative approaches to *Billy Budd*—eight, if you count subdivisions. I note them here for scholarly reasons, perhaps to forearm my critics, and surely to pay appropriate tribute to the enterprise—or at least industry—of literary criticism. (I will not include several prominent deconstructive readings as I think they fit, if perhaps imperfectly, within the general approaches identified.)

One approach sees the work as a *testament of acceptance*. The work manifests a "stoic" acceptance of an unjust social order and a rejection of older, more optimistic, ideals on the grounds that they are unproductive examples of naiveté, that they generate only destructive nostalgia. A second sees it as a *testament of resistance,* an ironic piece that portrays an unjust, repressive, even brutal social order that alienates everyone within it. A third, not surprisingly given the first two, sees the work as *systematically ambiguous.* Opinion divides as to whether Melville intended that ambiguity or just wrote a work that is both unfinished and too layered, too clogged with different meanings, to have a single meaning. A fourth approach sees it as a *tragedy.* Opinion divides, however, as to whether it is an Aristotelian tragedy involving pity, fear, catharsis, and perhaps a tragic flaw, or a Hegelian tragedy involving unavoidable and irreconcilable conflicts between competing goods. Finally, a fifth approach sees it as a *religious* work, but here again the religious meaning is contested. For some the meaning is Christian, a Christ-like sacrifice unleashes the mysterious forces of good that meet and overcome the forces of iniquity. For others, it is the retelling of an Indo-European myth in which a Celtic Apollo slays the serpent and then is ritually killed.

None of these approaches is obviously foolish, and that may be a tribute to the work itself. Nevertheless, none of them captures what I want to say about the work, although they do contribute to aspects of my interpretation.[10]

Melville is, I believe, portraying the fate of expressive, heroic virtue in modern times, especially in modern America. He does so by literary means, and this choice highlights crucial issues about the differing abilities of theoretical and literary works to present a topic like this to a modern audience. The question of genre is, then, an important one.

In fact, *Billy Budd* is an especially interesting example of the effect of genre because the literary work has been reproduced, and well-reproduced, in other genres: a film (based on a play) and an opera. Allow me to make a brief comment on these works as the presentations and changes made in them show much about what different genres can and cannot do.

The 1962 film, drawing on the play, has a splendid cast: Robert Ryan as Claggart, Peter Ustinov as Vere, Terence Stamp as Billy Budd, Melvyn Douglas as Dansker. The production is, in general, an excellent one, although the genre demands that important ambiguities be smoothed out and depths overlooked. Some changes, however, are pure Hollywood and reveal much about the fate of heroic virtue in yet another age in America. For example, after Billy Budd dies the crew is about to revolt, but a French ship appears and the crew turns to fight it while a voice-over intones pieties about justice.[11]

The Britten opera is an extraordinary piece and tells us much about what music alone can do.[12] The sea, for example, becomes a character in a sense it never could even in Melville's prose, and certain contrasts or even conflicts attain a harmony only music can produce. Some changes are most revealing—for instance, the opera starts with Vere as a lonely old man looking back at his life. Moreover, the surface message is telling, given Britten's own situation. The heroic lies in accepting the need for order whatever may be the tragic consequences for individuals.

Melville's own account is, of course, in prose. The prose is distinctive enough, however, that a few comments about specific features of Melville's literary style are in order. Melville treasures the concrete but sees it, first, as a locus of ambiguity and, second, as a carrier of larger meanings. The first feature is well captured by the poet Charles Olson's statement that "the secret of Melville as artist . . . [is] the presentation of ambiguity by the event direct."[13] A clear example of this is found in the famous scene in *Moby-Dick* when Ahab nails the dubloon to the mast and the crew's different reactions are inventoried, a situation that leads Pip to say "I look, you look . . . [we] are all bats."[14] *Billy Budd* is also full of examples, perhaps the most notable of which is the presentation of the different reactions to Billy's death, a presentation we will examine in the next section.

Indeed, in virtually all his mature works Melville portrays in virtuoso fashion both the cryptic density of significant events and the way in which people attempt to find false clarity. He will, for instance, lead readers to question why they failed to see more clearly than they did the ambiguities of a situation—or even, in some cases, the actual state of affairs. (The classic case of the latter probably arises in reading *Benito Cereno* when we realize that we should have recognized that the slaves, not the masters, control the ship.)

The second feature, the concrete as the carrier of larger meaning, appears in a technique, or better process, Melville often uses. He moves from the particular to the general by using linked descriptions and analogies. Many of these draw on mythic materials, and the procedure often produces a shower of allegorical sparks. Melville will, for example, expand the significance of a character by associating the character imaginatively with a wide range of interlocking allusions and resemblances.

The scene in which Claggart charges Billy Budd with mutiny illustrates this well. Here Claggart's eyes are described as "gelidly protruding like the alien eyes of certain uncatalogued creatures of the deep. The first mesmeristic glance was one of serpent fascination; the last was as the paralyzing lurch of the torpedo fish" (98). Billy Budd, in turn, when trying to speak to defend himself undergoes a struggle that "gave an expression to the face like that of a condemned vestal priestess in the moment of being buried alive, and in the first struggle against suffocation" (99).[15]

Melville believes only such literary techniques and uses of mythic materials can make present what actually happens and is at stake. They alone can focus our attention on both the ambiguity of concrete events and the more general meanings they may carry. The need to focus our attention is perhaps most pronounced when issues about heroic virtue are the subject; that is, when Melville deals with the highest and lowest reaches of human life, with the heroic in its finest and most twisted forms. Let us turn, then, to the actual presentation of this subject in *Billy Budd*.[16]

FOUR RESPONSES TO BILLY BUDD'S DEATH

The importance of these facets of Melville's literary imagination is especially clear in the portrait of the varied responses to Billy's life and death that make up most of the book's last chapters. These endings give concrete form to the narrator's own comment that "truth uncompromisingly told will always have its ragged edges" (128). Moreover, these ragged edges tell us much about the difficulty moderns, perhaps especially modern Americans, have in understanding those who display heroic virtue. They also show how such understanding rests, as it does in Aristotelian accounts, on the possession of a character that is heroic enough to allow a person to resonate with, and therefore to grasp, manifestations of the heroic.

The apparently disconnected last chapters, in my view, present four reactions to Billy Budd's death.[17] The first and most bitingly humorous reports the discussion of the purser and the surgeon about, in Melville's delicate language, the absence of a muscular spasm in Billy Budd. That is, why did the hanged man not have an erection? The purser, described as being more accurate as an accountant than profound as a philosopher, speaks with the surgeon, yet another of Melville's men of science.

The purser explains that the absence was due to will power, but the surgeon declares he is in error because will power is "a term not yet included in the lexicon of science" (125). The surgeon does agree, however, that it is a phenomenal occurrence "in the sense that it was an appearance the cause of which is not immediately to be assigned" (ibid.). The purser continues and asks if Billy Budd's death was then "effected by the halter, or was it a species of euthanasia?" (ibid.). (Euthanasia here seems to mean, among other things, a willed sacrifice of one's self for one's country.) The surgeon ends the conversation with his response, "*Euthanasia,* Mr. Purser, is something like your *will power.* I doubt its authenticity as a scientific term—begging your pardon again. It is at once imaginative and metaphysical—in short, Greek" (ibid.).

The surgeon especially but both these sensible men cannot, given their general frameworks, understand the event. Nor do they seem to see much reason to understand it. The proffered explanations are, to use the three terms of disapproval, at once imaginative, metaphysical, and Greek. Literature and related activities, philosophy or theology, and all that is represented by the pejorative use of "Greek" are beyond their ken and of no real use in understanding the world.

The second response is Vere's. Involved in a battle with a ship (and Melville cannot avoid a heavy hand when ship names are involved) originally called the *St. Louis* and now renamed the *Atheist*, he is killed. The compressed account only tells us that not long before his death Vere was heard to murmur "Billy Budd, Billy Budd," and perhaps more important that he was "cut off too early for the Nile and Trafalgar"—two of Nelson's great battles, the last the site of his heroic death (129). Moreover, with no preparation at all, a line about Vere appears that calls into question earlier portraits of him: "The spirit that 'spite its philosophic austerity may yet have indulged in the most secret of all passions, ambition, never attained to the fullness of fame" (ibid.). Was the judgment of the just judge, the person who aimed to protect the social good, poisoned by the pursuit of a warrior's fame?

The third and fourth responses present two public and seasoned accounts—and effects—of Billy Budd's death. One arises from the official report and is published in an authorized naval weekly. In its astonishingly twisted account of the "deplorable occurrence" (130) Claggart discovers a mutiny plot and Billy Budd stabs him to death. Moreover, Billy is not English but a foreigner, and Claggart is portrayed as respectable and discreet, a person whose life, it is declared, shows that patriotism is not the last refuge of a scoundrel. The report ends by noting that Billy Budd's prompt punishment ensured that nothing amiss occurred on the ship.

The last and most fragmented response—especially in contrast with the official account that precedes it—concerns the effect of his death on sailors, on those who cannot or do not read official accounts. It includes, for example, a lengthy poem about Billy Budd that circulates still among sailors and the fact that material objects from the execution are treated by sailors like "a piece of the Cross" (131). Objects and images associated with Billy Budd and his death move throughout the world the sailors inhabit.

Four responses that, among other things, contain Melville's view about how heroic virtue will be perceived in modern times. Four examples also of a fundamental idea in the Aristotelian tradition that accompanies the notion of heroic virtue: the "good person criterion." That is, a person's character determines what he or she is able to perceive and understand. Therefore the ultimate measure of a person or an act's excellence, or even meaning, is the excellence of the person who makes the judgment: the good person is the final measure of the good.[18]

The purser and surgeon are mystified by an odd physical fact but are unable, and unwilling, even to consider its implications. Their general views prevent them from grappling with the meaning of Billy Budd's death or life. Vere remains haunted by Billy but cannot bring that part of his experience into harmony with the rest of his understanding. Although the dead Billy Budd may be more alive for him than virtually all of the living who surround him, Vere's own alienation from himself leads to him only being haunted. And he may be haunted not just by Billy Budd but also by the fear that his ambition led to accepting reasons to kill him that were deeply flawed.

The official report has through ignorance, reasons of state, or sheer malice not only completely distorted the situation but also turned it into an official morality tale. It presents a simple tale about the danger of the dispossessed, especially if they are foreign; the role of patriotism; and the need for quick and violent action by those who lead a society. The last and most mysterious account concerns how certain aspects of Billy Budd's life live on in a dispossessed and uneducated group that suffers from rather than guides the society. His life, death, and example are still vital for them, although we ought not think that they—any more than the others—grasp fully either who Billy Budd was or what the actual situation was.

HEROIC VIRTUE AND THE MAJOR CHARACTERS IN *BILLY BUDD*

These endings manifest many of the problems that arise in understanding heroic virtue, especially understanding it in a modern society. Melville's most focused treatment of virtue of a heroic sort appears, however, in his depictions of the four major figures in the book. Three figures dominate the tale, and a fourth is significant although he hardly appears, a situation that reflects accurately the figure's perspective on heroism.

Each figure is one of those extraordinary people whom, Melville warns us, most normal people will have difficulty understanding. That is, Melville underlines again the way in which people's character determines what they can understand. Indeed, in what could be said to be the cautionary motto for *Billy Budd,* it is declared that in "an average man of the world, his constant rubbing with it blunts that finer spiritual insight indispensable to the understanding of the essential in certain exceptional characters, whether evil ones or good" (75). We are warned, then, that our own limitations may make us unable to grasp the manifestations of heroic virtue, or heroic vice.

The three dominating figures are Vere, Claggart, and Billy Budd; the fourth is an old sailor named Dansker. What we see in these figures, I think, is Melville's account of the forms, the stunted forms, that heroic virtue can take in America. Claggart is truly heroic—but is evil not good. Billy Budd is heroic but his heroism is flawed by a kind of naiveté that means not only that he must die but that he also will die having only imperfectly grasped the good. A third figure, Dansker, has chosen against heroism knowing what it is but believing the world no longer allows for its actualization. And a fourth Vere, pursues heroism as do most decent people but ends by destroying a good and dividing himself.

Let me begin with Dansker, a figure I have barely mentioned before now. An aged sailor who has displayed great heroism in battle, he seems to be the only person on the ship who understands Claggart and probably also Vere. Moreover, he warns Billy Budd about Claggart's plot to incriminate him. Yet he will do no more than offer the warning and then withdraw. He acts once, steps back, and lets the horror unfold. (The film, incidentally, cannot resist the temptation to make him a major character. In rejecting Melville's austere minimalism it shows, I think, a misunderstanding of who Dansker is and what he must do.)

Dansker is someone who can understand the heroic. Nevertheless, when the pains and ironies accumulate unbearably, he controls them, as did Ishmael in *Moby-Dick,* by adopting the laughing indifference he has observed in the hyena. Dansker is, if you will, a principled anti-hero. He believes that in the world he inhabits the attempt to nurture and express virtue must always be tempered, and even be trumped, by caution, detachment, and irony.[19]

Billy Budd, our next figure, is surely good in many senses of that word. Indeed, one crucial aspect of the story revolves around the presentation of how the kind of goodness Billy manifests has become either unrecognized or even a liability in the world in which he lives. Not only can his virtues become dangerous in that world, but they also lack most natural outlets. His virtues are finally realized only through a self-sacrifice that involves the seemingly simpleminded acceptance of the horrible injustices done to him, the apparently naive decision to bow to the representative of a twisted society and hierarchy.

If one were to speak of archetypes or at least general tropes, Billy Budd represents the robust, simple inhabitants of the countryside, the people whom Melville often pairs with the clever, indirect, often unscrupulous denizens of the city. More generally still, Billy Budd and his opponents recall the opposition Melville saw as basic to American self-understanding: the opposition between the ideas that animated the Declaration of Independence and those that animated the Constitution. And in the most general terms Billy Budd represents the kind of innocence which is good and not simply naive, which can motivate us in integral ways and not just produce sentimental nostalgia. As such he stands opposed to those whom experience has twisted either profoundly or partly.[20]

Such generalizations about what Billy Budd represents help to set the proper context, help to show us what is at stake. More crucial, however, are the actual features of his character. Billy Budd surely possesses qualities characteristic of innocence that most people would commend: he is, for example, without guile, envy, or the desire for revenge. These couple, however, with other qualities that show his innocence does not simply mirror an overly romantic picture of the childlike. He is, for instance, neither weak nor retiring. We are told of his great strength, his ability to fight, his excellence as a seaman. Moreover, he joins with these a demonstrated ability to bring peace and harmony to the seamen around him. These features of Billy's character are, at least in the abstract, admirable human attributes.

Other qualities many people normally associate with the ideally human are, however, lacking. He cannot read and he has a speech impediment, a stutter. Billy Budd lacks, then, abilities that many think must inform a flourishing human life: the ability fully to engage texts and people through reading and speaking. Furthermore, Melville portrays him at crucial moments with figures that recall animals or associate him directly with animals. He looks at Vere, for example, as would a St. Bernard dog— a dog, not so incidentally, that rescues human beings caught in difficulties they cannot get themselves out of. Melville's portrait of Billy Budd, then, raises questions about just what distinctive marks define the human, especially those human beings called to be heroically virtuous.

One of those central questions concerns the role of naiveté. Billy Budd is surely naive in at least some senses of that word. He finds it difficult to read other people's motives, particularly if those motives are twisted or even just complicated. This quality raises complex questions about just how suspicious one should be, an important question for Melville.[21] Most important here, however, it surely makes him vulnerable. Furthermore, it also means Billy's insight and even capacity to sympathize are limited. He cannot fully understand complex people, and therefore he cannot, at times, act appropriately toward them. Vicious people, moreover, will be opaque to him. The person he is least able to grasp is Claggart. Let us see what we, with our more suspicious nature or training, can make of him.

Claggart, the master at arms, is a man whose origins are mysterious and whose reasons for being on the ship are hard to fathom. What is clear, however, is that he is highly intelligent and well-educated. Moreover, he serves a necessary function in the society that is the ship. Therefore, he possesses what Melville calls a "mantle of respectability," a cloak born of the need to have someone like him maintain the hierarchical order of this crucial social organism (75).

Most important, the narrator declares that readers like us will have great difficulty in understanding him, and for two reasons. The first reason we have already referred to: the knowledge that arises in and undergirds ordinary life blunts the spiritual insight needed to understand exceptional characters. The second, however, arises from a distinctively modern situation. Modern people find it difficult to believe that real evil can define any person, much less to see that it does define a specific person. The narrator of *Billy Budd* plays with the reader here, telling us we are incapable of seeing what Claggart really is, noting that he will not mention the idea of the "mystery of iniquity" because of sophisticated people's attitude toward Holy Writ (76).

The narrator also makes it clear, however, that in considering Claggart we are dealing with no ordinary human being. There is no alloy of the brute in Claggart. Not only is he highly intelligent but he also suffers from no small or ordinary kinds of vice: no sordid but episodic kinds of sensuality, for example, no avaricious grasping after material gain. Claggart is free from all of this; he is intellectual, controlled, and self-contained. His viciousness is usually hidden and even when seen is not easily understood.

Claggart's overriding vice is envy, envy of Billy Budd's good looks, enjoyment of life, simplicity, physical abilities, and friendliness. In fact, Claggart can be said to personify envy as it has been portrayed in theological analyses in the Christian tradition's treatment of the seven deadly sins. Aquinas, for example, argues envy is the exact reverse of charity. The charitable wish goods for others and see goods as things to be enjoyed even if they are not possessed. The envious, in contrast, wish others did not have the goods they possess and react with pain to the goods that others have. Claggart exemplifies this kind of envy. He longs for but wishes to destroy the goods he cannot possess, he would rather a desert exist than that there be goods that are not his. Indeed, Melville frames Claggart in ways that recall the great enviers the Western tradition has seen; enviers such as the Adam of Genesis, Milton's Satan, and Shakespeare's Iago.[22]

Claggart's viciousness is as thorough, as single-minded, as is any state of virtue. And this is what leads Claggart to be heroic. That is, he will sacrifice himself to reach his goal: the goal that the goodness evident in Billy Budd ceases to exist. He knows, I believe, that only by forcing Billy to kill him will Billy die, and he acts so that will occur. He believes, then, in the expressive character of truly defining characteristics; he scorns prudential accommodations; he is a real lover. It is just that what he wants to express, what generates his imprudence, what he loves, is evil not good. He has, that is, all the marks of the heroic. But his aims and actions—step by step, quality by quality—are directed toward evil not good.[23]

The last of our figures, Vere, possesses no such singlemindedness, but he also aims at the heroic. Vere, however, lives in a world, and is the product of a society, in which virtuous heroism is almost impossible. Indeed, he represents just how inconceivable has become the pursuit of heroic virtue for responsible, decent people in America. The quandary he faces about whether to condemn Billy Budd cannot even become tragic; it can lead only to injustice and self-alienation. Let us turn, then, to the last of these four figures—the one Melville sees as representing the life of the responsible and respectable in his America.[24]

Two prefatory notes are in order, however, and each concerns the general background of Vere and his actions. Vere captains a ship operating in the British navy, one of the more brutal systems that modern times have seen. Moreover, the ship and he are part of the defense of a traditional hierarchical society (England) against one (France) that is, in some ways at least, trying to move society in more egalitarian and liberal directions.

Vere himself, it is true, does not act to protect the privileged classes. Rather he "disinterestedly opposed" such revolutionary ideas because they are "insusceptible of embodiment in lasting institutions: . . . [and are] at war with the peace of the world and the true welfare of mankind" (63). Vere is, then, a reflective perpetrator of the status quo. Moreover, he can be said to represent most of those reflective, decent people who in their exercise of power value order even if the price is injustice.

Vere is without question the single most important figure in the story if one approaches it looking for discrete examples of ethical deliberation and judgment, especially when they concern justice and the killing or saving of another human being. I think, however, much more than the textured description of discrete ethical conundrum is at stake in understanding Vere. Indeed, Melville's portrayal of Vere can be seen as one which criticizes, or at least situates in a larger context, any focus on ethical conundrums. The portrayal, therefore, also situates and criticizes those common approaches to literature by ethicists who use literature as a resource for reflecting on discrete ethical issues.

Allow me, then, to turn to Melville's depiction of Vere's character and perhaps also to overstate my case, to exaggerate in the direction of truth. Vere is a serious, well-intentioned person who is also intelligent, educated, and holds a significant position with remarkable responsibilities. Noted as bookish, dry, and rather distant, he particularly likes works that treat of actual people and events, and he favors commonsense philosophies and the settled convictions that arise from them. Vere is, then, a decent sensible man. He becomes or does evil because of deep flaws in his character and outlook, flaws that reveal much about Melville's views on the possibility of heroic virtue. Those flaws appear clearly, however, only in his reactions to unforeseen events, to those unexpected moments the responses to which, in an Aristotelian view, show the true character of one's soul.

Vere fails, in brief, because he is in the grip of conventional ideas and commonsense approaches, and they are not enough when heroic virtues are needed. A complicated character, he is aware of other alternatives. Billy's example, for instance, affects him deeply. Moreover, the recurring, seemingly inexplicable, motif of Nelson's life that weaves through the book conveys, among other things, the heroic ideal that haunts Vere. Nevertheless, he is finally a "utilitarian" or "Benthamite" in the special sense those words had for Melville. That is, he is a basically cautious person who can only calculate means to ends, serve mechanical processes, and reason from and about the useful as that is understood conventionally. And his failures represent the failures of that perspective, of the world that nurtures it, and of the kinds of virtue with which it wants to replace heroic virtue.

Vere's failures are object lessons that illustrate the problems in the perspective he represents. He does not see, for example, how malevolent Claggart is. He sets up the meeting where Claggart mesmerizes Billy Budd without even imagining that what did happen could happen. He cannot understand the evil within Claggart, especially the envy that drives him. Nor can he fathom the heroism that moves Claggart, the willingness to do anything, including dying, to extinguish Billy Budd's goodness. Vere fails to understand because he can neither imagine such evil might exist nor really grasp the true character of the heroic.

Moreover, Vere consciously subverts just procedures in order to achieve what he believes are good ends or goals—the avoidance of mutiny. Vere says, soon after Billy kills Claggart, that "the angel must hang" (101); he fails to take the case to the admiral although that is normal procedure; and he bullies or manipulates the court by using arguments of the most dubious or specious sort. Moreover, it is significant that he never even considers that Billy Budd alive is more likely to impede mutiny than Billy Budd dead. Billy had brought a new harmony to the troubled ship, and a possible mutiny seems to be avoided more by Billy's actions, especially by his final blessing of Vere, than by his execution.[25]

Several remarkable images or clusters of images capture Vere's character, and thus the fate of his grasp and pursuit of the heroic. One image portrays a crucial aspect of his character. Speaking of Vere's honesty and the directness it generates, he is said to be "a migratory fowl that in its flight never heeds when it crosses a frontier" (63). Vere's general perspective and the specific response he has when faced with the decision about Billy are like that of the migratory fowl who heedlessly and unknowingly crosses a basic border. He may try to pursue heroic virtue, but he lacks the imagination to see when frontiers are crossed. That is, he cannot see either when circumstances have changed fundamentally or when the people he faces are different from what he expects them to be. Moreover, Vere lacks imagination. He is unable either to imagine not following his own rules or to imagine fundamental questions about his own sense of the good to be achieved. In considering Vere, we see the force of Stuart Hampshire's argument that in the pursuit of the good, the ability to imagine is as important as is the ability to think.[26]

Nevertheless, Vere is a complex character—and he exemplifies a state shared by many moderns. His complexity is revealed in a set of figures that are presented at the time of Billy's death. Each is multivocal, and even ironic, in that each speaks of Vere's mental state, his ideas and emotions, but each also illuminates what he brought about both for himself and for others, however unwittingly. Shortly after Billy Budd's hanging Vere is described as "erectly rigid as a musket in the ship-armorer's rack" (124). Vere's service to the military needs of the state in hanging Billy has, he believes, strengthened that necessary if inhuman force. It has also, however, turned him into a rigidly inhuman creature.

Even more striking is the apparently odd image used to describe the coming of daylight just after Billy has been hanged: "And the circumambient air in the clearness of its serenity was like smooth white marble in the polished block not yet removed from the marble-dealer's yard" (128). After Billy Budd's death the world returns to a cold, hard, beautiful, and unformed natural integrity which has not yet been turned to truly human ends. This image reveals the personal and social order that much of Vere pursues. It also reflects, however, what Vere has done, or tried to do, to some of his own inclinations.

The force, and irony, of this image is heightened still further if we compare it to another image, presented just before this one, that is attributed to Vere. Vere rhapsodizes that "with mankind . . . forms, measured forms, are everything; and that is the import couched in the story of Orpheus with his lyre spellbinding the wild denizens of the wood" (128). Vere is self-deceived. Rather than being someone who plays a lyre to bring harmony to living animals, Vere in fact produces a world of smooth white marble. His measured forms are cold stone and they are created by violence. Moreover, he misses, characteristically, an important part of the Orpheus story. At the myth's end Orpheus is torn to pieces by Thracian women he will not love because he has forsworn love.[27]

Vere, then, injures or even destroys other people and the social forms he should protect. But Vere also injures himself, and that is an essential aspect of the tale Melville tells. The failure of the heroic we see in Vere does not simply harm others, it also harms Vere. Vere is deeply divided, something seen not only in his last words about Billy Budd but also, for example, in his agitation before the trial and in the images about him we have just examined. He not only creates victims but also is a victim of his own action and of the society in which he lives. He is unable to act either on his own benevolent impulses or on his impulses to see and honor a higher good. He cannot, then, express his own deepest understanding of virtue, however inchoate it may be, because two other features of his character are at war with that understanding. That is, he accepts (or the dominant part of him accepts) his role in a destructive society and he has a theoretical view that has no place for heroic virtue.

CONCLUSION

Billy Budd is a notoriously complex and ambiguous work. On my reading the book shows that Melville stands within a tradition about heroic virtue, is even caught by many of its most powerful ideas. And yet finally he is haunted rather than animated, much less consoled, by those very ideas. Put one way, Melville can be said to stand in the same stream Aristotle and Aquinas inhabit, but the stream is constantly changing. That is, Heraclitus' notion that one never steps twice in the same stream is part of this paper's point.

Melville's understanding of heroic virtue is usually closer to Aquinas' understanding than to Aristotle's. But often even more significant is the distance of Melville from both. Most important to us, however, is seeing the resemblances and the distinctions among these three figures, the similarities within differences and differences within similarities. They reveal much, I think, about both *Billy Budd* and the fate of heroic virtue in America.[28] I will conclude by examining that subject, but allow me first to sketch out a few things that provide the needed background for the examination.

Melville presents a picture in which the only alternative to the world represented by the warship, the *Bellipotent,* is the flawed heroic ideal represented by Billy Budd. We will return to the issue of how viable, or attractive, is the ideal Billy Budd represents. For now, however, let us consider the fact that the world of the warship is well adapted to the harsh, often dangerous realities that surround people.

The form of the warship's world can be well defended by solid, sensible people, utilitarians in Melville's sense of that word. Nevertheless, for Melville, living within that world can offer no real satisfaction to the best people. Those like Captain Vere who are drawn by, or even entertain, a higher goal than it allows must both act unjustly and become alienated from themselves. Moreover, they will always be liable to utilizing evil people like Claggart and to being manipulated by them. Dansker's principled antiheroism is yet another option, and one with considerable integrity. Nevertheless, that option involves being implicated in all the world of the *Bellipotent.*

Melville thinks, then, that we are faced with a "forced option," where not to decide is in fact to decide. One crucial feature of the forced character of the option is that truly evil people, incarnating truly evil forces, are active in the world the *Bellipotent* manifests. These people will usually be completely misunderstood or at best imperfectly understood by most people, especially by most decent, sophisticated people. These evil people will, moreover, be able to destroy much that is most worthwhile.

We must therefore, in Melville's eyes, either stand within, reaffirm, and make possible the death-dealing world of the *Bellipotent* or stand outside of it. The option remains a basic one. This is true even if standing outside the *Bellipotent*'s world has troubling features. It can endanger, in fact usually will endanger, those who do so. It will seem simpleminded to most people. Finally, it will be possible only for people who lack valuable traits or abilities. Melville has few illusions, then, about the likely fate of those who, in a modern situation, embrace the heroic, about how they will appear to many people, and even about their flawed characters.

He does, however, believe such heroes have a significant influence. It is difficult to specify, especially if we either use only the criteria that operate in the world of the powerful or the intellectually sophisticated or focus only on whether such people are influenced. Nevertheless, it can affect deeply those who do not run the society but rather are run by it, that is, the great mass of people. This becomes clear, I think, in the book's final chapters, those that deal with the different reactions to Billy's death. Billy's death has had a significant, and in some sense beneficial, effect especially on the common sailors but also on Vere. That remains true even if we ought not believe any of them fully grasped who he was and what occurred.

The effect the heroic has on other people is not, however, the basic measure of its worth. Rather it is the good that is expressed. In his understanding of that good's character Melville stands, as I said, in the same stream Aristotle and Aquinas inhabit. Although considerably closer to Aquinas than to Aristotle, he is, nevertheless, finally distant from both. Let us, then, examine the relationships among the three on the subject of heroic virtue, beginning with the ways in which he is closer to Aquinas than Aristotle.

Melville's imagery and references, mythic and otherwise, in *Billy Budd* often come from texts like the Bible that Aristotle would have found perplexing at best, and they carry much of the tale's meaning. Moreover, whatever Billy Budd's shortcomings, he remains in some sense attuned or adapted to "another" world, one that involves, for instance, the surrender of most kinds of aggression and calculation. Such an adaptation can only arise, I think, from a hope that at least resembles the religious hope Aquinas describes as a theological virtue and Aristotle would have thought peculiar at best and a vice at worst. This remains true even if Aquinas usually portrays that adaptation with an assurance and within a meta-physic that Melville would have found unintelligible and perhaps even comic.[29]

Furthermore, the depiction of evil's character and influence (if not of course its mere presence) reveals a world much closer to Aquinas's than to Aristotle's, even if the latter's views might accommodate aspects of it. Melville's world has dramatic fault lines, fault lines which reflect the powerful energies that created it and can unexpectedly tear it apart. The fault lines manifest potential powers, such as the dynamic that creates radical envy, which Aristotle would have difficulty accepting.[30]

Finally, the heroism Melville presents manifests a world in which intellectual sophistication of even a practical sort and a properly beneficent upbringing and sustaining community are nugatory. The lack of these features would, for Aristotle, make heroism virtually impossible. Aquinas, in contrast, is willing to declare that true spirituality may flourish in a person without either many intellectual gifts or the benefits of excellent nurture.

Nevertheless, despite the ways in which Melville is closer to Aquinas than Aristotle, he remains distant from both on much that is critically important. One general contrast has been discussed at length: the differences between theoretical and literary presentations. The distinctions between the two are immense, and those distinctions tell us much about the possibility of discussing, grasping, or manifesting heroic virtue. Indeed, the significance of this contrast can hardly be overestimated.

Also very different is the admirableness of the hero.[31] Melville stresses the deficiencies that, it seems, must accompany modern heroism. Moreover, he underlines the slim confidence that aspiring modern heroes will have. They will lack the reasons that once supported a more full-blooded confidence, reasons like those which either appear in a traditional Christian metaphysics or arise from the ethos of a coherent community. Finally, Melville underlines the immense difficulties that even decent people will have in approaching a heroic standard. He focuses on the obstacles, social and personal, that will impede, twist, and corrupt their pursuit.

Despite all these differences, connections among the three figures are still present. Some, such as the acceptance of the good-person criterion, are significant but less crucial to our subject. Others, however, are basic. For example, like Aquinas and perhaps also Aristotle, Melville believes a normal, nonheroic or antiheroic, perspective allows and justifies far too much horror. Moreover, and of crucial importance, they all believe a real alternative is present (for some people at least) however difficult it may be to grasp and live by and however frail it may be.

The alternative can appear only if three things are recognized. First, the character of the forced option must be seen. That involves, among other things, a recognition of just how much suffering and evil occur and just how easy it is to justify them. This understanding is not easily attained much less lived with, but it is possible. Second, people must embrace a hope that goes beyond what the forms of normal life would warrant. That hope rests on a grasp of heroism's character and the peculiar powers on which it draws. Third, people must understand that virtues have a heroic, an expressive aspect. Understanding that aspect should not only motivate action but also inform a correct understanding of the forced option, as well as aid and be aided by appropriate hope.

Seeing the alternative rests, then, on recognizing the forced option, adopting a distinctive kind of hope, and understanding the expressive aspect of virtue. Aristotle can embrace each of these three things in a fashion that allows him to believe that at least the best, and luckiest, people will be able to manifest heroic virtue. Aquinas can embrace each of them in a way that makes heroic virtue a real possibility for all people and in some situations even a fundamental demand on them. For Melville, however, the promise of each of the three has dimmed to the point where he can only be haunted by them rather than comforted by them.

After an 1857 visit from Melville in Southport, England, Nathaniel Hawthorne said the following about Melville: "[He] will never rest until he gets hold of a definite belief. It is strange how he persists—and has persisted ever since I knew him and probably long before—in wandering to-and-fro over these deserts. . . . He can neither believe, nor be comfortable in his unbelief; and he is too honest and courageous not to try to do one or the other. If he were a religious man, he would be one of the most truly religious and reverential."[32] Melville wanders and thinks all who truly understand will wander with him. The ghost of heroic virtue haunts or even bewitches him, but it brings only the consolation found in the twisted fate of Vere or the imperfect innocent who is Billy Budd.

NOTES

1. Terence Irwin's translation of the *Ethics* (Indianapolis: Hackett, 1985) is used here; incidentally "fine" is *kalos*. My thanks to Sally Gressens for her suggestions about how to approach this topic; to Mark Gonnerman for his general assistance; to the editors for their labors in bringing this volume together; to the anonymous reviewers for their comments; and to the symposium participants for their remarks. Finally, my thanks to Arthur Adkins, whom I came to know at a series of conferences, for his many perspicacious comments over the years. In ways that I would find difficult to trace, I believe this paper owes much to him.

2. St. Thomas Aquinas, *Commentary on the Nicomachean Ethics*, translated by C. L. Litzinger (Chicago: Henry Regnery, 1964), vol. 2, 831.

3. For martyrdom see St. Thomas Aquinas, *Summa Theologiae*, edited by T. Gilby and T. C. O'Brien (New York: McGraw-Hill, 1964), II–II, 124.3 and 124, 5 and 5 ad. 1; for charity see II–II, 23.1, 6, 7; 25.4–8; 26.2–8, 12.

4. Bernard Lonergan, *Collection*; edited by F. E. Crowe, S.J. (New York: Herder & Herder, 1967), 24–25.

5. Herman Melville, "Hawthorne and His Mosses," in *The Piazza Tales and Other Prose Pieces, 1839–1860* (Evanston, Ill.: Northwestern University Press, 1987), 244. Some of Melville's more theoretical speculations, however, can be extraordinarily good; see, for example, the "Supplement" to *Battle-Pieces (Battle-Pieces and Aspects of the War,* edited by Sidney Kaplan [Amherst: University of Massachusetts Press, 1972], 259–72), a piece that also is relevant to this paper. The relationship of literary works to ethical reflection has recently been treated in a number of excellent works. Especially relevant here are the accounts offered by Wayne C. Booth (*The Company We Keep: An Ethics of Fiction* [Berkeley: University of California Press, 1988]), Martha Nussbaum (*Love's Knowledge: Essays on Philosophy and Literature* [Oxford: Oxford University Press, 1990]), Judith Shklar (*Ordinary Vices* [Cambridge, Mass.: Belknap Press, 1984), and Bernard Williams, *Shame and Necessity* [Berkeley: University of California Press, 1993]); also note Charles Taylor, *Sources of the Self: The Making of Modern Identity* [Cambridge, Mass.: Harvard University Press, 1989, 456–93], on "epiphanies." The relationship of law and literature has also generated a substantial literature. Especially relevant here are the articles on *Billy Budd* in "Symposium on Billy Budd," edited by Richard Weisberg, *Cardoza Studies in Law and Literature* 1 (1989).

6. The idea of the heroic has, of course, a range of meanings, especially if it is treated in a framework that either spans divergent parts of a single tradition or draws from many distinct traditions. Nevertheless, I believe the expressive component informs a wide variety of admittedly quite different conceptions. For an examination both of the approach that underlies this kind of comparative endeavor and of an example of its application to courage, a virtue with close links to heroism, see Lee H. Yearley, *Mencius and Aquinas: Theories of Virtue and Conceptions of Courage* [Albany: State University of New York Press, 1990]; idem, "Theories, Virtues, and the Comparative Philosophy of Human Flourishing: A Response to Professor Allen," in *Philosophy East and West* 44, no. 4 (1994): 711–20; and Martha Nussbaum, "Comparing Virtues," book discussion of Yearley's *Mencius and Aquinas, Journal of Religious Ethics* 21, no. 2 (1993): 345–67; also see note 28 below.

In order to avoid misunderstanding, let me underline that I am not simply applying here any one person's idea of the heroic. For example, I am using neither a Homeric idea (see James M. Redfield, *Nature and Culture in the Iliad: The Tragedy of Hector,* expanded edition [Durham, N.C.: Duke University Press, 1994], 99–127) nor the very restricted notion of the heroic (or divine) kind of virtue that appears as one of Aristotle's six types of character at the beginning of Book Six of the *Ethics;* see especially 1145a19–29. I am, however, drawing on other aspects of, say, Aristotle's account; for instance, his analysis of the expressive component of virtue as it appears in his treatment of friendship.

7. For a more extensive treatment of this distinction, see Yearley, *Mencius and Aquinas,* 20–23; that analysis draws on Irwin's treatment in *Plato's Moral Theory: The Early and Middle Dialogues* (Oxford: The Clarendon Press, 1977). If this distinction is seen as simply descriptive, then any expressive motivation is

acceptable, but in traditional accounts evaluative elements are always prominent; for examples see *Mencius and Aquinas,* 129–43, 154–68. More important, I understand that a muted version of this distinction will always inform ethical action given that we never know for sure that our actions will generate the results we desire. Nevertheless, the uncertainly is much greater in the case of heroic virtue. This is especially true if self-sacrifice is involved, and the ultimate motivation is provided by the desire to manifest the valued state.

8. Herman Melville, *Israel Potter* (Evanston, Ill.: Northwestern University Press, 1982), 120. Melville also thought that when an industrial nation mobilized itself to fight, the inevitable result was an abridgment, formal and informal, of an individual's freedom. This abridgment for him was one great irony of the Civil War; the fight to free some people generated a process that enslaved most people in new ways. For a treatment of aspects of this issue, see John P. McWilliams, Jr., *Hawthorne, Melville, and the American Character* (Cambridge: Cambridge University Press, 1984), 201–11.

9. William James, *The Varieties of Religious Experience: A Study in Human Nature* (New York: Penguin Books, 1985), 364. For James's sense of heroism's liability to deformation, see, for example, ibid., 318. (James's first statement, incidentally, deeply affected Wittgenstein.) I examine James's ideas about heroism, a number of which relate in fascinating ways with Melville's, in "William James as Virtue Theorist: The Case of Voluntary Poverty," *Journal of Religious Ethics,* forthcoming. Heroism's character, role, and relationship to democratic ideas was a continuing issue in the America of this period; see George Cotkin, "The Discourse of Heroism," in *William James, Public Philosopher* (Baltimore: Johns Hopkins University Press, 1990), 95–122. Indeed, one could argue the tension between egalitarian and perfectionist ideals that Stanley Cavell, in *Conditions Handsome and Unhandsome: The Constitution of Emersonian Perfectionism* (Chicago: University of Chicago Press, 1988) and *This New Yet Unapproachable America: Lectures after Emerson after Wittgenstein* (Albuquerque, NM: Living Batch Press, 1989), sees as so crucial to American ethical thought revolves around an understanding of the heroic. (A related question is whether any focus on self-perfection necessarily generates cruelty toward other people, or at least a neglect of them; see Shklar, *Ordinary Vices,* 16, 38–40, 58–62, for a powerful argument that it does.) F. O. Matthiessen, in *American Renaissance: Art and Expression in the Age of Emerson and Whitman* (New York: Oxford University Press, 1941), 635–37, 643–44, 653–56, and especially McWilliams, in *Hawthorne, Melville and The American Character,* 155–225, treat well these issues in Melville; particularly relevant here is the analysis of Melville's poem "The Age of the Antonines" 217–19.

10. It is worth noting a few things about the history of the text. The manuscript for *Billy Budd* was found among other papers in Melville's desk when he died on 28 September 1891. Glued to the inside of the desk was a tiny clipping with the words "Keep true to the dreams of thy youth" (Harold Beaver, Introduction to *Herman Melville: Billy Budd, Sailor, and Other Stories* [New York: Viking Penguin, 1967], 38). The manuscript was not published until 1924, and questions about its exact form have provided many scholars with useful labors—as well as the opportunity to be involved in debates that would have provided Melville with wonderful materials for his acute sense of parody.

A thorough treatment of these issues is found in Herschel Parker, *Reading Billy Budd* (Evanston, Ill.: Northwestern University Press, 1990); also see the relevant materials in the edition that I use, *Billy Budd, Sailor (An Inside Narrative)*, edited by Harrison Hayford and Merton M. Sealts, Jr. (Chicago: University of Chicago Press, 1962). Although I will not pursue issues about the manuscript's correct form, let me note that I believe several cuts made in the edition I use, the generally accepted one, are questionable; see Milton R. Stern, Introduction and Appendices, to Melville, *Billy Budd, Sailor (An Inside Narrative)* (Indianapolis: Liberty Press, 1975), 149–60, for criticisms of the Hayford and Sealts edition, and see the example in note 22 below. Finally, the stages Melville went through in developing the story are worth noting. In the original, Billy Budd was an older sailor who was killed for actually fomenting mutiny; then the figure of Claggart was introduced; and finally the figure of Vere was added.

11. Other incidents in the film also illuminate ideas about heroic virtue in modern America. Billy Budd, for example, has a conversation with Claggart in which Billy declares that Claggart's loneliness occurs because he does not reach out to people or express his hostility. Some critics, incidentally, consider the play an improvement on the book largely because of the nuanced portrayal of Vere's dilemma. As will become clear, I think such a judgment manifests a misunderstanding of the book.

12. Benjamin Britten, *Billy Budd: An Opera in Four Acts*, libretto by E. M. Forster and Eric Crozier, vocal score by Erwin Stein (London: Boosey & Hawkes, 1952).

13. Quoted in *Billy Budd* (Harrison and Sealts ed.), 36.

14. Herman Melville, *Moby-Dick; or, The Whale* (Evanston, Ill.: Northwestern University Press, 1988), 434.

15. Page references to *Billy Budd* (Harrison and Sealts ed.) are cited in the text.

16. Wendy Doniger's response to my paper captures well, I believe, just how illuminating is an approach to *Billy Budd* that focuses on mythical elements. Bernard Williams's distinction, in chapter 2 of the present volume, between stark and dense literary treatment, is also illuminating because it clarifies how much of Melville's work can be seen as a successful combination of the two. Also worth noting is my judgment that the presence of both "ambiguity" and mythic elements does not involve a contradiction or even an opposition because the latter adds to the density the former presents.

The general question of how best to understand especially the mythic features of Melville's style is a vexing and controversial one; for representative earlier treatments see James Baird, *Ishmael: A Study of the Symbolic Mode in Primitivism* (Baltimore: Johns Hopkins University Press, 1956); H. Bruce Franklin, *The Wake of the Gods* (Stanford, Calif.: Stanford University Press, 1963); and Charles Olson, *Call Me Ishmael: A Study of Melville* (San Francisco: City Lights Books, 1947). A good general treatment of Melville's style in *Billy Budd* is found in F. Barron Freeman's Introduction to *Melville's Billy Budd* (Cambridge: Harvard University Press, 1948), 97–113. The issue of Melville's narrative techniques and the kinds of understanding they produce is also germane; see Ramon Saldivar, *Figural Language, in the Novel: The Flowers of Speech from Cerrantes to Joyce*

(Princeton, N.J.: Princeton University Press, 1984), xi–xiv, 110–55. Finally, an influential treatment of, among other matters, the significance of ambiguity is provided by Barbara Johnson in "Melville's Fist: The Execution of Billy Budd," *Studies in Romanticism* 18 (1979): 567–99.

17. Melville could also be said to present other responses to Billy's death. One is that of the sea birds, whose movements are carefully detailed. Another is by Dansker, a figure to be treated in the next section. As we will see, the text's silence on his response reflects his position on the almost inevitable character of what happened. Throughout both this section and the rest of the paper a major subject is the relationship between victims and victimizers. For an examination of how inextricably intertwined are the notions of victims and victimizers, see Shklar, *Ordinary Vices*, 15–23.

18. For an examination of the good person criterion that includes an attempt to meet the obvious criticisms of it, see my article "Conflicts among Ideals of Human Flourishing," in *Prospects for a Common Morality*, edited by Gene Outka and John P. Reeder, Jr. (Princeton: Princeton University Press, 1993), 238–43. It is interesting to speculate about what role, if any, this criterion plays when we evaluate different critical treatments of a work like *Billy Budd*.

19. See especially Hayford and Sealts's edition of *Billy Budd*, 85–86, for a treatment of Dansker, and note McWilliams, *Hawthorne, Melville, and the American Character*, 164–65, who treats the general motif in Melville. Also relevant to an appreciation of Dansker is the idea touched on by Bernard Williams in chapter 2 of the present volume, that is, that "forgetting" the horrible may be an acceptable human option.

20. On the first opposition, see, for example, Ethan Allan versus Ben Franklin in *Israel Potter* (Evanston, Ill.: Northwestern University Press, 1982). The second opposition, in Melville's mind, underlay the greatest tragedy in American history, the Civil War. The third could be said to be one of the fulcrums on which much in Melville, including this story, turns. McWilliams, *Hawthorne, Melville, and the American Character*, examines well many of these ideas. Stuart Hampshire's *Innocence and Experience* (Cambridge: Harvard University Press, 1989) contains an extremely sophisticated treatment of the ideas of innocence and experience and their various connections; he also discusses the relationship of the two to procedural justice. His book illuminates *Billy Budd* in many ways, although Hampshire never directly examines it or any of Melville's other works.

21. *The Confidence Man: His Masquerade* (Evanston: Northwestern University Press, 1984), for example, focuses on this problem, among others, and Melville saw it as an especially crucial one in the America of his day. He understood well the depth of the problem. That is, in many areas a lack of suspicion can generate harm to both the agent and other people, but too much suspicion can also corrupt both the agent and his or her relationships.

22. On the significance of envy, see Yearley, "Conflicts," 248–51. I think, incidentally, that an understanding of envy like Melville's shows us a place where Aristotle's and Aquinas's perspectives differ substantially. Helmut Schoeck, in *Envy: A Theory of Social Behavior* (Indianapolis: Liberty Press, 1966), 162–71, surveys many critical treatments of *Billy Budd* and focuses on how rare have been

sustained treatments of envy in considerations of Claggart; he also speculates on reasons for the absence. Matthiessen, however, in *American Renaissance*, 435–40, 504–6, offers an illuminating treatment of envy in Melville.

Relevant to the role of envy in *Billy Budd* is the fact that in Melville's manuscript a crucial chapter about Claggart was entitled "Pale ire, envy and despair"; the phrase is drawn from Milton's description of Satan in *Paradise Lost*. That title for chapter 12 is excised in the 1962 edition. Also relevant to the subject of envy is the textual evidence that erotic attraction is an important feature of Claggart's relation to Billy. I think, however, that considerably more than "simple" sexual attraction is at work. For an examination of aspects of this question, see Eve Kosofsky Sedgwick, "Billy Budd: After the Homosexual," in *Herman Melville: A Collection of Critical Essays,* edited by Myra Jehlen (Englewood Cliffs, N.J.: Prentice-Hall, 1994).

23. I well understand that someone could argue that there is little textual evidence for the notion that Claggart aims to have Billy Budd kill him, knowing that only such an act will ensure Billy's death. Nevertheless, I think such a reading not only is plausible but follows from a correct understanding of Claggart's character. (It also takes with due seriousness the narrator's comments about the likelihood of moderns misunderstanding Claggart.) Moreover, as discussed earlier (for example, in note 16 above), Melville's depiction of Claggart in this scene surely moves beyond a "realistic" description. Perhaps most important, even if someone questions this specific interpretative point, the general point about Claggart's belief in the expressive is largely unaffected.

24. My special thanks to Professor David Grene, whose comments at the conference helped me grasp complexities about Vere's character that I had missed. As the last of Melville's captains, it is worth noting that Vere has little of the heroic (if daemonic) dimension that Ahab displays, but he also has far more substance and grandeur than does Delano, the captain in *Benito Cereno* (in *The Piazza Tales and Other Prose Pieces, 1839–1860*), who literally cannot imagine that slaves may now command the ship he boards. For a well-argued presentation of an extremely negative view of Vere and what he represents, see H. Bruce Franklin, "From Empire to Empire: *Billy Budd, Sailor*," in *Herman Melville: Reassessments,* edited by A. Robert Lee (London: Vision Press, 1984).

25. Several vexing interpretative issues surround the trial, and I will not try to adjudicate them here. Let me note, however, that I think a compelling case can be made that Vere knows that in holding the trial on board his ship he is violating normal naval procedures. It is also worth remembering that initially only Vere knew that Billy killed Claggart.

26. See Hampshire, *Innocence and Experience,* 30–31, 45–48; also note Yearley, *Mencius and Aquinas,* 196–203, and "New Religious Virtues and the Study of Religion," *Fifteenth Annual University Lecture In Religion at Arizona State University* (American Academy of Religion, 1994), pp. 1–26. When considering especially the place of imagination but also other subjects related to heroic virtue, it is worth remembering what Melville said in an 1849 letter to Duyckinck about the "corps of thought-divers": "[I love] all men who *dive*. Any fish can swim near the surface, but it takes a great whale to go downstairs five miles or more.... [I am speaking] of the whole corps of thought-divers, that have been diving &

coming up again with bloodshot eyes since the world began" (quoted in Richard Roland and Malcolm Bradbury, *From Puritanism to Postmodernism: A History of American Literature* [New York: Viking, 1991], 164).

27. See, for example, Ovid *Metamorphoses* XI, 1–100. In a lost play by Aeschylus the maenad followers of Dionysus tear Orpheus to pieces because he failed to honor the god. Vere also applied the image of Orpheus to "the disruption of forms going on across the Channel and the consequences thereof" (128).

The contrasts between organic and inorganic images mirror, I believe, the conflicts that beset Vere. Other contrasts are also evident. For example, we are told before we have the image of Vere as a musket that Billy Budd lies prone in irons between two cannons. The two images are, I think, intended to contrast with each other.

28. The general approach used here draws on the comparative method or set of procedures I develop and use in *Mencius and Aquinas* (see especially 175–203); it works from the idea of analogical predication. Further discussions of it are contained in "The Author Replies," book discussion of *Mencius and Aquinas, Journal of Religious Ethics* 21, no. 2; and "Theories, Virtues." Also note the discussion in note 6 above.

29. The special character of this hope arises largely from the fact that people cannot know the source of the hope with even the assurance a probabilistic judgment provides. The hope fits, then, between normal assurance and doubt, or normal confidence and despair, and it must draw on something other than the judgment seasoned reason makes. To my mind such a hope must rest on love, not knowledge, because love can move a person into contact with something truly beyond the self rather than something that fits, however imperfectly, within the categories of a person's understanding. Little in Aristotle supports the idea that such a hope is other than an unwarranted inference, although that judgment about his views depends, in significant part, on answers to those questions about the needed basis for heroic virtue that we discussed in the opening section. Aquinas, however, at times speaks of religious hope in this fashion, although it is a vexing interpretative question as to how these formulations fit into the rest of his theological perspective; see Yearley, *Mencius and Aquinas,* 30–31; John Jenkins, "Yearley, Aquinas, and Comparative Method," book discussion of *Mencius and Aquinas, Journal of Religious Ethics* 21, no. 2 (1993): 377–83; and "The Author Replies."

30. Aristotle's views on these issues are, of course, complicated. Surely he is not simply optimistic about most people's capacities to understand and pursue goodness, even if slaves and women are excluded from consideration; see, for example, Aristotle, *Nicomachean Ethics,* 1162a 35–36, 1167b 13–16, and 28–29; and 1179b 5–32. Nevertheless, he believes that for at least some people such an understanding and pursuit is a readily available option. Moreover, he thinks the normal circumstances of life allow for a greater likelihood of a good life than does Melville, or some of Aristotle's own contemporaries; see Williams, *Shame and Necessity,* 160–64. (One might even say, if with hesitation, that for Melville Dansker represents the modern position most akin to the one Aristotle adopts.) Needless to say, despite Aquinas's views on the significance of evil he does not believe that evil's influence is ultimately equal to the influence of good.

31. Aquinas does acknowledge that the best religious people can lack important human qualities. He well knew that the Christian tradition contained many
examples of such people, and he explains it by arguing that grace imperfectly
forms natural features of the self; see Yearley, *Mencius and Aquinas*, 30. Nevertheless, the examples he uses as well as, of course, the explanation he gives differ
strikingly from Melville's portrait of Billy Budd.

32. Quoted in *The Confidence Man*, 314. Hawthorne's notebook account is
from Thursday, 20 November; the whole is well worth reading and is reproduced
in the Editorial Appendix to *The Confidence Man*. For a treatment of wandering
that arises from a perspective that contains remarkable similarities to Melville's
but draws very different conclusions, see my examination of that idea in the classical Taoist thinker Chuang Tzu, in Yearley, "Taoist Wandering and the Adventure
of Religious Ethics," the William James Lectures, *Harvard Divinity Bulletin* 24,
no. 2 (1995): 11–15.

RESPONSE

Wendy Doniger

Billy Budd is a most mythological novel; more than that, it raises questions about the intersection of heroism and love that is the subject of many
myths. My response will attempt to highlight and raise questions about
some of the points that Lee Yearley's paper makes on five mythological
topics: animals, love, heroic death, religious death, and multivalence.

First I should say why I think that the novel is a myth. Basically, it is
because the characters are presented to us in mythological and generic
terms rather than novelistic and individualistic terms and because the imagery and language are highly religious. Surely there is an intended ambiguity in the name of the Captain, "Vere," both as a pun on "truth" and as
a hint that this is a man who will "veer" from the truth (even in his final
encounter with that allegorical ship, the Atheist). Yearley notes the relevance of Shakespeare's Iago to Claggart, but he also notes, more tellingly,
I think, the relevance of Milton's Satan, and, most telling of all, the Adam
of the book of Genesis. The characters are what is nowadays called "larger
than life"—that is, mythological. To cite the quality of myth so wonder-
fully evoked by David Grene in his response to Stephanie Nelson's paper,
it is a story that makes us "participate in an unknowable certainty." The
story is, as one of the characters says (in debunking the concepts of "will
power" and "euthanasia" offered in explanation of Billy's lack of a "muscular spasm") "imaginative and metaphorical—in short, Greek." In short,
mythological.

1. Let us turn first to animals, the permanent repertory cast of most
myths. Lee Yearley evokes several of the many, many animal images in this
book. Claggart is like one of the "creatures of the deep," with "serpent

fascination" like a "torpedo fish." He tells us that some critics (who remain mercifully anonymous in his paper) interpret the novel as "the retelling of an Indo-European myth in which a Celtic Apollo slays the serpent and then is ritually killed." This is, I think, going too far, but we are certainly in the presence of a bestiary. Claggart is obviously an animal, but Vere is also an animal: Vere is said to be like a migratory fowl and also a Newfoundland dog—a good animal, more precisely a thoroughly domesticated animal. Of the two animals who come into heroic conflict, Claggart and Billy, it might be said that Claggart is a human animal and Billy a divine animal; neither is entirely or purely human. More important, given the central importance of self-knowledge and self-love in Yearley's analysis of this tale, Vere is an animal who doesn't know that he is an animal (which may make him even more dangerous than Claggart, who probably does know that he is an animal): Vere models himself on Orpheus, taming all the wild animals, ignoring the fact that he is himself one of the wild animals. Is there a continuum here linking wild animals with no moral sense, domesticated animals with some sense, human animals with a little more moral sense, and divine human animals with the most moral sense? Are the animals, as in a myth, positioned explicitly to delimit one end of the human species, with the gods positioned implicitly at the other end? Or should we be reminded of the noted capacity of certain animals, including but not limited to nursing mothers, for self-sacrifice for the sake of the survival of the group or species?

2. Second, love. Yearley argues that some variant of Aristotelian self-love is the key to Billy's death: "the true self-love that leads to the self sacrifice of heroic virtue." But he also notes Aristotle's "criticisms of false ideas of self-love" and "the dangers of false martyrdom," and I think this is even more relevant to Billy Budd. False martyrdom, rather than true heroic sacrifice, may have been Billy's unconscious motive, derailing his heroic self-love. Another, more positive explanation of Billy's actions is suggested by Yearley's discussion of the ways in which people perform heroic acts even when they know that they will do no good or even that they will do harm. This, too, happens all the time in myth, and in history, to people whom we can call Quixotic or Pyrrhic, the builders of the Bridge over the River Kwai. This is one of the things that may make a hero tragic, not merely that he dies but that his death is for nothing.

Self-love and love of god or country may be positioned at the two ends of the spectrum of love. Self-love is private, love of god and country public. In between, along the continuum, we find the love for another single human being and the love for a small group of human beings. What is the nature of the love and hate that motivate Claggart and Vere? Melville explicitly states that he does not expect us to understand Claggart's malice. Barbara Johnson, Eve Sedgwick, and other literary critics have suggested that Claggart's motive is a secret, and I think it is; they go on to suggest that it is a homosexual secret, and it may or may not be. Melville speaks of the "dark sayings" and talks of "the secret of all passions" in Vere (explicitly, envy, but perhaps implicitly the love that dare not speak its name). Yearley notes the Benjamin Britten opera, which has certainly been appropriated (if I may use the trendy word for a trendy thing) by gay studies, and he remarks, cryptically, "The surface message is telling given Britten's own situation." On the good ship Bellipotent, on the continuum between love of self and love of heterosexual other (which does not exist, even by suggestion, on that ship), we might position homosexual love, in this case the destructive, because repressed, love for the beautiful Billy conceived by Claggart and Vere. Claggart's love (for Billy) is secret, and Billy's love (for God? for the crew? for the world?) is, though mute, entirely public.

What is the importance of Billy Budd's beauty? In the literal terms of the plot, it excites Claggart's envy. In this it is mythological: in myths, the good are always beautiful; in myths, beauty and virtue and love are conflated. But Claggart may of course have had other reactions to Billy's beauty. And how does this motivate Billy? How does it make him willing to die? Mythological heroes often die *against* love, die in order to resist love or as a result of their failure to resist love: from Samson and Delilah to Superman/Clark Kent and the classic heroes of American westerns, the hero must remain chaste in order to remain powerful; when he is seduced, he dies. (Another, very different, fix on the relationship between love and not heroism but the related quality of justice is cited by Stephanie Nelson: Aristotle's dictum that, where there is *philia*, there is no need for *dikē*; or, as Itzak Rabin said about shaking hands with Arafat, you don't need a peace treaty to get you to shake hands with your friends.) Is Billy somehow compromised, not by Claggart but by Vere? Is this why he is willing to die?

Is the love-hate of Claggart and Vere for Billy the key to the unusually unerotic nature of Billy's hanging? What is the meaning of, in Melville's terms, "the absence of a muscular spasm"—that is, an ejaculation? And what is its relevance to euthanasia? Indeed, why does Melville introduce such a peculiar subject into his novel at all? What is he trying to call our attention to in this grotesque way? Yearley is too delicate to tell us what he thinks it means; like the purser and surgeon, he is "unwilling, even to consider its implications." Is it that Billy has no eroticism? That he is repulsed by both Claggart and Vere? That in death, if not in life, he takes charge of his erotic nature? Melville, as Yearley tells us, is always asking, "How suspicious should one be?" This applies, I think, not only to our real-life encounters, nor even merely to our encounters with the characters within the text (what is driving Claggart?), but, through a hermeneutics of suspicion, to our encounter with Melville himself. Claggart is a mad lover indeed, and perhaps not just a mad Platonic lover of virtue. His explicit envy of Billy's beauty, which is the reverse of charity, may also be an inversion of his implicit jealousy of Billy's love.

3. Let us turn now to the heroic death. Why are any heroes willing to die? To die willingly is the defining characteristic, what is nowadays called the job description, of heroes: "Nothing in his life / Became him like the leaving of it" (as Malcolm says of the Thane of Cawdor). Here the proper antecedent for Melville may be not Aristotle but Homer, with all those heroic deaths, culminating in the death of Hector, as a direct result of the complex moral dilemma of Achilles, rendered still more complex, perhaps, by his tragic love, of whatever nature, for Patroclus.

4. The religious death is one particular form of this heroic death. For where the heroic martyr dies for this world and for the people in it, the religious martyr may die for the other world, leaving this world altogether. Yearley tells us that Aquinas, on Aristotle, tells us "that any pursuit of a good that leads to one's death can be properly called an instance of martyrdom, a surrender of self to the genuine worship of God . . . charity is friendship with God." Love, Lee Yearley notes, and "love alone can move a person into contact with something fully beyond the self." But who is the God to whom Billy sacrifices himself? Is it merely some Durkheimian god incarnate in the fellowship of the ship, a.k.a. the ship of state, the social world, which, as Yearley points out, "is the world that we must, in this view, inhabit"? Yearley himself suggests the relevance of Aristotle's belief that "the ideal is alive in parts of the community." But if Billy's death is religious, what religion is it? Is Billy crucified? He hangs from the yardarm like Jesus on the cross, and the sailors treat the material objects from the execution as "pieces of the Cross." The puzzle of his lack of ejaculation/erection may be reflected in the controversy, thoroughly documented by Leo Steinberg, over depictions of the crucified Christ with an erection. Or does Billy die a more pagan death, more like that Indo-European python-killer? Melville likens him in his muteness to "a condemned vestal priestess (note the change of gender) in the moment of being buried alive." Yearley notes that heroes "stand between the *mysterious* gods and the limited truths manifested in normal life." Here we may recall David Grene's "*unknowable* certainty" of myth (emphasis mine): there are mythological secrets, after all, which need not be sexual. The recurrent references in Melville's text to the contrast between innocence and knowing, between those who see and those who do not see, is not merely sexual. It is also the theme of Eden. Melville used as one of his original chapter headings one of Milton's lines about Satan: "Pale Ire, Envy, and Despair." And Vere's

"lack of imagination," more important, in Stuart Hampshire's wise formulation, than his lack of any capacity to think, is what precipitates the tragedy.

5. Finally, multivalence. Yearley alerts us to the importance of the four endings, like the four Gospels, like the four interpretations of the rape (or was it a rape?) in *Rashomon*. He notes the equally fragmented division of opinion in literary criticism—does the novel mean this, or the opposite, or both at once? He cites Olson's dictum about catching the ambiguity of the event direct, a dictum which leaves us with a most ambiguous novel. Is this ambiguity by design, as Yearley argues in his statement that Melville purposely builds this layered and ambiguous theory of competing goods, this ragged edge of truth, this both stark and dense telling?

This sort of multivalence, or multivocality (which Roland Barthes and many others have written about), is a characteristic not of novels so much as of myths. The myth is a prism through which all moral views can be refracted. It invites moralizing, but does not provide it. Though the word "myth" is often used nowadays to designate an idea (particularly a wrong idea), the one thing a myth most certainly is *not* is an idea. It is a narrative that makes possible any number of ideas but that does not commit itself to any single idea. A myth is like a gun for hire, like a mercenary soldier: it can be made to fight for anyone. It tells us what happened, but it does not necessarily tell us *why* it happened or the meaning of what happened. It leaves each teller of the myth, each audience, to work it out individually. Each time a myth is told, it represents any or several of the many points of view that the myth allows. Yet, though it is not the task of myths to moralize explicitly, every myth implicitly invites the teller, the listener, the commentator, to moralize. And this is what makes *Billy Budd* seem to deconstruct all possible views of the construction of heroic virtue: it encompasses them all. There are many kinds of love and many religious reasons for self-sacrifice, and the myth refracts them all and challenges each reader, each of us, to make sense of it all. In this, Melville, as seen through the eyes of Aristotle, as seen through the eyes of Yearley, is not saying that there is no such thing as heroic virtue; he is not saying that just as different characters within his story have very different ideas about heroic virtue, so too different readers may have very different ideas about heroic virtue. Though these ideas are theoretically equal, in practice some of them are, like certain pigs in *Animal Farm*, more equal than others. Surely Melville felt that one of the many possible ideas about heroic virtue was better than the others (if not, perhaps, "true" in every sense of that word), but his story is constructed in such a way that it is not easy for us to know which one that might have been. And in the absence of that certainty, we must be content to find in it new insights into the construction of our own ideas about heroic virtue.

4

PLATO'S *CRITO:*
THE AUTHORITY OF LAW
AND PHILOSOPHY

James Boyd White

T HE *CRITO* IS ONE OF SEVERAL PLATONIC DIALOGUES about Socrates' last days: chronologically it follows the *Apology,* which consists of Socrates' speech at his trial, and it precedes the *Phaedo,* in
which he considers the possibility of an afterlife. Like many of the dialogues it receives its name from a person, Crito, an old friend of Socrates
who visits him in prison where he lies under sentence of death. Crito urges
Socrates to escape, claiming that the conviction and penalty, however legal
they may be, are unjust; that escape is perfectly practicable; and that Socrates therefore has a duty—to his friends, his family, and perhaps himself—to do it. Justice itself requires him to escape.

Socrates responds to these claims in many ways, but most famously
in a passage in which he asks Crito to imagine what the laws (*nomoi*) and
the common state of the city (*to koinon tēs poleōs*) might say to him about
the justice of his proposed escape. They would say, Socrates tells him, that
it would be unjust for him to escape against their commands, even if the
sentence against him is unjust, for he owes them an absolute duty of obedience. There are several reasons for this. First, the laws are like his parents, for they regulated the marriage of his actual parents and his own
conception, and they shaped his education too; he therefore owes them the
obedience of a child to a parent, or a slave to a master. Second, by continuing to live in Athens, when he could have left at any time, he has implicitly
agreed to obey all its laws and decisions. His only legitimate way out would
be to persuade the laws and the city that they are wrong, which he has tried
but failed to do. He is therefore obliged to obey the judgment of the law and
suffer death, even if the verdict compelling him to do so is unjust.

This summary of the speech of the Nomoi is imperfect, to say the
least, but for present purposes it will do, for it suggests that this set of
arguments, at least when stated in such a bald and unelaborated form, is
very weak indeed. Why, for example, does it follow from the fact that

Socrates has stayed in Athens that he has agreed to obey its laws and decrees, even when they are unjust? Why should we not read his actual conduct—particularly as it is summarized for us in the *Apology*—rather as agreeing to do what he can, at every stage and in every way, to advance the cause of justice? And why should this not mean correcting the city when it is wrong, including by disobedience when that is appropriate? For, as familiar Socratic doctrine tells us, the city can have no genuine interest in acting unjustly. Why, indeed, should an agreement to do, or suffer, something that is unjust be given any weight at all? And to turn to the even more problematic argument: For what reasons should we construe the relation between citizen and city as being like that of child and parent or slave and master? Even if we do take this step, why should these relations carry with them an obligation to do or suffer injustice?

Of course these questions might have answers, perhaps very good ones; no small part of Western political philosophy has been devoted to trying to work them out. But as the speech of the Nomoi is actually written, especially in its first version, it responds to virtually none of the questions we have about it, but consists instead of a series of conclusory declarations, with very little argument to support them, and that mostly, though not entirely, of low quality. We should not be misled by our familiarity with more recent and persuasive versions of these positions into misreading the way they are stated here.

The argument of the Nomoi is still more problematic when considered in light of the rest of Socrates' career, during which he has repeatedly argued that to live and act well is the supreme goal of life, and that "well" means, among other things, "justly."[1] The speech he imagines the Nomoi making and which he invokes as authoritative seems inconsistent with virtually everything else he has said and done, including in the *Apology*, where he boasts of his refusal to follow certain official orders and asserts an absolute commitment to leading the philosophic life. He says to the jury, for example, that he would not accept an acquittal that was conditioned on his giving up philosophy but would persist in this course of life against their command. The only constraint he recognizes in the *Apology* is that of his own *daimonion*, the spiritual force that, he says, always tells him when he is considering doing something that he ought not do.

Various stratagems have been devised to reconcile the *Crito* with the rest of what the Platonic Socrates has said and done: for example, that the command he described himself in the *Apology* as disobeying (to arrest Leon of Salamis) was itself not really law but lawless; or that the Nomoi speak only presumptively and thus recognize a host of unarticulated exceptions; or that the jury hasn't the power to make an acquittal conditional and that therefore his resolve, expressed in the *Apology*, to continue the philosophic life in violation of such conditions can be disregarded as merely hypothetical; or that the obligation "to do what the laws command or to persuade them otherwise" can be satisfied if one tries in good faith to persuade them, even if one fails; or, perhaps more sensibly than the other attempts, that there is a crucial Socratic difference between doing and suffering injustice.[2] But these attempted reconciliations are dubious at best, both because the inconsistency with the rest of what the Platonic Socrates says simply will not go away, no matter how much we wish it to, and because the arguments of the Nomoi, as I shall try to show, are on the merits weak and conclusory. Although they happen to persuade Crito, I think that one cannot really imagine them persuading any critically acute mind of the position they advance, that the Athenian citizen has an absolute obligation to obey the laws even when they are unjust.

* * *

Many of the difficulties we have in reading the *Crito* are due, I think, to a certain mistake commonly made not only in the reading of Plato but in the reading of other philosophic texts too, namely, to think that one can extract from a text a particular key passage—in this case the speech of the Nomoi—and read it as though it stood alone, as a set of arguments that could be abstracted from their context and assessed independently, rather than as a part of a larger text, with its own shape and rhythm and texture. At a more general level the mistake is to assume that the meaning of the text as a whole is propositional in kind, that is, that it can be reduced to a set of claims each of which can be independently tested for its truth or adequacy. May it not be that at least the *Crito*, and perhaps other Platonic dialogues, and indeed perhaps other texts we think of as philosophic as well, have a meaning of a richer and more problematic kind, one that cannot be reduced to the propositional? May it even be that our modern aspiration to produce philosophic texts that can be reduced to such forms is itself misguided, likely to fail, and perhaps an evasion of philosophic responsibility?

I want to ask: What happens, especially to its argument about the authority of law, if we read the *Crito* in a different way, as a composition of which we assume all the parts have a place and meaning, no one of which can be elevated above the others except in the terms, and on the grounds, that the text itself affords?[3] To take one example: the dialogue begins with Crito's visit to Socrates in prison, early in the morning, and with talk about a dream Socrates has just had. Can we not take this part of the text seriously, asking what it means, and not assume that it is just window dressing, or "setting the stage," or otherwise marginal or irrelevant to the matter at hand? We might even prepare ourselves to conclude, if the text so persuaded us, that this scene is more central to the text than the speech of the Nomoi itself.

The hope is that we may find a way to respect the text as it is composed, attending to its form, its methods, its various parts and their relations, and to discover the kind of coherence and meaning it then proves to have. We could put it, perhaps, that our object is to read this "philosophic" text not as a string of propositions but as "literature," that is, with an eye to possibilities of meaning richer and more complex than the propositional; but we would do this in part in the hope of being instructed in the falseness of the way we habitually distinguish between these two forms of thought and expression.[4] It may be that great philosophy is literary in many of its deepest commitments, great literature philosophic, and that what is called for is a way of reading both that attempts to recognize their full dimensions of meaning.

ANXIETY AND REPOSE

We can begin with the opening scene: Crito has come, very early in the morning, to the cell of Socrates, whose wholly understandable question to him is the first line of the dialogue: "Why have you come at this time of the day, Crito—is it not still very early?" The first part of Socrates' question—"Why have you come?"—will receive an answer a few paragraphs later, when Crito says that he is coming to bring the "bad news" that the sacred ship, during whose voyage to Delos Socrates cannot be put to death, will arrive that very day. For the present, however, Socrates focuses upon the other and apparently more trivial question, about what time it is. When he is told that it is indeed very early, just first light, he expresses surprise that Crito was able to get into the prison at such an hour. Crito responds that he was allowed in because, through his earlier visits, he has come to know the jailer and, besides that, because he has done him a favor of some unspecified sort. Crito reveals that he has been sitting there quietly some time, beside the sleeping Socrates. When Socrates asks why he did not wake him, Crito says: "I did not wish you to be in such grief and wakefulness [as I am]."[5]

The dialogue thus has its origins in Crito's complex response to hearing the news about the ship. He cannot bear to carry it alone but needs to communicate it to Socrates, no doubt in the hopes that somehow this will make it tolerable. This is in fact the unstated answer to the second part of Socrates' question, namely "Why did you come so early?" That Crito comes at all, is to tell the news; that he comes so early, rather than waiting till a more usual hour, manifests an anxiety or need, an incapacity to bear the news alone; this is in fact a rather appealing quality in him, attesting as it does to the depth and sincerity of his feeling for his friend.

But when he comes into the presence of Socrates, Crito does not wake him after all, in part no doubt out of a sense of consideration for him, lying peacefully asleep, but in part perhaps also because he discovers that merely to be in Socrates' presence gives him much of what he needs. For, he says, he has been sitting for some time beside him, full of wonder to perceive "how sweetly you sleep," and, as often before, "I have thought you happy in your character [*tropos*], and especially so in the present circumstance, [when I see] how easily and gently you bear it."

The issue thus presented by the opening of the text is the contrast between anxiety and repose, sleeplessness and sleeping, between the capacity to bear this apparent misfortune gently and the incapacity to rest once one has received the evil news. I think that this contrast is in fact the central topic to which the rest of the dialogue is addressed, and that to it the "obligation to obey the laws" is something of a sidelight.

Two important points about the character of Crito emerge in this brief opening. First, as we have seen, Crito is shown to be a friend of Socrates, and in two ways: he both needs to be with him in his distress, and can let him sleep. There are thus in Crito qualities both of dependence and kindness, and they will play their roles in the dialogue as a whole. Second, when Socrates expresses surprise that the jailer let him in, Crito says: "He is accustomed to me, I have come so often, and besides he has received a benefit from me." Here we learn that Crito is the kind of person who can establish a friendly relationship with a jailer; this in turn suggests an element in him of human warmth, or perhaps just a general agreeableness. Moreover, the "benefit" of which Crito speaks—whether by this is meant a bribe or present, or some past act of generosity—has converted this acquaintance into a relation of positive reciprocity. This was the archaic form of public community among the Greeks (and among others too) and it gave rise to the dominant conception of justice as doing good to one's friends and harm to one's enemies.[6] It is this understanding of justice, deep in the culture, that Plato is most at pains to undermine in the *Republic* and elsewhere;[7] an understanding closely tied to the aggressive egotism of the heroic and classical worlds alike, which Plato wishes to replace with another vision of what is good for human beings, individually and collectively. It is thus hinted here, what later becomes apparent, both that Crito is a highly competent member of his culture, at home in his world and able to manage its relations with skills, and that the conception of human relations, and of justice, to which he instinctively resorts is that of reciprocity in the service of the self and of one's friends.

          *   *   *

To Crito's comment about the ease with which he is facing death Socrates responds by saying that at his age it would be inappropriate (literally "discordant") to be vexed at such a thing. "But there are others," Crito says, "whom age does not release from such vexation." "That is true," says Socrates; "but tell me, why did you come, and so early?"

Here we have the first of a series of breaks or interruptions in the comfortable back and forth of question and answer between friends, an awkwardness of communication that will in fact become a major subject of the text. Here Crito suggests a point—it will be the main point of the dialogue in the end—that Socrates responds to age and death differently from other people, but Socrates turns away from it to something else, to his original question: "Why did you come?"

This repetition of the opening line marks not only its importance, which should be plain enough, but also the importance of the material that appears between its two occurrences—demonstrating Crito's emotional dependence, cultural competence, and fundamental kindness—for it invites the reader to ask why the dialogue does not begin here instead of with an apparent digression. This way of drawing attention to what seems at first unnecessary is a trope that will recur in the famous speech of the Nomoi, which goes on for several pages after the point at which it might naturally be said to conclude, namely, the point of Crito's first acquiescence in the conclusion it is urging. The text thus begins and ends with material that may seem otiose but which I think is by this very fact marked as having a special significance; part of its meaning, indeed, lies in its apparent gratuitousness.

* * *

Crito's response to the question why he has come is to say that he is bringing news—"bad news, not bad to you I suppose, but to me and all your friends, bad and burdensome; and to me I think a heavier burden than to all the others." This sentence at once expresses Crito's own distress and predicts that Socrates will feel differently. It thus renders explicit the tension from which the dialogue as a whole proceeds, the difference in feeling between the two men. And from what Crito says here we can see that Socrates' later response is not a surprise but a coherent manifestation of his known character.

To the news about the ship from Delos, when Crito gives it, Socrates responds rather oddly, not by the direct expression of any feelings he may have about the meaning of this event but by saying that he doubts Crito's prediction that the ship will arrive that day. He explains that this is based upon a dream that he has just had, in which a woman clad in white appeared to him and said: "O Socrates, on the third day you may fertile Phthia reach."

Crito: A strange dream, Socrates.
Socrates: Yet clear in meaning, or so it seems to me.
Crito: Too much, I fear. But Socrates . . .

And here Crito launches into a lengthy and formal speech of persuasion, to be discussed below.

What is the meaning of this dream, and, equally important, what is the meaning of the brief colloquy about it? At the most obvious level, the dream is read by Socrates as a prophecy that his death will happen in three days, not two. But what is the emotional significance of this fact, in this dream? The Greek reader would know that the words of the woman are a slightly modified quotation from a speech of Achilles in Book Nine of the *Iliad,* made when he is planning to quit the battle and go home to Phthia: "If the wind is fair," he says, "on the third day I may fertile Phthia reach." In the poem this is a moment of great poignancy, for it suddenly shows us how close is the homeland from which these warriors have been away so long, and which has seemed like another world; and it expresses a longing for home, and for peace, in the greatest and most violent warrior of them all.

As this dream defines it, then, the death that Socrates foresees is not an evil but a homecoming, a return to peace from the struggles of life. This is why he sleeps so soundly, why he is so calm in response to the anxiety of Crito. This is its bright meaning to him, which it will be the function of the rest of the dialogue to elaborate and make plain against the view of Crito that the imminence of the death is "bad news."

When, at the end of the passage, Socrates says that the meaning of the dream is clear, he in effect invites Crito to pursue with him the nature of that meaning, and with it the meaning of his impending death. But Crito fails to respond to this clue, and instead rushes headlong into his speech of persuasion. This is the second rupture in the flow of their talk.[8]

CRITO'S ARGUMENT

Crito's long speech, which follows next, has the earmarks of a prepared argument, like a lawyer's case. He begins with his thesis: "Still, even at this late date, be persuaded by me and save yourself." Then he gives his reasons.

Reputation

First, he says, if you die I shall suffer not one but two disasters, for "in addition to the loss of such a friend as I shall never find again," I shall appear, to those who do not know us well, as one who had resources sufficient to save you but did not care enough to do it, and "what [reputation] could be more shameful than to seem to care more for money than for friends?" In his response Socrates wholly disregards the first point and seizes upon the second, correcting his old friend and student on the most familiar of grounds: Why, he asks, should we care about the opinion of those who do not know the truth? People of judgment will see these things correctly.

> *Crito:* But the present circumstances themselves show that the many are able to inflict not the least of evils, but nearly the greatest, if someone is falsely accused before them.[9]
>
> *Socrates:* Would that they were able to inflict the greatest evils, Crito, for then they would have the power to do the greatest good as well, and this would be good for them. But they do not; for they cannot make a man sensible or foolish, but act upon him without thought or care.

Socrates here seems to speak from a distance, out of an amused yet sadly reflective state, with no apparent sense that he is involved in an emergency. His reference at the end to the "greatest good" is at once a refusal to accept Crito's sense of crisis and an invitation (his second) to explore their differences of attitude. He tries to engage his friend in conversation, with the apparent aim of leading him to a position from which the impending death can be seen, if not as a good at least not as a serious evil; but Crito will have none of it. He refuses this invitation too, and rushes on to the rest of his case: "That is all true, Socrates, but answer me this . . ." This is the third break in the conversation, another mark of its failure to get going.

When one reads this text in this way, with an eye to all of its parts and not merely to what seem to be its central speeches, it is full of difficulty and uncertainty, arising not least from the unsuccessful efforts of the two friends to engage on a common question in a common way. "How will Socrates respond to this man?" is the question we are invited to ask and to which the rest of the text, including the speech of the Nomoi, is a response.

✻   ✻   ✻

Notice that so far Socrates has made no response whatever to Crito's first claim, that he will lose an irreplaceable friend. How are we to read this silence: As suggesting that this is a trivial loss? That Socrates has no response to make to such a claim? If true, this would be a terrible deficiency of feeling and indeed of character in him. The question raised here and left unanswered is a thread waiting to be pulled that threatens to unravel the entire text—indeed more than this text, the premises of dialectic and the philosophic life itself—by demonstrating their lack of a simple element of humanity. It is one thing to greet one's own death with equanimity, quite another to dismiss the feelings of bereavement that those who love you will naturally have. Is this whole dimension of life—awareness of the feelings of others, acknowledgement of grief and loss, caring for another—simply missing from the ideal life Plato offers us here and elsewhere? Crito's unanswered claim is a nagging question, defining a tension that will run to the very end of the text and prove at last, I think, to be an essential part of its subject.

Competing Modes of Thought and Argument

The next piece of Crito's long set argument is rather endearingly inconsistent with what he has just said about the damage he fears that his reputation may suffer if Socrates refuses to escape: it is to tell Socrates to have no fear on his behalf, or that of their other friends, that if he escapes they will be accused by sycophants (roughly "informers") and forced to pay huge sums of money or suffer penalties beyond even that. "If you fear any thing of this sort, dismiss your fears; for we are right [*dikaioi*] I think, to run this risk in an attempt to save you, or if necessary an even greater one." The inconsistency is plain: only a moment ago Crito was asking Socrates to escape on the grounds that his, Crito's, reputation might suffer; now he says that Socrates should pay no heed to the possibility of a much more dramatic kind of suffering on his part.

What unites the two arguments, as any lawyer could see at once, is that they support the same position. But one argument enacts a kind of timorousness for which Socrates gently reproaches him—why fear the opinion of the many?—the other a kind of bravery and generosity of spirit, springing from his sense of loyalty and friendship, from the same place indeed as his sense of grief, and one can only admire it. In this frame of mind Crito has no concern at all for the many or what they might do to him. The split between these two impulses is an instance of what Socrates elsewhere calls being divided against oneself, and which he says is just the condition from which dialectic and the philosophic life may release us.[10]

In the speech that follows, Crito first disposes of the practicalities, explaining how easy the escape will be—there is plenty of money, the sycophants can be bought, Socrates can live with friends abroad, and so on—then makes his major claim: that it is not just (*oude dikaion*) for Socrates to allow himself to die. This as Crito knows is an argument that Socrates cannot let pass, for he has given much of his life to establishing the ethical centrality of justice and to giving it a meaning of his own. In raising the topic of justice, then, Crito is acting as a good student of Socrates; though perhaps there is an element of comedy here too, for the claim Crito makes—that justice requires Socrates to evade lawful punishment— is on the face of it bizarre.[11] And the particular conception of justice he invokes is exactly the one that Socrates has been trying most to repudiate and transform, namely, to do good to your friends and harm to your enemies. For Crito says that in refusing to escape Socrates will be doing to himself exactly what his enemies most wish to do to him, which is to bring about his death; and he will be abandoning not only his friends but his sons, to whom he owes a duty of care and education. He sums up his claim by invoking the standard language of value of his day and saying: "[W]hat a good and brave [*agathos* and *andreios*] man would choose, this you should choose, since all your life you have claimed to care for virtue [*aretē*]." Do not, he says, let us languish under the opprobrium or shame of having failed through cowardice of some sort (*anandreia*), you to escape, we to assist you.

Crito's argument is cast in the language of value characteristic of the world of Athens in which Socrates found himself, and indeed the earlier stages of that world as well. In terms that are deeply familiar, it embodies a kind of aggressive egotism, regulated by the principle of reciprocity, for it invokes both a conception of justice as retaliation—like the one that dominates the world of Aeschylus' *Oresteia*—and a related conception of positive reciprocity, which underlies the practices of hospitality that were so central to the ancient world. But as a statement of Socrates' idea of justice, or as an argument meant to appeal to him, Crito's argument is hopeless. Almost nothing could be worse.[12]

Crito closes his speech with a claim of emergency, an exhortation to act immediately or lose the chance forever; this is a pitch of the sort that one might find in the close of a lawyer's jury argument, or perhaps in a demagogue's speech to a crowd, a move made by a mind that is trying to overbear another. Its inappropriateness to the relation between Crito and Socrates could not be more marked.

In his distress, Crito has forgotten all he has presumably learned from Socrates about the opinion of the many, about the character of justice, and, what is of at least equal importance, about the kind of attitude and relation that is proper to a serious discussion between those who seek the truth, that is, to philosophic conversation.[13] In his definition of justice as helping your friends and hurting your enemies, in his concern for reputation, and in the kind of manipulative relation he tries to establish with his audience, this old friend of Socrates has collapsed from whatever education he may earlier have attained to the very position that Socrates has spent his life trying to refute and change. A depressing event for a teacher, to say the least, to see one's friend and student utterly fail to recall what you thought he had learned, and this precisely at the moment when it most matters, when the question of justice is presented as real and calls for action.

Socrates responds to Crito with great delicacy and accuracy. He, of course, refuses to reply to this speech with one like it—nothing could be less Socratic—and simply disregards for the moment the arguments and thesis it advances, focusing instead upon Crito's own emotional and intellectual condition: "Your eagerness is a fine thing," he says, "if it should prove to be rightly based; but if not, its very intensity makes it so much the worse." As for the merits:

All my life I have obeyed, of all things available to me, only the reasoned argument [*logōi*] that proves best to me as I think it out. I cannot now toss out the reasoned arguments [*logous*] of an earlier time just because this [my death sentence] has come upon me, but to me they continue to seem nearly the same as they did. I honor and respect them just as before. Unless we should find that we have something better than them now, understand that I will not agree with you.

And how are we best to determine whether we do have something better than our old arguments? Socrates suggests that they begin with the question Crito raised before, about opinions, namely, "Whether it is right to grant credence to some opinions and not to others."

The function of this brief speech is to transform the discourse, and the kind of community established by Crito's sincere yet overbearing and argumentative appeal, into another form, that of dialectic, in which two minds pursue a question together, seeking not to dominate each other but to discover the truth of it. This speech in fact begins to restore Crito to himself: it reduces the sense of urgency by dissipating it as irrelevant, and creates a sense of security in the very way the familiar and apparently detached investigation proceeds. In this sense it is a performance before our eyes of the way in which the philosophic life can lead one to disregard what others consider disasters.

A New Start

Socrates next offers Crito what might be called a short course in Socratics, reminding him of what he already knows. The discussion is too long to summarize here in any detail, but one can say that its form is that of question and answer, apparently meant not to explore new ground but to recall what has been established many times before, especially that we should attend to and respect the opinion not of the "ignorant many" but of the "one who knows." This is true of the body, with respect to which we follow the advice of the doctor and the trainer: How much more true must it necessarily be of that nobler part of us that is improved by justice and damaged by injustice? As for the claim that the many have the power to kill us, we answer that our aim is not merely "to live but to live well," which, as we know, means "to live justly."[14] And we are to live justly always, not sometimes to do justice and sometimes not. To act unjustly is evil (*kakon*) and shameful (*aischron*), in every case and every way, even when we act this way in response to injustice being inflicted on us.

All this is of course not to define justice but only to assert its importance. But when Socrates accepts Crito's implicit challenge and agrees that if it is just for him to escape he will try it, otherwise not, he commits himself to the question what justice is.

On this subject Socrates begins with the puzzling claim that to act unjustly is the same thing as to act badly towards (*kakōs poiein*) another. This is puzzling because there is a deep ambiguity here: How do we determine whether we are acting "badly"? If by consulting the person upon whom we act, then Socrates is defining injustice as the equivalent of injury, with injury in turn defined as "doing to someone something they don't like or want." But this would be to define injustice and injury, and necessarily justice too, in terms of human will and preference. This would be unimaginably inconsistent both with Socrates' usual insistence that we cannot trust our culturally determined instincts and with his position that a kind of restraint or self-control is central to the ethical life. It would entail an abdication of judgment precisely on those matters on which Socrates thinks it is most essential that we learn to judge rightly, namely, what counts as a true injury or true benefit. Yet if "badly" is to be determined not by the person we affect but by us in this very conversation, through dialectic, then the word is not very different, after all, from "unjustly": it marks an as yet unreached moral judgment. Thus we cannot say that the argument is much advanced by Socrates' definition; instead its function seems to be to introduce this very ambiguity concerning the proper role of the human will or preference in determining the meaning of justice—an ambiguity that will recur in the speech of the Nomoi.

Socrates takes Crito (and us) through two further very brief steps before he presents the famous speech of the Nomoi: first, he asks whether we ought not keep our agreements, if they are just. Upon receiving from Crito an affirmative answer to that, he asks: "If we go away [into exile], without persuading the city, shall we not be injuring (*kakōs poiein*) others, and those whom we least should injure?" And in doing this "shall we be adhering to our just agreements or not?" To this Crito responds that he does not understand what Socrates means. This is hardly surprising. After all, the second issue, about "just agreements," is a wholly new topic and contains deep ambiguities. (Must the act agreed to be done itself be "just," or is it enough that the conditions under which the agreement is made are fair ones? In either form the argument is at best incomplete.) And the ambiguity about the meaning of *kakōs poiein* discussed above—whether we see it from the point of view of the putatively injured, in which case it would be a revolution in Socrates' thinking, or see it from the point of view of "true harm," in which case it is nearly a tautology—is still with us and still also confusing. This means that despite what he will seem to say, Socrates introduces the speech of the Nomoi, not just to explicate what he has already said with adequate clearness but to do something else.

THE SPEECH OF THE NOMOI

In turning—at last—to this speech it is important to recall what we are perhaps too likely to forget, that Socrates is here speaking not to the world at large but to Crito, and not about the general issue of the obligation to obey the law, in any political state whatever, but about the propriety of his own contemplated escape. Crito has exhibited many things: an anxiety for himself, an impending sense of loss, tender concern for Socrates, a willing bravery to run great risks and to spend great sums, a collapse into the ordinary Greek morality of his day, and an amenability to Socrates' way of argument that has enabled him, for the moment at least, to be restored to some portion of his earlier attitudes and to his earlier relation with Socrates. He is a kind and brave man, concerned with what is right, but of limited intellectual power and thus unable to maintain a philosophic position with clarity and firmness.

The subject that has actually been established by the narrative and by the conversation is the gap between the anxiety of Crito and the repose of Socrates in the face of the latter's impending death. The topic of justice, normally one of Socrates' favorites, has been introduced not by him but by Crito, as a ground of argument meant both to justify his own willingness to run risks on behalf of Socrates and to attack Socrates' unwillingness to escape. The question before them is stated as one of justice because Crito has put it that way, not because Socrates has done so; Socrates has for the moment accepted this definition of the issue and the related claim that if it is just for him to escape he will do so. But in what follows he will try to turn the dialogue to its true subject and to bring Crito to see at the end what he could not at the beginning, the ground upon which his own repose in the face of death actually rests.

As I suggested earlier, the form in which the question of justice arises is on the face of it odd, indeed slightly comic: Crito is arguing not that justice permits Socrates to escape, a position defensible on many grounds, but that justice affirmatively requires him to escape, a far stronger and less likely case—so little likely, on the face of it, as to be itself a kind of paradox, perhaps in unconscious imitation of the famous Socrates paradoxes. Socrates treats it solemnly, as a serious claim; but it is significant that he is about to address it not in his own voice but that of the Nomoi.

The Nomoi in fact make not one speech but four (preceded by an introduction): at the end of the first, which is, in my view at least, wholly inadequate by any measure, almost a parody of bad argument, Crito announces that he is persuaded by it. This response defines by performance part of the problem that Socrates faces throughout, namely, Crito's limited intellectual capacity and consequent pliability in the face of any argument whatever. When Socrates then goes on to say more, this movement is not prompted by Crito's disagreement, as is usual in dialectic, but has another origin, the desire to move Crito from one set of understandings, from one way of talking, to another. What we see in the second stage of the speech, and even more in the third and fourth, is a gradual rewriting of it to bring Crito, and the reader, away from the false issue raised by the first stage of the speech to the question at the center of the dialogue.

Prelude

When Crito tells him that he does not understand what he has said about "injuring those he ought least to injure" and "violating his just agreements," Socrates says:

> If as we were about to run away from here (or however our escape should be called) the laws and the common state of the city might come and stand before us and say: Tell me, Socrates, what are you intending to do? By this deed which you undertake, do you intend anything other than to destroy the laws—that is, us—and the whole city too, so far as you are able? Or does it seem to you that the city can continue to exist, and not be over-turned, in which legal judgments [*dikai*], once made, have no strength, but are rendered powerless at the hands of private parties, and so destroyed?

Notice that in this brief argument the Nomoi assume that all acts of disobedience to the laws are morally the same, and all a kind of injury to them. They employ a non-Socratic definition of "injury" or "destruction," for they assert as unquestioned their own view of what is harmful and what is not, including their right to carry on in their own career of assumed injustice. They build, that is, on the version of *kakōs poiein* that means "to do something to someone that he does not like" rather than "to do someone an injustice." One could well imagine Socrates in another context responding that if the laws or other actions of the city are unjust, the city is not injured but helped by disobedience. This is in fact the kind of correction that human beings and human institutions often need, for an example of which one need look no farther than Socrates' own behavior, described in the *Apology*, when he refused the order of the Thirty to arrest Leon of Salamis. It fits with what else we know of Plato's Socrates that he would believe that no one has the right to compel another to do what is unjust.[15]

The Nomoi here speak of submission to the judgments of a court, and of the law that requires such submission, rather than of obedience to the laws more generally. This could be important, because a much stronger case can be made that judicial judgments ought not to be disturbed, at least if they have been reached in a fair way, than that positive laws requiring unjust action ought to be obeyed. In the former case one would argue that the person has had a chance to explain to the court why it should decide his way, and has failed. He must be bound by it, notwithstanding his disagreement with the outcome, or judicial judgments will have almost no weight: after all, the loser almost always thinks the judgment bad, and there would be no way to determine the rightness of his claim except by another proceeding, which would in the usual case be just as liable to error as the first one was. But all of this is of no avail to the case actually made by the Nomoi, for they will soon make plain that they are speaking of the duty to obey every law of the city, not just the one respecting the finality of judgments.

Moreover, the argument that one is bound by fair procedures even when a particular result is wrong, so familiar to us as almost to amount to second nature, rests on a kind of skepticism that it would be surprising to see either Socrates or Plato affirm. At least in its modern form, the argument claims that we are bound by the determinations of others largely because no one can really know the truth, or know what justice requires. This argument defines justice not substantively, in terms of ends or relations, but in terms or procedures and arrangements. On this view whatever the properly elected legislature or properly informed judge or jury do is by definition just; not in the sense that we must agree with it but in the sense that we must grant it authority, at least until it passes all bounds of acceptability. But, as I say, the Nomoi do not in fact develop this argument, and, equally important, the moral skepticism on which it rests is deeply inconsistent with the main thrust of Socrates' work here and elsewhere, which is that it is our deepest duty to discover the just and to do it.

Socrates himself does function out of a skepticism of a kind, his sense that we do not yet know what justice is. But his usual procedure for living with ignorance is not acquiescence in the judgments reached by the city—which is, after all, nothing but the opinion of the many "who do not know"—but dialectic, the heart of which is that the two parties to the conversation disown all loyalties except to each other and to the discovery of truth. Our ignorance is a ground not for refusing to make judgments about justice but for the imperative that we try to discover what it is and follow its commands; if the goal of moral knowledge eludes us, as perhaps it eludes both Socrates and Plato, we shall still have spent our lives in a way worthy of human beings. What is called for, then, as Socrates makes plain by performance into the *Apology,* is not simple obedience to the city but a kind of intellectual and ethical engagement with it.

The First Version of the Nomoi's Speech

About these opening remarks of the Nomoi, Socrates asks: "What shall we say, Crito, to these things and others like them? Someone—

and especially a rhetorician at a lawsuit—might have a great deal to say, especially on behalf of that law (*nomos*) now being destroyed [by us], which establishes that legal judgments once reached shall be authoritative.—Or shall we say against the Nomoi: 'The city has treated us unjustly and reached its judgment wrongly?'"—To this Crito agrees.[16]

This is the point at which Socrates presents the first full version of the speech of the Nomoi. The passage reads like this:

"O Socrates, is this [*i.e.*, that our injustice entitles you to act against us] what is agreed between you and us, or [is our agreement rather] to stick by whatever judgments the city reaches?" If we wondered at what they said, perhaps they might go on: "Do not be amazed at what is said, Socrates, but answer us, especially since you habitually employ question and answer yourself. Come now, what accusation have you to make against us and the city that you undertake to destroy us? Is it not true, first off, that we brought you into existence and that it was through us that your father took your mother and begot you? Tell us, have you any complaint to make about those of us [*i.e.*, the laws] who regulate marriage, that all is not well with us?"—I have no complaint, I would say—"But do you have any complaint against those laws concerning the nourishment and education of a child once he is born, in which you yourself were brought up? Or did those of us appointed to govern such things not provide well when we ordered your father to educate you in music and gymnastics?"—You did well, I would say.—"Well then. Since you were brought into existence and nourished and educated by us, can you possibly claim that you were not ours, both our child and slave, you and also your ancestors? And if this is so, do you think that you stand on an equal footing with us with respect to justice, so that whatever we might undertake to do to you, you think it right for you to do such things back to us?[17] For surely justice is not equal between you and your father, or your master if you have one, so that, whatever you might suffer, this you do back to them: being slandered you do no slander, being hit you do not hit back, and so forth. Shall you then be on equal footing with the laws and the city with respect to justice, so that if we should undertake to destroy you, thinking it just, you might undertake so far as you are able to destroy us, the laws and the whole country? And do you say that in doing these things you would be acting justly, you who have cared so much about the truth of virtue? Or are you so wise that you forget that the country is more to be honored than your mother and father and all your ancestors, and more holy and sacred and of greater importance, both among the gods and many right-minded people? And do you forget that it is more necessary to honor, and yield to, and serve the country when it maltreats you than your father, and either to persuade it [otherwise] or to do what it commands, and to suffer, if it should order you to suffer something, bearing yourself peacefully, whether it is to be struck, or bound, or if it should lead you into war, possibly to be wounded or killed, that these things are to be done, and justice is to be found here? Do you forget that one is not to withdraw or run away or leave one's position, but in war and in the courts and everywhere else one is to do what the city and the country should command, or persuade it which way justice lies? And that while it is a sacrilege to use force against either one's father or one's mother, a still greater sacrilege it is to use force against the country?"—What shall we say to this Crito? Do the laws speak the truth or not?

—The truth, it seems to me, says Crito.

This speech, though expanding on the opening remarks discussed above, still does not, in its present form at least, withstand much critical examination. It assumes throughout that to disobey the laws is to injure them and the city, when it may well be argued that to disobey an unjust law is to do the city, and the laws themselves, a service. Indeed in such a case obedience itself may be an injury. And in drawing an analogy to the duties owed by children to parents, and slaves to masters, the speech assumes that the obligation of obedience in those cases is both absolute and just, when in fact here too it might be that to disobey an unjust order is to serve, to obey to injure, and, more generally, that the obligation, whatever it is, should be conditioned on many exceptions, based on other standards of justice. And upon what does the domestic obligation rest in the first place? Not consent, for one does not choose a parent or a master, and obviously either might be vicious. The speech assumes that the duty to obey is self-evident; it thus works as an unreasoned appeal to the culture, to the way things are, of exactly the sort that Socrates' interlocutors often make and that he is normally at pains to expose as both intellectually and ethically inadequate.[18]

At the center of the argument of the Nomoi is the implicit claim that the city is like a person and that you are for it or against it in all things; whether you "help" or "hurt" is to be measured not by any external understanding of what justice requires but by the city's will or preference. The city is either your friend or your enemy, and this is in all respects. If the former, the Nomoi implicitly argue, as our help to you in the past demonstrates to be the case, you must help us; this means that you must do whatever we want, however unjust it may be to you or to others, for if you do not you will be hurting us. This is an implied invocation of the sense of justice as "helping your friends and hurting your enemies," which Crito has affirmed and Socrates always resists. The speech as a whole is thus as far from Socrates' own views, and methods of thought, as

one could well imagine—exactly the sort of jumble of unreasoned analogies and conclusory assertions, reaffirmations of cultural assumptions, of
which it is his habit to make mincemeat.[19]

* * *

Why then is it here? It is, I believe, a performance by Socrates of the sort
of argument that Crito's own earlier argument seemed to invite, a way,
that is, of meeting Crito on his own terms. You will remember Crito's set
speech, full of arguments why Socrates should escape; it was a kind of
lawyer's speech, invoking the common sense of morality and justice, and
this is a response in kind. (Socrates as much as tells us so when he speaks
of what "a rhetorician might say"; and he speaks throughout not in his
own voice but that of the Nomoi, who are dogmatic and authoritarian in
manner.) This speech actually mirrors the speech it is responding to, both
in its underlying conception of justice as helping friends and hurting enemies and in its conception of "harm" or "injury" described above. It
would not persuade you or me, or perhaps anyone else, but it persuades
Crito. It is a way of speaking to Crito in his own terms and at his intellectual level. As his acquiescence suggests, it "works"; yet in another sense
its evident defects call for further treatment. It is here not as a serious
statement of Socrates' own views—quite the opposite—but as a text that
catches Crito's modes of thought and argument, so that they may be
changed. It is not meant to stand as it is, but to be rewritten, transformed
into something else, and in such a way as to carry Crito with it; and this
process of rewriting is the center of life in this text.

Rewriting (I): The Citizen's Agreement

How do the rewritings of this speech work the transformations to
which I allude, and where exactly do they bring Crito and the reader at
the end?

In its next version—the second—the speech of the Nomoi develops
the idea that there is an agreement between Socrates and the laws which
obliges him to obey them. In the form in which we have already seen it
this argument is wholly conclusory, for who is to say that an agreement
exists or what its terms are? And to judge by Socrates' remarks in the
Apology, his own conception of the agreement he has in fact made, with
himself if not with the city, is that he should continue to lead the philosophic and dialectical life he there describes, wherever it takes him and
whatever should happen to him. And even if we assume that an agreement
to obey all the laws was made, explicitly or by conduct, why should any
respect at all be accorded an agreement which purports to require one to
do or to suffer something unjust?

What the Nomoi now say gives some content to the idea of agreement: since the laws permit any adult to leave the city at any time, taking their goods with them,

> whoever of you remains, observing the manner in which we decide cases and manage the rest of the city, we say he has already agreed with us by this conduct to do whatever we might command. And one who does not obey, we say acts unjustly in three ways, that he disobeys us who are his parents, that he disobeys those who nourished him, and that having agreed to obey us he neither obeys nor persuades us [that we are wrong]. . . . We give him two alternatives, either to persuade us [that we are wrong] or to do [what we order], of which he does neither.

This is a much more interesting and persuasive version of the argument, resting as it does not upon the authority of an *ipse dixit* but on the conduct of the citizen who has chosen to remain. But as an interpretation of this conduct it remains conclusory: Why should one, simply by remaining, be held to have agreed to obey all the laws of the city, including the unjust ones? The theory of the Nomoi would oblige anyone who stayed in the city to obey any imaginable law, say one prohibiting public speech or requiring one to carry out genocidal murders.[20] The relative importance of the city compared to parents and friends, referred to earlier, would only make more important the obligation to keep whatever agreement one did make, not in any way define its terms. And, more simply, why does past acquiescence commit one to future obedience? If the claim rests on simple consent, one should be able to withdraw it whenever one wants. And on what basis does this supposed agreement really rest? It is not as though the citizen has in practical fact the sorts of options the argument supposes, for all kinds of forces may keep a person in an Athens of which one deeply disapproves. This kind of argument has a vulgar twentieth-century version, expressed in the bumper stickers that say: "America: Love It or Leave It."

There is perhaps a qualification implicit in the remark that one has to do what the city orders "or persuade it," meaning persuade it that it is wrong. This has been read as meaning that one need only *try* to persuade the city of its error, but such a construction is (in my view) both linguistically incorrect as a matter of Greek and philosophically out of tune with the main thrust of the speech.[21] In fact it destroys the whole case that the Nomoi are making, for it would always be an out that one had argued seriously and honestly for the justice of one's conduct;[22] besides, in this case Socrates himself has tried to do exactly that and should, under this reasoning, be free of the very obligation the Nomoi are claiming he is bound by.

One might more plausibly modify the "persuasion" qualification by arguing that a city that failed to allow for regular processes of persuasion would not be entitled to obedience, for it would have violated a central term of the agreement itself. But this would not work to excuse Socrates' escape, for Athens has provided just such a process. And in any event there can be little support for reading such a qualification into this language, for it would really be just a sophisticated version of the claim that the Nomoi have already rejected, namely that Socrates is not obliged to suffer the penalty because the city has decided it unjustly. The very idea that the obligation to obey is dependent upon the justice of the conduct of the city, whether "justice" is defined substantively or procedurally, is antithetical to the main thrust of the Nomoi's argument. If taken seriously it would wholly undermine their claims, for it would invite us to ask what should be taken as the proper conditions of the obligation to obey the law, which might include a great many things: full participation as an equal in the making of laws, a fair distribution of resources and opportunities for political action, adequate procedures for speaking to the legislature or the judiciary, and so on. This is a line of thought natural to us in the twentieth century, and it can carry one very far in limiting the obligation to obey the law; but it is not how Socrates represents the Nomoi as thinking, nor indeed how he thinks himself.[23]

One more point about the repeated remark that the citizen is to do what the Nomoi command or to "persuade" them that they are wrong: the same word that in its active and transitive form is usually translated as "persuade" (*peithein*), in its middle or passive form means "obey" (*peithesthai*). There is no etymological connection between the two English words, and they would normally be thought of as having different complements: "persuade" and "agree" (or "yield," or simply "be persuaded"); "obey" and "command." This point is especially important in legal thought, where it has long been customary to think of rule of law as a "command," and of what it demands of its audience as "obedience." But the Greek term suggests that there is a deep connection between persuasion and obedience: that there is no obedience without persuasion of some kind, if only a threat, and no persuasion without something like obedience, or submission. *Peithein* might then best be translated as "to subject to verbal and intellectual force," *peithesthai* as "to yield to verbal and intellectual force." What this suggests about authority is that it is always created in part by those who are subject to it, that it is never total, and that it is present whenever we recognize the force of an argument or text. When the Nomoi say that Socrates has agreed "to obey us" but in fact neither "obeys" nor "persuades," all three verbs are from the same root, and the argument thus has a kind of punning or tautological form, which has in addition the effect of eliminating the possibility for education and community otherwise suggested by the idea of persuasion. The view of the Nomoi all boils down to a conflict of wills: either you must obey us or we you.

Rewriting (II): Socrates' Own Agreement

The third version of the speech of the Nomoi achieves a further trans-formation, in which it sheds at once the highly generalized sorts of argu-ments described above and many of the difficulties that they present. For the speech now moves from an argument based on the kind of agreement that any citizen makes with his city, by remaining there when the city per-mits him to depart, to the agreement that Socrates himself has made, not with any city but with Athens.

For Socrates, the Nomoi's imagined argument runs, more than any other Athenian, has made such an agreement by his conduct. He has lived at Athens more exclusively than almost anyone else, never going out of the city to see the sights, "nor ever for any other reasons, except on military duty," nor has he taken voyages as other men do, nor shown any interest in the laws of other cities.

> Still more: in this very lawsuit, it was possible for you to propose the penalty of exile, if you had wished, and then you could have done with the consent of the city what you now undertake to do against its will. [At trial] you preened yourself on the fact that you were not troubled if it were to become necessary for you to die, but chose, as you put it, death over exile. Now you are not ashamed (*aischunesthai*) of these words, nor do you have regard for us, the laws, whom you undertake to destroy, but you do what the most wretched slave might do, trying to run away against your undertaking and agreements, by which you agreed to live as a citizen under us.—But answer us this straight off, whether we speak the truth when we say that you have agreed, not in words but in your conduct, to live as a citizen subject to us, or not.

When the question is put to him, Crito once more says that he agrees with what the Nomoi are saying. But what he assents to here is vastly different from the earlier formulations, for now the ground of the argu-ment is the agreement Socrates himself has allegedly made with the city to which he has devoted much of his life. The question is no longer abstract or theoretical but particular; it is not about the meaning of residence in the city as a general matter but about the meaning of Socrates' own life, which might be—indeed it is suggested here it is—different in significant respects from the meaning of that of others. This is not abstract or legal-istic talk—from these predicates, these conclusions—but highly personal.

The speech really asks Socrates a question: "Isn't this the meaning of what you have done, and agreed to?" In doing so it necessarily concedes that on this point Socrates himself is the ultimate witness. In framing this part of the speech Socrates thus shifts his subject, from the forfeitures his conduct has arguably entailed to what its meaning is, both to him and to his audience. This is the ground upon which he will ultimately rest his case that his impending death is not the "bad news" that Crito sees it to be but an event that can be accepted with repose, even satisfaction, not only by Socrates himself but by his friends.

An even more particular ground for the duty not to escape is suggested by the closing reference to Socrates' behavior in this very proceeding, where his own choice of a proposed penalty in effect made it impossible for the city to order his exile. For under the procedures of Athenian law, the jury could not set its own penalty but had to choose between the two proposed by the parties: death, by Socrates' accuser; by Socrates, at first the "penalty" of a lifetime of free dinners, in recognition of his services to the city, then, upon prompting, a small fine. By failing to ask for exile, the argument would run, Socrates has waived his right to it, and in this sense agreed to his punishment. He cannot now take against the city's will what he might have had with its acquiescence; or, to put it slightly differently, the city should at least be given the chance to offer him, through the channels of the law, what he now claims the right to take on his own. This argument is a specification of the earlier ones—by remaining you agreed; you must submit or persuade—but with radically different force, for it is now grounded in a particular act, a strategic choice, to which he is being held. To speak of it as a species of agreement hardly stretches things at all. If the thrust of Socrates' own position were legalistic, it could perhaps rest on this waiver without more.[24]

But his position is not legalistic. What matters to Socrates far more than the "waiver" he might be said to have made is the meaning of that gesture as part of the meaning of his life as a whole. He thus brings us back to the reasons why he did not ask for exile in the first place, which for him are still in force and render irrelevant the whole conversation in which Crito has involved him when he claimed that it would be unjust for him not to try to escape.

Rewriting (III): The Meaning of This Life, This Death

In the final version of the speech, the Nomoi first sum up the argument from agreement (making plain that they are referring to Socrates' particular undertakings rather than to a general obligation of citizenship), then go on to argue in terms that remind us of Crito's initial concern with the opinions of others: they say that if Socrates obeys them (or: is persuaded by them) he will "not make himself ridiculous" in his escape from the city as he otherwise will. This theme is an odd one, for in its explicit form it is a direct appeal to the opinions not of the "one who knows" but of the many, an appeal in fact of just the sort that Socrates has rejected earlier in this dialogue and earlier in his life as well. But, as we shall soon see, this speech works at the same time in another way, to address the question Socrates has been pursuing from the beginning, namely how to explain to Crito—how to get him to see and feel—that what Crito now regards as a dreadful event is in fact not one, that the coming death is not to be deplored or feared but accepted as a fitting end to Socrates' life.

This is what the Nomoi say: If you escape, Socrates, "what good shall you do yourself or your friends? Your friends are likely to become exiles themselves, and deprived of the city and all their goods." And as for you, "if you go to a well-run neighboring state, Thebes or Megara, for both are well-governed . . . you will come as an enemy to their constitution; those who care for their own cities will be suspicious of you, considering you a destroyer of laws; and this will confirm the judges here in the rightness of their verdict, for whoever destroys the laws may very likely corrupt the young and unthinking" (which was the offense of which Socrates was convicted). Yet if you avoid well-regulated cities and orderly men, "will you have a life worth living? Shall you approach these men and speak shamelessly to them—saying what? Making the arguments you have given here, that justice and virtue are of the greatest value to human beings, and so are the established customs and the laws? Do you not think that the whole Socratic enterprise will then seem incoherent?" If you go to Thessaly, where Crito has his friends, which is the most disorderly place of all, perhaps you will enjoy hearing pleasant tales of your ridiculous escape from prison, dressed in disguise. And where will your arguments about justice and virtue be then?

And as for your children, the Nomoi go on, will you raise them in such barbarity? Or leave them to be raised by friends in Athens? But that of course you can do also if you die.

> So be persuaded by [or "obey"] us, Socrates, who are your nurses, and do not put children, or staying alive, or anything else, before justice, so that when you get to the lower world you have all these things to say in your own defense to the rulers of that place.[25] It is plain that if you do these things it will not be better or more just or more sacred for you here, or for those who belong to you, nor will it be better for you when you get there. As things are, you will depart [for Hades], if you should do so, as one treated unjustly not by the laws but by men. But if you should escape, shamefully repaying injustice with injustice and wrong with wrong, breaking your agreements with us, and doing harm to those whom you should least hurt— yourself and your friends and your country and us—we shall treat you harshly while you live, and our brothers, who rule in Hades, will not receive

you benignly, knowing that you tried to destroy us, so far as you could do so. So let not Crito, rather than us, persuade you what to do.

The point of this rewriting is to demonstrate to Crito not why escape would be "unjust" in the sense Crito supposes, but why it is that Socrates does not and cannot want the life that escape would give him. The claim in the end is a simple one and the same now as it was when he spoke in the *Apology*, namely, that for him to die now, in this effort to speak the truth to the city, is a fitting end for him; not so comfortable, and perhaps not so fitting, as to be maintained by the city at their expense for life, in recognition of his services, but fitting nonetheless. Socrates cannot wish to escape; and, in this conversation equally important, his friends cannot properly wish it for him either.[26] Perhaps, indeed, once they recognize that this is the way things are for him, they may come to feel the same essential repose that he does.

What the Nomoi say about his past does not establish that he has entered into an agreement, in character like a legal contract, that obliges him to stay in the city against his will, but that he has established a relationship with the city which it would be an abandonment of self to abandon now. For he has not merely resided in Athens, as the Nomoi say; he has made his relationship with Athens a central social concern of his life. He has tried to establish a dialectical relationship with the city—insofar as one can have such a relationship with a city—in which he seeks to say the truth, to refute and to be refuted, and this perhaps nowhere so clearly as in the *Apology*, where he argues for his acquittal but in terms that make it impossible for the jury to grant it without granting at the same time the truth and value of the goal to which he has directed his life.

A FITTING END

Why is this a fitting end? Not because it is of itself a good thing to suffer unjustly at the hands of Athens; but because this end, unlike escape, does not require Socrates to give up the major purpose of his life. Indeed, it is a way of fulfilling a major part of that purpose, which is to establish the value of thinking and talking about what we ought to be and do collectively, as a polity, and not merely as individuals: to establish, that is, the legitimacy of discourse about the nature of the just community. His success in doing this has been in fact the foundation of our own political thinking ever since, which depends upon our being able to imagine ourselves not merely as individuals who happen to be found together, our interests in temporary conflict or harmony, like rats in the maze of life, but as a larger polity, as a city or nation or society that has a moral life and career of its own of which we can ask the question, Is it just?

There are now, as there have always been, currents of opinion that wish to deny the value and coherence of that question and the legitimacy of the discourse based upon it. Yet this question is what has enabled us to think about ourselves as we have in the West, from Plato through Cicero and Aquinas and Machiavelli to the present time. If all were reducible to the individual (or to the family), to a calculation of individual costs and benefits, it would be impossible to talk, as Socrates did and as we have ever since, of a city or nation as having a character and moral life, which could be analyzed and judged by comparison to an ideal.[27] Socrates' death expresses his commitment to that possibility; to turn away would be to deny it. If he escaped to Megara or Thessaly, he could pursue questions of justice, if at all, merely as a theoretical matter, without the engagement with the actual that can make the pursuit real. For in his life Socrates has constituted Athens as an idealized dialogic partner, a moral actor for whom justice can be as central a concern as it is for an individual. It is this fictive creation, partly of his own making, that he would rather die for than deny, especially when the death, like this one, would do so much to make this fiction real.

Athens is his city: both the actual polis and, equally important, the vision of what it could become if it were to define itself by a concern for justice, if it were to ask the question Socrates taught individuals to ask— How are we to lead our lives in a just way?—and mean it.[28] This is what he cannot leave without abandoning himself. To walk away would not be to break an agreement to which he is held against his will but a commitment to a sense of himself and the possibilities of human life to which he has devoted his existence; it would indeed "injure those whom he ought least to injure," as the Nomoi claimed, but in a very different sense from theirs. To abandon his commitment to this conversation with this partner would be to destroy the meaning of his life.

Socrates thus dies in order to establish the value and coherence and meaning of a certain sort of conversation, in which we still participate and from which we still benefit. This is what he wants Crito to see. But it is not admiration for the Athens that actually exists, or for "the many" that run it, that motivates him. He is profoundly separated, in attitude and value, from those who dominate his culture. In speaking to Crito, for example, he has said that between those who think as he does, that one should never act unjustly, and those who think otherwise, there is such a difference that there can be no common deliberation but only mutual contempt. And his perpetually reiterated scorn for "the many," who do not think and do not know, as opposed to the few who do, expresses much the same feeling. In the *Apology* he acknowledges this sense of distance, explaining why he has never been politically active by saying that it would certainly have led to his death. The *Apology* can in fact be read as a kind of heroic attempt to do the impossible, to represent his life in ways that make it acceptable to the public, when in fact nearly everything he says seems likely to infuriate the jury all the more. It is not surprising that the vote goes against him, especially in a proceeding guided by standards so vague as to amount to a kind of ostracism; it is surprising instead, as Socrates said, that so many voted for him.

It would be a great mistake, then, to think of Socrates as operating out of a comfortable view of his city and its people. He is their most severe and troubling critic. Yet it has been a central part of his lifework to turn them in a certain direction, towards thinking of justice as their ultimate collective concern, and, though he is never optimistic about the prospect, it is the imagined possibility that he might succeed upon which he will not turn his back. He starts a certain kind of conversation with his city and will not give it up. This is not a conversation that can be translated to another city, another world; his engagement is with this particular city, just as it is with this particular Crito.

THE AUTHORITY OF PERFORMANCE

What, then, according to this text, *is* entitled to respect and authority? For, at least on the reading I have suggested, the laws are not, or not to absolute authority of the sort the Nomoi claim for them. Beyond that we can say rather little about the kind of authority Plato or Socrates regard them as having, and subject to what exceptions, for that question is not the one pursued here. In this dialogue, despite appearances, no very clear position is taken with respect to the authority of law.

But this is not to say that there are no claims to authority made here. In a sense any text makes a claim to authority, in that it makes a claim to attention and thus asserts the value of its own arguments and processes of thought, and this one is no exception. When we ask what kind of claims this one makes, we find that some of them are quite explicit. Socrates says early on, for example, that he will not now give up the "reasoned arguments" (*logous*) that have proved best in the past just because he faces imminent death, unless of course they are now shown to be defective. This is to invoke the authority of reason itself, and in two ways: the old arguments are entitled to respect because they are reasoned; but it is also true that he will now abandon them if he is persuaded that better reasons call for that. What one is properly to obey is reason, he seems necessarily to be saying, but this of course only suggests the question that his own performance must answer: "What is a good reason, and thus entitled to obedience?" That of which one is properly persuaded, he impliedly says, thus uniting the two meanings—persuade and obey—of the Greek verb *peithō*, and suggesting that here, as throughout the Socratic corpus, it is the process of philosophy itself, or what he usually calls dialectic, that is ultimately authoritative.

This is hardly a surprise, for elsewhere in the dialogues Socrates repeatedly tells us that he puts the authority of dialectic first, as the only thing we can, in our ignorance of the truth, rely upon. In the *Gorgias,* for example, he defines dialectic, opposing it to rhetoric, this way: in the dialectical conversation, unlike the rhetorical one, there are only the two parties to the process; they proceed by question and answer, not by making speeches; each promises to tell the truth as he sees it; each, knowing that his own knowledge is defective, actively seeks refutation from the other; and each, for the moment, is loyal only to that relation, calling in no others as witnesses, asking what they think, but calling only on the other party to the dialectic as his witness. Each speaker is to accept as authority, for the moment at least, only the relation so established with another and the activity it makes possible, the conversation itself, in the course of which, as Socrates practices it, our language, the very material of our thought and the ground of our connection to others, is broken down and remade.[29] A dialectic that sought to establish the superior authority of the laws, or of anything external to itself, would be a contradiction in terms. On this view, the true authority invoked here, that of dialectic, would be directly opposed to the one purportedly invoked, that of the laws of Athens.

But this view of dialectic will not work here, for in his relations both with Athens and with Crito Socrates modifies what he usually means by "dialectic": he does so because Athens is a constructed entity, with whom question and answer are impossible, and because Crito is simply not up to the demands of that kind of conversation and of life. With Athens it is a dialectic of a career, the performance of a way of life, which reaches its clearest and most challenging expression in the *Apology,* where for once the fictive construction of Athens has something like a real and momentarily united form in the jury, whom Socrates can address as a surrogate for the city as a whole. The essential thing is for Socrates to state as truly as possible what he has done and why, and to shift to the city the responsibility for dealing with it. He will seek not to please the jurors but to refute them, yet he will do all this out of a recognition of the incompleteness of his own knowledge. To ask for exile in that context would be to destroy his commitment to speak the truth in this relationship, upon which the meaning and coherence of his life depend; to seize exile now would do the same, only even more markedly so.

With respect to Crito—who is in some respects also a surrogate for the city more generally—Socrates cannot engage in dialectic in the usual sense, for Crito is not capable of it. Socrates is therefore not so much refutational as anagogic, leading Crito as it were by the hand from one position to another. He seeks not to mortify or humiliate (not in this sense to "hurt" dialectically and beneficially, and thus to correct, as he describes dialectic doing in the *Gorgias* and elsewhere) but to instruct in a softer way. He demonstrates the kind of friendship it is possible for Socrates to have with Crito, and thus addresses a central difficulty with the Socratic corpus, namely, what kind of relationship the dialectician can establish with one who is not himself fully capable of dialectic. This is itself a performance of kindness, and it respects the kindness of another; this enactment of kindness, reciprocal to Crito's own, works in the end as a response to the first claim that Crito made, which, as you remember, was not that it is unjust for Socrates to refuse to escape but that it would mean for him, Crito, the loss of such a friend as he would never find again.

Socrates made no response to that claim when it was made and has still not given it a formal answer. But, on the reading of the dialogue I have suggested, everything that follows, every question and speech, is meant as a response to it, both as an acknowledgment of the reality of Crito's sense of loss and as an attempt, in an act of friendship, to reduce that pain by bringing Crito to see the meaning of the event in different terms. What we see here is kindness responding to kindness, respect for what is worthy of respect in a person of limited capacity, and the exercise of an art at once intellectual and social, whose function is to teach by transforming his interlocutor's perceptions and understandings of the truth. Thus it is that the text has the form it does, leading Crito from one position to another: respecting his sense that he will lose a friend he loves and bringing him in the end to see that the continued existence of that friend, as the person he loves, is now impossible. He is not to grieve for Socrates, nor even for himself, at this verdict and its consequences, for it is not the verdict that deprives him of his friend but that friend's character, which is what he loves in him.

* * *

So what then is actually invoked as authority here? Not the laws; not the reasons for obeying the laws, for that topic is dropped when the argument is in a most unsatisfactory state indeed and transformed into another one; not even dialectic in its pure form; but another sort of conversation, another sort of philosophy, created by another sort of text, the *Crito* itself, defining its own idea of reason, its own way of being with language and with others.

What is this kind of reason? To start with the negative, the dialogue obviously rejects the mode of discourse offered by the Nomoi in their first speech, which is abstract, propositional, conclusory, and unreasoned in character—as authoritarian in performance as it is in its message—just as it rejects the methods of Crito's first speech too. These two speeches make

a pair that captures much of the contemporary state of Athenian discourse, Crito invoking the "ordinary Greek" conception of justice (helping your friends and hurting your enemies), the Nomoi marshalling another set of appeals that would also seem compelling in "ordinary Greek,"
based upon one's self-evident duty to one's city.[30] In this way these two
speeches define the kinds of argument that it would be second nature for
an educated Athenian to make. And by kinds of argument I mean not only
the particular positions taken but the way they are explained and justified,
the reasons offered as persuasive, including the tone of voice, the attitude
towards one's audience and towards countering arguments, in short, the
whole intellectual and ethical performance of the text. Imagine trying to
engage the Nomoi in philosophic conversation, and I think you will see
how impossible it would be and perhaps, something as well of Socrates'
difficulty in addressing Crito himself.

The dialogue works with these two voices in different ways, using
one—that of the Nomoi—to answer the other, Crito's, then rewriting it
to make a very different case indeed. The mode of thought performed in
the dialogue as a whole is thus dramatic and literary, in contrast to Crito
and the Nomoi alike, both of whom seek to argue from the top down,
from general principle to particular conclusion, in a standard rationalist
way. The kind of reason for which authority is claimed in the dialogue as
a whole is very different in quality: its idea is not to make arguments good
for all time, in all contexts and languages, but to carry on a conversation
that is appropriate to this relation, with this person—or city—and this
language, under these conditions of ignorance and uncertainty. This is
true at once of Socrates' conversation with Crito and of Plato's with us,
his readers. Both place at their center not abstract propositions of fact or
value but the enactment of character and relations; both make the difficulty of thought and speech itself a central issue; both insist upon the pri-
macy of the related questions, "What kind of person should I be?" and
"What kind of city should Athens be?"

The movement is corrective, from the authoritarian and the propositional to the authoritative and enacted. The life of the text is in this movement, in its transformations of one way of thinking and being into another, like music. In a sense the ultimate ground of this dialogue is
narrative, for it all depends upon one's acquiescence in Socrates' claim that
this is a fitting end to such a life. Its ultimate value, like the value of Socrates' own career, lies not in any theoretical scheme or system but in the
kind of life it invites and makes possible.[31]

In its relation to us as readers the text is challenging, for it presents us
with a real puzzle: a set of pieces that do not fit together, though we may
try again and again to force them, until we see it not as an intellectual
structure but as a piece of social and political action. It offers us no firm

place to stand—certainly not in the first speech of the Nomoi—but a difficulty, in the working out of which we must assert our own mind against the incompleteness and defectiveness, not of the text as a whole, but of certain arguments within it.

The effect of this dialogue, like many, is not to offer the reader a system, a structure of propositions, but to disturb and upset him in a certain way, to leave him in a kind of radical distress—even while leading Crito to greater repose. For what is the right attitude, after all, to take towards laws that require us to suffer what is unjust? That require us to do it? Can we fashion arguments, better than those of the Nomoi, out of their materials of status and agreement? In a sense, Socrates is refuting a version of himself when he refutes Crito's claim that justice requires escape, for this is just the sort of paradoxical thing he likes to urge, and he certainly thinks that the claims of justice are paramount—or are they, when the law requires its opposite? [32]

Such tensions are not a peculiarity but a standard feature of the Platonic dialogues. Think of Socrates' perpetual insistence upon proceeding by question and answer, for example, rather than by long speeches, a principle violated as often as followed; or his apparent assumption that the questions he asks, say about the nature of justice or courage, can be satisfactorily answered in their own terms, which is countered by his repeated resort to myth and fable as ways of talking; or his claim that he "knows nothing," contradicted constantly by his certainty on many questions, substantive as well as procedural; or his obvious love for poetry, against his rejection of it; or his respect for inspiration, answered by his insistence on reason; or, of special relevance to the *Crito*, his claim for the exclusive authority of dialectic and philosophy, answered by his repeated engagement in traditional religious and civic observances; or, again of relevance here, his unremitting contempt for "the many," who rule Athens and dominate his culture, and his equally unremitting loyalty to, and love for, his city.

Despite what is sometimes claimed for the *Crito*, this kind of writing grants authority to no proposition, to no institution—not even to dialectic—but to the life of thought and imagination enacted here by which the questions of rightness and wrongness, authority and no authority, are addressed. It does not precipitate out into system or doctrine but is always a fresh demand upon the particular moment, the particular mind.

The dialogue at once stimulates and frustrates the reader's own desire for an authority external to himself. We want Plato (or Socrates) to tell us what authority the law has, and a part of us wants this to be very great indeed; but he will not do that and offers us instead contradictory and paradoxical movements of the mind, with respect to which we can locate ourselves only by becoming active, affirming and rejecting the various claims from our point of view. As we do this, we find our affirmations and rejections are themselves subject to challenge. Instead of an authority out there in the world—the law—and instead of an intellectual authority, a mode of reasoning that will proceed ineluctably from general principles to particular conclusions, this text offers us a mode of thought that is inherently inconclusive and puzzling, and thus transfers the problem to us. Like Crito, we look for arguments that will constrain like iron bands; we are naturally susceptible to voices like those of the Nomoi, telling us how things are. It is the great art of this dialogue both to bring these aspects of the reader to life and to challenge them. The ultimate meaning of this text lies in the way it constitutes its reader: more deeply puzzled, more fully alert, more wholly alone.

This text offers us the experience of incoherence partly resolved, then, but resolved only by our seeing that our own desires for certainty in argument, for authority in the laws—or in reason, or in persuasion—are self-misleading; that we cannot rest upon schemes or formulas, either in life or in reading, but must accept the responsibility of living, which is ultimately one of establishing a narrative, a character, a set of relations with others, which have the kinds of coherence and meaning it is given us to have, replete with tension and uncertainty. This is what Plato means by philosophy.

*   *   *

What is troubling about the *Crito* in the end is not its absolutism, or its elevation of the institutional, but the reverse: that in its claim to make the dialectical conversation the only authority it tends to erase the value of every formal institution, every other aspect of culture. Quite the opposite of a treatise in favor of an authoritarian view of law, then, its tendency is to erode respect for everything outside the present conversation, including law itself, as law is usually conceived. Another way to put this point is to say that the kind of conversation it enacts and celebrates has no place, or almost no place, in the world outside itself.

But suppose that the law we saw in the world, or imagined, was not the authoritarian, unreasoned, conclusory voice of the Nomoi but a conversation that met the standards of the *Crito?* Would it then be possible to write a text in favor of the authority of law which enacted, and thus claimed authority for, a conversation that continued in the public places of the community, a conversation in which the law itself mirrored the processes of thought here enacted and held out as authoritative? The claims for the authority of the present conversation and that of the larger conversation, the larger institution, would then cohere, not split apart. This would require a different sort of law from any imagined by Socrates, and perhaps a different kind of dialectic too. The movement would be from

"You should grant authority to the commands of the law if there are good reasons to support it," to "You should grant authority to the law, because it is itself reasoned in a proper way." And by this we would not mean merely logical coherence but that its conversational processes met the requirements of comprehension, openness, respect for the other, kindness, and devotedness to truth that characterize the performance of Socrates here.

NOTES

1. In speaking of "Socrates" here and throughout I do not mean the historical person but the character created in this and the other Platonic dialogues, especially the early ones. I assume that one of Plato's goals is the definition of this complex person, or persona, and, therefore, that it is right to read these dialogues against each other.

2. See John Burnet, *Plato's Euthyphro, Apology, and Crito* (Oxford: Oxford University Press, 1924), 253–54 (the order of the Thirty to arrest Leon of Salamis no law at all); Terence Irwin, "Socratic Inquiry and Politics," *Ethics* 96 (1986): 400–15 (Nomoi's claims only presumptive); Thomas C. Brickhouse and Nicholas Smith, *Socrates on Trial* (Princeton: Princeton University Press, 1989), 143–47 (the hypothetical character of his vow to continue to philosophize against a conditional verdict); Richard Kraut, *Socrates and the State* (Princeton: Princeton University Press, 1984), 65–73 (on "persuade" as "try to persuade"); A. D. Woozley, *Law and Obedience: The Arguments of Plato's Crito* (Chapel Hill: University of North Carolina Press, 1979), 30–31, 32, 44 (disobedience permissible if punishment accepted) ("try to persuade") (hypothetical character of vow in *Apology*); Gerasimos Santas, *Socrates: Philosophy in Plato's Early Dialogues* (London: Routledge & Kegan Paul, 1979), 45–54 (distinction between *prima facie* and all-things considered cases) (*Apology* and *Crito* involve different issues, the first conscientious disobedience, the other secret evasion); R. E. Allen, *Socrates and Legal Obligation* (Minneapolis: University of Minnesota Press, 1980), 109 (distinction between doing and suffering wrong).

On the distinction between doing and suffering injustice: while it is true that Socrates in the *Crito* suffers injustice, and that this is, as he says in the *Gorgias*, far less serious than doing it, the Nomoi themselves make no such distinction. They quite clearly say that the obligation is to do (*poiein*) whatever they command.

3. For a fine reading of the *Crito* on such premises, see Ernest J. Weinrib, "Obedience to Law in Plato's Crito," *American Journal of Jurisprudence* 27 (1982): 85. For a fuller account of that article, and my debt to it, see James Boyd White, *Acts of Hope: The Creation of Authority in Law, Literature, and Politics* (Chicago: University of Chicago Press, 1994), 310–11.

4. Another way to put this would be to suggest that for Plato at least "philosophy" does not mean the creation of an intellectual system, supported by arguments—although that is how he has often been read—but rather an activity of mind that he at once exhibits in his dialogues and stimulates in his reader. After all, in his Seventh Letter—if that is indeed by him—Plato said that his real phi-

losophy is not to be found in his writings but in his teaching, in the living engagement of mind with mind. One might read his writing, then, as attempting to replicate in his relation with the reader the dialectical activity that in its fullest form exists only in living conversation. In the terms suggested by the *Phaedrus,* where Socrates attacks writing, it may be Plato's object to create a text that, unlike most, does not simply say the same thing always but shifts its meaning as it is more deeply understood (*Phaedrus* 275d–e). This is possible because its meaning is not propositional in character but performative, residing in the activity in which it engages the reader.

For a development of this line of argument with respect to Plato's *Gorgias,* see my *When Words Lose Their Meaning: Constitutions and Reconstitutions of Language, Character, and Community* (Chicago: University of Chicago Press, 1984), chapter 4. For a similar argument with respect to Wittgenstein and Kierkegaard, see James Conant, "On Comparing Wittgenstein and Kierkegaard" (forthcoming). For a general approach to the relation between philosophy and literature, see Martha Nussbaum, *Love's Knowledge: Essays on Philosophy and Literature* (Oxford: Oxford University Press, 1990). On the other hand, it would hardly do simply to say that "philosophy" should be regarded as a kind of "literature," without doing more. Both of those terms require definition, at its best performative, in the text that says such a thing.

To put it the other way round and say that literature is, or can be, philosophic is not to say that its experience can be translated into a set of propositions and arguments on philosophic themes. The point rather is that the activities and practices of literature can be seen to be of general, and not merely particular, value, as they instruct us about the conditions upon which life must be led, the nature and limits of language, the capacities of our minds, and so forth.

5. In summarizing portions of the *Crito* I have sometimes translated directly, in which case the extract is set off with quotation marks or in block paragraphs, sometimes paraphrased roughly, in which case there are no such marks.

6. For further discussion see generally A. W. H. Adkins, *Merit and Responsibility: A Study in Greek Values* (Oxford: Oxford University Press, 1960); K. J. Dover, *Greek Popular Morality in the Time of Plato and Aristotle* (Berkeley: University of California Press, 1974), 180–84; and Mary Whitlock Blundell, *Helping Friends and Harming Enemies: A Study in Sophocles and Greek Ethics* (Cambridge: Cambridge University Press, 1989), especially chapter 2. Socrates of course questions this "ordinary Greek" morality.

7. The *locus classicus* is the position advanced by Polemarchus in Book One of the *Republic.* Compare also what Meno says in *Meno* 71e. Gregory Vlastos, *Socrates: Ironist and Moral Philosopher* (Ithaca: Cornell University Press, 1991), 179–99, argues that the *Crito* is a central text in Socrates' revolutionary rejection of the ethics of retaliation. The major issue is whether justice is to be thought of as a code of individual behavior, as a species of honor in fact, or as a quality of whole human community and its life.

8. Earlier it was Socrates who refused to follow up a line began by Crito, who had remarked on Socrates' distinctive attitude towards his own death. Now Socrates seeks to pursue this very question: Why then did he not do so earlier? Perhaps the reason is that the dream provides a better context for thinking about this issue,

for the dream is a direct expression of Socrates' own feeling rather than a comparison with others. We might read the text, indeed, as suggesting that Socrates brings up the dream deliberately, in order to present this issue in a more satisfactory way than Crito did.

9. In making this point Crito expressly identifies those "who do not know" or the "many"—whose opinions followers of Socrates have long known they need not respect—with the jurymen of Athens, who have just condemned Socrates to death and done so unjustly. What may seem in other contexts to be an abstract point about the "one who knows" and "the many who do not" is thus here given significance of another kind, for now the many have real power. The issue is no longer "mere knowledge," as Crito might put it, but "life and death," assuming—as Socrates would not—that the latter is far more important than the former.

Both speakers seem here to urge inconsistent attitudes: Crito that the verdict of the jurors be disregarded, but on the grounds of reputation, which itself grants authority to "the many"; Socrates that only the opinion of the one who knows matters, but that the verdict of the many, even though unjust, should be honored. This unmarked but real tension gives the text much of its life and energy.

10. In *Gorgias* 482b–c.

11. Maybe in this too Plato meant Crito to remind us of Socrates, who often argued for positions felt by his interlocutors to be impossibly paradoxical—for example that it was "better" to suffer injustice than to do it. See *Gorgias* 474b–79c.

12. Except to claim that justice itself has no meaning or value as Thrasymachus and Callicles do, as represented by Plato respectively in the *Republic* and the *Gorgias*. For more sympathetic treatment of these sophists, and the sophistic movement in general, see Eric Havelock, *The Liberal Temper in Greek Politics* (New Haven: Yale University Press, 1957) and G. B. Kerferd, *The Sophistic Movement* (Cambridge: Cambridge University Press, 1981).

13. I base this assumption about their prior relationship partly on what we, and the original audience, can be assumed to know about their friendship and partly on the way in which Socrates later uses arguments that he explicitly assumes to be familiar to Crito.

14. In Greek the phrase "to live well" has much less by way of moral connotation than it does in English; it might better be translated as "flourish" or "succeed." To say that to live "well" is to live "justly" is thus far more contestable in Greek than English.

15. It is true that here Socrates is asked to suffer rather than to do injustice. This is plainly the lesser evil, but it is still an evil; moreover, there is nothing in the speech to suggest that it does not apply to affirmative conduct and much, including the repeated use of the verb "to make" or "to do" (*poiein*), to suggest that it does.

16. In suggesting that they might say to the city that it "has acted unjustly towards us," Socrates temporarily invokes the conception of justice that Crito has earlier articulated, namely, that it is right to repay injustice with injustice, and at least in this way to "harm one's enemies." But Socrates will later reject this view of justice, as he has done before; his use of it here can then be read as meeting Crito on his own ground.

17. The Nomoi here take Socrates' imagined response—"My conduct is justi-

fied by your injustice"—as a version of the conception of justice Crito invoked, namely, "hurting your enemies." "The verdict made our city the enemy, hence retaliation is justified"; such is the argument that the Nomoi are answering.

18. Notice also that to concede that one has no complaint to make about certain laws—here those relating to marriage or education—is no argument at all on the question whether one is obliged to obey other laws that are unjust.

Part of the puzzle of this text arises from the circumstances that Crito and the Nomoi, imagined by Socrates as speaking against each other, are in fact both representatives of the culture to be refuted by Socrates. Crito and the Nomoi agree on more than they differ, and it is with this area of agreement that Socrates will mainly concern himself, refuting both at once. But it will not look much like refutation, for in transforming the speech of the Nomoi into another mode Socrates' aim is not so much to defeat Crito as to instruct him.

19. I speak here of the speech as it is composed in the text. Of course one could say a great deal as a general matter about the bearing of status and contract upon the obligation to obey the law, and these topics are deep in our own thought. But the Nomoi say virtually nothing beyond the assertion of their bald conclusions; this is in fact a large part of Plato's point in composing the speech as he does.

20. There is also perhaps the qualification that the city must think what it is doing is just. But this would apply to almost all laws, perhaps all laws, for as Plato has shown us more than once, it is virtually impossible for a person to admit that what he is doing is truly unjust.

21. See Kraut, *Socrates and the State*, 65–73, for the best statement of the argument I am resisting. It is true that the present tense "may express an action begun, attempted, or intended" (Herbert Weir Smyth, *Greek Grammar*, rev. ed. [Cambridge, Mass.: Harvard University Press, 1956], par. 1878), but it does so only when the context requires it, and whether that is so is the question in issue here. As Smyth puts it, "The idea of attempt or intention is an inference from the context and lies in the present only insofar as the present does not denote completion." For Kraut's contrary view, see 72–73 of *Socrates and the State*.

22. This is true, of course, only if one's conduct is indeed just; but the whole argument assumes that. The subject of argument here is the duty to obey laws and decrees that are concededly unjust.

23. As I suggested above, it would be in principle possible to distinguish between two kinds of injustice, and say that injustice in the particular result is no ground for disobedience of the laws in general, but that injustice in the process by which laws are made or applied is such a ground. This would appeal to those who want to distinguish between an unjust system and unjust results, and to say that allegiance to an essentially just system requires toleration of results that seem unjust, either because they are inevitable in an imperfect world or because the judgment as to whether they are truly just can never be confidently made. In this sense whatever the reasonably fair system does is as "just" as anything human can be.

But this line of argument is not I think present in the speech of the Nomoi; and if it were it would remain very far from the position normally advanced by Socrates for the argument of the Nomoi requires the citizen (at least of a state which permitted him to depart) to comply with all its laws, however unjust they might be, including laws requiring him to commit affirmative injustice. Crito may be swung over to such a position by this speech, but that should not be said either of Socrates or of the reader.

24. But the merits of this argument should not be overstated: to ask for exile would mean foregoing asking for what justice requires. And why should the city be able to compel such a waiver? As Socrates puts it in the *Apology,* to propose such a penalty would be to accuse himself of a crime, when he is guilty of none (*Apology* 37b). For a vivid account of the evils of exile, see *Lysias* 7.41 ("On the Olive Stump").

25. Compare *Gorgias* 523–27, where Socrates imagines himself addressing his judges in the afterlife, saying that this is the court he cares about, and *Apology* 40e4–41a5, to much the same effect.

26. It is true, however, that he said that he would attempt it if he were persuaded that justice so required: Is the dialogue then necessarily about the justice of escape or submission after all? Surely Socrates would not remain if he thought it unjust to do so, and we can therefore take it that he genuinely does not think that "justice requires him to escape." But this is actually a rather unlikely position; as I said above, it is part of the comic tone of the dialogue that Crito should urge it upon him. It is to be distinguished from the much stronger argument that justice *permits* him to escape; but the latter is irrelevant since Socrates prefers, for very good reasons, not to do so.

The whole argument about the requirements of justice presupposes, in an unstated way, a conflict between the will and the right, affirming the claims of the latter over the former. But Socrates is saying that he does not experience this conflict and therefore—except in the unlikely form in which Crito presents it to him—the issue of the justice of his proposed conduct is simply not before him. The question whether justice forces him to stay, like the question whether it forces him to leave, just doesn't come up. Compulsion is not his topic, but choice and meaning.

27. Plato is of course building on earlier visions of the city as having a moral life. Think of the beginning of *Oedipus Tyrannos,* for example, where all of Thebes suffers from the moral pollution brought upon it by one man, or of Thucydides' *History,* which imagines the cities as moral actors in another way, as capable of making and breaking treaties, of mass murder, of supreme folly, and so on. Plato's achievement is to see the city as a moral actor from the inside, as he sees the human soul as well; justice becomes a term for its essential health, including the proper distribution of role and competence to its various parts.

28. In the *Apology* 29d he said: "As long as I am alive and able, I will not stop doing philosophy and advising you and pointing out errors to whomever of you I happen to meet, saying, as I usually do, 'Oh, my most excellent friend, you are an Athenian, a member of the city greatest and most well-known in wisdom and power: do you not take shame at caring about money, seeing to it that you might have the most you could, and about reputation and honor, but you neither care about nor plan your life being mindful of self-discipline or the truth or your soul, how it might be in the best state it could be?'" (Translation by Susan Prince.)

29. For further accounts of dialectic, see especially Vlastos, "The Socratic Elenchus," *Oxford Studies in Ancient Philosophy* 1 (1983): 27–58 and Richard Robinson, *Plato's Earlier Dialectic,* 2d ed. (Oxford: Clarendon Press, 1953).

30. Owing partly to its small size, partly to its inherent susceptibility to civil

war, the polis was perceptibly fragile. This perhaps gave a kind of self-evidence to the duty not to impair its capacity to survive as a functioning unit, even at the cost of doing or suffering injustice. Think of the practice of ostracism, by which a person would be exiled by a special vote (apparently without any claim that this action needed to be based on any principles of justice), or the way in which Thucydides presents as treasonable Alcibiades' claims to have a right to retaliate against the city that harmed him.

I am grateful to Arthur W. H. Adkins for this point. He has also suggested in correspondence that one purpose of the *Crito* may have been to defend Socrates against the charge that he was responsible, as Alcibiades' teacher and lover, for this conduct and its justification. One can read the speech of the Nomoi as responding directly to the claims of Alcibiades, in Thucydides VI.92.2. On civil war, see especially Thucydides' account of the civil war in Corcyra—his image of the chaos with which every city was in principle threatened—and recall that Athens itself was torn by internal war more than once during the last years of Socrates' life.

31. Indeed it makes doubtful whether any conversation that is as abstracted from experience and particularity as that proposed by the Nomoi (and readily pursued by philosophers ever since), say on the question whether "the citizen has a duty to obey the law" and if so "whether that duty is absolute or qualified," could meet the standards of thought and discourse established by the *Crito*.

32. Compare here the *Euthyphro*, where Socrates' interlocutor similarly engages his attention by claiming that what he is doing—prosecuting his father for causing the death of a slave—is just and holy, even though unpopular, a classic Socratic position. In the *Euthydemus*, the effort is to distinguish Socrates from others who are similar to him in a different respect, namely the teachers of eristic argument, who succeed in confusing their auditors, as Socrates also does, but by logical tricks rather than dialectic. See Thomas H. Chance, *Plato's Euthydemus: Analysis of What Is and Is Not Philosophy* (Berkeley: University of California Press, 1992), especially 13–21.

RESPONSE

Charles M. Gray

Professor White usefully compares critical writing to travel literature. What follows is an account of my revisitation of the *Crito*, a trip inspired by Professor White's account of his. We differ on one "issuable" point— the strength of the speech by which the Athenian Nomoi try to dissuade Socrates from escaping his penalty. This difference affects how each of us sees other features of the dialogue. There is no disputing that Professor White has made many interesting discoveries. What I shall offer is little more than guidebook fare, in contrast to a highly original and imaginative exploration. I do think, however, that underestimation of perhaps over-celebrated sights has led Professor White to look for and find too much of the city's charm—that is to say, the dialogue's moral gravity—off the beaten track.

Although I agree that the *Crito* does not reduce to the speech of the Nomoi, I am not convinced that their position is weak. They do not establish "propositional truth" demonstratively. As Socrates does in his own behalf in the *Apology,* they mimic dialectic in what is more a forensic speech than a philosophical investigation. It has the looseness and multifarious resourcefulness of such speeches. This does not mean, however, that the Nomoi fail to state fairly clearly the best available arguments for the conclusion they want. That conclusion may of course fall short of the highest standard of truth attainable in moral thinking. I am skeptical as to whether—save in an obvious way I shall eventually discuss—a solider moral truth lurks in the interstices of the dialogue, but Professor White has impressively opened the possibility of finding one through a literary analysis that makes use of many neglectable features.

The Nomoi expressly defend the rightness of abiding the sentence of the law whether or not one accepts it as just. By emphasizing (51:B–C) that evading death by escaping from death-row is like shirking service in war or deadly duty in battle, they extend the argument to the obligation to risk one's life as a citizen-soldier whatever one thinks of the war's justice or expedience. The hard facts of Greek life—states' precarious existence and the threat of enslavement—seem to justify making that a more categorical duty than it might be in other historical circumstances. Further extension to the duty of not using force to overturn the law and the existing polity seems implied. I see no reason, in construing the position of the Nomoi, why a line should not be drawn here, substantially the line that is familiar from Christian "non-resistance" or "passive resistance" theory: it is *not* implied that one should otherwise obey unjust laws or unjust official commands warranted by law; it is at least a right, and usually a duty, to disobey, provided one is willing to pay the appointed penalty. While it is hard to find that line articulated in Greek sources, we do have the example of Socrates practicing a little "civil disobedience" (*Apology,* 32:C–D.)

For this conclusion, the Nomoi use two arguments of principle. (The speakers go beyond the principles of citizenly duty, appealing both to Socrates' interests and to other moral considerations, such as how he can best serve the welfare of his friends and children. I shall not comment on these further points in a "multifariously resourceful" speech, except as they can be folded into the deeper arguments.) The first I shall call "the argument from quasi-contract and asymmetry." This is what the language about the laws' having begotten, nourished, and educated Socrates comes to.

The major premise for this argument is that we owe a debt for benefits even when they have not been contracted for. The minor premise is that one owes the state one has been born and brought up in—however open to criticism it may be—for benefits analogous to those conferred by parents: existence itself, what one is genetically, and all that parents pass on as the primal transmitters of culture. The Nomoi speak fancifully, indeed fallaciously, of Athenian marriage law as the begetter of Athenians; the serious point is that being born under some particular set of institutions is fundamentally formative. One might have been born under better (at the deepest level, the analogy with parents breaks down here, because one could not have different parents and still be oneself, but at the level of cultural transmission it holds); the benefit of having been shaped in the beginning as what in some aspects one simply is could have been a greater benefit if innumerable human choices out of one's control had been different. But not to consider that primal shaping a benefit at all strains the identification of self with self.

Both premises seem to me to have serious claims, though they present a few problems. The first—good should be repaid with good—is close to irresistible in itself, but it has to be cleared of association with the inverse: bad may be requited with bad. Socrates rules out the latter as a form of just conduct in the *Crito* (49) before he listens to the Nomoi. It is a sign of the looseness of their tactics that the Nomoi do not always remember this stipulation, for some of their rhetoric seems to attack Socrates for proposing to "destroy" them in exchange for their trying to "destroy" him, which he cannot intend if he remembers a principle he has already embraced. It is a weakness in the argument that there is no real exploration of whether evading the consequences of unjust or misapplied law is necessarily harmful to the law. What might appear "destructive" is arguably beneficial in the same way that hurting a wrongdoer with a rehabilitative purpose is a benefit to him, and even hurting him with a deterrent one is different from retaliation. In either case, what the punished person suffers for a good end is only an off-setting bad if pain is counted as bad per se. Even if it is, it can only be a bad to the sentient, not to such abstractions as "the Laws," though personifying them masks this. The *Crito*'s implied position on the insufficiently discussed issue must therefore be that the obvious social evil of law subverted cannot be outweighed by any kind of good to the legal order that might ensue. That is a hard doctrine, but respectable, the more so the more carefully it is stated as "abide the penalty" rather than "always obey," for it is difficult to see how "visible martyrs" could fail to be of more service than any alternative to law so bad that full submission to it, pending lawful reform, is unacceptable.

The minor premise involves a questionable, but defensible, jump from biological parents to "parental" institutions. I take it that no one wishes his parents had not coupled at the moment that produced him. At any rate, saying one so wishes is only a way of expressing the wish that one had never been born. Wishing that one had been born into a different set of socially constructed arrangements (including the supra-biological role of literal parents) is not wishing the impossible or the equivalent of a wish for non-existence. Nevertheless, the sincerity of professed desires to be different in the most basic ways dependent on history—public or personal—rather than on oneself is open to doubt. To take the simplest example, would anyone really want his "mother tongue" to be different? Renaissance dreamers imagined children isolated from the local vulgate and brought up speaking Latin as naturally as Vergil did: surely the dream belongs in the gallery of infatuations—ultimately a dream that the children might be like Vergil if only they could speak as he did. Of course the line is uncertain that runs between our "most basic" dependencies on the history that other people made for us and the features of one's inheritance it is rational, if impractical, to deplore. Equating the gifts of the Nomoi with those of what would now be called "culture" seems justified in view of the breadth of Greek *nomos*—more "humanly created normative structure" than merely "law." Greek thought about norms was controlled by a picture of societies coterminous with states being established in one comprehensive form, the *nomothetēs* functioning as much more than a "legislator."

The third component in the argument—the "corollary of asymmetry"—says that justice as reciprocation is conditioned by special relationships. In the case of peers, one owes back in proportion to what one has received. In the paradigm exceptional case, parents, one owes back indefinitely more. That case generalizes to the principle that some benefits are so basic, vast, and diffuse that commensurate reciprocation cannot be specified. They can be met only by piety, submission, and self-abnegation, by gratitude unamenable to limitation. By force of the analogy between the parental and the nomic "gift of life," the state is cut in on the Greek intuition that parents cannot—as if they were like other free and equal persons with whom one happens to have dealings—deserve only calculated fair value in recompense for their role in one's life.

Aristotle states the principle of asymmetry clearly (*Nicomachean Ethics*, V:v, 1–7). It is explicit in the *Crito* (50:E) when the Nomoi ask Socrates whether he thinks *to dikaion* is *ex isou* for him and for his parents or master: Reciprocal justice can be *ex isou,* but in special relationships it is not. The argument depends to a degree on a valuation of filial piety that is of course not only Greek, but that is cultural. There is abundant testimony that the Greeks put this virtue close to the heart of morality and prescribed a double standard, going to behavior deeper than surface manners, as between parents and others. Whether a philosophic argument for "asymmetry" generally or for filial piety in particular can be made from scratch I hesitate to say. Modern attitudes to the contrary are no doubt corrective of real evils.

The second argument made by the Nomoi is contractual, a version of the argument that political obligation derives from the same moral fountain as the duty to keep contracts. The Nomoi do not, however, assert that living in any state, or accepting membership in any political society, implies agreement to submit to its laws even when one's judgment disputes the justice of the laws themselves or of results ensuing from their procedurally correct application. In their version, that duty depends on the fairness and openness exemplified by Athenian institutions: One is free to emigrate as an adult and to remove one's property; one is free, in several contexts, to do by persuasion what one has forgone the right to do by force or trickery—to try persuading those who make the laws and those who apply them to conform their acts to one's ethical beliefs, and indeed to one's mere interests and preferences. Even with these special advantages given in consideration of one's surrender of private judgment, consent is not lightly inferred. No minimum evidentiary standard is specified, but the Nomoi take it as part of their job to show that Socrates has exceeded any plausible minimum. Whatever exactly has moved him, he has displayed an exceptional fondness for living in Athens and has all but said he would prefer death to exile for his punishment.

The Nomoi are intelligent in not pushing contractualism too far. Granting its force, contract theory has trouble keeping the citizen's or subject's obligation neither too weak nor too strong. If private judgment is alleged to have been bargained away absolutely for mere security, some will say that the price is too high. Others, though attracted to the deal as stated, are apt to discover in a pinch that security has not been delivered and that a promise manifestly failing to produce the end for which it was given can no longer bind. Death-row is the most obvious pinch, but once the idea has dawned sundry defaults of law and government can be made out as clear and present non-performances. In short, it is hard to give away private judgment altogether. The Nomoi are wise to rely on their supplementary hook, "quasi-contract and asymmetry." They see that to yield as strong an obligation as they want to urge contract needs reinforcement. Athens can demand more complete obedience than a state that offered less liberal conditions; but nevertheless—if in the hour of death it seems unconvincing that one could have *agreed* to submit to *this*—then Athens, like less generous states, can call on the uncontracted debt of filial piety. It is a virtue of the latter to be vague—stronger than a contract in that it does not invite asking when the voluntary, purposive act of contracting has failed of its purpose but weaker in the sense that *just* what must be done to fulfill the debt cannot be pinned down. Raising violent hands against parents or quasi-parents, failing to defend them to the death in the scrapes they have dragged you into, even deception and verbal disrespect, are harder to make acceptable than what is immediately at issue in the *Crito:* quietly staying out of the way of unjust wrath, saving the parents who have forgotten themselves bitter regret in the future. For this reason, in Socrates' situation, contract-proper perhaps shoulders the larger half of the task. In the abstract, however, promissory obligation is easier to rid the conscience of.

The liberality of the terms on which Athens is said to have purchased submission is worth dwelling on, whether or not the picture the Nomoi give is historically accurate. As the picture is drawn, the emigrant needs no passport which someone has discretion to deny and is charged no fee to compensate for the services and property he removes from Athens. So far as appears, he is free to liquidate real property and remove the proceeds, and presumably he can take his wife and minor children along, as well as property in the form of slaves. Nothing is said to rule out his leaving property behind and retaining his right to the revenues from it, nor to suggest that he is excluded from the benefit of any outstanding contracts. For a further specified detail, the emigrant is not debarred from settling in an Athenian colony (nor, apparently, restricted to emigrating there.)

More important than this freedom to terminate the contract without penalty is freedom to protect one's interests and promote one's beliefs by persuasion. It is strange for this to come from a Platonic source, for it amounts to a positive defense of Athenian *tropoi* and ultimately of democracy itself. Such defenses are rare. It is questionable whether Pericles' funeral speech is a plea for democracy and "Athenianism" so much as a boast that the Athenians' natural superiority allows them to get away with social and political deviations from the conventional wisdom. The *Old Oligarch* is the classic left-handed defense: By any acceptable standard of what ought to be, democracy is terrible, but its critics should not comfort themselves by assuming its ineptitude and transcience. There is a defense of sorts in Aristotle's *Politics,* but with plenty of left-handedness and the proviso that democracy not reach the extreme of assembly-sovereignty. Fragments suggest that deeper justification, to counter the abundant criticism, had some currency, but do any go so far in moral argument as to say in effect "The claim of a regime to loyalty, to the degree it depends on the citizen's giving up something in order to get something, is plausible only when part of what he gets is freedom of speech and a political role"?

The Nomoi are not precise about what the open door to persuasion means, but three aspects seem distinguishable: (a) One's "day in court." It is an irony (which the Nomoi could not have had the perspective to see) that the defects of the Athenian legal system are bound up with the advantages Athens offers. The law's looseness—huge *dikastēria,* the strong im-

probability of being caught on a technicality, the courts' freedom to construe the law toward their notions of substantial justice or merely to
exercise their mercy or their whims—gave the persuader a wide choice of
fronts to fight on. If one was in danger of condemnation without a firm
basis in law and without proper scrutiny of the facts, at least one could
scarcely claim not to know the game or complain if one was too stupid or
too proud to devise the best strategy.

(b) *Parrēsia;* tolerance of endless talk in and out of official contexts;
the absence of clearcut legal restraints on criticizing laws, state policies,
and politicians. So far as these were realities in Athens, the Millian point
holds: *De facto* opportunities to persuade the public that its collective
doings and shared prejudices are mistaken count for as much as formal
political institutions. The dark side—less apt to show in more conventional or more regulated societies—comes to Socrates' case: The persuader against the grain may fail, may incur keener enmity in the end than
if he were shunned or censured earlier; law that is slack about limiting
what one is permitted to say or do may prove slackly open to vague accu-
sations and politicized justice. But if it is too easy for the persecutors to
use the courts, the persecuted are free to use them in the same open-ended
way. They are perhaps better off than if their enemies could dispense with
the outward processes of law and go directly to politically imposed sanc-
tions or if pressures outside the political apparatus, from Mrs. Grundy to
murder, could choke any chance of dissent's prevailing.

(c) Every citizen's right to take part in the assembly; to propose and
speak for new laws and policies and to oppose in speech; in a less direct
way, universal eligibility for office, including membership of *dikastēria*
and councils. (Though in exercising the powers of their offices magistrates
rather speak for the laws than persuade them, it matters to those attempting to persuade governing atuhorities that they are not addressing representatives of the laws pre-selected for bias against the probable views of
some citizens. When the officer, as in collegial bodies, must himself persuade, he is in possession of a special opportunity to persuade to effect.
Random distribution of such special opportunities helps toward convincing the citizen, whoever he is, that in exchanging the right to coerce or
evade the laws for the right to persuade them he has not received a smaller
share of the latter than more privileged citizens.)

In sum, although they do not talk about them, the Nomoi must be
thinking about the formal features of democracy when they call attention
to the scope they allow to persuasion. However commendable with respect to the other forms of "willingness to listen" oligarchic Nomoi might
be, their generosity must be suspect in that they deny to some of those
from whom they demand obedience the forums where ideas and desires
can be directly translated into *erga.* Although all that Socrates and Crito

say to each other is hostile to the *dēmos,* and by implication to giving it any role in government, acquiescence in the political theory of the Nomoi involves a kind of concession.

What is to be made of Socrates' especially pronounced acceptance of Athens? What, in the first place, should one conclude when any person who is not coerced to live under a set of institutions or to abstain from peaceful, aboveboard efforts to manipulate them in his favor, not only elects to stay in but shows no sign of having even casually considered opting out? Possibly he has modest expectations from political association—little beyond the everyday law and order most regimes can supply. Or perhaps he likes the climate, the hunting, the food—anything the institutions have little to do with, apart from permitting the enjoyment of such natural or accidental comparative advantages (freer enjoyment than the Platonic planner would prefer to tolerate, be it said). Suppose next that we know he is far from uncritical of the local institutions (though in a rather unempirical fashion—not given to travelling, literally or intellectually, in search of actual evidence of better institutions and their feasibility). Nor is our character a political activist, working for change in the assembly, aspiring to office, serving on juries. Have we got a conservative, convinced you cannot leave home though part of you hardly feels *at* home there? Or are the faults of Athens bound up with the unique opportunity it gives Socrates to be Socrates? Obviously it is not a safe place to be his kind of critic. But could it be the only country where a person can undertake to risk his life for the chance of making a critical dent where one is really needed?

The passage in the *Crito* most illuminating on this range of questions is 83:Bff., where the Nomoi show Socrates that he could only be wretched if he were to escape to another city. The Nomoi look at two opposite types of place, arguing that in either Socrates' life would be worthless to him: On one side are cities with *eunomia.* (Thebes and Megara are specified, owing to their proximity to Athens, but practicalities aside, stronger examples would be Sparta and Crete, said in the *Crito* at 52:E to be admired by Socrates, as they were by others of the right-thinking). On the other side is Thessaly, proposed by Crito because of his connections there, a place which, according to the Nomoi, is characterized by *ataxia* and *akolasia.* I shall suggest a possible *tertium quid,* but let us first inspect the polar types.

If Socrates were to escape to a city with *eunomia,* he might be grudgingly accepted but would be considered an enemy of the local laws and could not with a straight face conduct the ethical conversations that were all-in-all to him. The implication is that part of a state's having *eunomia* is having, as at least a very widely shared cultural postulate, the attitude that running away from the law's sentence is wrong, for reasons in the range of those the Nomoi give. To test one's intuitions on the convincingness of this point, one should perhaps think about the following proposition: Decent states do not countenance a right of revolution in their prevailing political morality, much less in their express law; orderly states, with a high incidence of voluntary law-abidingness—and when compliance fails, enforcement that is both sure and fair—are such because the law is genuinely respected. The law need not be considered perfect, but the citizens must believe it was made with a serious regard for the general requirements of justice and for local appropriateness; self-respect on the part of the personified Nomoi of such a state would forbid their indulging resistance by persons pretending to a higher morality. (*Eunomia* and *eunomeomai* are elusive terms. "Decent and orderly state," the decency and the orderliness involved with each other, seems to me about right.)

What if Socrates had gone to a state with *eunomia*, not to escape punishment, but by way of exercising his option to withdraw from his commitment to Athens? One can only say that if his relationship with his adopted city would still have been unsatisfactory, though perhaps less so, it must be because eunomic states, unlike Athens, do not give you an out. In other words, part of being eunomic is taking the grounds for political submission very seriously. Someone who chose to opt out of a state permitting it need not be wicked in eunomic eyes, but he would be second-rate, despised as a moral philosopher if tolerated as a resident.

Thessaly, at the other extreme, has nothing to offer Socrates. The inhabitants are represented as childish savages. If Socrates escaped there, and if the natives whimsically took to him, they would find him amusing—a funny stranger with a tall tale about a jail-break in his past. If he got on their wrong side, they would taunt him. They are too underdeveloped morally to worry about the political principles of someone they like, but they have a moral resource enabling them to taunt when hostile feelings prompt them to. The resource is what savages would be expected to have: primitive respect for courage. With the acute cruelty of children, they would see how to cause painful shame to an old man afraid to die. If Thessaly were the alternative, it seems obvious that no deficiencies of Athens could induce a citizen not under dire pressure to emigrate. Someone odd enough to do so would not be tauntable in the manner of the cowardly refugee, but he would still be a slave to whims ungoverned by ethics.

Are states with *eunomia* and the Thessalies of this world the only choices? I can imagine another. Let us call it the Thrasymachan state. This place is not disorderly on the surface; the people you meet are not savages; the *homme moyen* would rather live there than be dead (or if not particularly fearful of death, but indignant at abusive treatment by his home state, he might make his protest by moving there and have reasonable hope for an undisturbed existence). The place is just Thrasymachan and therefore not eunomic. For the prevalent beliefs are that the law, here or anywhere, is as it is because some person or class was strong enough to shape the law in his or its interest; that usually your best bet is to acquiesce in the facts of power and carry on with your business in the framework that exists; but that of course if you can take over and reshape the institutions in your own interest—or shirk your military duty to save your skin or evade a disagreeable sentence—you would be a fool not to. The law of such a state may be observed and enforced reliably enough, at least in the short-run within which lives are led, and its substance need not be intolerable, but *eunomia* is lacking if, as I hypothesize, morally based respect for law— even if it proceeds from deluded or confused morality—is essential for that quality. "Respect" for power, a slave's tribute, is not respect.

How would Socrates fare in such a society? As an escapee, he would not incur censure, as in eunomic states (or, unless lucky enough to be adopted as a pet, as in Thessaly), for he would seem to have done the sensible thing. If he came as a fully voluntary immigrant, people would probably at first sight commend him as an enterprising fellow on the look-out for a power structure offering better opportunities for a person of his sort than the one he left behind. But what would happen when Socrates set out on his inevitable career as a moral questioner? I do not find it easy to predict. Possibly, by making the inhabitants uncomfortable with their Thrasymachanism, he would provoke hatred comparable to that which caught up with him in Athens. But would the inhabitants have the emotional stake in their clearheaded cynicism that some Athenians had in their confusion? Would everyday Thrasymachans en masse be harder to needle by exposing incoherences in their thought than the solo professional sophist, with a stake in his theory, in the *Republic*? I can imagine Socrates dismissed without malice as an eccentric, his ideals seen as attractive if they were only relevant, his logic admired as brilliant play in a game unconnected with life. Either way—persecuted all over again or trivialized— Socrates is better off back in baffling, unclassifiable Athens. He is trammeled in consent to stick with Athens, no matter what—partly because he has visibly waived his right to withdraw, partly because he is inwardly estopped.

The arguments above on Socrates's obligation to go through with his punishment are not clinching at their best nor developed to their best. Their originality, however, seems to me to excuse their shortcomings. For example, the step from the stipulated point that promise-keeping is generally speaking part of just conduct (49:E) to the idea that one is bound to the state or one's fellow citizens by a promise—or is in a position vis-a-vis the state that is ethically indistinguishable from being bound to a person by a promise—is not seriously justified. But as an intuition is it not quite novel? Greek political writers were worried about *stasis* and unlawfulness; they were acute in analyzing the distemper's causes and cures.

With modern hindsight, it seems strange that they focus so little on submission as a moral duty, or on failure to understand that duty as a cause of instability, that they look so exclusively to prudence and "art" for such hope as they have of mitigating unrest. (See, for example, Aristotle, *Politics,* V and Thucydides on Corcyra). Plato and his Nomoi deserve credit for divining an idea with a future—that something like promissory obligation to political obedience trumps weighty competing moral imperatives. They elevate the idea above a vulgar "love it or leave it" attitude, and they state it in a form that may avoid some of the pitfalls of later contractualism, although they do not explore the grounds of that approach adequately. Those grounds may ultimately, of course, be unestablishable. Without "The powers that be are ordained of God," there may be no sufficient reason why Socrates should not escape.

If the speech of the Nomoi is the *Crito's* strong center, it certainly has a foil; it is in a story, and the rest of the story counts for what the dialogue finally says. I am inclined to find the heart of its power in the ironies it weaves around the first commandment of the Socratic faith: Follow the *logos,* never mind the circumstances in which the *logos* is uttered, for if the *logos* is valid, so far as you can see, it is valid whatever the circumstances. This is formulated succinctly at 46:B: "not only now, but always, I am such a person as to be persuaded by (or obey) nothing (*tōn emōn*) but the *logos* which to me (*logizomenōi*) seems best." *Tōn emōn* is touchingly broad: nothing else that belongs to me, not my body, my life, my goods, my interests, my friends and family, can prevail against the *logos.* Should we add my hunches, visions, voices, culturally inbred responses, conscience? How far will *tōn emōn* reach? I leave the famous word for, *inter alia,* "word" untranslated, because the instability of its meaning is in play in the *Crito.* Of course the sense one is supposed to think of first is "argument" (in the philosophical, dialectical, "logical" style) not of such structures made of *logoi* as oracles, poems, speeches designed to win the case or take the prize. Socrates is no doubt sincere in professing his commitment to follow the best *logos* he can hear, as much in present circumstances as if they were different: if the sentence were not mortal; even were it so, if there were plenty of time to consider the options and the reasons for them; if Socrates' conviction were unexceptionable. The trouble is, the circumstances will not go away. The Nomoi do not address an ideal type, but a septuagenarian with a thought-out belief that death is actually good; who has an exceptionally firm grasp of what most people grasp with the head, though animal emotions may drown good sense in the crisis; who believes that it is silly for a man of such age to take trouble to salvage a bit of further life, especially when the time saved would be miserable and the means of salvation costly to his friends. Moreover, Socrates has just had a visionary experience, wherein a figure bathed in the effulgence of divinity beckons him home. The dream, he says, is better evidence (44:A–B—*tek-mairomai*) than, at any rate, one humble *logos*—the everyday inference that if some men have walked from Sunium and reported a ship there bound for Athens, the chances are the ship will arrive any minute. No doubt a demonstrative *logos,* too, would prevail against anything so empirical. But what that is humanly sayable would prevail against "a woman, fair and lovely to look at, clothed in white garment" and what she has to say, quoting Homer? As it is, the *logos* Socrates hears from the Nomoi only flows into the stream that is carrying him. Should it persuade someone differently circumstanced? Well, yes—a heroic *logos*-follower would probably follow that *logos*. Socrates cannot be blamed because a sound *logos* concurs with his voices. But does it concur? Yes, so far as results go; at another level, not so well. The Nomoi appeal to a moral bond with Athens that cannot be broken; it is a bond for Athenians through-and-through. Socrates is not one. His home is not here, but "fertile Phthia." Athens is a way-station, an outpost. The *logos* is sound, temporally speaking. Submission to the parents and the Nomoi who gave one this life, and to the state to which one has committed oneself in order to secure the blessings of this life, is a duty, but it is not of ultimate importance. It is important only because how one handles a provisional life—as someone in particular, in a specific culture, with human needs to which the *polis* answers—is a test for one's readiness to move on. It is fitting that at the end of the dialogue Socrates hears the *logos* he will follow as the flutes that Corybants "think they hear" (in the *dokousin* the rationalist blinks) and is confident that "the god" is leading him. That is what he has been listening for.

5

KANTIAN IMPERATIVES AND GREEK VALUES

Paul Schollmeier

I

FEW PHILOSOPHERS HAVE DONE AS MUCH to enhance our understanding of ancient moral value as has Arthur W. H. Adkins. His strategy of analyzing what form and role responsibility assumed in ancient Greek society especially presents modern scholars and students alike with many insights into ancient morality and its beliefs.[1] What I would like to do in the present essay is to build upon this understanding of these ancient values. My purpose will be not so much to increase our understanding of the ancients but rather to increase our understanding of ourselves. In particular, I want to examine and to evaluate the modern Kantian view of our moral selves.

Without a doubt, Immanuel Kant has cast a very long shadow over modern philosophy. This shadow is particularly deep in the field of moral philosophy. We almost always couch our discussions of the most basic moral problems in Kant's very terms. And we do so with good reason. Kant clearly invented ethical concepts that have enabled us to improve our understanding of ourselves. Nevertheless, these very concepts as Kant employed them do have their limits, and these limits have prevented us from understanding ourselves even better.

The Kantian concepts most influential are those of imperatives, both categorical and hypothetical. These concepts are frequently used to determine the nature of moral injunctions. The question usually asked is, Are moral imperatives categorical or hypothetical? The answer, whatever it might be, relies with only rare exceptions not solely on Kant's definitions of these imperatives but on his particular applications of them as well.[2] Though loyalty to his theory is commendable, I want to suggest that

Kant's specification of his imperatives in application obscures a moral position worthy of our consideration.

We may, I think, shed new light on the Kantian imperatives by returning to ancient Greek moral theory. For my evaluation of these imperatives, I propose to examine and to compare the concept of intrinsic value presented in Kant's moral theory with that presented in Plato's and Aristotle's theory. I thus intend to reverse the strategy of Adkins. My strategy will be not to bring a modern moral concept to ancient Greek philosophy in order to view it from a new perspective but rather to take a concept from the ancient Greeks in order to gain a new perspective on modern moral philosophy. The result, I hope, will be a moral outlook as admirable as Kant's in its essentials but as adroit as Aristotle's in its applications.

II

I, too, shall ask the usual question about moral imperatives, whether they are categorical or hypothetical. My answer will be that moral imperatives are categorical but that these imperatives need not be Kantian. We shall indeed discover that categorical imperatives can take a variety of forms. How many kinds there are depends on how we conceive of the subject of moral imperatives, that is, on how we conceive of ourselves.

But I want first to review our definitions of categorical and hypothetical imperatives and then to examine our usual applications of these definitions. We tend to follow Kant very closely in defining imperatives, and I think that we are right to do so. We distinguish categorical from hypothetical imperatives by their ends. Both categorical and hypothetical imperatives express commands. But a categorical imperative commands an action as good for its own sake; a hypothetical imperative commands an action as good for the sake of something else. In other words, the one imperative requires an action as an end; the other requires an action as a means (*Gr.* 2. 414).[3]

Examples are ready to hand. Let us assume that we have a moral obligation not to commit suicide. Suppose, then, that someone is in deep despair and no longer desires to live. He in fact wishes to die (compare *Gr.* 1. 397–98).[4] If he yet preserves it without caring for it, this poor person clearly preserves his life merely for the sake of fulfilling an obligation to do so (*Gr.* 1. 399–400). He can hardly preserve it for the sake of satisfying a desire, for he has no desire to live. He thus acts for the sake of lawfulness itself (401). Or, more precisely, this individual acts in accordance with a categorical imperative, for he conforms his action to a universal law solely for the sake of conforming to it. That is, he acts in such a way that he can will his maxim to be a universal law (402).

But imagine someone with a strong desire to live—someone with a *joie de vivre*. If he preserves his life, this happy fellow in all likelihood acts merely for the sake of satisfying his desire to live. This person seeks the pleasure that this satisfaction gives him. He thus follows a hypothetical imperative, for he engages in an action solely for the sake of its effects. And he does not act for the sake of conforming to moral obligation itself. His action does conform to a universal law, but it conforms for the sake of pleasure (compare *Gr.* 1. 397–98).

Behind the Kantian distinction between categorical and hypothetical imperatives lie two models of human action. Behind the categorical imperative is an assumption that we ourselves and our actions are essentially rational.[5] As rational beings, we can act in accordance with our idea of a law. We can do so only because we have a will, for our will is nothing other than practical reason, which enables us to derive actions from laws (*Gr.* 2. 412–13). We consequently seek what is objectively good, for we use reason to recognize the good, and reason is the same for us all (413).

A different assumption about ourselves and our actions lies behind the hypothetical imperative. We and our actions can also be irrational, for we have a will which is fallible. Our will is not always in harmony with moral law because it is exposed to subjective conditions. These conditions are, in a word, our desires.[6] And so we may act for the sake of the pleasure which fulfilling a desire can give us (*Gr.* 2. 412–13). But pleasure influences our will only through our senses. Pleasure is therefore subjective, for the senses are not the same for everyone (413).

Consider our example again. The person who does not care to live acts out of sheer will power for the sake of acting in accordance with moral law since he does not have any desire for life. His action essentially conforms to moral law and hence is objective. The person with a desire to live acts out of an inclination for the sake of its pleasure. His action might conform to moral law but only by accident. It is essentially subjective.

We may sum up by considering the Kantian concept of a good will. A categorical imperative commands an act of good will. An action of this sort arises from the will for the sake of its own activity (*Gr.* 1. 397–400). A hypothetical imperative does not even command an act of will. Its action arises out of desire for the sake of its satisfaction (see *Gr.* 2. 413–14 n., where Kant distinguishes between a practical and a pathological interest).

We thus follow Kant in defining categorical and hypothetical imperatives. We also tend to follow Kant in applying his definitions of imperatives, but I think that we are mistaken in doing so. Before I can show why we are mistaken, I must first be clear about the Kantian application of these imperatives, especially the categorical. A good place for us to begin is in the middle of things with the second formula of the categorical imperative. The second formula is probably the most popular with contemporary philosophers, though Kant himself commends the first (*Gr.* 2. 435–37). This formula will also be the eventual focus for my evaluation of the imperative.

The second formula of the categorical imperative states that we must act in such a way that we treat humanity in any person ever as an end and never as a mere means (*Gr.* 2. 429). Insufficient attention is paid, I think, to the fact that this formulation rests on a supposition that something exists which is an end with absolute value in itself. This something, Kant proclaims, is humanity itself: "Now I say: humanity and in general any rational being exists as an end in itself, not merely as a means for the arbitrary use of this or that will, but must in all its actions, both those directed toward itself and those directed toward other rational beings, always be viewed at the same time as an end" (*Gr.* 2. 428).[7] As if to give it special emphasis, Kant reiterates this assumption even more succinctly: "The ground of this principle is: *Rational nature exists as an end in itself* (*Gr.* 2. 428–29).[8] The principle referred to in this statement is of course the categorical imperative. We would also note that rational nature is the proper moral subject; human nature is only the proximate subject (see *Gr.* 425, for example).

How does this assumption yield a ground for the categorical imperative? The assumption provides an objective ground for the will in two senses. An end valuable in itself first of all provides an object for the will; it is something that the will can make its end. But the will also finds in this end an objective principle. For an end of value in itself is the same for all humans and even all rational beings. Every rational being is by nature absolutely valuable in itself (*Gr.* 2. 427–28).[9]

A hypothetical imperative finds its ground in an end which is not absolutely valuable but only relatively valuable. It has an end which is objective in only one sense. Though not an object of the will, its end is an object of impulse. Only in relation to a desire can a hypothetical imperative command an action as a means to another end. But this end is accordingly a mere subjective principle, for its worth is relative to the desire of a subject (*Gr.* 2. 427–28).

Consider our example again. A person who does not commit suicide, though sorely tempted, regards humanity in himself as an end of absolute value. But someone who commits suicide uses his humanity as a means to another end of only relative value. Though he does not pursue pleasure, he does seek to avoid pain by ending his life. The one person acts on the second formulation of the categorical imperative; the other acts on a hypothetical imperative (*Gr.* 2. 429).

So, humanity exists as an end in itself. We might now ask, What is this end in itself? Recall, now, that a categorical imperative commands an action as itself an end. But the second formula of the categorical imperative declares that we must treat our humanity as an end. Humanity would therefore appear to be an activity which is itself an end. But what activity? Presumably, a rational one. But, then, what rational activity is an end with value in itself?

The first formula of the categorical imperative tells us what this rational activity is. This formula states that we must act only in such a way that we can will our maxim to be a universal law (*Gr.* 2. 421). Recall, again, that a categorical imperative commands an action as an end in itself. To act so as to will a maxim to be a universal law would therefore be an end in itself. Such an action is in fact an absolute end, for universal law is unconditioned (420–21). But the proximate absolute end is humanity, according to Kant. And so humanity is the activity of willing universal law.

A hypothetical imperative, by contrast, aims only at an end conditioned by desire (*Gr.* 2. 420–21). And of course its maxims are not moral commands but merely rules of skill or counsels of prudence (416–17).

Consider the poor soul contemplating suicide one final time. By declining to commit suicide, this person acts so as to treat his maxim as a universal law. He thus takes as his end the activity of conforming his maxim to lawfulness. And he regards this activity as absolute, for he is without desire. He thus acts on the categorical imperative in its first formula. But someone who commits suicide does not treat his maxim as universal law. By ending his life, he acts on a rule of skill. Nor is his end absolute; it is relative to his desire. His action thus rests on a hypothetical imperative (see *Gr.* 2. 421–22).

The third formula confirms our inference about the first two. Indeed, this formula of the categorical imperative, Kant explicitly argues, sums up the first and the second formulas (*Gr.* 2. 430–31). It states that we must act in such a way that we treat humanity as having a will which makes universal law (see 430–31). This formulation thus suggests that we as well as others exist as an end in ourselves when we are self-legislative. In a word, the only end of absolute worth is self-legislation.[10]

To conclude, I would like to point out how limited Kant's application of his categorical imperative is. Kant recognizes only one end which is valuable in itself: a rational being or more proximately a human being. What makes such a creature an end in itself is its rationality. But rationality itself has only one practical function: the activity of making law for its own sake.

Kant himself believes that these two limitations are in the nature of things. He asserts that through its proper nature a rational being is determined as an end in itself and therefore as a legislator (*Gr.* 2. 435–36). He also states that the natural end of the human will is universal legislation (432–33). That would appear to be why Kant prefers the first formula, which states this function most explicitly.[11]

III

I would now like to address the question, Are moral imperatives categorical or hypothetical? My answer is, Moral imperatives are categorical, but categorical imperatives need not be Kantian. I shall accept the Kantian conception of the categorical imperative but reject Kant's narrow application of it. That is, we may act on categorical imperatives, but we need not act solely for the sake of making moral law. We can act instead for the sake of other activities that have value in themselves. We may thus widen our application of the categorical imperative.

To show that we may widen our application, I shall first make explicit a distinction implicit in our discussion of moral imperatives and in Kant's own discussion as well. This distinction takes us back at once to the ancient Greeks: it is that between intrinsic and instrumental value (*Rep.* 2. 357b–57d; *Eth.* 1. 7. 1097a25–34).[12] An action has intrinsic value if it is choiceworthy for the sake of itself; an action has instrumental value if choiceworthy for the sake of something else. For example, dancing is choiceworthy for its own sake. Country dances, ballroom dances, even the jitterbug, we can perform for their intrinsic value. But we put on our dance slippers for the sake of something else—for the sake of dancing. Putting slippers on has instrumental value.

A categorical imperative obviously commands an action that has intrinsic value, for it demands that we perform an action for its own sake. Kant argues, as we have seen, that this action is law-making. According to the first formula of his categorical imperative, we must act on a maxim that we could will to be a universal law. But a hypothetical imperative commands an action that has only instrumental value, for it requires an action for the sake of something else. An action of this sort a person usually pursues for the sake of pleasure, according to Kant.[13]

Now, I can only ask, Is making law the only activity with intrinsic value? And does law-making have the highest intrinsic value? I think that our answer to both questions must be negative. Law making is not the action with the highest intrinsic value, nor is it the only action with intrinsic value. We may perform many other actions which have value in themselves. These actions constitute our happiness in the Greek sense of the term. By definition, happiness for Plato and Aristotle is an activity which is itself an end (*Eth.* 1. 7. 1098a16–17; *Rep.* 4. 419a–421c, for example, though Plato simply assumes what Aristotle asserts). And this activity for humans can only be action (see esp. *Eth.* 2. 1–2).

We can glean an indication of what these intrinsically valuable activities are by glancing at some Aristotelian and Platonic virtues, for happiness on their account is an activity in accordance with virtue (*Eth.* 1. 7. 1098a16–17 and *Eth.* 2. 6. 1106b36–1107a2; see *Rep.* 4. 427a–434c and 441c–442d).[14] Happiness in the Greek sense presents its clearest example in the activity of theoretical knowledge. To know theoretically is to know for the sake of knowing. Aristotle is probably the most ardent proponent of pure science and its intrinsic value (*Eth.* 10. 7. 1177b1–4). We must strain every nerve, he declares, in the pursuit of theoretical knowing (1177b31–1178a2). Activity of this kind is the best; it is the most continuous, the most pleasant, and the most self-sufficient (1177a18–1177b1). Plato, of course, recognizes the intrinsic value of pure knowledge, though he views it more as a dangerous distraction. The guardians of his ideal city, he argues, must study mathematics and dialectics especially in order to develop and to understand models of their city (*Rep.* 7. 521c–535a). But so delightful are these studies in themselves, he fears that his guardians will have to be coaxed and coerced, if necessary, to return to political life (519b–521b).

Though we do not always recognize the fact, we, too, pursue science for its own sake. An astrophysicist, for example, does not seek to determine the nature of black holes for the sake of any application. There is none, despite some fanciful claims to the contrary. He is determined to account for the amount of matter in the universe. Nor does a particle physicist search for the missing quark for the sake of any possible utility. His purpose is to isolate the ultimate elements of matter. On occasion, a scientist may argue that his investigations will ultimately issue in practical applications. But these applications are of no real concern to him; they are merely spinoffs, most often sought by others.

Practical knowledge can also be an end in itself. Plato takes pleasure in poking fun at those who pursue knowledge of this kind for it own sake. He dubs them philodoxers because they confuse theoretical knowledge with practical and pursue practical knowledge as if it had theoretical value. These characters are the lovers of sights and sounds who seek out every Dyonisiac festival (*Rep.* 5. 475d–480a). Aristotle recognizes a similar pursuit in a less disparaging manner. He distinguishes theoretical sharply from practical knowledge and identifies a virtue for this activity. Understanding, he argues, is an ability to judge practical matters without issuing commands (*Eth.* 6. 10.).

We also enjoy practical knowledge in itself, but, again, we often fail to realize that we do. Journalists, for example, bring us live telemedia reports about political and other matters from around the world, and yet the information thus proffered has little, if any, practical bearing on our lives. We have our own philodoxers too, though they are known by other names. For example, fans of movie stars, rock stars, and sports stars ardently seek practical knowledge as if it were the only kind. So does the neighborhood gossip. Bird watchers and those who enjoy wild flowers take a similar, if more reserved, attitude toward other creatures.

The Greeks argue that even practical activity has its value for its own sake. Plato's very purpose in the *Republic* is to show that justice has intrinsic value in addition to any instrumental value that it may have (*Rep.* 2. 357a–358d). Justice, he argues, consists in all citizens performing their own functions, and each citizen finds his happiness in the performance of his function (*Rep.* 4. 419a–421c and 427c–434c). Aristotle argues in general that one must choose moral actions for their own sake as well as perform them with knowledge and from habit (*Eth.* 2. 4, especially 1105a30–33). More specifically, he explains that an action is not just if done only instrumentally—that is, for the sake of its effects. If we act out of fear, say of punishment, we do only what a just person would do (*Eth.* 5. 8. 1135b2–1155b8).

Despite some contemporary pessimism, we still do find intrinsic value in just actions. We surely approve of people who do what they ought even though their actions may not yield any advantages for themselves. We admire not only the citizen who refuses a reward for coming forward but also the criminal who decides to come clean. And we take a dim view of people who exhibit a legalistic attitude toward the law, such as those who search out tax loopholes for themselves or hire lobbyists to carve them out.

Other practical activities, such as courageous and temperate actions, also have intrinsic value. Persons who act courageously do what must be done for its own sake with little thought of risk to themselves. Consider the proverbial reply of the police officer or fire fighter who, upon receiving an award for heroism, protests that he was only doing his job. That we may perform temperate actions for their own sake is most obvious on social occasions—for example, a banquet we do not normally attended for the sake of satisfying appetite. Attending a banquet is a ceremony undertaken for its own sake. And so is a cocktail party and a backyard barbecue.

Nor do the Greeks overlook the intrinsic value of these activities. A courageous person, Aristotle observes, is one who stands his ground against pains and may even delight in doing so; a temperate person delights in abstaining from pleasures. What they can both enjoy is their virtuous activity itself and a pleasure which supervenes upon it (*Eth.* 2. 3. 1104b2–8; see also *Eth.* 10. 4. 1174b31–33). Courageous and temperate activities for Plato also have value primarily in themselves rather than in avoiding pain or in seeking pleasure. The guardians and other citizens, he argues, all find their happiness in fulfilling their functions and not in living as if they were revellers at a festival (*Rep.* 4. 419a–421c again).

Finally, there remain what I think are perhaps the most obvious instances for us—the arts as well as sports and games. Dances, concerts, plays, movies, and games of all sorts we all enjoy for their own sakes, not merely as spectators but also as performers or players. Rare is the person who does not enjoy a gala ball or a square dance. Amateur musicians and actors perform in our cities and towns purely out of their love for the arts. Until recently the modern Olympics were quite rightly limited to amateurs, who participated without a thought of compensation.

The Greeks, of course, advocate the intrinsic value of these activities as well. Aristotle argues at length that music is an important leisure activity, pursued for its own sake (*Politics*, 8. 3. 1337b27–1338a30). He disagrees about sports, unfortunately. Games, he argues, are mere relaxation—medicine for the soul (1137b35–1338a1). Plato suggests that when properly blended, music and gymnastics both are important leisure activities, though he points out their instrumental value (*Rep.* 3. 410b–421c). And he clearly encourages the guardians to engage in imitation—but only of objects consistent with their function (394d–397b).

The Greek conception of happiness, then, shows that we may perform many activities of various sorts for their own sakes. But I must acknowledge that philosophers today do engage in controversies about what kind of value our intellectual and moral activities have. Any question about the value of science as such Plato and Aristotle would find philosophically moot. Science itself can only be pure because it concerns eternal truths valuable for contemplation alone (*Rep.* 5. 475d–480, for example; *Eth.* 6. 3. and 6. 6.). But contemporary philosophers argue that science essentially has not intrinsic value but rather instrumental value. John Dewey does, for example. He argues that we must define ideas "in terms of operations to be performed" and that we must test their validity "by the consequence of these operations." [15]

We also concede that practical knowledge is, of course, practical. The Greeks themselves esteemed it for its applications. Aristotle is more explicit than Plato about practical wisdom and its functions. Both theoretical and practical wisdom grasp truth, he argues, but practical wisdom can also control desire (*Eth.* 6. 2. 1139a21–31; *Eth.* 1. 13. 1102b13–28). But even Plato recognizes the practical value of opinion. The guardians, after their philosophical education, must return to politics and accustom themselves to its idols (*Rep.* 7. 519b–521b).

Clearly, we would like to know more about our contemporaries and their cultures in order to be better able to live together with them. This aspiration I take to be the motive behind current cries for political correctness and cultural diversity. The environmental crisis, in fact, requires other applications of us. We need to know better the natures and functions of plants and animals in order not to harm them but to preserve their species and ecosystems.

That practical activities have instrumental value is most obvious, especially in our acquisitive era. But Plato himself classifies justice as a good of the best sort precisely because it is valuable not only for itself but also for its effects (*Rep.* 2. 357c–358a). Aristotle argues that only theoretical activity has value for itself alone and that practical activity we value for itself and its effects (*Eth.* 10. 7–8.).

Nevertheless, I would aver that, in addition to their instrumental value, all human activities, theoretical as well as practical and productive, still have intrinsic value. And we may surely engage in these activities for the sake of such value. Even Dewey acknowledges what he calls the play of ideas. He thus acknowledges that theoretical activity has some intrinsic value, though he emphasizes its instrumental effects.[16] Can we not equally recognize the playful nature of our other activities as well and perform them for their own sake?

In these examples, then, we find activities which are choiceworthy for the sake of themselves. Activities of knowing, doing, and making, to put the matter in more general terms, all have intrinsic value.[17] And even law-making too still retains its intrinsic value. Kant himself points out that to determine the will in accordance with universal law has value for itself even if it issues in unsuccessful action or in no action at all (*Gr.* 1. 394). We all recognize this intrinsic value when we are able to uphold our principles under trying circumstances.

But we also see how multifarious our identity as rational beings actually is. Scientist, citizen, artist, sports fan, bird watcher, hero, host, prima donna, or center linebacker, we are each and every one of us one or more of these intrinsically valuable beings. And of course I have hardly exhausted the list of intrinsically valuable activities and their corresponding identities.

We need not, then, view moral selves merely as law-makers who make law for the sake of making law. Admirable though acting from the Kantian imperative is, to engage in these other activities for the sake of engaging in them is equally noble. Their worth shines out, as does that of Kantian duty, when we overcome a temptation to pursue these activities merely for the sake of something else, such as personal gain or pleasure (see, of course, *Gr.* 1. 394).

Making universal law is thus not the sole activity valuable as an end in itself. But neither is making law the activity with the highest intrinsic value. The Greeks themselves argue that theoretical knowledge is the activity which has the highest value in itself. They cite in support of their contention the properties of this activity, as already noted, as well as the properties of its object (again, *Eth.* 10. 7. 1177a18–1177b1; also *Eth.* 6. 7. 1141a17–1141b8; *Rep.* 7. 519b–519c). Plato uses the lowly cicada as an image of our devotion to this activity. As the cicada sings from birth until death without need of sustenance, so too those devoted to philosophy argue with one another and quite forget food and drink (*Phaedrus* 259b–259d).

Most, if not all, contemporary philosophers would argue that even activity of a practical sort has greater value than an activity of lawmaking.[18] Making laws and following them, they argue, are of value not for themselves primarily but for their effects in action. Unfortunately, philosophers today often overlook the intrinsic value of practical activity in favor if its instrumental value.[19] The pragmatists especially do. Dewey, for example, argues that practical activity, like practical knowledge, has value primarily for its consequences.[20] But we clearly do admire individuals who act justly or courageously without regard for what the consequences might be for themselves.

Many people would find the highest intrinsic value in the arts and their products. Theater goers and concert goers as well as musicians and actors find greater intrinsic value in the performances of high culture than in either of the investigations of science or the machinations of politics. The same may be said of the plastic arts and more recent genres, such as jazz. And I need not mention again the devoted fans of popular culture and the spectacles of mass media. Aristotle himself argues that tragedy is its own end; its plot is its soul, as it were (*Poetics* 6. 1450a22–23 and 38–39).

By importing the concept of an intrinsically valuable activity from ancient Greek philosophy, we can thus cast a new light on modern moral philosophy. We can now see how restricted Kantian moral theory appears to be. Kant considered only one activity to have intrinsic value, and he focused on an activity that does not have the highest value of this kind. We see, too, that we in fact perform many intrinsically valuable activities, though we may fail to recognize in theory that we do.

So, I would now ask, Does an activity which is an end in itself but which is not making universal laws entail a categorical imperative? I think that it does. An eudaemonic activity in the ancient Greek sense makes a categorical demand on us, for it is an activity with an intrinsic value, and such an activity can be rational ground of choice. We can thus be obliged to engage in many activities of this kind, for they alone constitute our value as an ends.[21]

This argument is essentially Kantian in one respect. It agrees with what Kant states in the second formula of the categorical imperative, that an intrinsic value is a ground for a moral demand. But the argument is decidedly not Kantian in other respects. It disagrees with what Kant states in the first formula, which requires universal legislation. I am arguing rather that we can be required to engage in thought, action, or art. In other words, I suggest that we are essentially activities of knowing, doing, and making, for in these activities we realize ourselves most fully. We are not merely self-legislating creatures, as the third formula asserts.

The non-Kantian categorical imperatives that result from this analysis are objective in two senses. Though they are *a posteriori*, these imperatives do rest on objective knowledge of ourselves. I thus assume that empirical knowledge is the same or very similar for us all. But this knowledge, since it is empirical, is subject to the usual caveats. That is, we may be mistaken about what our function in given circumstances is or about what our circumstances are. But as categorical, these imperatives command an action as an end in itself. They thus provide an object for the will. We act on them because we recognize that an activity has intrinsic value, not because we wish to satisfy a desire.[22]

The analysis also assumes the Kantian model of a will which is rational and rejects any concept of an irrational will. As beings with a rational will, we act in accordance with a concept of an intrinsically valuable activity. Do philosophers, for example, engage in inquiry for the sake of the pleasure that it might give? Even if impelled by a desire to know, we most often find the pleasure of satisfying our curiosity outweighed by the pains of doing so. Rather, we engage in theoretical activity for its own sake; we wish to know for the sake of knowing. Any pleasure is adventitious.

But of course people can shirk non-Kantian obligations. We can act irrationally, for our will remains fallible. We most often do so when we treat an intrinsically valuable action as an action with instrumental value. That is, someone may perform an action with intrinsic value for the sake of an ulterior end. He usually seeks profit or pleasure and thus pursues a subjective good dependent on greed or another desire. He thus subjects himself not to a categorical imperative but to a hypothetical one. And this imperative is hypothetical in the Kantian sense.

I would assert, therefore, that humanity is by nature a knowing, doing, and making creature. Specific activities of these sorts entail categorical obligations because they are ends in themselves.

IV

My argument does require some sacrifices of us, however, if we are to maintain it. We must sacrifice some cherished prejudices inherited from Kant. The first sacrifice required is our notion of a moral agent; we must modify it. Kant argues that all rational beings as such are ends in themselves with absolute value because they are self-legislative (see *Gr.* 2. 425–26, for example). I agree with Kant that rational beings are ends in themselves, but I do not agree that rational beings as such have intrinsic value. I am arguing that other activities besides self-legislation—activities which are empirical—have intrinsic value. The subjects of morality are thus not all rational beings but merely human beings as we know them. That is, only rational animals of one species are moral agents.

What is more, the rational animals in question do not have absolute value as ends in themselves. *Homo sapiens* has an intrinsic value which is merely relative. What has absolute value is the whole of which we are but a puny part. We can of course experience only intermediate wholes with relatively greater value than ourselves. These wholes make up our social and natural environments.[23] But the ultimate whole with absolute value in itself can only be the universe itself.[24]

The second sacrifice required by this analysis is the universality of moral imperatives. Kant argues that categorical imperatives are both universal and necessary (for example, *Gr.* 2. 420–21). The necessity of moral imperatives of course remains. Categorical imperatives are necessary because they are required of us as beings who engage in intrinsically valuable activities. Though without absolute value, these activities constitute what we are. We are, again, creatures engaged in knowing, doing, and making in all their variety and particularity.

But moral imperatives can be only generalities because they rest on empirical knowledge. How do we know what is incumbent upon us? We ourselves experience activities which have value in themselves, and we observe others engaging in them. Our knowledge of our moral obligations is thus limited by our experience and its scope, though these limits can be probed with imagination. Our knowledge of moral obligations is also limited by its objects. Empirical objects are subject to change and depend on their environment. What we find intrinsically valuable today may indeed have disvalue tomorrow.

Finally, we can have a kingdom of ends on this account. But I would prefer to call such a society a community of ends. With this change in nomenclature I mean to draw attention to the members of society. We again are not rational beings legislating universal laws for ourselves; we are rather human beings participating in human activities within human situations. Any moral laws that we make are not primarily ends in themselves; they are rather means to actions valued as ends in themselves. And what these actions are we determine only by experience within a given environment.

V

Today philosophers are not as sanguine about rationality and its activity as was Kant in his day. Kant advocated one absolute rational standard for all moral conduct. Many contemporary philosophers are so disillusioned with his project that they eschew any rational standard for conduct. They often advocate what amounts to little more than an intellectual fad. But without taking the "high priori" road of Kant, I think that we can keep our rationality and take a "low posteriori" road. We need not seek one rational activity with absolute intrinsic value; we may pursue many activities which have relative intrinsic value. Indeed, we must.

NOTES

1. Arthur W. H. Adkins, *Merit and Responsibility*, 1960 ed. (Chicago: University of Chicago Press, 1975).

2. Two exceptions known to me are Williams and Foot. Though they both quarrel with Kant's conception of emotion, Williams discovers a new application for the categorical imperative, Foot finds one for the hypothetical imperative. See Bernard Williams, *Ethics and the Limits of Philosophy* (Cambridge: Harvard University Press, 1985), chapter 10, 189; Philippa Foot, *Virtues and Vices* (Berkeley: University of California Press, 1978), chapter 11, 158–59.

3. Immanuel Kant, *Groundwork for the Metaphysics of Morals*. Akademie edition of *Kants Werke* (Berlin: Walter de Gruyter, 1968), vol. 4, 385–64. All references are to this edition.

4. That we can never be completely sure of the motives for any action, I do of course realize. See *Gr.* 2. 406–407.

5. Williams challenges this assumption. He argues that a categorical imperative is not unconditional in the sense that it depends only on reason and not on desire. This imperative is unconditional rather in that it depends on a desire essential to our very character. It thus does not depend on any desire we may merely happen to have. Williams, chapter 10, 189.

6. This assumption Foot challenges. She argues that a hypothetical imperative can be conditioned by a desire for a long-term project as well as by a passing inclination. And we may be said to want a long-term project even though it might at a given moment leave us cold. Foot, chapter 11, 158–59.

7. The translation is mine.

8. Patton's translation.

9. I thus differ significantly with Korsgaard on the interpretation of this formula. Borrowing terminology from Moore, she argues that our humanity as a choice has intrinsic, or unconditioned, value and that humanity as an end has only extrinsic, or conditioned, value. She explains that when we choose rationally, we confer value on our humanity as an end. Kant thus avoids, according to her, the "ontological task" of identifying rational ends. See, for example, Christine M. Korsgaard, "Two Distinctions in Goodness," *The Philosophical Review* 92 (1983), 169–95, especially 177–84. But Kant not only declares emphatically, as we have seen, that our humanity exists as an end in itself, he also clearly argues that humanity alone exists as an unconditioned end (see again *Gr.* 2. 428). Far from avoiding it, Kant tackles the ontological issue head on.

10. Kant also argues that the three formulas are the same in that they express the form, the matter, and the complete determination of our maxims. See *Gr.* 2. 436–37. For an elaboration of this argument, the reader may consult Warner A. Wick, "Introduction: Kant's Moral Philosophy," Immanuel Kant, *Ethical Phi-*

losophy, translated by James W. Ellington, (Indianapolis: Hackett Publishing Company, 1983), xvii–xxi.

11. Williams is thus quite right to lament this impoverished conception of our moral selves. See Williams, chapter 4, 64–69, for example.

12. Plato, *Republic;* Aristotle, *Nicomachean Ethics.*

13. Korsgaard's attempt to map Moore's terminology onto Kant's moral theory appears to be what leads her astray. I have used the terms "instrumental" and "intrinsic" merely to indicate values that are means and ends. Without using "intrinsic," Korsgaard also opposes the instrumental values to those which are ends. But she goes on to oppose the term "extrinsic" to "intrinsic" in order to distinguish objects which have value from something else or in themselves. See Korsgaard, 169–70. For this distinction Kant prefers the terms "relative" and "absolute" or "conditioned" and "unconditioned." Kant accordingly indicates that our humanity has value as an unconditioned end (see n. 9 above). But Korsgaard denies that Kant takes a position of this sort, though she recognizes it as a possible one. Kant's position, according to her, is that our rationality is an extrinsic end. This is, a conditioned end. See 170–71 and 172–73. Korsgaard's utilization of Moore's terminology thus obscures in Kant's theory the very distinction that she meant to illuminate.

14. This definition of happiness differs from that of Kant. Though he at times ascribes it to Aristotle, Kant appears to define happiness as an activity that is at bottom strong-willed or even weak-willed, for he identifies it with the pursuit of pleasure. Compare, for example, *Eth.* 1. 13. 1102b13–28 with *Gr.* 2. 442–43; and *Eth.* 7. 1–10. Also see Roger J. Sullivan, "The Kantian Critique of Aristotle's Moral Philosophy," *The Review of Metaphysics* 28 (1974), 24–53. Foot and Williams too both remark how narrow Kant's discussion of nonmoral action is. Williams, chapter 4, 64–65; Foot, chapter 11, 158–59 and 164–65.

15. John Dewey, *The Quest for Certainty* (New York: G. P. Putnam's Sons, 1929), chapter 5, 114.

16. Dewey, chapter 6.

17. This conception of action and its intrinsic value agrees with what MacIntyre says about a practice and its internal goods. Alasdair MacIntyre, *After Virtue,* 2nd ed. (Notre Dame: University of Notre Dame Press, 1984), chapter 14, especially 187–90. But MacIntyre parts company with us when he argues that a value intrinsic to action is socially teleological. See 196–97. I would argue that intrinsic value is naturally teleological because it is something that we discover by means of empirical knowledge.

18. Williams argues of course that a desire essential to an agent is the source of the highest practical value. Again see chapter 10, 198.

19. See Foot, chapter 11, 164–66. If one cares about others, she argues, then one will seek not the role of helping them but their good.

20. For example, John Dewey, *Reconstruction in Philosophy* (Boston: Beacon Press, 1948), especially chapter 7.

21. McDowell is thus on the right track to argue that an action may be presented as practically necessary by our view of a situation. John McDowell, "Are Moral Requirements Hypothetical Imperatives?" *Proceedings of the Aristotelian Society,* sup. vol. 52 (1978), 13–29; for example, 14. But he explains that we view

an action as morally required merely because our upbringing teaches us to see its situation in a special light. See 20–22. McDowell thus overlooks the intrinsic value of an action and its moral significance.

22. Ricoeur argues merely that Kant's moral theory provides a framework for Aristotle's theory of action. Kant's ethics of right incorporates Aristotle's ethics of good because their judgments intersect. Both normative and evaluative judgments apply to fundamental human goods, which, he claims, are nothing more than external goods. See Paul Ricoeur, "The Teleological and Deontological Structures of Action," *Contemporary French Philosophy,* edited by A. Phillips Griffiths (Cambridge: Cambridge University Press, 1984), 99–111; especially 108–111.

23. Plato and Aristotle of course place great emphasis on our social and political nature; today we must also take into account our ecological nature. For example, see Aldo Leopold, *The Sand County Almanac* (Oxford: Oxford University Press, 1949).

24. On this topic one might consult Marcus Aurelius or Spinoza.

RESPONSE

Candace Vogler

1. There is much of interest in Paul Schollmeier's paper, and there is a lot to say about his work. Professor Adkins famously remarked that "we are all Kantians now,"[1] and my response to Schollmeier will center on Kant, but I should say at the outset that the interest I take in Kant is more purely philosophical than historical. I approach him with a kind of mercenary spirit, anxious to take hold of what I find in order to make sense of practical reason. I am glad for the chance to engage with another reader of Kant, uneasy with Kantianism, in search of insights which bear on current philosophical perplexities.

2. Schollmeier begins his discussion of Kant by suggesting that a categorical imperative commands an action as good for its own sake, while a hypothetical imperative commands an action as good for the sake of something else. An action commanded for its own sake is commanded as an end, whereas an action commanded for the sake of something else is commanded as a means. The implicit command carries with it a sense of requirement, a 'must' of sorts. Kant suggests that there are at least two kinds of necessitation involved here. The first sort is to be found in rules of skill which tell how a kind of thing is done and in pragmatic suggestions about what to do in order to be happy (*Gr.* 415–18).[2] Kant takes it that plain happiness consists of something like maximal desire satisfaction over the whole course of one's life: if my only aim was happiness, and I knew what I wanted to pursue and when, then figuring out how to attain

happiness would be a case of technical deliberation in the face of uncertainty about future events (*Gr.* 173, *KU* 417–19, *KpV* 25, 73, *MS* 482).[3] The result of my deliberation would be a very detailed life-plan—a sort of agenda or calendar covering the whole term of my prospective life. For Kant, what links techniques to pragmatic considerations is that both concern ends in the sense of desired *outcomes, aims,* or *stopping-places* for courses of action wanted because of their perceived connection with happiness. These practical considerations are about getting results. This is not exactly what the Categorical Imperative is about.

The second sort of practical 'must' is categorical, "concerned, not with the matter of the action and its presumed results, but with its form and the principle from which it follows" (*Gr.* 416). The Categorical Imperative belongs, of course, to morality and is the basis for self-legislation. I am uncomfortable with Schollmeier's suggestion that Kant thinks that self-legislation is the *only* thing we do that is valuable in its own right, if self-legislation is understood as *law-making* rather than conducting oneself in accordance with what is objectively necessary. Kant does indeed cast a long shadow over moral philosophy. I still find much of what is covered by that shadow obscure. While I find Kant incomprehensible at various key points, however, I try always to keep my faith in Kant's claim that he does not introduce new moral principles but merely offers a new, systematic treatment of the old ones (*KpV* 15). To suggest that law-making is the only intrinsically valuable activity *would be* to introduce a new principle of morality, I think, even in East Prussia—as though paying one's debts, or helping the lame dog over the stile, or doing one's part in the community devoted to mutual aid for dependent rational beings was somehow a *distraction* from the business of rational morality.

Is self-legislation even *among* these activities which Kant takes to be valuable as such? Even this more modest claim seems to me peculiar, although it looks to have more solid support than the claim that self-legislation is the only activity which is valuable in its own right. "Self-legislation" could be just another name for autonomous practical reason in action, of course, in which case it would matter for Kant because it was expressive of our natures as dependent rational agents. But if we understand self-legislation in this way, then, self-legislation will have more to do with *how* one is supposed to understand one's doings than with *what* gets done. It won't concern particular kinds of activities as much as it does the *spirit* in which we enter into them. Robbing Peter in order to pay off one's debts to Paul, for instance, will *not* count as the Good Will "straining . . . every means" to do its duty in the face of obstacles raised "by some special disfavour of destiny or by the niggardly endowment of step-motherly nature" (*Gr.* 394). The impermissibility of *this* way of discharging debt is part of what we grasp when we grasp categorical practical necessity. At least, this would seem to be the most charitable reading of Kant on these matters. Many scholars, however, concur with Schollmeier in understanding self-legislation as having something to do with *commanding oneself* to do this or that, and here self-legislation as valuable in its own right looks more shaky.

Presumably, self-legislation involves the self-initiated, principled guidance of one's pursuits. Pursuits guided by the right sort of principles in the right sort of way are what we are after on the Kantian scheme. To assign moral worth to the activity of *commanding* ourselves to act well on the basis of sound principles adds the extra step which renders the whole mysterious. Surely if paying debts out of a sense of duty is good, we don't have to add that dutifully *telling oneself* that one ought to pay up also is good. The debt-paying principle grounds the telling, the paying, and any disposition to do either one, as near as I can tell. The debt-paying principle is meant to find the formula which reveals its ground in the Categorical Imperative. If Kant meant us to think that *commanding ourselves* to do our duty, or even *getting* the formula which shows the sense of acting from the motive of duty, is a *further* activity to be prized in its own right, then Kant needs a better story about why this is so. He would be on more solid ground if his point was rather that once we have framed matters in a Kantianly respectable way, the indicated action ought to flow from seeing the sense of it, and, insofar as we are determined to be only as happy as we are good, the indicated course of conduct ought positively to attract us.

3. Schollmeier's argument involves moving from considerations about ordinary doings of the sort explored extensively in ancient Greek philosophy back into the Kantian framework in order to use the former to enlarge upon the latter. But ordinary doings are about ends in the sense of stopping-places, even if the end in question is the pleasure of engaging in one's ordinary activities. Because of this, the distinction between things done for the pleasure of doing them and things done in order to advance some further interest doesn't map tidily onto the Kantian distinction between categorical and hypothetical imperatives. *All* considerations about ordinary ends of action—what Kant calls the "matter" of the actions— whether the actions are done for their own sake or for the sake of attaining some further end, ought to fall on the *hypothetical* side of the divide for Kant.[4] At least, all such considerations ought to belong to the realm of the hypothetical unless Kant means us to think that self-legislation is a special kind of ordinary activity to be prized in its own right (a thought which, I have argued, he should *not* be pressing upon us). Hypothetical

imperatives are about how to attain ends the attainment of which will make one happy. If I swim for the sheer pleasure of swimming, then the relevant hypothetical imperatives will concern how one swims, when, and where, and what sorts of steps must be taken in order to get to the swimming hole. What the Categorical Imperative will add is something about whether or not I am permitted to swim under the circumstances (for example, I *won't* be permitted to swim if I have made some grave promise and swimming will prevent me from keeping my word, or if I owe you the money I'd have to pay out in order to go swimming). The Categorical Imperative will add this whether I am swimming for the joy of it (where the activity of swimming *itself* is my objective) or swimming because my row boat got away from me and I need to retrieve it quickly (where securing the boat is my objective and swimming is my *means*).

By the very same token, a Kantian end-in-itself (*Zweck an sich selbst*) is *not* an end of action (*Absicht*).[5] Here is what I mean: on the Kantian scheme, my friend is an end-in-himself. Kantians will make much of my friend because he is a dependent rational being (*Gr.* 430). Personally, I'm more inclined to prize him for his mercurial temperament, excellent wit, and utter horror of moral dogmatism, but I hope that neither Kant nor I would take it that my friend was anybody's *objective*. Making my friend laugh or showing up for his birthday party might be objectives, but *he* isn't an objective. Now, in all fairness I suppose that he might be an objective for some crazed geneticist armed with a tattered copy of Dr. Spock. But it seems safe to assume that this *can't* have been what Kant had in mind in his discussion of ends-in-themselves. Even if we restrict our attention to my friend's spare Kantian humanity, the object in which we find value isn't an end of *our* actions in the sense of an objective, outcome, or aim (*MS* 386). He may be a laudable human because of things that *he's* done, of course, but he can't be an end for *me* in the way that, say, improving my golf game or cheering him up could be an end for me.

The Categorical Imperative has us attending to others as ends-in-themselves with an eye toward acting in accordance with reason. Attending to others as ends-in-themselves requires taking it that they could *share* my ends (*Gr.* 430, *MS* 388), not taking it that they *are* my ends. Because I look to the wider context of humanity when I frame Kantian principles to guide my actions, and because neither other people nor their humanity could be my reason-given objectives, I suspect that Kant's ends-in-themselves aren't direct ends of action at all. Pursuits undertaken noninstrumentally, in the way that Scrooge hoards his money, *are* direct ends of action, however. Schollmeier's discussion of activities pursued for their own sakes is a discussion of direct ends of action—objectives, results, outcomes, stopping-places—those things which Kant is at pains to *distinguish* from the business of the Categorical Imperative.

4. Whatever we are to make of Kant on the topic of ends-in-themselves, Schollmeier is surely right to direct our attention to more ancient thought about ordinary activities and how they belong to a life of excellence or flourishing in order to illuminate ethics. Morality is one aspect of modern life. We can agree with Professor Adkins that morality in the distinctively Kantian sense did not belong to ancient thought about excellence or flourishing whether or not we agree with his diagnosis of the divergence. What Schollmeier celebrates in the Greeks is their thought that a life worth living has a certain kind of shape and that very many activities take their significance from the place they have in the living of various kinds of lives. Schollmeier reminds us that it is a *distortion* to treat those pursuits which have no share in traditionally conceived, spare Kantian morality as all belonging alike to the realm of the merely permissible.

I do not agree with the way in which Schollmeier tries to broaden the Kantian picture, but I take it that the direction of a significant part of recent work on Kantian ethics has been toward fleshing out Kant's thought about what makes life worth living.[6] Whether this involves re-working a basically Kantian framework or merely recovering what Kant meant to do from the obscurity of past interpretations is a matter for historians. Such work can only help us to continue to learn from Kant, and tempering what we learn from Kant about the rationality of ends with a healthy dose of respect for ancient thought about whole lives can only help us in the effort to compass more of the ethical in modern moral philosophy. In closing, I will make some suggestions about how Kantian sensibilities might be tempered by appreciation of more ancient sources for ethical thought.

On the Kantian scheme or at least on the received interpretations of it, there are two human practical spheres which it is our job to shape into one harmonious totality: the sphere of happiness (where every practical 'must' has the kind of force belonging to hypothetical imperatives) and the sphere of autonomy, rationality and morality (where the practical 'must' has the full force of the Categorical Imperative behind it). What belongs to the sphere of happiness carries the taint of arbitrary desires or inclinations with it. What belongs to the sphere of morality is not similarly tainted. While some ancient conceptions of how it befits a man to live narrow the options for the kind of life worth living down to one, place tremendous emphasis on human reason, and appear to treat deliberately doing ill as a kind of error or mistake, even these views do not depend upon the kind of radical isolation of reason from everything else about a person's powers or capacities of the kind learned about in introductory course lectures about Kant's moral philosophy. What is reasonably wanted as an ordinary end in, say, Aristotle, is wanted as conducive to or part of doing well. But even if wanting to attain what belongs to doing well is wanting something which will be deeply satisfying, it isn't wanting aimed at plain happiness of the sort Kant describes. The closest Kantian cousin of this sort of wanting is wanting happiness in proportion to virtue.[7] And while virtue proper involves a shepherding of inclination such that we can measure the strength of virtue by how great a hindrance to duty is posed by inclination (*MS* 405), there is underneath it all a thought that untutored Nature and reason are at odds for us in action (*KpV* 111, 113).

Part of the Kantian emphasis on self-legislation—the part which inclines one to imagine that self-legislation is commanding oneself to do one's duty—takes for granted that men must work to subject inclination to the rule of reason. Very crudely, things seem to go the other way around in, say, Aristotle. Unlike Kant, Aristotle seems struck by the thought that a *struggle* between inclination and reason in a grown-up man is exceptional and requires either a diagnosis of faults in the system of moral education (if the internal war is waged often in many apparently well-educated citizens) or else a special story about how the inclinations have separated themselves off from everything else (if the problem belongs to, say, an individual man's occasional incontinence). In general (but again, crudely), the Greeks appear to have avoided the thought that doing what one wants is one thing, doing what one must is another, and it is hard to bring the two together. Further, they seem to have managed to avoid this thought without supposing that human beings could be happy come what may if only they were good. Like Kant, they recognized that no matter how good you were, you were going to be unhappy if a great pile of rocks fell and crushed your leg.

Now, Greek ideas about harmony in thought, action, and feeling are notoriously linked to Greek ideas about the natural functions belonging to different kinds of human beings. We have no such ideas. But, like Schollmeier, I would suggest that it might be better to think in terms of whole human lives (and such harmony and discord as is to be found in the various pursuits which characterize them) than to start from the idea associated with Kant that there's morality on the one side, and everything else on the other and, in order to get the twain to meet, one must have as an object of the will a kind of totality which one cannot attain by one's own efforts.[8] Kant, after all, is only able to get "everything else" lumped onto one side by having a thin conception of happiness and by concentrating on the 'must' of moral obligation for most of his ethical theory. The reader of surviving fragments of ancient Greek thought and culture might well suppose that it is the peculiar narrowness of Kant's understanding of happiness which, when coupled with the special emphasis on obligation in ethics, is partly to blame for the supernatural effort he thinks is required in order to get a kind of totality in place which is neither narrowly self-interested nor narrowly moral, but broadly ethical.

NOTES

1. Arthur W. H. Adkins, *Merit and Responsibility: A Study in Greek Values* (Oxford: Clarendon Press, 1960), 2.

2. References to Kant's work will be given parenthetically in the text as follows: *Grundlegung zur Metaphysik der Sitten* (*Gr.*) Direct citations refer to *Groundwork of the Metaphysics of Morals*, translated by H. J. Paton (New York: Harper and Row, 1964); *Kritik der Praktischen Vernuft* (*KpV*); *Kritik der Urteilskraft* (*KU*); *Die Metaphysik der Sitten* (*MS*). All page references are to the appropriate volumes of *Kants Gesammelte Schriften* (Berlin: Königlich Preussische Akademie der Wissenschaften, 1902–).

3. Happiness in proportion to virtue is another matter entirely, of course, but plain happiness seems to have been something like maximal desire-satisfaction for Kant.

4. This is in Bernard Williams's splendid phrase, "the cunning of the Kantian construction" (*Shame and Necessity* [Berkeley, California: University of California Press, 1993], 76).

5. Occasionally, Kant uses different terms for the two, as I've indicated. For example, he uses *Absicht* in discussing objectives or outcomes at *Gr.* 393, 414–17, associating *Zweck* with the Categorical Imperative and with consideration about whether or not some action (course with an aim/*Absicht* as its intended stopping-place) is good. I think that there is little textual evidence that he would have made the distinction I've made by pointing out that the 'end' as it appears in "end-in-itself" is a homonym for 'end' in the sense of stopping-place and some evidence that two sorts of ends were strangely entangled for him. See, for example, uses of *Zweck* to cover both at *KpV* 108–9. Untangling the two and seeing how they work together in Kant's theory of practical reason would require explaining how thought about ends-in-themselves is meant to be expressed, or otherwise to inform, determinate courses of action with ends-in-the-sense-of-stopping-places, which just *is* the problem of explaining the relation between the categorical framework for practical deliberation and the contemplated actions that constitute the matter of deliberation itself. Far better scholars than I disagree about how this works, and a few are skeptical that the framework *can* enter into the content of deliberation in the right sort of way to make a go of Kantian theory. For such skepticism among scholars see, for example, Thomas E. Hill, Jr., *Dignity and Practical Reason in Kant's Moral Theory* (Ithaca, New York: Cornell University Press, 1962), 97–122.

6. See, for example, Stephen Engstrom, "The Conception of the Highest Good in Kant's Moral Theory," *Philosophy and Phenomenological Research* 52 (1992): 747–80; Christine Korsgaard, "Kant's Formula of Humanity," *Kant-Studien* 77 (1986): 183–202; Barbara Herman, *The Practice of Moral Judgment* (Cambridge, Mass.: Harvard University Press, 1993), especially 184–207.

7. See, for example, *KpV* 110–11, 129, and *KU* 453.

8. On the relevant object of pure practical reason, universal happiness in proportion to universal virtue, see *KpV* 110–11, 122. On the impossibility of obtaining this object by one's own efforts see *KpV* 115–16 (other thinkers have mistakenly thought they could find the highest good in this life), *KpV* 118–19 (the synthesis of happiness and virtue belongs only to the Supreme Being), *KpV* 125 (we can only conceive the highest good in this world on the supposition that a supreme moral intention is the cause of the natural order of things).

6

PLATONIC LOVE AND COLORADO LAW: THE RELEVANCE OF ANCIENT GREEK NORMS TO MODERN SEXUAL CONTROVERSIES

Martha C. Nussbaum

I

IN E. M. FORSTER'S NOVEL *Maurice*, two young men, strongly attracted to one another, begin their university study of Plato:

They attended the Dean's translation class, and when one of the men was forging quietly ahead Mr Cornwallis observed in a flat toneless voice: "Omit: a reference to the unspeakable vice of the Greeks." Durham observed afterwards that he ought to lose his fellowship for such hypocrisy.

Maurice laughed.

"I regard it as a point of pure scholarship. The Greeks, or most of them, were that way inclined, and to omit it is to omit the mainstay of Athenian society."

"Is that so?"

"You've read the *Symposium?*"

Maurice had not, and did not add that he had explored Martial.

"It's all in there—not meat for babies, of course, but you ought to read it. Read it this vac."

This essay was delivered as a McCorkle Lecture at the University of Virginia Law School and published in a much fuller form in the *Virginia Law Review,* October 1994, together with an Appendix coauthored by me and by Kenneth Dover. I would like to thank Julia Annas, Douglas Baird, Victor Caston, David Cohen, Andrew Koppelman, Elena Kagan, Kenneth Karst, David Konstan, Anthony Price, David Strauss, and Cass Sunstein for their helpful comments on a previous draft and,Christopher Bobonich, Terence Irwin, Anthony Price, and Richard Sorabji for giving me written statements on points of scholarship. I am especially grateful to Kenneth Dover for his detailed comments on my draft and, even more, for his generous assistance and his written statements on many points relevant to the issues surrounding this trial. All translations from the Greek are my own, unless otherwise noted. Reprinted by permission.

. . . . He hadn't known it could be mentioned, and when Durham did so in the middle of the sunlit court a breath of liberty touched him.

In 1990, an American judge, a Reagan appointee to the United States Court of Appeals for the Seventh Circuit, fulfills Clive Durham's assignment, reading the *Symposium* for the first time, in order to "plug one of the many embarrassing gaps in my education."[1] In his 1992 book *Sex And Reason,* Richard Posner describes the impact of this experience:

> I knew it was about love, but that was all I knew. I was surprised to discover that it was a defense, and as one can imagine a highly interesting and articulate one, of homosexual love. It had never occurred to me that the greatest figure in the history of philosophy, or for that matter any other respectable figure in the history of thought, had attempted such a thing. It dawned on me that the discussion of the topic in the opinions in *Bowers v. Hardwick* . . . was superficial.[2]

Discussing those opinions later in his book, Posner argues that they betray both a lack of historical knowledge and a lack of "empathy" for the situation of the homosexual, the two being closely connected: "The less that lawyers know about a subject, the less that judges will know, and the less that judges know, the more likely they are to vote their prejudices."[3] Thus he suggests that the "irrational fear and loathing"[4] expressed in the Georgia statute under which Michael Hardwick was prosecuted, and endorsed in the opinions, might have been dispelled by a study of history—beginning, it would appear, with a study of Plato. *Sex and Reason* was his own attempt to advance this educational process and "to shame my colleagues in the profession"[5] for failing to educate themselves in this area. In at least one subsequent judicial opinion of his own, Posner has shown the effects of his own classical education: for in a recent blackmail case he speaks eloquently and with empathy of the special vulnerability of the closeted homosexual in contemporary American society, describing in some detail the non-necessary and non-universal character of the prejudices that make this class of persons so painfully susceptible to the blackmailer's schemes.[6]

On 15 October 1993, I found myself on the witness stand in a courtroom in Denver, Colorado, telling State District Judge H. Jeffrey Bayless about Plato's *Symposium*. Since I had a very short time to testify as an expert witness, I focused above all on the speech of Aristophanes—which I had elsewhere argued to be one of the speeches in which Plato expresses views that he wishes his reader to take especially seriously.[7] I told the Court the story of how human beings were once round and whole—but now, cut in half for their overambitiousness, they feel a sense of lost wholeness and run about searching for their "other half."[8] There are, Aristophanes tells us, three types of search, corresponding to three original species of human beings. There are males whose "other half" is male; females whose "other half" is female; and people whose "other half" is of the opposite sex. The speech describes the feelings of intimacy and joy with which the lost "other halves" greet one another,[9] and describes the activity of sexual intercourse as a joyful attempt to be restored to the lost unity of their original natures. This is so no less for the same-sex than for the opposite-sex couples: in all cases, lovemaking expresses a deep inner need coming from nature, and in all cases the couples, so uniting, have the potential to make a valuable civic contribution.[10] Through this text and many others, I suggested that a study of history reveals a wide variety of judgments about same-sex acts and attachments and a valuable array of reasoned arguments on this topic, which should cause us to ask what our own arguments in this area are and how far they are based on reason.

Taking my Colorado experience as a basis, I shall argue that ancient Greek texts relating to sexuality are radical and valuable for us in just the way Clive Durham and Richard Posner say they are. They have the potential to make a valuable contribution to our contemporary legal and moral thought, and this in four ways. First, they force us to confront the fact that much that we take to be necessary and natural in our own practices is actually local and nonuniversal; this, in turn, forces us to ask whether we have good reasons for what we legislate and judge. Second, they permit us to question certain empirical claims that are commonly made in this domain today, such as the claim that when same-sex acts and relationships are widely tolerated the family and the social fabric will be subverted. Third, the Greek texts provide us with some valuable concrete arguments concerning the important human goods a sexual relationship of this sort may promote. And, finally, they promote what Posner found so sorely lacking in recent judicial treatments of this topic, empathy for the hopes and fears and human aims of those who are involved in such relationships.

II

In 1992 the State of Colorado passed by referendum, with the support of 53 percent of those who voted, what is now famously known as Amendment 2: an amendment to the State Constitution that makes it illegal for any state agency or any local community within the state to "adopt or enforce any statute, regulation, ordinance or policy whereby homosexual, lesbian or bisexual orientation, conduct, practices or relationships shall constitute or otherwise be the basis of, or entitle any person or class of persons to have, any claim of minority status, quota preferences, protected status or claim of discrimination." Since Aspen, Boulder, and Denver had in fact passed civil rights ordinances aimed at protecting lesbians and gays from discrimination, the Amendment nullified those ordinances. A group of plaintiffs went to court for a preliminary injunction against the law; such an injunction was granted by Judge Bayless and upheld by the State Supreme Court by a 6–1 vote. The Supreme Court sent the case back for trial, holding that the State must show that Amendment 2's prohibition of special protections on the basis of homosexual or bisexual orientation is "supported by a compelling state interest and narrowly drawn to achieve that interest in the least restrictive manner possible." Both the trial court and, on appeal, the Colorado Supreme Court found in favor of the plaintiffs, declaring Amendment 2 unconstitutional. The case will shortly be heard by the United States Supreme Court.

In the course of attempting to establish its claims of "compelling interest," the State called a wide range of expert witnesses, whose arguments were contested by expert witnesses for the plaintiffs. Among the State's witnesses were several experts on moral philosophy who offered testimony about the views of the ancient Greeks. I was asked to rebut both their historical contentions and their moral arguments.[11] Here I shall focus most closely on the arguments of John Finnis.

Finnis's moral argument—the argument he traces to "Plato and those many philosophers who followed him"[12]—begins from the premise that it is morally bad to use the body of another person as an instrument for the purpose of one's own private pleasure or satisfaction.[13] Although the legal relevance of this claim remains unclear to me, it is at least a plausible moral contention. He then continues with the assertion that a sexual relationship is able to avoid this sort of manipulative use of another person only through the openness to procreation characteristic of a marital relationship in which no artificial contraception is used:

> Marriage, with its double blessing—procreation and friendship—is a real common good. Moreover, it is a common good that can be both actualized and experienced in the orgasmic union of the reproductive organs of a man and a woman united in commitment to that good. Conjugal sexual activity, and—as Plato and Aristotle and Plutarch and Kant all argue—*only* conjugal activity, is free from the shamefulness of instrumentalization that is found in masturbating and in being masturbated or sodomized.[14]

All beliefs on the part of nonmarried couples that they are in fact actualizing a "common good" such as love or friendship are called "the pursuit of an illusion,"[15] on the grounds that there is no "biological reality"[16] to the uniting that takes place, as there is in the "orgasmic union of the reproductive organs of husband and wife."[17] Finnis goes on to argue that such relationships are not merely unproductive but actually destructive of the personalities of the participants[18] and also of the community. Appeal to Greek antiquity is crucial in getting Finnis to this conclusion.

One may wonder what difference it makes whether Finnis did or didn't get the Greeks right. For surely his argument must stand or fall on its own merits, not by any such appeal to authority; and so too must the argument that rebuts it. This is all true. And it is possible to rebut the Finnis argument in general philosophical terms as well; my testimony emphasized that point. And yet I shall argue that getting the Greeks right does, in the ways I have suggested, help us in no small measure to get our own arguments right—by removing a false sense of inevitability about our own judgments and practices,[19] and by showing us moral arguments of great rational power.

III

It is difficult to study Greek views of sexuality, for the reason so eloquently given by Forster: in this area scholarly puritanism and evasiveness have exerted a pernicious influence, eclipsing or distorting what Clive Durham quite rightly holds to be a straightforward matter of scholarship. The omissions perpetrated by figures like Clive and Maurice's imaginary tutor—whether prompted by shame or by the desire to make the revered Greeks look more like proper Victorians[20]—make their way into the editing and translating of ancient texts, into the making of lexica and other technical tools of scholarship, and thence into the interpretation and understanding of the ancient world. Until very recently there were no reliable translations of Greek and Latin texts involving sexuality and no reliable scholarly discussions of the meanings of crucial words, metaphors, and phrases. As Kenneth Dover writes, in a document addressing the issues of scholarship that arose in the Amendment 2 trial, "On sexual behavior, and homosexual behaviour in particular, translations and authoritative-sounding statements until quite recent times are not to be relied on, because turbulent irrationality impaired the judgement of translators and scholars."[21] In every instance, then, we need to approach these matters with rigorous scholarship, scrutiny of all the occurrences of a term, and freedom from influence and prejudice.

What, in general, does the Greek evidence show us, so approached?[22] As we approach the evidence, let us bear in mind the claim that Finnis wishes to make about ancient Athenian culture:

> In classical Athens, there was amongst the Athenian upper classes an ideology of same-sex "romantic relationships" which were specifically man-boy relationships (inherently lacking the genuine mutuality of equals) and which in a certain number of cases doubtless resulted in sexual conduct. But even at the height of this ideology, a speaker addressing the Athenian Assembly-Court in 346/5 BC could confidently assume that the bulk of his audience would regard sexual *conduct* between males as involving at least

one of the partners in something "most shameful" and "contrary to nature," so that that partner, at least, must "outrage (*hubrizein*) himself." I
refer to Aeschines, *Against Timarchus* especially paragraph 185 given in
K. J. Dover, *Greek Homosexuality,* page 60.[23]

Let us bypass for the present the inherent oddity of citing Dover in connection with an interpretation of Greek norms that Dover painstakingly
demolishes, arguing both that this part of Aeschines' speech is in important respects misleading concerning both legal and moral norms and that
even Aeschines' antithesis itself "cannot rest on a simple assignation of
homosexuality to the category of the unnatural,"[24] but rests, instead, on
an alleged unnaturalness for males of subordination and passivity. (And,
as we shall see, Dover is far from holding that one party in a Greek homosexual relationship must subordinate himself in a shameful way.) But
let us instead turn first to more basic matters.

We must begin by enumerating the types of sources on which a
scholar can draw in reconstructing the historical picture.[25]

(A) *Visual Art.* Of special importance are the numerous vase paintings
depicting erotic and sexual activities. Most of these were produced between 570 and 470 B.C., thus prior to most of the literary evidence (the
first surviving Greek tragedy being 472). Most derive from Corinth and
Boetia, from which there is little literary evidence. Thus caution needs to
be exercised in linking the vases with Athenian culture, but they can illuminate many aspects of the Athenian cultural scene. Vases have the advantages of explicitness in their depiction of sexual conduct: literary sources
are typically more reticent.[26]

(B) *Oratory.* The central text in Dover's argument is a law-court
speech from the year 346 B.C., Aeschines' *Against Timarchus.* Oratory is
excellent evidence for popular attitudes, since the speaker had to persuade
a jury of citizens chosen by lot, in matters in which much was at stake for
his client.[27] In the absence of rules of relevance, any sort of innuendo or
moral rhetoric might be used; and if we often can discern little about what
was really true in the case, we can learn a lot about what a jury might have
been expected to find persuasive. Dover shows, however, that rhetorical
distortions of fact can extend even to the presentation of the legal picture—so, again, caution is needed.

(C) *Comic Drama.* The comedies of Aristophanes (and fragments of
other comic poets) are filled with frank sexual material.[28] The material is
aimed at amusing the average audience, so it relies on some norms of what
would be acceptable and what found shocking. But Aristophanes must
be used with extreme caution in reconstructing what people seriously
thought and did, just as would the humor of a scathing sexual comic of
today.

(D) *Other Literary Evidence.* One may also draw on the poems of Sappho (6th century B.C.); the erotic poetry ascribed to Theognis, of highly dubious and possibly mixed date (possibly extending from the seventh century B.C. to the Hellenistic period, that is, after the fourth century B.C.); the erotic poems of the so-called Greek Anthology, composed from the third century B.C. through, probably, early centuries A.D., though the most important texts derive from around 100 B.C.

(E) *Philosophy.* Philosophers are in general not reliable sources for popular thought; but there are exceptions. Plato's dialogues contain, I would argue, no speech that Plato does not wish his reader to ponder seriously. On the other hand, some speakers are identified more clearly than others as spokesmen for popular views of the day. Among these, Dover is right, I think, to single out the speaker Pausanias in the *Symposium;* I would add the speeches of Phaedrus and Aristophanes, though the latter seems to me an especially serious part of Plato's own design—and, as well, though with caution, the speech of Lysias and the first speech of Socrates in the *Phaedrus.*[29] Aristotle's thought can sometimes be used, with caution, to reconstruct the reputable beliefs of his day.

(F) *Artemidoros.* A writer of unusual interest for the student of sexuality is the dream interpreter Artemidoros of Daldis, who wrote during the second century A.D. Dover did not use Artemidoros, since his cut-off date was the end of the Greek Anthology; but the seven or so centuries covered by his reconstruction is a far longer span than the gap of two centuries separating most of the Greek Anthology from Artemidoros.[30] Given the diversity of his clientele, Artemidoros is a fine source for popular thought; and Winkler provides convincing arguments "that Artemidoros' categorization of sexual acts corresponds to widespread and long-enduring social norms—that is, to the public perception of the meaning of sexual behavior."[31] In general the sexual attitudes and customs of the Greek world do exhibit a remarkable constancy across place and time.[32]

What, then, does this evidence show us? First, it shows us a culture in which the sexual appetite is not found per se problematic or shameful. Here I agree with both Kenneth Dover and Michel Foucault:[33] there is a great distance here from the Christian problematizing of sex, both in the general culture and in the philosophers. No appetite is per se wicked; all appetites need careful management. Sex, like any other pleasure, may be "used" either well or badly.[34]

Second, and again in agreement with the picture presented in Dover, there is neither general condemnation of same-sex acts as such nor a view that the desire to perform such acts is the sign of a wicked or depraved character. Dover's book amply demonstrates that "the Greeks regarded the sexual arousal of an older male by the sight of a beautiful younger male as natural and normal."[35] Homosexual copulation was not viewed as per se immoral or as criticized by the gods. Dover summarizes: "The Greeks in general believed that many kinds of behaviour, notably fraud, perjury, robbery, and the like, were offensive to the gods and incurred divine punishment in this world or the next. They certainly did not include homosexual copulation among these modes of behaviour; indeed, the gods themselves enjoyed it."[36] Dover correctly contrasts Greek attitudes with "the sentiment of a culture which has inherited a religious prohibition of homosexuality and, by reason of that inheritance, has shown (until recently) no salutary curiosity about the variety of sexual stimuli which can arouse the same person."[37]

We may go further: in Greek culture and practices, the gender of the partner assumes far less importance than it does in our own society, and is usually taken as less salient than many other facts about a sexual act. Nor are people very often categorized socially in accordance with their orientation toward partners of a particular gender. It is assumed that abundant appetitive energy may find an outlet in intercourse with either gender, and the two possibilities are frequently treated as more or less interchangeable for moral purposes, youths and women being coupled together as likely pleasures for a man to pursue. To cite just one example analyzed by Dover, in Aristophanes' *Acharnians* the delights of peace are praised in a hymn to Phales, god in whose honor a phallus is carried in procession. These delights include sex with young men, adultery with married women, and the rape of a pretty Thracian slave girl—all being listed without distinction, as more or less interchangeable pleasures for the male hero.[38]

As for actual practices, in Sparta we find evidence of a strong encouragement of male-male relations in connection with the military culture, and also of female-female relations, as evidenced in erotic parts of young girls' choral poetry.[39] For female-female relations elsewhere, the primary evidence is the poetry of Sappho, correctly interpreted by Dover and John J. Winkler as giving clear evidence of sexual acts as well as romantic friendship.[40] Aristophanes' speech in Plato shows that such relationships were familiar to Athenians as well.[41] Although all such arguments must remain rather speculative, the surviving evidence being so slight, Winkler has argued that the lyrics of Sappho give evidence that female-female sexuality was less asymmetrical, less governed by the dichotomy of penetrator-penetratee, and more mutually sensuous than other sexual relationships in Greek society.[42] It is interesting to note that Artemidoros, who otherwise does not bother to mention female-female acts in his elaborate list of sex acts (presumably because his clientele was all male), does include in the category of acts "contrary to nature"—a category of weird and counterfactual rather than vicious acts, and one that includes the perpetual fantasy of making love with a god or goddess—the description "a woman penetrating a woman."[43] He evidently finds this so weird as to be impossible, though there is no sign that he believes anything one way or the other about other sex acts between women.[44]

But for Athens, most of our evidence, both literary and artistic, pertains to male-male relations. Here we find—again I am agreeing with Dover—no general condemnation of male-male relations, a fortiori not a general *moral* condemnation. Indeed Dover, like David Halperin, produces and stresses the evidence that visiting both male and female prostitutes was considered perfectly acceptable for a citizen male,[45] and male prostitution is treated as a perfectly routine matter in texts of many kinds. Even in the midst of his moralizing denunciation of Timarchus (a citizen) for prostituting himself, Aeschines hastens to reassure his audience that he has no intention of discouraging the general practice of male prostitution; his aim, instead, is to guarantee that people who want casual sex with young men "turn to foreigners and resident aliens so as not to be deprived of what they prefer."[46]

Where relation between two male citizens are concerned, we find, again, no general condemnation, but, instead, a complex system of caveats or reservations. We must begin by noting that these relations, even when they involve people close to one another in age, always involve an asymmetry of roles: the *erastēs* or "lover" is the older partner, who actively pursues and courts the younger, drawn by the sight of youthful male beauty. He is expected to be keenly interested in sexual contact, and this interest, and the (active, penetrative) conduct that follows from it, is taken to be perfectly normal and natural. The younger partner, the *erōmenos* or "beloved," is likely to be pleased at being the object of admiration and interested in benefits such as friendship, education, and political advancement that a relationship with an *erastēs* may bestow. The relationship may in this sense involve a real reciprocity of benefits and mutual affection based on this. But the cultural norm dictates that he is not to have a keen sexual interest in being penetrated, nor to develop habits of enjoying that sort of penetration: for that would be, in effect, to be turned into a woman, and one could expect that this would unfit him from playing, later in life, an active manly role.

This being the case, the relationship between an older and a younger male citizen is hedged round with a complex series of caveats and reservations. What are these reservations? (1) No citizen may receive money for sex. Proof that one does is disqualifying for citizenship, because it is connected closely with the idea that one has put one's own body up for sale to and use by the highest bidder, hence with the idea of treason. In a democracy where most major offices are filled by lot, one does not want to have a citizen who is up for sale.[47] Receipt of many gifts may also give rise to the suspicion that one's favors are being bought. (2) There are grave strictures against sexual violence and enticement, especially against the young. As Dover shows, *hubris* need not mean actual sexual assault. It usually does mean that, when the subject of the verb *hubrizein* is an adult male and the object a woman or a boy. But the term may be at times extended to include "dishonest enticement, threats, blackmail" and other forms of nonphysical coercion.[48] It seems wrong, however, to assert that a fully consensual relation between *erastēs* and *erōmenos* could be stigmatized as *hubris*—except by someone alleging that it did after all contain one or more of the forbidden forms of coercion.[49] (3) Habitual passivity, that is, habitually the one who gets penetrated, is much criticized, as I have said, and is taken as evidence that one is not fully manly. (The Aristotelian *Problemata* says it shows that the person is physically malformed, with his fluid-bearing "ducts" going to the anus rather than to the penis.[50]) As a result, there is strong anxiety about passivity in general. Finally, (4) there is widespread criticism of those who seek casual bodily pleasure in their interactions with younger males without caring for friendship and other values.

Where the relationship between an older and a younger male citizen is concerned, therefore, much care needs to be taken. The penetrative role is per se nonproblematic, and if one goes to penetrate a male prostitute, it is perfectly all right, just as if one goes to penetrate a female prostitute. It was not just common, but widely approved, for married males to visit prostitutes of either sex. But with a young male who is going to be a citizen, much caution must be exercised not to corrupt him by excessive gifts and not to encourage habits of passivity. For this reason, a cultural ideal, prominently depicted in visual art, prefers intercrural intercourse, that is, intercourse in which the older partner achieves orgasm by friction of the penis between the younger man's tightly clenched thighs.

It is clear, however, that this is not the whole picture. In Greek comedy, anal penetration is taken to be the norm, as Dover stressed in his first edition. In the postscript to his second edition he now grants that this fact may well indicate that the vase-painters' preference for the intercrural mode may be "highly conventional."[51] In the Greek Anthology and the dream book of Artemidorus, anal intercourse is again taken to be the norm, and intercrural copulation is not mentioned. (Artemidoros classifies both active and passive anal acts as acts that are both "according to nature" and "according to custom.") So it would appear that both in fifth-century Athens and in the later period represented by the Greek Anthology and Artemidoros, anal acts between citizens occurred. How were these acts viewed? The evidence of comedy must be read with much caution, for, as Dover shows, the comic genre depicts human motivation as venal and selfish consistently, not only in the sexual domain. It would be wrong to infer from comedy that in popular thought generally the penetratee was thought to have been bought. On the other hand, it is also clear that the fact of anal passivity would be a source of anxiety and possible shame, if it were seen as part of a picture in which the young man is thought to be developing habits of passivity. The best solution to this problem seems to me to be one that invokes conventions of public and literary evidence already demonstrated by Dover. The suggestion is that anal acts were assumed to occur between the *erastēs* and his citizen *erōmenos,* but they were not in general to be publicly mentioned. To speak publicly of what everyone took for granted would incur shame for the youth, where the fact itself would not. This conclusion is fully consistent with Dover's analysis. The important point to stress, in any case, is that such shame as was potentially at issue was shame not about the fact of same-sex copulation but about the "womanish" position of passivity and its potential connection with being turned into a woman. No such shame, it would seem, attached even potentially to conduct that did not involve this penetration, thus not to conduct involving intercrural intercourse, apparently the most common mode of copulation.

As for oral sex, the Greeks seem to have had some aversion to this form of conduct, and especially to the receptive role, but their condemnation appears to have been aesthetic rather than moral.[52]

We must now insist on the question of age, for Finnis repeatedly called the relationship of *erastēs* and *erōmenos* a "man-boy" relationship, alleging that nobody has bothered to inquire how young the "boys" actually were.[53] But this is not so: Dover and others have commented on this matter at length, assisted by the clear evidence of visual art. To modern American ears the word "boy" suggests someone between the ages of, say, four and twelve. But the *erōmenos* of Greek custom was typically, and ideally, a young man between the time of full attainment of adult height and the full growth of the beard: so, if we go by modern growth patterns, perhaps sixteen to nineteen; but more likely, since the ancient Greek age of puberty seems to have slightly later than ours, the age of a modern college undergraduate.

One should also consider what the typical *erōmenos* was expected to do and to be, for our own children grow up much more slowly than young people in the ancient world. Looking at famous couples such as Achilles and Patroclus, the tyrannicides Harmodius and Aristogeiton, and the famous Sacred Band of Thebes, an elite military corps made up of male-male couples, we can conclude that the *erōmenos* is generally old enough for mature military and political action.[54] (And since the popular thought of our day tends to focus on the scare-image of a "dirty old man" hanging around outside the school waiting to molest young boys, it is important to mention, as well, that the *erastēs* might not be very far in age from the *erōmenos.* One can begin to play that role, as Halperin correctly insists, even while he is still playing the other role—though he will not play both roles in relation to the same person.) There is, moreover, some evidence of couples in which the *erōmenos* was even older than the standard norm, especially in relationships of long duration. Pausanias and Agathon continued for at least twelve years a relationship that began when Agathon was eighteen.[55] The Stoics apparently held that a relationship should continue until the *erōmenos* was twenty-eight.[56] We should also consider the relationship between Plato and Dion of Syracuse, which is at any rate widely (and sympathetically) represented in the evidence for Plato's life as a sexual relationship, and which evidently began when the parties were about fifty and thirty-five respectively. We have, as well, the fact that Plato's Pausanias and Aristophanes speaks of their norm as that of a lifelong partnership;[57] Pausanias insists that it should not begin until after the growth of the younger party's beard. Aristotle, finally, following Pausanias, defends a long-term alliance as morally best.

We must now also address the issue of mutuality, since Finnis claimed that the *erastēs-erōmenos* relationship was inherently exploitative. It is true that the *erōmenos* is depicted typically as deriving no *sexual pleasure* from the conduct—although this may well be a cultural norm that conceals a more complicated reality.[58] What is more important is that it is perfectly clear that a successful relationship of this sort produced many advantages for the younger man—education, political advancement, friendship—and that he frequently felt intense affection for the *erastēs* as a result. The tales of courageous self-sacrifice with which Plato's Phaedrus regales his audience would not have seemed surprising. Furthermore, the young man can be expected to go promptly on to active sexual pleasures of his own, in a phase of life that will last much longer than his *erōmenos* phase lasted.

IV

We now turn to the philosophers. Finnis claims that "all three of the greatest Greek philosophers, Socrates, Plato and Aristotle, regarded homosexual *conduct* as intrinsically shameful, immoral and indeed depraved or depraving. That is to say, all three rejected the linchpin of modern 'gay' ideology and lifestyle."[59] He repeatedly suggests that they do so using, or at least suggesting, an argument similar to his own, namely, an argument that relies on the moral centrality of the potentially procreative marital bond. I shall argue that none of the philosophers I shall discuss takes the position described by Finnis; nor does any endorse his positive view of the marital relationship. Even those texts that do rank nonconsummated same-sex relationships over consummated relationships do so not because they find anything shameful or degrading in homosexual intercourse as

distinct from heterosexual intercourse but for other reasons—in the case
of some works of Plato, out of a general suspiciousness of the power of
sexual passion to interfere with reason and a consequent desire to reduce
all orgasmic sexual expression to a minimum. In fact, we shall find that
same-sex relationships are usually ranked ahead of heterosexual (and, frequently, marital) relationships, on the grounds that they are more likely to
be linked with spiritual goals.

Socrates

It is very difficult to reconstruct the views of the historical Socrates on
sexual relations. For Socrates' views in general we have four major
sources: (a) the dialogues of Plato; (b) several works of the writer Xenophon dealing with Socrates; (c) the Aristophanic comedy *Clouds*, which
offers a satire on Socrates; and (d) various scattered statements by Aristotle. From now on we may ignore (c) and (d), which offer no help with
the issue of sexuality. Xenophon's testimony is generally recognized as
much less reliable than that of Plato, where they conflict. Xenophon,
though an able man of affairs, an intrepid military leader, and a literary
stylist of some skill, was not a subtle philosopher.[60] Plato, by contrast, was
of course a very great philosopher; and he is doubtless the best source we
have for Socrates' life and activity. The use of Plato as source, however,
poses further problems: for Plato uses Socrates as a character in dialogues
of varying dates, in many of which we have independent reason (Aristotle's testimony above all) to think him to be developing ideas of his own
that were not Socrates' ideas. Further complexity derives from the fact
that in some of the works that are usually judged "Platonic" rather than
"Socratic," there may be narrative and biographical material that gives
genuine illumination about Socrates.

In brief, I solve this problem as Vlastos solves it—giving the Platonic
Socrates pride of place where he and Xenophon do not agree and dividing
the works of Plato, as Vlastos does, into a group that represents (more or
less) the thinking of the historical Socrates, and those that are Platonic. In
the former group I would place dialogues such as *Apology, Crito, Laches,
Lysis, Charmides, Protagoras,* and *Euthyphro;* in the latter group, *Symposium, Phaedrus, Republic, Philebus, Laws,* and many others that will
not concern us here. Unlike Vlastos (and concurring in arguments of T. H.
Irwin[61]), I treat *Gorgias* as containing much material that may be called
Platonic. Like Vlastos, however—and like Dover—I regard the portrait of
Socrates' life and activity painted in the speech of Alcibiades in the *Symposium* as a genuine source for the historical Socrates, if used with proper
caution, despite the presence of clearly Platonic doctrines in other portions
of that dialogue.

What can we know about Socrates' attitude to same-sex relations?

Very little, as it turns out. In Plato's dialogues, Socrates takes his place in the "strongly homosexual ambience" of Athenian society.[62] Socrates' friends are routinely depicted as involved in erotic relationships with younger men, and he responds with sympathy to their situations.[63] Socrates himself is depicted as having strong sexual attractions to younger men: for example, he is "on fire, absolutely beside myself" when he looks inside the cloak of the young Charmides (*Charmides* 155C–E, cf. *Protagoras* 309A).[64] We know that Socrates was married[65] and had children; but he never alludes to his or anyone else's marital sexual life, and in general his sexual interest in women appears to have been slight, so far as Plato's portrait is concerned.[66]

Did Socrates engage in male-male sexual relations? And if he did not, did he have a general reason for this policy, and, if so, of what sort? Xenophon provides him with two general reasons against homosexual conduct, which Socrates is prepared to commend to others as well: the pleasures of sex can enslave reason (*Symposium* 3.8–14); and sexual gratification is "not a good thing" because it is something like scratching an itch—that is, a way of relieving tension, but not good in itself (*Memorabilia* i.2.29ff.).[67] We may remark that neither of these arguments singles out homosexual activity for special blame: Xenophon's Socrates would presumably say the same of erotic passion generally, given the reasons he advances. It just happens that his friends are far more passionate about young men than about women and so need more counseling in that regard. Nor do we hear any mention of a view that marital sex is in any way superior to other forms of sex, heterosexual or homosexual (although we may remark that the usual assumption would be that the husband would not be passionately in love with his wife, and marriage would to that extent escape the blame reserved for passion). Finally, the blame involved does not involve the idea that such copulation is wicked or depraved. Like the scratching to which it is compared, it may be inferior, but, as Dover says apropros of this material, " 'Inferior' does not mean 'wicked.' "[68]

As for Plato's Socrates, there is no clear evidence for a general attitude on the matter that Socrates is prepared to recommend to others. In several passages, through a metaphorical use of erotic language, Socrates insists that his own most intense passion is for wisdom, a higher goal that the pursuits of bodily intercourse distracts him from (*Protagoras* 309B–D). As Dover remarks, "It does not follow logically from this that homosexual copulation should be avoided, unless one also believes that any investment of energy and emotion in the pursuit of an inferior end vitiates the soul's capacity to pursue a superior end."[69] Does Socrates think this? Note that even if he does, he would not be singling out homosexual copulation for special condemnation, and the grounds of his condemnation would not be that he finds the activity wicked or shameful. Once again: "inferior" does not mean "wicked." But does he think this? Dover argues in the affirmative—but only by drawing on the *Republic,* an unquestionably Platonic rather than Socratic text, and by putting the evidence of Xenophon together with that of Plato, a method that I would consider defective; Dover now grants my methodological point.[70]

The primary piece of evidence we have is the story told by Alcibiades in Plato's *Symposium,* concerning his own failed attempt to seduce Socrates, in which Socrates sleeps all night beside the beautiful young man without evident arousal (216C–219E). This story must be used with caution as a source for the historical Socrates, given its context in an unquestionably mature Platonic dialogue and its close relation to other arguments of that dialogue; but even scholars such as Vlastos who insist on the distinction between Plato's Socrates and the historical Socrates as depicted by Plato so use it. What, then, if so used, does the story show? It certainly does not show that Socrates has disgust at Alcibiades' proposal or thinks the orientation of his desire diseased; he clearly treats the proposal as quite natural and normal. Nor does it offer any evidence that he thinks the proposed conduct depraved or wicked or different in kind from an attempted seduction by an attractive young woman (except that Alcibiades is seen as exceptional in beauty in a way that no woman would probably have been seen by Greek society of the time). Socrates seems to think sexual relations inferior to the course he actually follows—for what reason? Two reasons are suggested in the passage. The first is that (as suggested in the *Protagoras*) he feels the lure of philosophy so strongly that he simply doesn't get aroused by anything else.[71] The second reason is that he notices Alcibiades' youthful vanity and wants him to find out the hard way that he cannot get what he wants through good looks alone. The seduction of this charismatic teacher would have turned him straight away from philosophy; Socrates' refusal creates a painful stimulus to self-examination.[72] In short, his reasons for refusal are internal to his conception of the value of philosophy and of his role as philosophical teacher.[73] There is no evidence here even for Xenophon's Socrates' general claim that sexual conduct is always inferior, a distraction from better pursuits. And there is no evidence whatever, even in Xenophon, for Finnis's conclusion that Socrates "regarded homosexual *conduct* as intrinsically shameful, immoral and indeed depraved or depraving."[74]

Plato

Plato is a philosopher of enormous complexity. Since in his suspiciousness about all appetitive pleasure he diverges more than any other Greek philosopher from the cultural pattern I have described, his views need to be probed with special care. Sensitivity is also required in posing questions about Plato's own relation to his varied characters; we cannot assume that the character Socrates is the only one whose views we should connect with their author. I shall have my eye on three questions: (a) What, if anything, is said about homosexual conduct? In particular, is it singled out from other forms of sexual conduct as unusually shameful or depraved? (b) What, if anything, is said about the social contribution of such relationships? (c) What, if anything, is said about marriage? Is there any sign of the positive view of the worth of procreative intercourse that Finnis appears to trace to Plato?

Gorgias

Toward the end of this dialogue, Socrates is criticizing Callicles, who has held that the best life is the life with the largest desires, provided one always has the opportunity to satisfy them. Socrates compares this to the wish that one always had the greatest possible itches, provided one always had the power to scratch. In this and the succeeding series of examples, he tries to get Callicles to grant that no pleasure is per se valuable just because, like scratching, it replenishes a lack or removes an antecedent pain. Eventually he will ask Callicles to think this way about the central bodily activities—eating, drinking, and sex. A turning point in this argument is reached when, after Callicles has gamely tried to defend the scratcher's life as a good thing, Socrates provides a further example, the pleasure of the *kinaidos*. Callicles is outraged and tells Socrates he should be ashamed to mention such an example (494E2ff.). Finnis took this case, it would seem, as a reference to homosexual conduct in general.[75] But the *kinaidos* is clearly a person who chronically plays the passive role. Dover translates as "pathic"; in my published treatment of the dialogue, I used the phrase "passive homosexual"[76]—meaning by this to denote someone who habitually plays the passive role. More recently, I have been convinced by arguments of the late John J. Winkler that *kinaidos* usually connotes willingness to accept money for sex, as well as habitual passivity;[77] therefore rendered the word as "male prostitute" in my affidavit. But there is in any case no doubt that we are dealing here with not an isolated act but a type of person who habitually chooses activity that Callicles finds shameful.[78] That, and no view about same-sex relations per se, is the basis of his criticism. In fact, Callicles is depicted as having a young boyfriend of his own. (It would be assumed that he would practice intercrural intercourse with this boyfriend, thus avoiding putting him in anything like the *kinaidos'* shamed position.) Socrates expresses no view of his own on these matters, although he seems to suggest that all appetitive activities, including eating and drinking, are inferior to activities (whatever they be) that do not simply relieve an antecedent tension or lack. Once again, "inferior" does not mean "wicked."

The *Gorgias* contains no discussion of the marital bond.

Symposium

The dialogue is set at an all-male drinking party attended by a group that includes pairs of lovers.[79] Its speeches express conventional views about love, most of which Plato depicts in an appealing and serious light. The speech by Phaedrus points to the military advantages that may be derived by including male-male couples in a fighting force: because of their intense love, each will fight better, wishing to show himself in the best light before his lover (178D–179B). Such an army, he concludes, "though small in size would pretty well conquer all of humanity" (179A).[80] Shame is mentioned as a motive closely connected, in a positive sense, with passionate sexual love: each will be ashamed of doing anything cowardly before his lover (178E). Phaedrus does mention two cases of marital love and self-sacrifice, giving high praise to the courageous actions of Alcestis; but he expresses some surprise that a male-female love could have the same features he finds in male-male love.[81]

The speech of Pausanias (convincingly argued by Dover to be one of our central pieces of evidence for prevalent Athenian attitudes) criticizes males who seek physical pleasure alone in their relations with younger males and praises those who seek deeper spiritual and moral goals. Strong interest in sex with women is connected by Pausanias with a preference for the body over the soul (181BC). A sexual act, says Pausanias, like any other act, is not right or wrong in and of itself: for everything depends on the manner in which it is done (180E, 183D). If the *erastēs* demonstrates that his primary concern is for the character and education of the *erōmenos*, rather than merely for bodily pleasure, then it will be a fine or noble thing (*kalon*)[82] for the younger man to "gratify" the older (*charizesthai*, a word that, as Dover has shown, clearly connotes intercourse). Such a lover should look for a young man whose beard has already started to grow, since that is the age of good judgment (181D): after all, the goal is "to love as people who are going to be together their entire lives and to live together" (181D), and this goal requires careful selection. The young man should not let himself be caught too quickly, since he must test the lover's character and regard for his education (184AB).

Pausanias is aware of a variety of different customs regarding male-male intercourse. He makes fun of regions where it is held *always* to be a good thing to "gratify" a lover, without regard to the moral concerns he has enumerated. This custom, he says, suits unrefined people who lack the capacity to persuade one another of virtue and good intentions (182B). But he also condemns the opposite custom, and more strongly, associating it with Asian despotism. He mentions that tyrants will sometimes promulgate the view that same-sex relations are shameful, in order to discourage the sort of devotion to political liberty that such relations, as exemplified by Harmodius and Aristogeiton, can foster (182BC). Marriage plays no part in Pausanias' thinking, except when he mentions laws that forbid sleeping with other people's wives (181E). It would be assumed, however, that the relations he describes could be compatible with marriage on the part of the *erastēs*. The lovers Pausanias describes are both happy and socially responsible.

Since Eryximachus' speech is concerned more with cosmology than with human beings, I omit it. Aristophanes' speech I have already described: it situates same-sex longings deep in nature, describes intercourse as a way of being restored to a natural wholeness and unity, and argues for the civic benefits of male-male love in particular. There is absolutely no doubt that lovers of all three types are envisaged as engaging in intercourse—intercourse, indeed, is a central topic of the speech. Although the speech does recognize the distinction between the *erastēs* and the *erōmenos*, it is remarkable for its suggestion of mutual desire and pleasure: for both partners feel "friendly love and intimacy and passionate love" (192BC), and the younger "halves" of original male-male "wholes" are said to enjoy "lying with and being embraced by men" (192A). (Indeed, the whole conceit of the myth leads the mind in the direction of an uncustomary symmetry and reciprocity.) Relationships between "other halves" are said to endure throughout life (192C). Aristophanes remarks that custom may force such male-male couples to marry, though they "do not turn their thoughts to marriage and begetting of children by nature . . . but it is enough for them to live unmarried with one another" (192AB).

Agathon's speech contains little to interest us. Socrates' speech recounts a process of religious-mystical education in which male-male love [83] plays a central guiding role. Whether or not it is abandoned when one reaches the summit of philosophy's vision—and Anthony Price has now convinced me that it is not [84]—this erotic bond offers a primary insight and inspiration into the nature of the good and beautiful. The speech argues that a preference for women and marriage betrays an inferior type of creativity, focused on bodily rather than spiritual goals: these people want offspring of the body, rather than of the mind and character (298E). [85]

Will the lovers in the Socratic ascent have sexual intercourse? Certainly, as they fix their minds increasingly on the whole of beauty, rather than simply on individual exemplars of beauty, the tension and strain involved in erotic passion will cease; Socrates' imaginary instructor Diotima remarks that Socrates will no longer have to pursue the young men that now "strike you out of your mind" (211D). She uses the language of sexual "being-with" for the aspiring philosopher's relation to the eternal form of Beauty, having used it earlier of his relation to those same young men (*sunontes,* 211D, *sunontos* 212A)—again implying that a new form of intercourse displaces the old as the object of the philosopher's most intense interest. One could, of course, imagine intercourse continuing without intense passion—a possibility explored in Plato's *Phaedrus*. But the result is likely to be the stonelike unaroused Socrates of whom Alcibiades so bitterly complains, feeling Socrates' unresponsiveness as a kind of rape.[86] I have argued that the reader of the dialogue is intended to feel more than a little ambivalent about a proposal in which so much of human passion is given up, and is intended to feel, therefore, some sympathy with Alcibiades' preference for flesh-and-blood intercourse.[87] Through appeals to empathy in both Aristophanes' and Alcibiades' speeches, the text recalls to its reader the world of ordinary Athenian judgments, making clear the costs, as well as the benefits, of Diotima's therapy. But even if we disregard that issue, as we should not, and give Socrates the final word in a simple way, his argument in no way shows the view that homosexual conduct is depraved, wicked, or shameful. It is at least as good as any other sort of sexual conduct, though all such intercourse may be uninteresting once one "has intercourse" with the form.

Republic

In this work (and the roughly contemporaneous *Phaedo*) we first encounter in a clear form that suspiciousness about all appetitive expression that will figure so largely in Plato's thought after this time. The appetitive element in the soul—the one that is responsible for eating, drinking, and sexual activity—is compared to an insatiable "many-headed beast" whose demands grow the more they are gratified (442A) and whose pursuits are a constant threat to good reasoning.[88] People who live by their appetites are said to resemble animals—"like cattle . . . they pasture, grazing and mounting" (586A). Although the sexual appetite is singled out as the greatest and sharpest and most "madness-producing" of the appetites (402C), the three major appetites are treated throughout the work (for a typical example, 580E), and Plato's strictures apply to them all. In a passage in which he is making proposals for the control of the dangerous erotic appetite, Socrates suggests that in the Ideal City the *erastēs* should kiss the *erōmenos,* if he persuades him, and touch him as a father might touch a son, "for the sake of the fine" (presumably, to encourage his educational development), but go no further (403BC): "If not, he will incur the blame of being uncultivated and lacking comprehension of the beautiful" (*amousias kai apeirokalias,* C1–2). This, of course, is far from the Finnis claim that these sexual relations will be regarded as shameful and depraved. And Plato's argument is altogether different from the Finnis argument, since it applies perfectly generally to all sexual relations, especially those accompanied by real passion.

Notice, as well, that there is no mention of what men will and will not do outside of the *erastēs/paidika* relation, which was of special concern to Plato because of the intensities of passion to which it typically gave rise.

For example, we are not told that males will not make love with both male and female prostitutes, as in most Greek cities they could routinely be expected to do. This would presumably have been seen as a smaller danger than intercourse with the *erōmenos*, given that, rather like eating a boring meal, it would be done for release only, and not with passion. In the *Phaedo*, Plato does seem to take the position that the wise man will not have sexual intercourse at all; but in the *Republic* he follows a milder program, permitting indulgence in all the appetites "up to the point of health and well-being" (558Dff., mentioning sexual intercourse at 559C6, after eating and drinking).[89] Given the right restrictions on potentially procreative sex that are mandated by Plato's eugenic schemes,[90] it seems logical to suppose that some form of sex for release, presumably with male and/or female prostitutes,[91] would be permitted. As for the positive side of Finnis's sexual program, it is nowhere to be found, in a work that sets out in a relentless manner to extirpate the traditional family and the traditional bonds of marriage that sustained it.

Phaedrus

The dialogue contains a praise of the intellectual, political, and spiritual benefits of a life centered around male-male love, with considerable stress on the positive role of bodily desire in awakening the personality to its highest aspirations. It begins with Phaedrus reading to Socrates a speech allegedly written by the well-known orator Lysias.[92] The speech argues that a young man should give his sexual favors not to a person who is passionately in love with him, but to one who is not in love with him. The argument plays cleverly on tensions and paradoxes inherent in Athenian conventions of the time. (Notice that "Lysias" begins from the realistic assumption that an attractive young man with many suitors will "gratify" one of them, the only question being which. Rightly or wrongly, he treats the question, "Shall I at all?" as already resolved.) When the speaker holds up the advantages of an alliance that is based on excellence and friendship on one side, an interest in one's education and advancement on the other, he utters familiar truths. When he argues that these advantages are more likely to be present when the *erastēs* is not passionately in love with the younger man, but is "in control of myself," he says something not implausible; for his observations concerning the instability and inconstancy of *erōs* would themselves have seemed to the audience familiar truths. The advice to avoid the passionate suitor and to gratify the nonpassionate one is, then, on the one hand bound to seem eminently sensible[93]; on the other hand, it leaves out the wonder and divinity of *erōs*, which the Greeks strongly felt, even while they felt its dangers.[94]

After giving his own version of "Lysias'" argument, Socrates tries to leave. He is stopped by his famous *daimōn*, who always stops him when he is going to do something bad. It would be bad, he now acknowledges, to leave the blame of *erōs* unretracted. He now proposes to "purify" himself before *erōs*, whom he asserts to be a god,[95] by uttering a speech of recantation. The moving and beautiful speech that follows argues that some forms of "madness" can be the source of the greatest good for human beings, and that among these, the madness of love is the best. The arousal of the soul by a visual response to bodily beauty—a response that is described in unambiguously sexual terms and that is said to involve "the entire soul" (251B, C, D), that is, its appetitive as well as its rational elements—is said to be a crucial step in the soul's progress toward insight and metaphysical understanding.[96] The awakening is imagined throughout as that of an older man by the beauty of a younger; Socrates argues that the highest form of human life is one in which a male pursues "the love of a young man along with philosophy" (249A). He describes the experience of falling in love in moving and erotic language, rich in imagery of receptivity as well as activity (being melted, being watered, even drawing a stream of desire into oneself as through an irrigation trench [251E]).

Nor is passionate arousal a mere stage in the soul's progress: for it gives rise to an enduring relationship in which physical infatuation is deepened by conversation and the pursuit of shared spiritual goals and in which the "mad" lover's state gives rise to generous and stable friendship, rather than to the dangers warned of by "Lysias." Most remarkable of all, it also gives rise to a reciprocation of sexual desire on the part of the younger man,[97] who, taking note of the unparalleled generosity of his lover, finds himself suffused with a stream of desire from "the source of that stream which Zeus, in love with Ganymede, called 'passionate longing,'"[98] and conceives a longing and desire for his *erastēs*, "having a 'reciprocal-love' [*anterōs*] that is a replica of the other's love. But he calls it, and thinks that it is, not *erōs* but *philia*. He has desire similar to the other's, albeit weaker, to see, to touch, to kiss, to lie with him" (255D). Greek homosexuality conventionally involves reciprocity of a sort: for the *erōmenos* receives kindliness and education in return for his beauty. Plato here constructs—in a way that indicates the culturally unusual nature of the proposal, for the young man doesn't have a word to use for his own desire—a more thoroughgoing reciprocity, extending to the body's longing for beauty.[99] The relationship is envisaged as a long-lasting one, in which the two "associate with touching in the gymnasia and in other places of association" (255C).

Plato expresses views about this touching that will seem to a modern audience rather peculiar. On the one hand, he strongly endorses the lovers' bodily desire as god-sent and good, when it is a response to the way in which a body manifests traces of the soul within. (Thus, like Pausanias, he does not endorse desire that stops short at the body's surface, so to speak.)

The dialogue is remarkably erotic, and commentators of many different types have responded to it, rightly, as marking a new stage in Plato's attitude to the passions.[100] The part of the soul that represents the soul's emotions is imagined as good and as motivated by reverence and awe toward the boy's beauty. And the bodily arousal of appetite itself at the sight of bodily beauty is given extraordinary significance in the soul's progress, for it is Plato's contention that this response to bodily beauty is a crucial stage in starting the soul going on its way to truth and understanding (250DE).

But the familiar Platonic suspiciousness of the bodily appetites remains, producing the thesis that it will be best for the contemplative couple, in their search for metaphysical insight, to stop short of orgasmic gratification, although they gratify their bodily desire regularly in caresses that stop short of this. Plato's reasoning seems to be, once again, that orgasmic gratification derails the soul from its pursuit of wisdom, and also, it seems, from reverence toward the image of divinity within the younger partner. In effect he seems to believe, as in the *Republic,* that one must starve one part of the soul in order to feed another. His reasoning applies perfectly generally to all sexual activity and does not single out homosexual activity in particular, except for special praise and interest; procreative sex was quickly dismissed in a sentence as the occupation of people deficient in spirituality, rather like animals (250E). Furthermore, Plato shows much sympathy for couples who continue to have full intercourse from time to time and who think of this intercourse as a central element in their relationship.[101] These lovers, too, will recover their wings and reenter the heavens, "so that they carry off no small prize for their erotic madness" (256D). They "will live in the light and be happy traveling around with one another, and will acquire matching plumage, when they acquire it, because of their love" (256DE). Those who have avoided this sort of love will be condemned to "roll around and beneath the earth for nine thousand years" (256E–257A). Plato is very likely wrong to think that sexual activity derails aspiration and even reverent emotion; but the views he does hold here do not come close to the claim that homosexual conduct, as such, is inherently shameful and depraved. Once again: "inferior" clearly does not mean "wicked," as he unambiguously shows in his depiction of the afterlife rewards of the sexually indulgent couples.

I must now confront one remaining issue: the occurrence of the difficult phrase "contrary to nature" in an obscure description of sexual activity at 250E. The sentence reads as follows:

> The one who has not been recently initiated or whose vision has become corrupted is not sharply carried toward the vision of beauty-in-itself when he sees its earthly counterpart, so that he does not revere it when he looks

on it, but, giving himself over to pleasure, attempts to mount in the manner of a four-footed beast and to beget children, and associating with wantonness he neither fears nor is ashamed to pursue pleasure contrary to nature (250E).

Two things can be insisted on from the start. First, the reference to begetting children is really that, not some more general reference to ejaculation. This has been convincingly argued by Dover, who also points out that the picture of mounting like a four-legged animal would not surprise the Greeks, who by preference depicted (and no doubt practiced) heterosexual copulation in the *a tergo* position.[102] Second, the character who does whatever he does "contrary to nature" is the same person, a fact that most translations obscure. Plato is describing not two distinct types of people, but a single type. It is also clear what, in general terms, this type is: the type of person who pursues only bodily pleasure, a type resolutely condemned not only by Plato but by Greek cultural norms.

What, however, is meant by the reference to "contrary to nature"? Commentators have been quick to interpret the passage in the light of the modern ideas of the unnaturalness of homosexual copulation in some moral sense. Dover, with greater sensitivity to historical context, reads it in the light of the appeal to the behavior of animals in Plato's *Laws*—which, as we shall see, is itself by no means easy to understand. What we must understand is that the appeal to nature is a very slippery topic in Greek philosophy.[103] To say that something is "in accordance with nature" may indeed mean "in accordance with the behavior of other animals." But such appeals to the animal kingdom are typically associated with hedonism and immoralism—certainly they are so by Plato, who ascribes such appeals to Callicles and Philebus,[104] in defense of their self-serving hedonistic programs. Other prominent examples include the son Pheidippides in Aristophanes' *Clouds*, who learns from his new-fangled philosophical education that appeals to the animal world can help him justify beating his father.[105] To the son's gleeful assertion that the rooster fights its father, the father replies, "Why then, since you imitate the rooster in everything, don't you eat shit and sleep on a perch?" A good question—and Plato would have sympathized with it. In dialogues as diverse in date as *Gorgias, Republic,* and *Philebus,* he shows himself to be resolutely opposed to such appeals to the animal kingdom, which would establish norms for an ethical thinking creature by appeal to the behavior of a nonthinking creature. In the *Philebus* he concludes that appeal to the animal world does indeed support a hedonist thesis,[106] but that we will not give that life the first place

> even if all the cattle and horses and all the other beasts speak in its favor by their pursuit of pleasure—creatures trusting in whom, as diviners trust their

birds, the many judge that pleasures are the most important thing in living well, and they think that the passionate loves of beasts (*tous thēriōn erōtas*) are authoritative witnesses, rather than the loves of those arguments that are divined on each occasion by the philosophic muse (*Philebus* 67B).

Nor do nonhuman animals fare well in the *Phaedrus* itself: for Socrates holds that a soul that saw nothing of the eternal Forms would be put into an animal body, since being human requires the intellectual grasp that only a sight of the Forms would deliver (248D, 249B). The people described in 250E, then, are human beings who are on the borderline of the human-animal divide, incapable of the loves of those who are further away from the beast. So it would be very odd to find their sexual behavior criticized on the ground that it is *not animal;* and of course the child-begetters have just been criticized, predictably, precisely on the ground that their behavior *is animal*. We may add that the term *phusis* is used elsewhere in Socrates' speech not to designate the animal kingdom but to designate the specific "nature" of the divinity within each human (253A1) and the "nature" of the beauty that each pursues (254B5–6).

The best solution to this problem seems to be the one offered by Christopher Rowe and now accepted by Kenneth Dover: the pleasure of these people is "against nature" "because it is the pleasure of an animal, not a man."[107] In other words, it is against their specific nature as humans (which Plato, as often, understands in a particularly intellectualistic way). This makes the criticism a unity: both in child-begetting and in other sexual activity, the person in question behaves like an animal, in that he pursues pleasure without an interest in the soul. But what other sexual activities are mentioned in the second part of the sentence? Are they both heterosexual and homosexual, exclusively heterosexual, or exclusively homosexual? There seem to be three possibilities: either the sentence means, "he begets children, and in so doing wantonly pursues pleasure in an animal fashion," or, "he begets children, and in general wantonly pursues pleasure in an animal fashion in all of his sexual activities," or it means "he pursues pleasure animalistically with women, begetting children, and also animalistically with men, having sex for pleasure only, unconstrained by shame and reverence for the soul." The third reading seems to me preferable,[108] and we note that one and the same person, or type of person, may well be envisaged in both roles: for it is standard to think of hedonism and wantonness as giving rise to an indiscriminate pursuit of both females and males.[109] What we have, then, is a commonplace of the culture, given a new Platonic sharpness: a stern criticism of the hedonist, who in all his sexual acts behaves like an animal, indifferent to the soul. The departure from standard cultural norms consists in understanding child-begetting itself as a merely animal act; this is to be explained by Plato's tendency to equate human nature with intellectual Form-seeing nature. None of this implies that all homosexual copulation is "contrary to nature" in some normative sense; and indeed that suggestion would be hard to square with Plato's treatment of the intercourse of the second-best couples.

In short: the *Phaedrus* offers a stirring defense of male-male desire and love and gives an extraordinary role to erotic love within the life of philosophical aspiration. If full genital intercourse is viewed with standard Platonic suspiciousness, this does not arise from any particular condemnation of homosexual relations; other types of sex fare worse. And bodily acts stopping short of orgasm are endorsed in vivid and moving terms.

Laws[110]

It is sometimes thought that in the *Laws* Plato offers a general condemnation of homosexual relations in a way that singles them out for special moral blame. Even if this were true we would at most be able to say that he had for some reason changed his mind, and we would have to look for his reasoning.[111] But I believe that once we establish the Greek text of the two problematic passages in the most accurate way—a difficult paleographical and text-critical challenge—and peel away layers of mistranslation and overtranslation, things look different. Here I can only summarize my conclusions:[112]

(1) Plato's overall worry is, once again, about bodily pleasure generally and its ability to take over the personality, disrupting reason.[113] He appears to have, in addition, a special worry about the loss of male bodily fluids that are important for reproduction, in connection with his persistent worries about population.[114] (2) Homosexual conduct is not singled out for special blame. The final law regulates all forms of extramarital activity. Married sex, furthermore, does better not because it is thought to *be* better (morally) but simply because it is necessary for the city.[115] (3) Insofar as particular attention is devoted to homosexual relations, it is because they are thought to be especially powerful sources of passionate stimulation, not because they are thought to be especially depraved or shameful.[116] The criticism of those who indulge in the active role is that they are intemperate and overindulgent, not that they are wicked. Nor does Plato suggest that the *desire* for such relations is diseased, depraved, or anything but natural and normal. As for the younger partner, the fear, as elsewhere in Greek culture, is that he will be turned into a woman; and it is this worry about passivity, rather than any worry about same-sex conduct in particular, that inspires that aspect of Plato's critique. (4) Plato's characters suggest that the surrounding society will find regulation of homosexual conduct unacceptable. (5) The passages contain several peculiarities that must make us cautious in our assertions. These include: (a)

the expression of doubt as to whether the proposed regulations are a joke or in earnest—in close connection to an appeal to animal nature, which might arouse some skepticism in a chronic reader of Plato; (b) the idea—made part of the proposal—that it is "noble" to engage in such conduct provided one does not get caught; (c) the fact that the eventual legislation is addressed only to males envisaged as having wives and thus has no clear implications for premarital behavior or the behavior of women (whose involvement in same-sex activity has been prominently mentioned before). (6) Plato clearly does not hold Finnis's view either about the high moral worth of marital sex or about openness to procreation. He thinks marital sex necessary, not fine; and elsewhere in the *Laws* he is an enthusiastic supporter of methods traditionally used to keep population size down if it is likely to get too high. Such methods would include contraception and abortion. The "greatest and most honorable" ministry in the city oversees *both* fertility treatment and contraception/abortion (740D).

For all these reasons, it seems wrong to think that we find, even here, any basis either for the positive Finnis view of marital sex or for the view that homosexual conduct is any worse morally than any other sort of sexual conduct.[117] The most important thing to realize about these passages is how difficult they are to interpret and how mistaken it would be to put forward any simple view without recognizing all the difficulties I have mentioned, and others.

In general, Plato is, among the philosophers I consider here, by far the most suspicious about the bodily appetites; he thus diverges more from ordinary Greek norms. But the divergence is not total: as I have argued, we may still find ample continuity between his norms and the views of Athenian society, together with a rather extraordinary account of the philosophical dividends of male-male erotic desire.

Aristotle

Aristotle speaks far less about sexual matters than does Plato. It is evident that like most Greeks he does not find the sexual appetite per se problematic. Indeed, he argues that the innate desires of a human being incline toward virtue: "All the virtues of character seem to belong to us from birth in a way. For we are just and moderate and courageous and the rest straight from our birth. . . . Even children and animals have these natural dispositions, though they evidently prove harmful without rational guidance" (*Nicomachean Ethics* VI.13, 1144b3ff.). The virtue of moderation includes proper balance in choices with respect to sexual conduct: so Aristotle is holding here (among other things) that we are inclined from birth to balanced and appropriate choice in the sexual realm—though of course it requires much education for those inclinations to mature into a fully virtuous disposition.[118] In general, then, Aristotle lacks Plato's intense anxiety about our bodily desires in general and our sexual desires in particular.

If we turn now to his account of the virtue of moderation, we find that for him it "concerns those pleasures that we have in common with the other animals" (*EN* 1118a23–5): he explicitly mentions eating, drinking, and sexual intercourse, and states that the bodily senses involved are, above all, those of touch and taste. Because we share these pleasures with the other animals, it becomes especially important to characterize, and strive for, a specifically human way of performing them (see *EN* 1118a25). This way will be to manage the use of these appetites by one's own practical reason. The vicious person Aristotle imagines is totally indiscriminate in his choice of pleasures (1119a1–3). The virtuous person, by contrast, integrates bodily expression into the framework of an overall plan of life governed by reason. But this does not mean that he seeks to reduce bodily expression to a minimum. For there is a deficiency of another sort that a virtuous person must also avoid: having too little pleasure in these forms of bodily expression. Aristotle mentions that this deficiency has no common name in the language, since "that does not happen very often" (*EN* 1119a6, 11). Indeed, he continues, "such a lack of feeling is not human; in fact, even the other animals make selections of food, and take pleasure in some types and not in others. If there is someone to whom none of these things is pleasant, and one thing does not differ from another, he would be far from being a human being" (*EN* 1111a6–10). (Although Aristotle's example here is eating, the passage as a whole leaves no doubt that he is making a general claim about all the bodily appetites, since he generalizes throughout the passage.) The person who strikes the correct balance, he concludes, will "desire as many pleasures as conduce to health or well-being, in a balanced way and as he should, and other pleasures insofar as they do not impede these or do not contravene the noble or exceed the limits of one's material resources" (*EN* 1119a16–18).[119] In other words, one's sexual choices, like others, should not lead one into excess or ill-health or disgrace or extravagance; properly managed, however, sex can actually be valuable and choiceworthy for its own sake. It is important to note that every virtuous action is, by definition, an end in itself, chosen for its own sake apart from any relation it bears to other ends. This is Aristotle's position about reason-governed sexual activity. It need not be justified by any further end it may promote, such as reproduction; properly chosen, it is good in itself.

Aristotle's views are closely related to the popular Greek norms I have previously discussed. As in the popular culture, we find (1) a refusal to treat sex as specially problematic in moral terms—it is just one of the appetites to be managed, like the appetite for food; and (2) the absence of any special connection between the management of sexual appetite and the topic of marriage. In fact, marriage is not mentioned in the entirety of the discussion of appetitive moderation. Aristotle nowhere urges husbands to practice sexual monogamy, though they should not go after the wives of other citizens. Nor is any reservation expressed concerning the gender of one's sexual partner.[120]

There is one passage in which Finnis has repeatedly claimed[121] to find an Aristotelian condemnation of same-sex activity, and I shall now discuss it. In *Nicomachean Ethics* VII.5, Aristotle lists some forms of conduct that are not "pleasant by nature" but result from some "deformities or habits or corrupt natures." First he discusses a sub-class of these that he calls "bestial," and the examples are a man who takes pleasure in slitting open pregnant women and eating their children, the cannibalism of the wild people of Pontos, the sale of children for sexual services, and Phalaris, who liked to boil people in cauldrons. That, he says, is the "bestial" category, but then there are other related forms of conduct that come about through disease—for example someone who ate his mother and someone else who ate another man's liver, when these people were mad; and then, finally, there are some that arise from either sickness or habit, "for example pulling out one's hair and biting one's nails, and eating coal or earth, and, in addition to these, the of [*sic*] sexual intercourse toward men. For some of these things are by nature, some happen from habit, and some to those who are subjected to abuse from childhood" (*EN* 1148b28–31). He continues, "Concerning all those things for which nature is responsible, nobody would hold that these are akratic [cases of blameworthy knowing-the-better and doing-the-worse], just as one would not hold this about women, on the grounds that they do not mount but are mounted" (1148b32–3).

The first thing to notice about this list is the way Aristotle carves it up. In none of the cases does he assign moral blame, since he thinks these people in the grip of a diseased state for which they cannot be held responsible (1148b33–49a2). But the crimes come in various categories; and the male-male case, whatever it is, is grouped not with the hideous and gory crimes but with familiar if somewhat gross habits like hair-pulling and fingernail biting. There is absolutely no evidence that Aristotle wished to regulate such forms of behavior by law or that he thought them a danger to society.[122] Second, the treatment of nature in the passage is in fact complex. It appears to me that Aristotle is shifting from a normative and universal sense of nature—these things are not "pleasant by nature" in the sense of "in accordance with our ethical end as human beings"—to a descriptive and particular sense, in which many of these actions are in fact "according to nature" for particular individuals, in the sense of being in accordance with the (odd or diseased) constitution that they happen to have. Once again, we must be on our guard when nature is mentioned, for it is a slippery concept in ancient thought. Aristotle here holds that the fact that something is in accordance with one's "nature" exempts one from moral blame for it—although that will not stop people from rightly regarding the conduct in question as gross or offensive.

What is the conduct in question, in the male-male case? The phrase is simply "the of sexual intercourse toward men." The "the" is a feminine article, which presumably introduces an unstated noun; this noun, to judge from context, would appear to be *hexis*, "stable state," "disposition." Kenneth Dover, Anthony Price, and Terence Irwin have all argued independently that what is referred to is a stable or chronic state of preferring passivity toward other men and that what Aristotle is saying about it is that this state can be produced by repeated sexual abuse in childhood. Dover argues as follows:

> Perhaps distaste for the subject has prevented translators and commentators from discussing the curious words, "the of sexual intercourse for males" and has induced them to translate it as 'pederasty', 'faire l'amour avec les mâles,' etc. If that translation were correct, Aristotle would be saying that subjection to a passive role in homosexuality when young disposes one to take an active role when older. This would be a strange thing for a Greek to say; it would also be strange for a Greek to suggest that pleasure in an active homosexual role is 'disease-like' or unlikely to be experienced except in consequence of involuntary habituation; the example of the passive sexual role of women as naturally-determined behaviour which cannot be reproached as a lack of control over bodily pleasure indicates that Aristotle's mind is running on the moral evaluation of sexual passivity.[123]

It should be noted that Dover translates the relevant phrase in the *Ethics* passage as "those who were first outraged in childhood," making it clear that he believes that child abuse or assault is at issue. Dover then goes on to adduce as further evidence a passage in the *Problemata*, a work produced by pupils in Aristotle's school, in which the male taste for *habitual passivity* toward males is explained in a similar manner, as resulting either from a defective physiology or from habits of passivity.[124] Dover now comments further on Aristotle's cryptic expression of the point at issue. He suggests that the odd dative may mean "the sexual pleasure *of* males," and that it is dative only because *tōn aphrodisiōn* is already in the genitive. He continues:

> It seems to me likely that A. expects us to understand *tōn aphrodisiōn* here as referring to *sexual enjoyment in the passive role;* and it doesn't occur to him that it could be ambiguous, because when he's introduced the subject in the category of things that go wrong he wouldn't expect any reader to

regard *penetrating* as going wrong—it's something that all males must naturally like!

In other words, the phrase means a chronic disposition *in a male* to find sexual enjoyment in the passive role.

In a similar manner, Price[125] interprets the passage as referring to a man's "playing the female role" in a way caused by "some pathological state produced by habituation to sexual abuse from boyhood." (By abuse he means not only actual rape but also seduction at an age too young for meaningful consent.) He observes that Dover "rightly stresses that Aristotle is thinking of sexual inversion in particular (which the Greeks disparaged), and not homosexuality in general (which they were far from conceiving as a unitary quasi-medical condition). It is striking that he is not concerned, as we might be, that a sexually abused boy may abuse other boys in his turn; it is habitual passivity, and not imitative activity, that he sees as the danger."

Note that for neither Dover nor Price does the passage condemn the role that an adolescent male might play toward an older male in approved intercrural intercourse (or even, perhaps, the occasional anal act—see above); the problem is developing *habits* of enjoying passivity.[126]

Aristotle so far, then, does not differ from the standard beliefs of Greek culture regarding homosexuality. But he says so little about the topic that we might remain dissatisfied. Anthony Price has now shown, however, that he in fact says much more than previous commentators had realized. By supplementing the meager data of the ethical works with scattered remarks on the topic of erotic love in the logical and rhetorical treatises, Price assembles a composite picture that places Aristotle very close to the speech of Pausanias in the *Symposium* and close as well (although Price does not say this) to the view of the Greek Stoics who followed Aristotle; all, in turn, are close to the Greek popular norms I discussed. Price's argument has the drawback that it does rely to some extent on examples given in the logical works, where Aristotle is not clearly developing a view of his own but may simply be using hypothetical examples to make a logical point; the use of the *Rhetoric* is open to similar criticism. But insofar as Price has been able to link these remarks to passages in Aristotle's ethical writings—and in most respects he has successfully done this—we may cautiously put the picture forward as what may have formed the contents of Aristotle's lost writings on erotic love.[127]

The picture that emerges, briefly stated, is as follows: male-male erotic relationships are frequently deficient in mutuality and friendliness because of the inherent inequality of the parties. On the other hand, the real aim of (at least some cases of) *erōs* is not intercourse, but friendly love: intercourse is "an end relative to the receiving of affection" (*Prior Analytics*

68b6). Sexual love, unlike other types of friendly love, must be inspired by a visual response to bodily beauty (*EN* 1171b29–31, 1167a3–4), and the way this beauty awakens imagination (*Rhet.* 1307b 19–25). But lovers naturally seek not just the satisfaction of their desire, but also its return (*EE* 1238b32–9): thus erotic love points toward a certain degree of mutuality in affection and perhaps also in desire. Thus, over time, "Aristotle envisages the emergence of that reciprocal concern and respect which constitute the best kind of friendship, linking individuals not merely as satisfiers of one another's incidental needs, but as partners in a life of personal self-realization. The moral end of love is to transcend itself in friendship." [128] Or, as Price puts it more recently, "Aristotle allows that a homosexual relationship may fuel a mutual familiarity that leads in time to his ideal of friendship—the cultivation of a shared moral character in and through cooperative activities." [129]

Will sexual intercourse be a part of this picture? Price stresses Aristotle's anxiety (an anxiety that he shares with Greek culture) about the development of habits of passivity in the younger partner. He inclines to the conclusion that—not out of moral or metaphysical concerns, but out of medical concerns—Aristotle will want pederasty to focus on "'looking rather than loving', as Plato had put it" (citing *Laws* 837c4–5). I see no evidence at all in the text for this conclusion, and if Aristotle had intended a conclusion so far from conventional Greek practice one might have expected him to state it. As Price himself states, "Aristotle's moral attitudes, as all agree, were more typical of the Greeks of his time than Plato's." [130] The only evidence for anxiety about the young man's passivity is the passage I have already discussed, in which Price rightly argues that the danger is the production of a certain sort of womanish habit by repeated coercion in childhood. Surely the intercourse envisaged by Pausanias—which begins when the young man has reached the age of judgment and which presumably carefully avoids engendering "womanish" habits (focusing on intercrural intercourse)—would not court this risk. I see no reason to conclude that Aristotle differed from Pausanias, from the Stoics, and from the prevalent cultural norm, regarding the conditions under which sexual intercourse would be appropriate. [131]

To summarize, it is perfectly clear that the active homosexual role is judged by Aristotle (as interpreted by Dover, by Price, and by me) to be morally unproblematic; for an adult man to visit a male prostitute would incur no blame—except in the sense that it will be better to have, as well, at least some relationships in which one links desire with friendship and kindly intentions. [132] Nor, as Price and I now agree, would sexual conduct between an older male and an adolescent of the appropriate *erōmenos* age be problematic, provided it observed the cultural protocols discussed above. We may add that marital fidelity could not supply the Aristotelian husband with a motive for avoiding male-male conduct, since Aristotle never mentions a duty of sexual fidelity in marriage.

The Hellenistic philosophers who followed Aristotle are an extremely important part of the general history of attitudes to sexual conduct in the Greco-Roman world. Since they were not central to Finnis's claims, however, and since I examine their contribution elsewhere, I shall not discuss them here.[133]

We may summarize: All of the major Greek philosophers concur in and develop the Greek popular norm, according to which erotic relationships are better if they focus on the soul rather than simply the body and seek stable friendly love rather than unstable and promiscuous passion. And all believe that same-sex sexual desire, including a characteristic orientation of that desire, can be an extremely valuable element in human life, expressive of goods of love and friendship and powerfully linked to other social and intellectual ends. Relationships that involve sexual desire of this kind can be a major vehicle of human aspiration and are generally deemed more valuable as vehicles than are marital relationships, whose ends are generally assumed to be less profound. Aristotle, like Plato's Pausanias and Aristophanes (and like the later Stoics), has no objection to sexual conduct, either homosexual or heterosexual, provided that it is performed with the right motives and ends. Plato's position on orgasmic gratification is complex and varies during his career. He never holds that same-sex touching and caressing are bad things, so far as I can see; nor does he ever hold that orgasmic gratification is wicked and depraved. But he does, in *Phaedrus* and *Laws,* hold it inferior to a nonorgasmic eroticism, in which the appetitive part of the soul offers fewer distractions to reason. He holds this on grounds of his general suspiciousness of appetite, not on grounds of any special worries about the same-sex acts. Marital acts fare worse than same-sex acts in *Symposium* and *Phaedrus* (in the latter of which same-sex copulators get rewards from the gods, but child-begetters are simply condemned as animal). The position of the *Republic* is unclear, for the reasons I have given. Marital acts fare better than same-sex and extramarital acts in *Laws*—not because they are thought to be finer but because the city has to have them; and the text has the many peculiarities that I noted.

V

I now return to my four claims about the relevance of the ancient philosophical tradition; in the process I shall be able to answer the moral arguments produced by Finnis.

Looking at ancient Greek culture should have for us today the same result it did for Richard Posner: that is, if we look at the Greeks not as projected images of ourselves but as they really were, in all their differences from us, we will be shaken into seeing that many things we are accustomed to think neutral and natural are actually parochial. As Michel Foucault wrote in the introduction to his study of Greek sexuality, the Greeks "free [our] thought from what it silently thinks, and so enable it to think differently." [134] We see, in particular, that it was possible not to single out the sexual appetite from the other appetites as a source of special anxiety and shame; that it was possible not to categorize persons in accordance with a binary division between the homosexual and the heterosexual; that it was possible to regard the gender of one's sexual partner as just one factor in a sexual coupling and not the most morally relevant at that; that it was possible to hold that same-sex relationships are not only not per se shameful but potentially of high spiritual and social value. None of these need make the committed Christian change his judgments; it does, however, make the Christian ask on what evidence and argument the judgments are based. This is especially important for the Catholic natural-law tradition, which claims to derive its conclusions from reason, not from authority. We need, then, reasoned argument, since we see that our own judgments are not the only ones in the world. We need to be sure that we have distinguished between prejudice and reasoned argument.

Second, when we look at the Greeks—and in general we look at them as a culture that we admire, that we consider successful as a culture, the source of some of our deepest ideas and most cherished cultural artifacts—we notice that the presence of same-sex relationships in both Athens and Sparta did not have the result so frequently mentioned in modern debate, not least in Colorado: the result, that is, of eroding the social fabric, or, as Professor Harvey Mansfield argued, causing the downfall of civilization. In fact we find widespread in Athens—as witness, for example, the speeches in Plato's *Symposium* and *Phaedrus*—the view that encouraging such relationships is a fine way of building up or strengthening the social fabric, since such pairs of lovers, through their special devotion to courage and political liberty, contribute more together than each would separately. Indeed, we notice that Pausanias, in Plato's *Symposium*, spoke of the resistance to such relationships in Asia as a strategy adopted by tyrants, for the purposes of discouraging "high aspirations in the ruled—[and] strong friendly loves and associations, which . . . *erōs* is especially likely to create" (182C). (For similar reasons, they discourage gymnastics and philosophy!) Once again, we are put on guard against the possible presence of prejudice and bias in our arguments.

In addition to the use of history to "free thought" and to test social hypotheses, I have said that this particular part of philosophy's history is significant because of the intrinsic interest of the moral arguments it develops on this issue. I believe that, although Finnis's moral argument might be criticized independently, a consideration of ancient Greek arguments give us great help in developing that critique. For Greek texts show, and show repeatedly, that the passionate love of two people of the same sex may serve many valuable social goals apart from procreation. They may communicate love, friendship, and joy; they may advance shared political, intellectual, and artistic ends. Finnis has no argument to rule this out: he has only the bare assertion that such people are in the grip of an illusion because their reproductive organs are not forming a genuine biological unity. The Greeks show us that this is not the only sort of unity in passion that may promote a human good.

Kenneth Dover, having read Professor Finnis's account of Greek homosexuality, comments upon it in the same vein:

> The Greeks were well aware that many homosexual relationships did what the participants hoped and imagined, neither more nor less. If the participants imagined that they were achieving something which for biological reasons they could not achieve, then of course they would have been pursuing an illusion; but why should they have imagined that? [135]

Finally, reading the Greeks has value in our moral and legal deliberations on this issue for the way in which they invite us to share the passionate longing of these same-sex lovers, to be moved by their hopes and anxieties and their eventual joy. The reader of the *Symposium* and the *Phaedrus* is not very likely to remain someone who thinks of people who choose same-sex partners as altogether alien and weird—as do, for example, the majority and concurring opinions in *Bowers v. Hardwick*. Indeed, reading these moving narratives is itself a form of emotional and imaginative receptivity; to allow those stories, those people, inside oneself is not only to gain an education in empathy for those particular people. It is to exemplify some of the very characteristics of receptivity and sympathetic imagination that homophobia seeks to cordon off and to avoid.

I might add that I believe the compassionate imagining of another person's suffering and joy lies at the heart of what is finest in the Christian ethical tradition. In that sense, studying the Greeks might promote Christian virtue.

VI

There are several objections one might make to this appeal to history. I cannot deal with every possible objection here, but let me address what seem to me to be the most prominent.

The first objection says that the high-minded couplings depicted by Plato have little in common with today's promiscuous gay scene. [136] I think that I do not need to spend so very much time on this one, since it contains a distorted picture of today's world and the aspirations of men and women within it. Even in Plato's time, promiscuous relations were well known, and Pausanias criticizes them; today, on the other hand, deep love and friendship are very well known, so that, on this side too, the asymmetry has not been demonstrated.

And in fact, studying the Greek world may tell us something interesting about the issue of promiscuity: for it tells us that a society that in general tolerated same-sex relationships could be as critical of promiscuity as any and as interested in deeper relationships based on friendly love. The Greeks therefore make us ask skeptical questions about any hasty claim that same-sex relations are inherently linked with promiscuity or superficiality, claims that were sometimes made in the context of Amendment 2.

A second objection is far more interesting. It is that the ancient sexual scene is so different in its basic categories from our world that there is no straightforward mapping of today's homosexuals onto ancient Greek actors. What was salient then is different from what is salient now, and to that extent the ancient world lacked the modern conception of "the homosexual," a person with a lifelong disposition toward partners of the same gender. This point, which has been developed by some writers I admire,[137] says important things about the two cultures, with many of which I agree. But three observations must now be made. First, this asymmetry does not help the argument of John Finnis: for when he criticizes homosexual conduct in his Affidavit, he individuates actions extensionally, not taking into account the thoughts of the parties about the sort of act they are committing. For many people if not most, he holds, are in the grip of illusion; what is really morally relevant is the classification by gender and marital relation that can be performed by a neutral observer. And in this sense there will be no problem in comparing the two cultures, as Finnis enthusiastically does. Second, we must now observe that this asymmetry between cultures is exactly what reading the Greeks is supposed (in my argument) to reveal to us: namely, it is supposed to reveal to us the fact that a society may tolerate and even encourage sexual acts between members of the same sex *without* regarding this as the most morally salient feature about the act and without problematizing same-sex desire itself in a special way. The presence of asymmetry does not defeat the comparative project, it is what makes it interesting. Finally, we should note that any characterization of the Greeks that pushes this discontinuity to the limiting point of total noncomparability, denying that the Greeks had any conception of an erotic preference for members of one's own gender, is clearly refuted by the evidence of Plato: for both Pausanias and Aristophanes know and casually refer to people who have such stable preferences, indicating as they do so that they are referring to a widely accepted fact about human life. Such people may, they assert, also marry and have children, while continuing to have same-sex relations: to that extent their form of life is indeed different from that of many modern homosexuals, though certainly not all. But their preference for same-sex acts is held to be both stable and a deep fact about their personalities.

The third and most interesting objection to the cross-cultural comparison is the claim that the Greeks' high evaluation of same-sex activity is inseparable from Greek misogyny and the widespread Greek belief that one's deepest loves and aspirations and political goals could not possibly be shared with a mere woman. To that extent, shouldn't we rule out using the Greeks as a sign of what we might be, even in the very limited sense of that idea suggested by my argument?

I see no reason why one should draw this conclusion. First of all, the historical evidence indicates that encouragement of same-sex relationships varies to a large extent independently of women's role. In Sparta women had far greater freedom and power than at Athens; but Spartan culture gave especially prominent endorsement to same-sex relationships, both female and male. And we must recall at this point that the existence of same-sex relations among women also complicates the picture.

Second, the philosophers give us strong reasons for doubting that an interest in sex-equality need be linked with a tendency to denigrate same-sex relations. Plato probably taught women in his school and certainly argues most seriously for their equal education; he praises relationships that are rich in spiritual and intellectual value, and in his own culture these are most likely to be between males. But there is nothing in his argument itself to prevent an extension of the norm of love, in connection with the extension of the educational norm. In Aristotle too, although the woman remains incompletely equal, there is an ideal of friendly love and reciprocity in both same-sex and opposite-sex relations. As Anthony Price puts it very well in his recent book, in both same- and opposite-sex relations "Aristotle envisages the emergence of that reciprocal concern and respect which constitute the best kind of friendship, linking individuals not merely as satisfiers of one another's incidental needs, but as partners in a life of personal self-realization." [138] Such Platonic and Aristotelian norms deeply influenced later Stoic and Epicurean reconceptualizations of marriage as a genuine partnership. And the Stoics evidently wished their ideal city to contain not only male-male but also male-female (and possibly also female-female) sexual partnerships, in connection with their norm of gender equality. Indeed, in their view a just city will minimize gender as a salient feature, adopting, for example, a unisex style of dress. All this suggests a close connection between women's equality and an indifference to the gender of one's sexual partner. [139] Equally important, both Platonic and Stoic arguments tell us that the encouragement of same-sex relations of the best sort will promote a general attention to questions of social justice and that a concerted attention to social justice will lead, down the road, to women's equality. This seems to be a set of connections well worth exploring.

Finally, we can all think for ourselves, and see that the Greeks' defense of same-sex relationships as containing important human goods is in fact completely independent of misogyny, both logically and empirically, no matter what the Greeks themselves thought on this point. For we can see, among other things, the great support that feminism has received from same-sex relations, both female and male. And we can notice that desire to enforce traditional gender boundaries has been a major source of resistance to the goals of both feminists and lesbian and gay people, in closely connected ways: so it seems reasonable to suppose that the historically guided rethinking of the sexual-orientation boundary may also free our minds to think differently about gender more broadly.[140]

In short: the equation of the ancient with the modern should not be done in a facile and historically naive way. Indeed, we will not reap the benefits of the comparison if we do not remain vigilant for difference, for it is difference from which we wish to learn. But with the proper caution the comparison may be extremely fruitful.

VII

There are many morals that I could draw in concluding. I could talk about the importance of incorporating this sort of study of the history of sexuality into the liberal arts curricula of universities, so that judges will not have to get this material from expert witnesses but will know it already. I could talk, too, about the urgent practical importance of more philological and historical work on these texts and issues, work that would make available to the legal profession and the public at large the full and accurate story about ancient sexual norms. Dover's wonderful book is indispensable, but it is not sufficient. We need a companion volume on the philosophical tradition.

But instead of dwelling further on this point, I wish to turn, instead, to a different Platonic point in concluding. It is the importance of facing this issue with reason. Plato shows us nothing more clearly, time and time again, than the way in which prejudice can be dispelled by rational argument. His dialogues show us people who intensely disagree. But so long as they are willing to stay in the argument and participate in it sincerely, there is every reason to think that prejudice will eventually fall away and what is of real moral interest will remain. As he has Socrates remark in the *Republic*, apropos of the equal education of women, things that are strange at first inspire mockery or loathing; but over time this is dispelled by reason's judgment about the best.

I do not deny that forces impervious to reason can be identified in this situation. I have seen some of them up close, and it has made me vividly aware of a world that is not the world of scholarship. But I do say this: that if the game is simply power, the powerless will always lose; that to defend the basic civil rights of the powerless we need, therefore, reason, a force whose dignity is not proportional to its sheer strength. I am convinced that reason does support basic civil rights on this issue. If we fight with any other weapon we will have given our adversaries the greatest victory that they could possibly win, that of debasing our humanity. But I believe that if we face the issue with good history, precise scholarship, and valid moral argument, we will prevail over prejudice in our judicial system.

NOTES

1. Richard A. Posner, *Sex and Reason* (Cambridge, Mass.: Harvard University Press, 1992), 2.

2. *Sex and Reason,* 2. Posner here says that the superficiality of the opinions does not imply that the decision is wrong; but later in the book he does argue the later position, as we shall see.

3. *Sex and Reason,* 347.

4. *Sex and Reason,* 346, states that "statutes which criminalize homosexual behavior express an irrational fear and loathing of a group that has been subjected to discrimination, much like that directed against the Jews, with whom indeed homosexuals . . . were frequently bracketed in medieval persecutions. . . . There is a gratuitousness, an egregiousness, a cruelty, and a meanness about the Georgia statute that could be thought to place it in the same class with Connecticut's anti-contraceptive law."

5. *Sex and Reason,* 4.

6. US v. Siekny Lallemand, 7th Circuit Court of Appeals, 29 March 1993. The question before Posner was whether Lallemand, who had deliberately set out to blackmail a married homosexual with two children, deserved an upward departure in sentencing under the Federal guidelines for what is called "unusually vulnerable victim." Given that all blackmail victims are persons with guilty secrets, what was special about this one, a married government employee who had attempted suicide when approached by Lallemand with the blackmail demand? The answer lies, Posner argues, in current American mores, which do treat this sexual secret as different from many others.

7. See *The Fragility of Goodness: Luck and Ethics in Greek Tragedy and Philosophy* (Cambridge: Cambridge University Press), chapter 6. Hereafter *FG*.

8. Plato, *Symposium* 189C–193D.

9. "They are struck in a wonderful way with friendly love and intimacy and passionate desire, and are hardly willing to be apart from one another for even a short time." (192 BC).

10. Aristophanes clearly prefers the male-male pairs, whom he characterizes as motivated to intercourse "not by shamelessness but by bravery and courage and

manliness, welcoming one who is similar to themselves" (192A). He claims that only this sort become *politikoi*—and says that they will marry only if coerced by the law. But his description of the joyful love of the reunited "other halves" is explicitly said to apply to all three types: "both the lover of youths and any other one," 192B7. Kenneth Dover (*Plato: Symposium*, Cambridge 1980, note on this passage) argues that Aristophanes is joking here, along the lines of other jokes in comedy that make fun of an alleged similarity between politicians and those who give sex for money. But in that case we would not expect Aristophanes to say, as he does, that the *erōmenoi*, when older, become active *erastai*; we would expect him to focus on chronic passivity, as he does not. Since Aristophanes' statements here are so much in line with what Phaedrus and Pausanias seriously say, it would be difficult for a reader to take them as joking, without a much clearer signal. I would therefore argue that we have Plato making fun of his foe Aristophanes but putting his own serious ideas (ideas Aristophanes would have treated comically) into Aristophanes' own mouth. Dover now agrees with this argument.

11. Much of my testimony concerned an entirely different issue, the status of same-sex domestic partner law in Scandinavia, where I have spent some years as a consultant with a United Nations institute concerned with quality-of-life issues.

12. Finnis, Affidavit of 8 October 1993, para. 47.

13. Ibid., para. 46. Far less plausible, however, is the premise that Finnis also endorses, that it is always morally bad to use one's own body as an instrument of one's pleasure. As Kenneth Dover and I argue in our coauthored statement, Finnis has no consistent way of assailing masturbation while approving of such innocuous activities as hiking, or going for a swim, or smelling a rose.

14. Ibid., para. 46.

15. Ibid., para. 47.

16. Ibid., para. 47.

17. Ibid., para 47.

18. Cf., for example, para. 4: "it harms the personalities of its participants by its disintegrative manipulation of different parts of their one personal reality."

19. Here see Kenneth J. Dover, "Greek Sexual Choices," a review of David Halperin's *One Hundred Years of Homosexuality*, in *The Classic Review* (1991): "choice of sexual object has a history which becomes intelligible in proportion to our readiness to shed our belief in the inescapable naturalness of our own assumptions."

20. Cf. Dover, *Greek Homosexuality* (Cambridge, Mass.: Harvard University Press, 1980), hereafter *GH*, vii: "A combination of love of Athens with a hatred of homosexuality underlies the judgments that homosexual relations were 'a Dorian sin cultivated by a tiny minority at Athens' (J. A. K. Thomson, ignoring the evidence of the visual arts) or that they were 'regarded as disgraceful both by law and . . . by general opinion' (A. E. Taylor, ignoring the implication of the text to which he refers in his footnote)." In a personal communication of 11 February 1994, Dover calls Taylor's statement a "grossly false statement." On the history of British classical scholarship on this topic, see Linda Dowling, *Hellenism and Homosexuality in Victorian Oxford* (Ithaca, N.Y.: Cornell University Press, 1994), passim.

21. Dover, letter. In the longer version of the article I give numerous examples

of these phenomena, many of them taken from my experience as assessor of the philosophical translations of the Loeb Classical Library, which, as it happens, was the series of translations relied upon throughout by Finnis.

22. On all major points I am in agreement with the conclusions of Kenneth J. Dover, *Greek Homosexuality* (Cambridge, Mass.: Harvard University Press, 1978, second edition 1989); see also Dover, *Plato: Symposium* (Cambridge: Cambridge University Press, 1980), a work less fully available to the lawyer because it is a commentary on the Greek text; but the main points can be easily grasped.

23. Finnis, Affidavit of 8 October, para. 32.

24. Dover, *GH,* 67–68.

25. See Dover, *GH,* 1–17, and also Dover, *Greek Popular Morality in the Time of Plato and Aristotle* (Oxford: Oxford University Press, 1975); hereafter *GPM.*

26. The degree of reticence varies, of course, with the genre; and even in lyric and tragedy, one discovers passages of an explicitly sexual character (see remarks below on Sappho and Aeschylus' *Myrmidons*). Interestingly, these two examples of explicitness are both homosexual; I cannot recall a case of similar heterosexual explicitness in early lyric or in tragedy.

27. See Dover, *GPM.*

28. Aristophanes' surviving plays were produced in Athens between 425 and 388 B.C.; few surviving comic fragments in general can be positively dated earlier.

29. See my "Eros and the Wise: The Stoic Response to a Cultural Dilemma," *Oxford Studies in Ancient Philosophy* 1995.

30. The best treatment of Artemidoros on sex is in John J. Winkler, "Unnatural Acts," *The Constraints of Desire* (New York: Routledge, 1990), 17–44. Winkler also translates the relevant passages in an Appendix, 210–16. The only complete English translation, by Robert White (Park Ridge, New Jersey: Noyes Press, 1975), is seriously defective and should not be trusted.

31. Winkler, 24.

32. See Dover, *GH,* 8.

33. In *The Use of Pleasure,* volume 2 of *The History of Sexuality,* translated by R. Hurley (New York: Pantheon, 1985), 38–52.

34. For some examples from the philosophers, see below, and Aristotle *EN* III.5–6, Plato, *Republic* 436 Bff., *Phaedrus* 238AB, *Laws* book I, which moves rapidly from a discussion of sexual *sophrosune* to a discussion of drunkenness. Other examples are cited in Foucault, loc. cit. and passim.

35. Dover, person communication of 11 February 1994, summarizing the argument of *GH* 60–68, where much evidence of the perceived naturalness of this desire is assembled. For just one example, Xenophon, *Hienon,* 1.33, where Hiero tells the poet Simonides that his passion for a youth "is for what human nature perhaps compels us to want from the beautiful."

36. Dover, personal communication of 11 February 1994; cf. *GH* 196–203. Dover notes that "Pindar's gods are too refined to digest anything but ambrosia, but never so insensitive that their genitals cannot be aroused."

37. Dover, *GH* 203.

38. Aristophanes, *Archarnians* 263–79. For many more examples, see Dover, passim, and see David Halperin, "One Hundred Years of Homosexuality," in *One*

Hundred Years of Homosexuality and Other Essays on Greek Love (New York: Routledge, 1990), 15–40.

39. See Dover, *GH,* 179–82, 183–88.

40. Dover, *GH,* 171–80; Winkler, *Constraints,* 162–87. On 175–76 Dover argues that one fragment refers to an orgasm.

41. Plato, *Symposium* 191E. This would appear to be the only passage in Athenian literature to describe female-female relationships.

42. Winkler, *Constraints,* 162–87.

43. Artemidoros, in Winkler, p. 221. The acts are "contrary to nature," it would seem "because to perform them would involve violating the usual rules of what is possible. The other main examples in this section are self-fellatio, presumed to be physically impossible; sex with the moon; sex with a dead person— again, presumed impossible (Artemidoros is presumably thinking not of necrophilia but of the fantasy that one actually succeeds in having regular intercourse with someone who is lost), and sex with various animals, especially wild animals. This last case may be possible in a way the others aren't—though it all depends how wild the animals are! It is not too clear what leads Artemidoros to classify it with the impossibles, except that he may be concentrating on the vast majority of cases, where the animals are too wild or are otherwise unavailable.

44. As to the sex acts that occurred or were believed to occur, Dover, on the basis of the evidence about the sexual practices of the women of Lesbos (involving both men and other women), concludes as follows: "they are likely to have been credited with all such genital acts as the inventive pursuit of a piquant variety of pleasure can devise, including homosexual practices together with fellatio, cunnilinctus, threesomes, copulation in unusual positions and the use of olisboi" (184). On *olisbol* (dildoes) and female masturbation, see *GH,* 176, n. 9.

45. The most extensive treatment of the evidence on this point is in "The Democratic Body," in David Halperin, *One Hundred Years of Homosexuality and Other Essays on Greek Love* (New York: Routledge 1990), 88–112, and notes 150 ff.; see especially 180, n. 3.

46. Aeschines, *Against Timarchus* 1.195; see Halperin, 180, n. 3.

47. For the best treatment of this set of connections, see Dover, *GH,* 20–109. See also John J. Winkler, "Laying Down the Law: The Oversight of Men's Sexual Behavior in Classical Athens," in *The Constraints of Desire* (New York: Routledge, 1990) 45–70.

48. Dover, *GH,* 36.

49. David Cohen, in *Law, Sexuality, and Society: The Enforcement of Morals in Classical Athens* (Cambridge: Cambridge University Press, 1991), argues that a father could bring a prosecution of *hubris* against the consensual lover of his son. Dover points out in his recent review of Cohen (*Gnomon* 1993, 657–60) that we know of not a single case in which this actually occurred. He also criticizes Cohen for generalizing hastily from passages in Aeschines that are likely to contain self-serving distortions of popular norms. Cohen's book was repeatedly cited as a central authority by Finnis, although it appears to offer no support to Finnis's positive thesis regarding the marital bond, and although it insists, consistently with Dover's analysis, that the penetrative homosexual role is not per se problematic (see 182). Like Dover, Cohen insists that it is passivity that involves stigma—although

he differs from Dover in his account of the circumstances under which such stigma was incurred. Dover's two counterarguments show, I believe, that Cohen has not given us any good reason to diverge from Dover's own analysis. On the other hand Dover gives Cohen's book high praise, as I would also, for its treatment of the seclusion of women.

A larger issue should now be mentioned, as David Cohen has emphasized to me (letter of 27 April 1994). The thesis of Cohen's book, and especially of its final chapter, is that the notion of a private sphere, immune from interference by the state, was absolutely essential to the Athenian notion of radical democracy (218–40). The Introduction to the book (2ff.) opens with a strong attack on contemporary American and English statutes that penalize consensual sexual behavior, and, specifically, homosexual conduct. Cohen holds that the proper way to use his book in the context of these public issues is to argue that the state has no business trying to use the law to enforce morality. To this end he deliberately drew attention to the contrast between ancient Greek views on privacy and modern sexual legislation.

50. *Problemata* iv.26, see below.

51. Dover, *GH* 133–51, 204.

52. See discussion in the longer version.

53. For example, Rebuttal Affidavit, para. 23: "Nussbaum is further inviting the Court to admire a culture in which the primary, and perhaps the only, socially approved sorts of same-sex sex acts were between adult men on the one side and boys on the other. Nussbaum herself, and the several pro-'gay' writers on classical Greek sex whom she praises in her publications, display no noticeable interest whatever in the question whether there was an age of consent for the young boys between whose thighs grown men (with or more likely without social approval) performed what she calls 'inter-crural intercourse' (graphically described by Dover at page 98). Neither she nor the others inquire how young such boys might therefore be in practice." Note that Finnis, as usual, completely bypasses the possibility of penetrating a prostitute or a non-citizen, which would be widespread and socially approved forms of same-sex conduct; and he also, as usual, omits same-sex relations among women.

54. On Achilles and Patroclus, see Plato, *Symposium* 180AB: Phaedrus says that Aeschylus is wrong to make Achilles the older, on the grounds that Achilles was clearly beardless, and was also the most beautiful of all the heroes. (The *erōmenos* is assumed to be more beautiful than the older *erastēs*.) The fragments of Aeschylus' lost *Myrmidons* give clear evidence that he saw the relationship as one involving sexual conduct, presumably intercrural intercourse: Achilles, mourning for the dead Patroclus, speaks of the "many kisses" they have shared, and of "god-fearing converse with your thighs." See translation of the fragments in Dover, *GH*, 197–98. Aeschines interprets Homer's silence on the sexual side of the relationship as a kind of cultivated knowing reticence about what would have been obvious to "educated" hearers: see Dover, *GH*, 41, 53. In Xenophon, *Symposium*, Socrates denies that Homer intended any erotic element in the portrayal of the friendship; as Dover and I agree, he is correct about the heroic age, but, as Dover remarks, Socrates "lived in an age when legend owed its continued hold on the imagination at least in part to the steady importation of homosexual themes"

(*GH,* 199). On Harmodius and Aristogeiton, see Dover, *GH,* 41, and especially Plato, *Symposium* 182 C. On the Sacred Band, see below, on Plato's *Symposium.*

55. For the evidence, see below on Plato's *Symposium,* and Dover, *GH,* 84.

56. See below, on the Stoics.

57. It would not be obvious that the partners would be expected to continue sexual relations throughout that time—although Aristophanes' picture, which makes intercourse central to the benefits of the relationship, strongly suggests this. But it is also not obvious that in long-term marriages the parties continue having sex throughout.

58. Dover aptly compares the situation of the *erōmenos* to that of a young woman in Britain in the time of his adolescence (the nineteen thirties) (*GH,* 88). He might have extended the comparison to take in this point: just as a proper British woman, from the Victorian era until rather recently, was publicly expected not to enjoy sex, but frequently did in private, so too it is possible that the *erōmenos* derived more pleasure than is publicly depicted. In his Postscript to the second edition, Dover grants that there is some literary evidence that the *erastēs* stimulated the penis of the *erōmenos,* and that one vase shows an *erōmenos* with an erection (205).

59. Affidavit, para. 35.

60. The best treatment of the entire issue of sources is Gregory Vlastos, *Socrates: Ironist and Moral Philosopher* (Cambridge: Cambridge University Press 1991), passim; Xenophon's testimony is discussed at 99–106. See also T. H. Irwin, "Xenophon's Socrates" (review of Leo Strauss), *Philosophical Review* 83 (1974): 409–13.

62. Dover, *GH,* 154.

63. See the discussion in Dover, *GH,* 154ff., and especially *Lysis* 205D–206A.

64. As Dover notes in *Symposium,* 5, there is a tradition—reported by Aristoxenus in the fourth century—that Socrates' heterosexual appetite was abnormally strong; it is conspicuous that Plato does not represent this fact—which, of course, would not have been incompatible with unusually strong homosexual response.

65. To at least one woman: for the story that he had a second wife on account of laws intended to remedy underpopulation, see Diogenes Laertius, *Life of Socrates.*

66. At *Apology* 41C, however, he does announce his attention to engage women as well as men in philosophical questioning—when he reaches the underworld, where, presumably, women would be less secluded! And he does, of course, converse with the learned Aspasia in *Menexenus.*

67. See Dover *GH,* 159–60. Note the close resemblance of this argument to Socrates' argument against Callicles in the *Gorgias*—see below.

68. Dover, personal communication of 11 February 1994.

69. *GH,* 159.

70. Dover, *GH,* 159–60; compare Dover, personal communication of 15 March 1994: "I accept the criticism that in *GH* 153–164 I ought to have drawn a distinction between Plato's Socrates and Xenophon's Socrates. I think there were two reasons why I failed to do so. One was my long habituation to thinking of Socrates in terms of the contrast between the Socrates of comedy and the Socrates

of serious literature (Plato, Xenophon, Lysias, etc.); the other was that in *GH* I was not primarily interested in the real Socrates, but simply in the views of homosexuality to be found in philosophical contexts, no matter to whom they were attributed. However, this is a suitable opportunity to sort things out."

71. See Vlastos, 40ff.: "A maxipassion keeps all the minipassions effortlessly under control."

72. See Vlastos, 42: "The irony in his love for Alcibiades, riddling from the start, persisted until the boy found the answer the hard way, in a long night of anguished humiliation, naked next to Socrates, and Socrates a block of ice."

73. In *Symposium*, Dover argues in a similar way, writing of the incident (165): "Plato undoubtedly wishes to suggest that physical relations are inimical to the pursuit of metaphysical truth with the same partner on other occasions. This may not be true, and even if it is true not everyone will regard it as a good advertisement for metaphysics, but it is dictated by Plato's psychology." Dover now clarifies: "In that passage of my *Symposium* commentary I did not intend any inference, positive or negative, to be drawn about the views of Plato's Socrates on homosexual copulation in circumstances where no philosophical teaching or co-operation is contemplated. Since he consistently assumes that homosexual temptation is universal, natural and normal (and in *Charmides* 155C–E he amusingly describes its impact on himself), we can hardly imagine that he regarded its consummation as 'monstrous', 'evil', 'depraved', or any adjective stronger than would be applied nowadays to a heterosexual 'lapse'."

74. Finnis, Affidavit, para. 35, see above. As for Xenophon's own attitudes to homosexual conduct, see the excellent discussion in Dover *GH,* 61ff., where he argues that "evidently Xenophon did not think the impulse to those reasons a blemish in a character for which he had an unreserved admiration" (64); the worries about conduct expressed by Xenophon's characters focus on the issue of passion as threat to reason, not on any notion of intrinsic shamefulness, wickedness, or depravity.

75. At the conclusion of his general line of argument that homosexual conduct can never actualize a genuine good because it lacks "biological unity," he writes: "Hence Plato's judgment, at the decisive moment of the *Gorgias,* that there is no important distinction in essential moral worthlessness between solitary masturbation, being sodomized as a prostitute, and being sodomized for the pleasure of it." It seems very dubious that any reference to masturbation is intended in the passage. Dover (personal communication of 15 March 1994) writes that he knows of "no explicit reference to masturbation in Plato or Aristotle." He points out that if Plato had intended such a reference to be understood from 494C6ff., Callicles' protest would have come at D1, rather than at E7, after the reference to the *kinaidos.* (I note here that masturbation would have elicited protest for a different reason: it was thought to be a habit of slaves who did not have the means to find a sexual outlet—see Dover, *GH* 97.)

76. Dover, personal communication of 15 March 1994. Nussbaum, *FG,* chapter 5, 142–43.

77. Winkler, "Laying Down the Law," in *The Constraints of Desire,* 45–70; on the idea that addiction to this sort of pleasure will lead one to sell oneself, see especially 57. Winkler stresses that the *kinaidos* is a scare-image defined contex-

tually, usually as the polar opposite of the stout-hearted patriotic manly soldier (45–54).

78. Finnis accuses me of "inherent unreliability" (Rebuttal Affidavit, para. 17), on the grounds that I say one thing in my book and another in the trial; he interprets the book's term "passive homosexual" to mean a person who is anally receptive in a single act. All I can say is that if my statement in the book was indeed ambiguous enough to permit this interpretation, it should not have been ambiguous; no scholar will doubt that a *kinaidos* is a type of person who habitually behaves as a pathic. And it seems reasonable enough that I should be allowed to learn from the work of others and modify my claims accordingly.

79. Pausanias is the *erastēs* of Agathon: see 177D, 193B7–C2, and also *Protagoras* 315DE; the relationship is historical, and was well known for its long duration: it is attested both when Agathon is eighteen and twelve years later, when Pausanias followed him to Macedon. See Dover, *GH* 84, *Symposium* 3. Intimacy between Phaedrus and Erixymachus is less clearly suggested, 177A ff. Finnis asserts without evidence that all the relationships depicted in the dialogue are "intended by the author to be understood as consistent with Socrates' and his own firm repudiation of all forms of homosexual genital activity" (Rebuttal Affidavit, para. 19). Surely if Plato wished to make such a point he would hardly have introduced Pausanias as a character, since he not only is well known for a sexual relationship but gives the rationale for it eloquently in his speech. Dover remarks, justly, that the language of serious Greek literature is "always circumspect" in matters of sex, but that this should not mislead the reader: "The ultimate 'service' or 'favour' desired by the older male is bodily contact leading to orgasm, though no doubt a smile or a friendly word would be treasured by the besotted lover as an interim favour" (*Symposium*, 3).

80. This is likely to be a reference to the well-known Sacred Band of Thebes, formed around 378 B.C. Dover (*Symposium*, 10 and *Phronesis* 10 [1965]: 1–20) argues that the dialogue must have been composed after that date, since Phaedrus describes the idea in "entirely hypothetical terms." But Plato more than once plays on the gap between dramatic date and date of composition, making his characters hint at things that, by the date of composition, would have been known to be reality. Thus the *Republic*'s allusions to the abuse of justice by those seeking power, on the part of characters who somewhat alter the dramatic date, would have been heard by its audience to contain ironic reference to events which had in the mean time occurred. Similarly, the fact, in the *Charmides* that characters known to the audience for their lack of moderation are shown (at a dramatic date well before the relevant events) calmly discoursing on moderation would very likely be read as containing ironic reference to those well-known (to the reader) events. I believe that the reference here is like that: Phaedrus, at the dramatic date 416, refers in entirely hypothetical terms to what an audience of the 370's would know to be a current reality. Dover now accepts this point: letter of 11 May, 1994.

81. 179A: "And indeed lovers are the only ones who are willing to give their lives—not only the males, but even women." It is culturally interesting that Alcestis is depicted as the *erastēs* of her husband, though no doubt she was imagined as younger and as behaving sexually in the usual female way. The reason seems to lie

in the intensity of her love, as contrasted with her husband's self-absorption—so Phaedrus maps them onto the *erastēs-erōmenos* dichotomy in a way that makes this distinction paramount, sexual role subordinate.

82. Dover points out (letter of 11 May) that *kalos* sometimes means just "okay," "in order," "(perfectly) are right," etc. I am happy enough with this; but in a dialogue whose central topic is the *kalon* and in which the high moral connotations of the word that are common in Platonic philosophy predominate, I would be still be inclined to render the terms as I have. This is certainly the only way to translate the term consistently throughout the dialogue, something that translators have on the whole rightly sought, despite the dialogue's plurality of speakers.

83. As often in Plato, we simply do not know whether some of the insights developed using this example might be intended to be generalizable to male-female and female-female loves as well.

84. Price, *Love and Friendship in Plato and Aristotle* (Oxford: Clarendon Press, 1989), 15–54, especially 47–49, where Price argues that a type of close personal intimacy characterized by "educative pederasty" is present throughout the ascent. (By "pederasty" Price means something quite different from pedophilia, sex with young children; he means sex with adolescents of roughly college age.)

85. See the comments of Dover, *GH*, 163, and of Vastos, "The Individual as Object of Love in Plato," in *Platonic Studies* (Princeton, 1981, 2nd edition).

86. *Hubrisen*, 219C5; on these metaphors, see the excellent treatment in M. Gagarin, "Socrates' *hubris* and Alcibiades' failure," *Phoenix* 31 (1977): 22–37. His charge against Socrates seems unfounded: for *being used* seems an essential feature of rape, and Socrates has humiliated him in a way that expresses not only no intent to use, but probably also a sincere concern for his well-being.

87. *FG*, chapter 6.

88. My own account of these familiar issues in *FG*, chapters 5 and 7; see especially 436A ff., 583C–84A, 533CD, 586AB.

89. This passage is in the middle of the discussion of the oligarchic city and man, but it is introduced as a digression, necessary to clarify a concept that will be used in that discussion. There is no reason to think that Socrates' articulation of the concept of "necessary desire" itself holds good only for the oligarchic city. He says simply that such desires "might justly be called necessary" (558E).

90. The best treatment of these, with all their contradictions, is in Halliwell.

91. But the latter only if Plato thought he could rely on the contraceptive devices in use at the time. Masturbation would be another possibility, but I am not certain that the term *aphrodisia* could, without strain, designate masturbation.

92. Scholars are not agreed on whether the speech is a real speech by the historical Lysias or a Platonic invention that captures Lysias' style well. I am inclined to the latter view.

93. One might here register another complaint against A. E. Taylor (see above n. 20), who writes, "the thesis of Lysias, we must remember, would be an offensive paradox even to the section of Athenian society which practiced 'unnatural' aberrations" (*Plato: The Man and His Work*, 1927).

94. One excellent place to study this is Euripides' *Hippolytus*, in which *erōs* is depicted as bringing an extraordinary mixture of beauty and danger to human life, and in which the hero's decision to avoid its claims is shown to be both impious and impoverishing.

95. In contrast to the *Symposium*, which had denied the divinity of *erōs*. On all these issues I have presented a fuller argument in *FG*, chapter 7.

96. See Dover *GH*, 163–65, who comments on the extraordinary emphasis given to the erotic response to bodily beauty in Plato's metaphysical system. In his forthcoming autobiography, Dover comments further on this theme, in a manner that makes evident the wide difference between his own moral intuitions and those of Finnis.

97. See David Halperin, "Plato and Erotic Reciprocity," *Classical Antiquity* 5 (1986): 60–80; and see the exchange between Halperin and me in *Proceedings of the Boston Area Colloquium for Ancient Philosophy* 1989.

98. 255C. What is at issue is a complicated etymological play in which the word *himeros*, "passionate longing," has been etymologized (251C) as deriving from "particles" (*merē*) that flow (*rhein*) from the beloved to the lover. The dialogue is suffused with this sort of word play, much of it erotic. See also *Cratylus* 419E.

99. We need not suppose that such reciprocity was unknown before this; Socrates describes the experience as one that is likely to follow upon the young man's perception of his lover's generosity. But what is clear is that the cultural vocabulary lacks a description for it.

100. For an excellent treatment of the shift from *Republic* and *Symposium* to *Phaedrus* in this respect, see Vlastos, *Socrates,* chapter 1, and "The Individual as Object of Love in Plato," in Vlastos, *Platonic Studies* (Princeton, 2nd edition 1981), especially Appendix, "Sex in Platonic Love." See also Price, *Love and Friendship,* 54–102, my *FG*, chapter 7, and the briefer comments by Dover, *GH*, 164–65, who describes well the persistent sexual imagery of the dialogue.

101. Interpreting 256D, "thinking that they have given and received the greatest pledges," with Price (following a suggestion by Edward Hussey), to refer to their sex acts, which they believe (wrongly) to be the greatest thing they have exchanged with one another: see Price 92–93, criticizing Dover, *GH*, 163, n. 16, who takes the "pledges" to be the rest of their relationship and their "thinking," therefore, to be correct. Dover now accepts correction on this point: letter of 11 May 1994.

102. Dover, *GH*, 163, n. 15, criticizing Vlastos, "Individual," 23, n. 76. Concurring see Rowe, 184. I would add that in *Republic* IX (see above) "mounting" has been used as a general description of animalistic sexual activity, just as "grazing" is used of animalistic eating.

103. For one sensitive exploration of a passage using "nature," see Dover, *GH*, 60ff. I am in effect arguing that Dover has not read the present Plato passage with the same sensitivity to context and argument that he there argues to be an essential requisite of interpreting the appeal to nature.

104. Callicles, in *Gorgias* 483C8ff.; Philebus, in *Philebus,* passim.

105. *Clouds* lines 1421–32. There are many similar examples. For a good

overview of the "nature/convention" debate, see W. K. C. Guthrie, *A History of Greek Philosophy,* volume III (Cambridge, 1969).

106. What is probably in question here is the hedonism of Eudoxus, who is reported by Aristotle (*Nic. Eth.* 1172b9–11) to have argued that pleasure is the supreme good by appealing to the behavior of "all creatures, both those endowed with reason and those without it."

107. Rowe, commentary, 184; see Dover, letter of 11 May 1994, praising Rowe's suggestion as "certainly excellent."

108. The first is now defended by Price (letter of 7 May 1994).

109. See, for example, Pausanias' speech at 181B.

110. Here it is especially important to note that problems of establishing the Greek text correctly and problems in translating it beset all available versions. Thomas Pangle's is by far the most adequate, going well beyond Bury and especially Saunders in accuracy; but in the crucial passage he reverts to inadequate manuscript readings at a pivotal juncture.

111. Thus what we should *not* say is what Finnis says, *Notre Dame Law Review,* 13: ". . . to know or tell Plato's views on the morality, the immorality, of all such nonmarital conduct as homosexual sex acts, one need go no further than these unmistakably clear passages in the *Laws,* texts with which every other text of Plato can readily be seen to be consistent."

112. See Appendix 3 of the longer version of this article for a full philological and philosophical discussion, including numerous references to unpublished new work of Dover and other scholars.

113. See Dover, *GH* 167: "Plato's main concern is to reduce to an unavoidable minimum all activity of which the end is physical enjoyment, in order that the irrational and appetitive element of the soul may not be encouraged and strengthened by indulgence. . . ." He spends at least as much time on drunkenness as on sex.

114. Dover (letter of 11 May) suggests that loss of semen plays such a large role in folklore and psychopathology that one may wonder whether Plato thought that semen is a nonrenewable resource.

115. Plato does not always distinguish these two categories, certainly, but he is capable of doing so, as in the notorious discussion of the rule of the Ideal City by the philosophers, a task they view "not as something fine (*kalon*), but as a necessity" (*Republic* 540B).

116. See here Dover, *GH,* 164.

117. Compare Price, pp. 230ff.; Price has now altered his translation of the relevant passage.

118. This does not imply a belief in infantile sexuality, which does not seem to be present in any ancient thinker. What Aristotle means is that things are in good order at our birth, in such a way that, with the proper support and development, virtue will in due time result.

119. The word I have, for want of a perfect equivalent, translated "material resources" is *ousia,* which means one's estate, fortune, property, possessions. In other words, "material" is not meant to refer to one's own body.

120. Marriage is mentioned only twice in the entirety of the *Nicomachean*

Ethics: as the occasion for an especially big party (1123a1); and as an occasion, like a funeral, to which one will want to invite one's relatives (1165a18). There are, of course, numerous references to the (friendly) relation of husband and wife, but not in contexts where the end of sexual activity is discussed. In two passages Aristotle cites sleeping with someone else's wife as an instance of unjust or wrongful action (1134a20–1, 1137a19–20), but this should be understood not as a reference to any intrinsic immorality in nonmarital relations, but rather as a violation of the rights of the woman's husband. Aristotle does hold that *moicheia* is bad in itself—see *EE* 1221b, *EN* 1134a19, 118a25, *Rhet.* 1375a; but *moicheia* includes only sleeping with someone else's wife or concubine and possibly (though this is disputed) sleeping with unmarried women of good family who are citizens' daughters or wards. (For examples of recent debate, see Dover, *Greek Popular Morality* [Oxford 1974] and Cohen, 98ff.) It is an injury against "the husband's claim to exclusive sexual access to his wife" (Cohen 109); thus it does not bear on the propriety of a married man's visiting a prostitute or *hetaira*, neither of which would be disapproved at the time. The only passage I know of where Aristotle calls a form of sexual conduct "contrary to piety" is in a reference to incest at *Politics* 1262a27, criticizing Plato's ideal city.

121. Affidavit, para. 38; Rebuttal Affidavit, para. 18. He follows Thomas Aquinas's interpretation of the passage.

122. Finnis fails to note these distinctions in his affidavit, simply saying that the male-male case is "the last item on the list of unnatural pleasures"; nail-biting and hair-pulling receive no mention in his account. In fact, in Affidavit paragraph 38, he cites the present passage as evidence that "Aristotle . . . represents such conduct [by which Finnis means all homosexual conduct] as intrinsically perverse, shameful and harmful both to the individuals involved and to society itself." Will we have a new referendum on the civil rights of nail-biters?

123. Dover, *GH*, 169.

124. Dover, *GH* 169–70, discussing *Problemata* IV.26. This being Dover's interpretation, Finnis's summary in Affidavit, para. 38, is very odd: "Dover's discussion of the views of Aristotle (born 384, died 322 B.C.) is incomplete and may be judged evasive, discussing only one of several relevant passages in Aristotle's works. But even Dover does not contradict the scholarly consensus that Aristotle rejected homosexual conduct. In fact, Aristotle on a number of occasions (in some cases directly and in other cases by a lecturer's hint) represents such conduct as intrinsically perverse, shameful and harmful both to the individuals involved and to society itself. I refer to his *Nicomachean Ethics* VII,5: 1148b29, his *Politics* II,1: 1262a33–39, together with the hints in II,6: 1269b28 and II,7: 1272a25." But of course it was precisely Dover's purpose to argue that the *EN* passage *does not* contain a general condemnation of homosexual conduct but rather a condemnation of child abuse leading to chronic passivity; nor does Dover mention any of the other three passages cited by Finnis. These passages would not have changed his case if he had. *Pol.* 1262a33–39 is a discussion of the danger of incest in Plato's ideal city. Aristotle notes that, making all children in the city the children of all the adults, Plato seeks to prevent incest by prohibiting intercourse between the generations, but he does not prohibit "passionate love and the other practices that would be most unfitting between a father and a son, or between a brother and a

brother." This hardly amounts to a general condemnation of homosexual conduct; and it doesn't have to do with conduct at all, in Finnis's narrowly defined
sense. 1269b28 is a discussion of the warlike customs of Sparta and Crete, which
Aristotle links with sexual excess; he mentions that most warlike peoples are excessively bossed around by their women at home (1269b24–5), "with the exception of the Celts and others who clearly give honor to male-male intercourse."
Honoring male-male intercourse, it would seem, is here seen as a way some
warlike nations have of not being excessively woman-dominated. Next, in the line
actually cited by Finnis, he says that it is reasonable that mythographers linked
Ares to Aphrodite: "for all people of that kind [viz., warlike people] are dependent
on intercourse either with males or with women." I fail to see what Finnis thinks
he finds here to support his claims, since male-male and male-female intercourse
are treated exactly alike. The last passage mentioned by Finnis is 1272a 25. Here
Aristotle has been discussing the Cretan custom of public meals; he mentions that
the Cretan lawgiver holds *oligositia*, deliberate undereating, to be healthful and
"philosophizes" about it at length; he also philosophizes about holding down the
population size by having men reside separately from their wives, "making them
associate with the males" (*tēn pros tous arrenas poiēsas homilian*). Aristotle concludes, "concerning which [that is, this associating], as to whether it is an inferior
custom or not inferior, there will be another occasion to conduct a thorough inquiry." Now presumably Finnis understands *homilia* to refer to sexual intercourse
with males and takes Aristotle to be hinting that he is going to condemn it somewhere else. Of course the bare statement that one is going to look into something,
as to whether it is good or not, hardly tells us how the inquiry will come out. But
a more important difficulty is that the passage is plainly discussing the custom that
men do not *reside* with wives but *reside*, military fashion, in all-male barracks.
This custom is neither necessary nor sufficient for sexual intercourse with males.
We know that an army may have single-sex barracks without encouraging same-
sex sexual conduct; on the other hand, sexual intercourse between males, at
Athens and elsewhere, standardly occurred while the older party was residing with
a wife. And of course it is the custom of separate residence that Aristotle actually
does discuss elsewhere, producing arguments that it is good for the upbringing of
children for families to dwell together. Finally: *homilia* is not, as *sunousia* is, a
standard euphemism for sexual intercourse; and the statement that the legislator
"makes" or "causes" this "associating" would surely be odd if it meant sexual
intercourse—we know of no laws for mandatory male-male intercourse; whereas
it would not be odd if it meant what I think it clearly means, requiring men to
reside with their fellow males.

125. *Love and Friendship,* 248–49.

126. Translator Terence Irwin concurs in this reading of the passage: see the
longer version of this article.

127. Reproducing a list of Aristotle's writings that probably reflects an early
collection in the Peripatetic school, Diogenes Laertius has an "*Eroticus,* 1 book,"
a "*Theses on love,* 4 books" (*Diogenes Laertius* V. 22–27).

128. Price, 249.

129. Personal communication, 16 December 1993.

130. Personal communication, 16 December 1993. Later in the same docu-

ment, Price describes those Greek attitudes as follows: "As Nussbaum correctly asserts, what generally troubled the Greeks (like all macho Mediterranean males) was that a man should play the woman's role, especially habitually. It is that, and not the nonprocreativity, which the orator Aeschines, for instance, once calls 'unnatural' (i.185)."

131. In correspondence, Price now accepts this point, saying that his remarks about chaste pederasty were meant to apply only to relations with boys too young for meaningful consent.

132. And, as Dover points out (letter of 11 May), except in the sense in which men who pay because they are no good at seducing "incur a certain degree of ridicule and contempt in all cultures."

133. See the *Virginia Law Review* version of this article; but also, Nussbaum, *The Therapy of Desire: Theory and Practice in Hellenistic Ethics* (Princeton: Princeton University Press, 1994), chapters 5 and 12, and *"Eros* and the Wise: the Stoic Response to a Cultural Dilemma," *Oxford Studies in Ancient Philosophy,* 1995.

134. Foucault, *The Uses of Pleasure,* 9.

135. Kenneth Dover, personal communication of 15 March 1994.

136. For a related point, see Finnis, Rebuttal Affidavit, para. 29., quoted above in note 122.

137. In particular by Foucault and Halperin, in the works cited above.

138. Price, *Love and Friendship in Plato and Aristotle* (Oxford: Clarendon Press, 1989).

139. For the evidence on gender equality, see Schofield.

140. For an eloquent statement of this position, see Andrew Koppelman, "Why Discrimination against Gays and Lesbians Is Sex Discrimination," *NYU Law Review,* 1995.

RESPONSE

Richard A. Posner

I am a great admirer both of Professor Adkins, whose Greek reading group I was a slow-witted and struggling member of before my appointment to a judgeship deprived me of the leisure necessary to prepare for and participate in its demanding sessions, and of Professor Nussbaum, from whose classical learning and philosophical insight I have learned a great deal in recent years. So I am honored to have this opportunity to comment on her fascinating paper in this conference in honor of him.

Americans have difficulty distinguishing "may" and "can." My comment will illustrate the difference: I *may* not talk about the Colorado case because judges are not permitted to make public comments on pending cases, and I *can*not talk about Professor Nussbaum's philological points because I am not a classical or any other kind of philologist, despite my learned disquisition on the difference between may and can. I might take issue with a few points of detail in her paper. We can't infer the age distribution of a population from the average age at death, since high infant mortality can lower the average while actually raising the longevity of those who survive infancy and childhood by screening out those with the weakest constitutions. And the fact (if it is fact, as I greatly doubt—I think it is a bit of hyperbole) that a child is 100 times more likely to be molested by a heterosexual than by a homosexual says nothing about the relative propensity of heterosexuals and homosexuals to molest children, since that depends on the ratio of heterosexuals to homosexuals. If it is 100 to 1, the propensities would be the same.

But these are trivial details, and what I want to comment on, and what I can with propriety and with an approach to competence comment on, is the role of classical learning in relation to the question of how we ought to view homosexuality in American society today. This is both a sociological and a normative question. The sociological aspect of the question is how far Americans will be influenced in their view of homosexuality in American life today by what the Greeks and Romans thought or did. The answer is probably not at all, or not enough to count. There may be other judges and public officials besides myself in whose mental world Plato and Aristotle figure largely, but if so I don't know any. And between computer-style modernity and multiculturalism I believe the role of classical civilization in American thinking is going to shrink rather than expand in the coming years.

The normative question is the one I'll focus on. To what extent should what the Greeks and Romans thought or did about homosexuality influence modern views? I think we have to make three distinctions. The first is between critical and constructive analysis. I think the proper role of philosophers in public debate is pretty much limited to knocking down bad philosophical arguments made by other participants in the debate; and similarly with classicists. If participants in the debate over homosexual rights make arguments based on the classical texts, it is entirely appropriate for a classicist to point out the mistakes in those arguments. It does not follow that the classicist can mine those texts for good arguments either in favor of or against homosexual rights.

The second distinction I want to make is between the reportorial and the analytic or evaluative content of the classical texts. One can mine Plato and Aristotle and the rest of the classical authors, along with vase paintings and statues and every other source of historical or anthropological inference, for information about the customs, practices, and attitudes of the Greeks and Romans. Or one can study the texts for the authors' own views and arguments. The reason for maintaining the distinction is that there is a danger of confusing these two uses: the danger of thinking that an idealized relationship depicted in the philosophical texts is an accurate description of typical behavior in the society.

The third distinction I want to make is a threefold distinction among ways in which the texts and other sources that constitute the materials of classical studies can influence the modern reader. One way is simply to enforce the lesson of relativism—that other civilizations have had different practices and different norms from our own; that things we might consider unthinkable and unnatural have seemed otherwise to other cultures. The second source of influence consists of arguments, demonstrations, or data of a logical or scientific character. And the third way is inducing sympathy in the reader by presenting an alien practice or norm in a sympathetic light, lit from the inside so to speak.

The first way, enforcing the lesson of relativism, seems to me the most important, but although Professor Nussbaum mentions it she does not emphasize it. Discovering that other cultures, especially admired ones or (what is often the same thing) ones that we consider ancestral to or continuous with our own, have done or do things that we unreflectingly consider unnatural or unthinkable is likely to give us at least a momentary jolt and invite us to reexamine our views. But often the jolt is indeed momentary. After all, the Greeks and Romans were casual or approving not only about homosexuality (more precisely, male homosexuality, for they disapproved strongly of lesbianism) but also about infanticide, slavery, censorship, xenophobia and ethnocentrism, religious and sexual discrimination, and the absence of professional judges, and discovering the ancient Greek views of these matters is not likely to lead to any deep reexamination of our own views on them.

Professor Nussbaum stresses arguments, remarking at one point in her paper that we must attend to the "concrete arguments" in the Greek texts concerning the morality of homosexuality, arguments that she describes as moral arguments of great rational power. But she does not identify anything that I recognized as arguments; and I am not myself aware of any. Aristophanes' charming parable of the separated halves in the *Symposium* is not an argument, but a parable, illustrating the literary side of the Platonic dialogues. Professor Nussbaum says that Plato "shows" that homosexual love can serve worthwhile goals apart from procreation, but showing is not the same thing as logical or scientific argumentation. I know that rhetoric buffs like to merge the syllogism with the metaphor and everything in between, but I think there are useful distinctions between science and poetry. I do think, and here is where the showing comes in, that the dialogues foster a certain empathy for homosexual relations by presenting them as normal and rewarding, but the demonstration is clouded by Plato's evident preference for sublimated over executed homosexuality, and by the disapproval, which I will come back to, of habitual passivity in sexual relations. Plato seems to have thought that the only unproblematic function of sex was procreation (not that procreation was unproblematic, but that procreation was the proper function of sex), facilitating its divorce from love, including Eros. Moreover, although as Nussbaum points out there are a number of examples of fully adult long-term homoerotic relationships in the Greek texts, the standard form of Greek homosexuality seems to have consisted of relations between a man in his middle or late twenties, or older, and (at least at the onset of the relationship) a teenage boy. We call that, when it has a physical dimension, pederasty (the Greek word, for the Greek practice), and it is about as difficult to get Americans to view pederasty with anything but horror as it would be to get them to approve of infanticide. Even states that have repealed their sodomy statutes retain a higher age of consent for homosexual than for heterosexual intercourse.

Pederasty is not pedophilia or child molestation. The boy is pubescent or postpubescent. So it is not as bad. But Americans consider it bad enough.

Then there is the standard problem with examples. We must ask how *representative* are the ideal homosexual relationships found in Greek culture. If the question is whether homosexual orientation is conducive to a happy life or a stable relationship, pointing at Achilles and Patroclus or Socrates and Alcibiades or Pausanias and Agathon is not going to provide many clues to the answer. For in discussing social problems we are naturally most interested in typical rather than exceptional situations.

I want to come back to, and conclude with, what I called earlier the lesson of relativism. I do think that the Greek and Roman evidence shows, along with much other evidence both anthropological and biological, that homosexuality is not "unnatural" in any nonconclusory sense of the word. But I am not sure what more it shows. Professor Nussbaum suggests that it refutes arguments that homosexuality leads to the downfall of civilizations. I think those arguments are ridiculous, but we must remember that the decline and fall of the Roman Empire was long attributed to its toleration of "vice," that the Athenian Empire had a calamitous collapse too, and that Sparta followed shortly. So the people who make those arguments will not be assuaged by close study of Plato and Aristotle.

But I think the real problem with arguing from ancient Greece and Rome to today is the following, and here I am repeating an argument I have made in my book *Sex and Reason* and elsewhere: There is evidence not only from Greece and Rome but also from the entire Mediterranean and Latin world (as far afield as the Philippines) and even from Japan that homosexuality is likely to be relatively unproblematic in a society in which marriage is not companionate, that is, in which the husband and wife are not expected to be intimates, confidants, and close friends, associating continuously, taking meals together, etc. Usually in these cultures there is a big age gap between husband and wife, and the wife is cloistered, sometimes almost literally sequestered, and uneducated. In such cultures men form close bonds with other men, which sometimes spill over into homosexual relations, especially when women, being sequestered, are unavailable before marriage and marriage is late for men; then we get opportunistic homosexuality, the homosexuality of men (or women) who prefer heterosexual relations but will settle for homosexual in a pinch: the sort of thing common on naval vessels and in prisons. This is penetrators' homosexuality; often the receptive partner is either a preference homosexual (a term I am about to define) or a male prostitute.

I am more interested in the situation of the "real" homosexual in such societies. I mean the man (for like Nussbaum I'm speaking of male homosexuality) who prefers homosexual relations, the Kinsey five or six; for Kinsey's famous scale is an index of homosexual preference or orientation, not of activity. When modern Americans speak of homosexuals they have in mind primarily these preference or orientation or Kinsey homosexuals.

The point to be emphasized is that the situation of such a homosexual is an easier one in a society of noncompanionate marriage. So little is demanded of the husband that it is easy for homosexuals to have stable marriages and pursue erotic satisfaction on the side. So easily do homosexuals blend in that they are socially unproblematic, even invisible (without concealment), so that to this day people in Mediterranean or Latin societies will sometimes deny that there *are* any homosexuals in their society. They are as inconspicuous as left-handers, because like left-handers their peculiarity, their "deviance," has little or no social significance. Yet they tend to be looked down on, as something less than full men. This is an echo of the ancient reservations about habitual passivity in sexual relations of which Professor Nussbaum spoke; for those habitual passives, people who *enjoy* being penetrated, presumably were what I am calling "real," Kinsey, homosexuals.

It is difficult for homosexuals to have successful companionate marriages. Marriage (I mean of course with women) by male homosexuals in societies such as ours in which companionate marriage is the dominant and approved form are usually undertaken for disguise or out of self-deception, and are rarely successful. A society in which companionate marriage is the norm tends therefore to extrude "real" homosexuals from a basic social institution, making them for the first time deviant in a socially significant sense, forcing them into their own subculture, making them strange and even threatening, creating the hostility to homosexuals that is a conspicuous feature of our own society as it was for long of England, perhaps the earliest European nation to adopt companionate marriage as the norm.

I am painting with a broad brush, omitting important qualifications and also the evidence; but if I am at least broadly correct in my analysis of the impact of companionate marriage on the situation of the homosexual, this implies that we can be misled by taking the ancient descriptions of homosexuality as illustrative of the possibilities for homosexuality in our culture. Even if such legal barriers to full equality for homosexuals as remain are dismantled, so long as our society is dominated by an ideal and a practice of companionate marriage it will be difficult for homosexuals to fit in as easily as they did in the civilizations depicted in the classical texts.

To conclude these brief remarks, I agree with Professor Nussbaum that the treatment of homosexuality in the classical texts can illuminate the modern debate over the issue for the handful of people who take or can be induced to take an interest in the classical texts. I think it can do this primarily by making us more reflective and self-critical concerning our priors about the matter rather than by furnishing a source of arguments or even by promoting a sympathetic understanding of the homosexual experience. But I think that in the end we may be more struck by the differences between the social context of ancient homosexuality and our own than by the resemblances.

7

The "Speech of Lysias" in Plato's *Phaedrus*

Arthur W. H. Adkins

Plato's *Phaedrus* begins with a series of *erotikoi logoi,* set speeches on the subject of *erōs* (230e5–234c5, 237b2–241d1, 243e9–257b2). Its position and length mark the final speech as the most important in Plato's eyes; but the earlier speeches have their own part to play in the economy of the dialogue. In this paper I shall study the first of these *erōtikoi logoi,* which has received short shrift at the hands of interpreters of the *Phaedrus.*

When Plato wrote the *Phaedrus,* the *erōtikos logos* was already an established genre of Greek epideictic oratory. Its popularity, in the general context of Greek life and mores, requires little explanation. Such speeches were put in the mouth of the *erastēs,* the lover, and addressed to the *erōmenos,* his beloved, a handsome youth; and it is hardly surprising that charm and ingenuity, dexterity of thought and elegant choice of word, not to mention trickery and sophistry, were the criteria by which the *erōtikoi logoi* were judged.[1]

But the popularity of the genre seems an insufficient explanation of Plato's having begun one of his most carefully wrought dialogues with an *erōtikos logos,* and with this one in particular, allegedly by Lysias. In the Bollingen Foundation translation of Plato's dialogues Edith Hamilton's editorial comment on the speech is: "Love is the first matter they take up. Phaedrus has with him a piece of writing about it which he greatly admires and reads it to Socrates who objects to it as making love chiefly a physical desire."[2] The version of the *Phaedrus* printed in the Bollingen translation is by R. Hackworth. Hackworth's own editorial comments on his translation are: "The speech . . . consists mainly in adducing a large number of prudential considerations. In every way it will be to a boy's good—to his

Professor Adkins kindly offered to contribute this paper to our anthology, even though he did not present it at the symposium. With the assistance of Mrs. Adkins, we corrected the copyedited manuscript and the page proofs of his contributions.—Editors.

material advantage, his security, his repute, and even his moral improve-ment—to yield not to a lover, that is to one who feels *genuine* passion for him, but to one who is moved by physical desire *and nothing else.*" Hack-worth, having thus characterized the lover and the nonlover, gives the nonlover's account of the lover: "The lover's passion is a malady, preclud-ing him from all self-restraint, and no *permanent satisfaction* can be ex-pected from him" (emphases mine).[3]

What Hackworth means by "mainly . . . prudential considerations" and "genuine passion" he does not explain; but his terminology in general suggests that he is starting from a position and perspective very different from that of "Lysias." In that speech the distinction between the lover and the nonlover seems to be identical with, or very close to, that expressed by the distinction between "being in love with X" or "having fallen in love with X" and "loving X." The latter expression can certainly, in appropri-ate contexts, include physical desire, but not to the exclusion of rational control. The latter condition is characterized by exclusion ("nonlover") here. I shall discuss below whether any Greek word is available to char-acterize it positively, and if so, whether there would have been any prob-lems in using it here.

In this paper I wish to argue that the customary characterization of the speech is unjustified, whether by the standard of Plato's contemporaries or our own, and to suggest motives for Plato's having set a speech on this topic claiming to be by Lysias at this point in the dialogue. Whether the speech is by Lysias or not is unimportant for my argument. It suffices that Plato chose Lysias as an appropriate author to express such sentiments.

Phaedrus tells Socrates that Lysias maintains in his *logos* that a youth should grant his favors to a man who is not in love with him rather than one who is. Socrates' immediate response is "Splendid! I wish he would add that a youth should grant his favors to a poor man rather than a rich one, to an elderly man rather than a young one, and in general to ordinary people like myself. What an attractive democratic theory that would be!" This can be read as banter; but it may be banter with a purpose. At the very least it reminds the reader of the differences between Socrates and the wealthy and lavish lovers, the *kaloi kagathoi,* who were usually promi-nently involved in such relationships in Athens. It seems clear that the historical Socrates was much to be seen in the company of handsome youths, and that this speech of the Platonic Socrates is related to that situ-ation; but its purpose will become apparent only as the dialogue develops. It may also seem reasonable to conclude that a speech by Lysias will be in some sense "democratic"; but more will be said of this later.

Plato goes to great lengths to claim that the speech on the nonlover is a verbatim report of a speech by Lysias. When Socrates asks Phaedrus to tell him what was in Lysias' speech, Phaedrus begins by denying that he can possibly remember enough of such a carefully wrought speech to do justice to it (227d6ff.). Socrates says he is sure that Phaedrus has made every effort to get the exact text by heart (228a5ff.); and Phaedrus does not deny it. Finally, it transpires that Phaedrus has the actual text under his cloak. (None of this compels us to believe Plato's claim of Lysian authorship; but it is not unreasonable to inquire what Plato hoped to gain by pretending that it was by Lysias.)

If we are to be able to make even an educated guess about Plato's motives, we must consider how Lysias appeared to his contemporaries in Athens. He was a resident alien, a metic, son of the wealthy metic Cephalus who appears in old age in Plato's *Republic*. Cephalus' sons Polemarchus and Lysias were affected by the rule of the Thirty (404 B.C.). Polemarchus was killed by them for his wealth; Lysias escaped and fled, along with many other democrats, to Megara.[4] To assist the return of the democrats he supplied them with 200 shields (the family probably owned a shield factory) and with Hermon raised a force of 300 men. When the democrats returned, he seems to have been granted Athenian citizenship on the motion of the democratic general Thrasybulus, but to have lost his citizenship when Archinus brought a suit for *graphē paranomōn* against Thrasybulus. As a metic, Lysias could not himself appear in court;[5] but he became famous and prosperous as a writer of forensic speeches to be delivered in court by one of the parties in the case.[6]

Let us now turn from editors' comments to the Greek text. The nonlover (230e6ff.) says that the youth understands the nonlover's *pragmata*, and that the youth has heard that if these things should happen it would be to their mutual advantage.[7] The nonlover claims (230e7ff.) that his not being "in love with" the youth should not be grounds for his failure to obtain what he is asking for. The nonlover will treat him much better than would the lover. When desire has departed, lovers regret the benefits they have conferred upon their beloved; but nonlovers never need to regret what has transpired. They have not acted under compulsion (of desire) but voluntarily, in a condition in which they would be most able to reason about their own resources, they confer benefits on a scale that matches their capabilities. Then again, lovers consider the material loss they have suffered as a result of their passion and the benefits they have conferred (on the beloved); and reckoning in the toil they have expended, they think that they have long ago given the appropriate *charis* to their beloved. The nonlovers, however, cannot allege any neglect of their personal affairs as a result of their relationship, nor set past toils on the debit side, nor complain about quarrels with their relatives (presumably over the lavish presents that the lover showers on his beloved). When these great troubles are absent, nothing remains other than zealously devoting themselves to doing whatever each thinks will gratify the other. Again, suppose that it is a reason for valuing lovers highly, that, as they say, they do good to (*philein*) whomever they love (*eran*) and are ready through their words and deeds to gratify their beloved while making enemies of everyone else. It is easy to understand, if they are speaking the truth, that they will set a higher value on anyone with whom they later fall in love, and it is evident that, if the new beloved so desires, they will do harm to the former beloved. Again, how is it reasonable to squander *toiouton pragma* on someone suffering from *toiautēn sumphoran,* which no one who knew anything about it would even try to remove.[8] Lovers themselves admit that they are ill (*nosein*) rather than in their right minds (*sōphronein*), and that they know that they are mentally disturbed, but are unable to control themselves. So, when they return to their senses (*eu phronēsantes*), how could they suppose that these matters were well done on which they were deliberating while they were in such a frame of mind? Again, if you were to choose the "best" (*beltistos*) of your lovers, your choice would be restricted to a few; but if you were to choose the *epitēdeiotatos* of the rest, you would be able to choose from many.[9] Consequently, there is a much greater chance of finding someone worthy of your *philia* (231e2).

The nonlover has still some points to make in his disparaging comparison of the relationships a youth might have with a lover rather than with a nonlover; but it may be useful to evaluate what has been said so far. *Pace* Hackforth, the nonlover is certainly not trying to reduce the relationship between lover and beloved to a financial transaction, in which the *erastēs* is to make due payment for services rendered by the *erōmenos.* Nothing in Lysias' Greek suggests it; and both law and morals ruled out such behavior for an Athenian citizen or a prosperous metic. The youths whom the nonlover was pursuing were scions of the best Athenian families; prostitution, male or female, was incompatible with citizenship. The terms of comparison must be different.

In fact the speech itself makes the situation quite clear. At 232a Lysias assumes that the youth accepts *ton kathestēkota nomon* (custom, of course, not positive law) of the Athenians under which it is understood that the lover is to pursue his beloved openly, but that the beloved should not gratify him, or rather not be known to have done so. The beloved should avoid becoming the topic of gossip.[10] The passionate lover with his flamboyant pursuit and lavish gifts will have staked a great deal, in competition with other similarly flamboyant and lavish lovers, on the success of his suit. Lysias' speech indicates that some lovers were more lavish than they could afford to be; and they were also investing a great deal of self-esteem in the success of their suit, in a highly competitive society. Once successful, such a lover will be likely to "kiss and tell," to the detriment of the reputation of his beloved; but the nonlover will be discreet, so that his relationship with the youth whom he is trying to persuade may escape notice altogether. If they are seen conversing (*dialegesthai*) together, people who see them will reflect that 'Whether one's motive be *philia* or some other pleasure, one has to converse with other people."[11]

Again, the nonlover makes it clear that the youth would get more lavish gifts from a lover: Lysias' nonlover cannot be attempting to win over the youth by competing in his offer of precious objects. The difference emphasized so far is that the lover is guided by passion alone, and by a drive to outdo other lovers. The passionate lover wants the best of the year's young men, the Reigning Beauty; and this may cost the lover a fortune in gifts to win him over.

Why should the handsome youth be deterred from accepting the suit of a passionate lover? Surely not by the thought that the lover is courting financial ruin by his behavior. The values of the Athenians, or at all events those of the leisured *kaloi kagathoi,* circumscribed the behavior of the beloved in several ways; but the acceptance of lavish gifts from his lover was not proscribed, and much less the acceptance of such gifts on the grounds that the lover could not afford to give them. Such gifts constituted a kind of *charis* from the *erastēs* to the *erōmenos* that was socially acceptable.

"Socially acceptable," that is to say, at the social level with which we are concerned here. In Aristophanes' *Plutus,* 149–159, Chremylus, socially and financially at the opposite pole, cites Corinthian courtesans among the purchasable pleasures available only to the rich. His slave Cario adds that "the boys" do the same thing, "not for the sake of their *erastai,* but for money." Chremylus claims that only the "boy-tarts," not the *chrēstoi,* ask for money. The *chrēstoi* ask for a good horse or a pack of hounds. Cario comments "They are ashamed to ask for money, and 'bake a crust' around their baseness with a name." Evidently *chrēstoi* is used to denote the young men of good family to whom *erōtikoi logoi* are characteristically addressed. The Chremyli of Athens are not directly affected; but their response, as mere spectators, lends vividness to the sketch of the attitude of the *erastēs'* family. (Note that these outsiders seem to think that a nonmercenary *erōmenos* might gratify his *erastēs* for the *erastēs'* own sake and that the slave Cario collapses into one the categories of mercenary and nonmercenary while the Athenian Chremylus accepts the distinction.)

We may think that some of the nonlover's warnings about the *erastai* are excessive, and unlikely to convince; for example, that after the beloved has fallen out of favor with his *erastēs,* a subsequent beloved will work on his admirer to do the former beloved harm. But it should not be forgotten that we are concerned with a small group of wealthy, prominent, and powerful persons in a small political community, constantly meeting each other face-to-face; and that if a relationship has ended acrimoniously, the persons concerned will be deemed to be displaying both *aretē* and *dikaio-sunē* if they benefit their (new) friends and harm their (new) enemies.

It should also be clear that at this level of society in a small community a comparatively small group with new friends and new enemies might suffice to bring about the realignment of political factions. If it is borne in mind that Plato may intend "Lysias" here not merely to be addressing handsome youths but making general political points which are relevant to the situation in Athens and other Greek poleis of the time, some of the obscurities of the speech may be clarified. Before turning to this question, I shall complete my brief analysis of the speech.

Lysias continues (232b5ff.) by supposing that the youth may fear that any *philia* he may form with an older man may well not be lasting; and that if the two were to "fall out" for some other reason, both would be the losers; but if they should fall out after the youth has "sacrificed what he holds most dear," the youth will suffer a great hurt. This fear evidently concerns the behavior of lovers and nonlovers alike; for Lysias responds by describing the paranoid behavior of the lover, who is always afraid that someone else may lure his beloved away, and keeps him away from maintaining his earlier friendships and from forming new ones.

Lysias contrasts whose who are not lovers (232d4ff.), but "achieved what they asked of you" on account of their *aretē*. A nonlover would not feel jealousy (*phthonos*) toward those who flocked around the youth, but would feel hatred for those who were unwilling to do so, thinking that the latter are looking down on him whereas the others are benefitting him.[12] Lysias concludes that there is much more hope that *philia* will be the result of this rather than *echthra*.

Lysias next points out to the youth (232e3–33a4) that "many of the lovers desire your body before they get to know your character or become familiar with *tōn oikeiōn*,[13] so that it is unclear to them whether they will still want to be your *philoi* when they no longer feel passionate desire for you. Whereas the nonlovers were *philoi* to one another already before they engaged in these acts, and it is not likely that any pleasures they experience will diminish their *philia*, but that these things are left behind (in the memory) as reminders (*mnēmeia*) of what is to come."

At 233a4 the nonlover claims that it is to be expected (*prosēkei*) that the youth will become *beltiōn*, more *agathos*, by taking the nonlover's advice rather than that of a lover. For *erastai* praise the things that are being said and done contrary to what is for the *beltiston*, most *agathon* (to their partner), in part because they are afraid of arousing hostility in their partner (if they oppose his desires), in part because lovers themselves come to worse (*cheiron*, more *kakon*) conclusions on account of their passion.

Lysias continues to describe the behavior of lovers, 233b1ff. When they have ill-fortune (*dustuchountes, sc.* in their relationship with their beloved), *erōs* causes them to regard as painful (*aniara*) things which cause no pain to the rest of mankind (*sc.* nonlovers, or themselves when not in love); and when they fare well (in their relationship), *erōs* compels them to praise even the things that it is not worthwhile to take pleasure in. So it is much more fitting to pity *tois erōmenois* (those with whom at least one other person is in love) than to emulate them.

Lysias contrasts the behavior of the nonlover (233b6ff.). If the youth takes the nonlover's advice and accepts his suit, in the first place the non-lover will not make it his goal to pander to the youth's immediate pleasure, but will concern himself with the benefit that is to come, for the nonlover is not overcome by passion but self-controlled. He does not stir up powerful hostilities on small pretexts. Only under strong provocation does he display even a little anger, and that reluctantly.[14] He shows forgiveness (to the youth) for what was not intended, and tries to deflect him from hurtful actions that were intended. For these are the signs of a *philia* that will last for a long time.

The nonlover realises that the youth may have absorbed certain presuppositions from the gymnasia, 233c5ff. For example, he may uncritically accept that it is not possible for a strong *philia* to come about unless one of the *philoi* is in love with the other; but he should reflect that in that case we would not make so much of our sons as we do, nor of our fathers and mothers; nor indeed would we have (as we do) faithful *philoi* who do not become our faithful *philoi* as a result of such desire but from different pursuits.[15]

At 233d5ff. the nonlover draws analogies with other situations. If one should gratify especially those who are most in need, it is appropriate (*prosēkei*) in other contexts to benefit (*eu poiein*) not the *beltistoi* but those who are most in need. For if *they* are freed from the greatest hardships, they will feel the most gratitude (*charis*) to their benefactors. And indeed on this argument it is not appropriate to invite one's *philoi* to one's private festivities but rather those who ask and need to be satisfied. For *they* (233a1ff.) will feel affection for the one who invites them and will follow him and come to his door and will feel the greatest pleasure and will be the most grateful (*charin eisontai*) and will call down many blessings on their benefactor's head.

Needless to say, this argument is a *reductio ad absurdum*. The Athenians of Lysias' and Plato's day did not behave in this way to those who were literally destitute. The notion of "going out into the streets and lanes of the city, and bringing in . . . the poor, and the maimed, and the halt, and the blind" to a feast (Luke 14:21) did not occur to any ancient Greek moralist, even allegorically and even after the guests originally invited had declined. The beggar is not to be turned from the door, but he, and other suppliants, are *hiketai,* "those who come," (*hikneomai*). There is no moral requirement that they should be sought out or given preference at table over one's *philoi,*[16] as the nonlover indicates (233e5ff.).

The nonlover now recapitulates his list of those whom the youth should and should not gratify: not those who will merely enjoy his youthful beauty, but those who will give him a share of their *agatha* when he becomes older; not those who once they have had their way with him will boast of their conquest, but those whose sense of propriety will keep them silent to all persons; not those who will *spoudazein,* make much of him, for a short time, but those who will be his *philoi* in just the same way throughout his life; not those who when desire is past will seek a pretext for a quarrel, but those who when his youthful beauty is past will then display their *arete.* The nonlover also repeats his advice to the youth, to remember that lovers (*erontes*) are reproached by their families and *philoi* (234b1ff.) on the grounds that the practice is harmful (presumably to lovers, family and *philoi* alike); and also that no relative or family member ever yet found fault with nonlovers on the grounds that they had come to decisions (*bouleuesthai*) contrary to their own interest.

Much of the nonlover's advice to the youth has been in terms of behavior towards nonlovers no further defined. This may be the reason why (234b6) the nonlover now imagines the youth asking whether his advice is to gratify all nonlovers as such. The nonlover's immediate reply is rather odd: "I don't suppose that even the *eron* would bid you to have this attitude to all the *erontes.*" (Is the nonlover supposed to have forgotten his own vivid account of the paranoia of the *erastes?*) But the remainder of the speech sustains the prudential tone of the nonlover's earlier advice. If the youth gratifies all and sundry of the nonlovers, the *charis* received is not worth an equal *charis,* and it is not equally possible to escape the notice of the others; and it is the goal that there should be no harm (*blabe*), but benefit for both, from the relationship. The nonlover concludes, 234cff. "I think that what I have said is sufficient. If you still crave [*pothein*] anything else, and think it has been left out, ask."

This speech, whether the words are Plato's or Lysias', is only the first move in a long and complex dialogue; but it is all that I am concerned with here. Before continuing with the discussion, it may be useful to analyse what has been said. In the first place, the nonlover is not concerned with a merely physical attraction. Such relationships are mentioned; but they are ascribed to the lover who "falls in love" with a handsome youth "at first sight," before he knows anything about him or his circumstances (232e3ff.), so that it is not clear whether they wish to be *philoi* once desire has faded. The nonlover, on the other hand, is the *philos* of the youth before he attempts to persuade him to gratify his desires; and the *philia* is based on compatibility of character and interests.

Philia is a thread which runs through the nonlover's speech from beginning to end; and it will be useful to consider the meaning of the term in Greek.[17] "Friendship" is too narrow, since "friendship" in English is usually restricted to relationships in which there is some emotional warmth, whereas *philia* in Greek encompasses all cooperative relationships. The breadth in Greek results from the social and political conditions in which the Greeks lived. Even in Athens of the fifth and fourth centuries B.C.—the polis frequently claimed as the source of the idea of a democracy whose citizens live under the rule and protection of law—a surprising amount of self-help remained necessary if the citizen head of household was to survive and ensure the continued existence of himself and his family. Few if any citizens could hope to achieve this goal without allies, *philoi.* One of the definitions of justice at this time was "helping one's *philoi* and harming one's *echthroi*." In the small, face-to-face community of the polis, the citizen was always aware of the presence of his *philoi* and *echthroi;* and he must have been aware that his *echthroi* would take any opportunity offered of being just in terms of the definition given above. In contrast, his *philoi* were those people on whose cooperative behavior toward him he could, or should have been able to, rely.

Consequently, *philoi* were needed for *mutual* aid in helping one another and harming their enemies. The quality, power, and number of one's *philoi* is of far more importance than any emotions or desires one may experience in one's relationship with them. "Can I rely on the help of X in a crisis?" is the relevant question. It should be noted, however, that this is the *minimum* requirement for the existence of a relationship which can be termed *philia*. Warm affection, "love" in the sense described above and contrasted with "being in love," may be present. The "nonlover" of Lysias' speech *philei* in this sense, and sexual desire—but not infatuation—is certainly present. (Lysias de-emphasizes this fact, for it would blunt the edge of his rhetoric to give it its due weight.) The "nonlover," as described, has the long-term interests of both partners at heart.[18] Warm affection may produce not cold but warm calculation.

Philoi could be derived from a number of sources: one's blood kin, which should be interpreted in the sense of the extended family, though enmities within the extended family were naturally not unknown; and relatives by marriage were important sources. The need for effective help made marriage far too important to be left to the chance affections and desires of two young people. Marriages were contracted with a view to the well-being of the two families concerned.[19] The couple would be *philoi* in the Greek sense, but were unlikely to be even friends, and indeed might be virtually unknown to each other, at the time of the marriage. (Nothing of course ruled out the development of deep emotional ties between husband and wife after their marriage.)

Many *philoi* were inherited, as a result of blood ties and marriages contracted in earlier generations. But new links could be formed in the present generation by marriage. If *erōs*, passionate desire, played any part in Greek marriage, it was a phenomenon not planned for by those who arranged the marriage. In Xenophon's *Oeconomicus*, Ischomachus, the wealthy gentleman farmer whose views on marriage and the household in peace and war constitute a definition in use of *kalokagathia*, there is no mention of *erōs*. One cannot reply that such a theme is no more to be expected here than in Mrs. Beeton's *Household Management*. Ischomachus begins his address to his bride—who is not yet fifteen years old—by asking her whether she already knows why he took her in marriage and why her parents gave her to him, "for I know that it is as clear to you as it is to me that there was no lack of possible sleeping partners for each of us" (7.11–12). Ischomachus deliberated on behalf of himself, and his bride's parents on behalf of their daughter; and the subject was "whom we should select as the best *koinōnos* (partner, sharer) in the *oikos* and the children, should the god grant them any." They will then deliberate about the best education for the children, an education that will render them an *agathon* (benefit), in that they will be the best possible *summachoi* (fellow-fighters, allies) and care-givers to Ischomachus and his wife in old age.[20]

This is not now a fashionable view of marriage, in the English-speaking world at all events; but it has been the prevalent one throughout recorded history and is widespread over much of the planet today. Xenophon is certainly not portraying Ischomachus as cynical. Greeks expected marriage contracts to be based on prudential considerations. *Erōs* was feared for its possible disruptive effects.

How successful the Greeks were in maintaining stable marriage relationships we do not know. But we do know that *erōs* migrated to the gymnasia, where it held very visible sway. It should not be forgotten, however, that the Greeks did not create the gymnasium to facilitate erotic relationships between youths and older men, but as part of the traditional education of their political classes. The gymnasium contributed both to the maintenance of physical health and to the political education of the youth of the leisured class by their elders from the prominent political families, who were, before the advent of the sophists, Socrates, Plato, and Aristotle, the repositories of such political wisdom as was available. Since the men and the youths who met there were members of the more leisured families, the youths were likely to be socialized into the values of oligarchy. That these competitive values were conducive to civil strife was realised by Herodotus (3.82), and a particular example of such strife was vividly portrayed earlier in the *Theognidea*, an oligarchic anthology ascribed to Theognis of Megara. Many of the poems to be found there express the writer's relationship with a youth named Cyrnus.

The relationship was both sexual and political. In the situation I have described, it was almost inevitable that the youth was socialized also into the mores of the gymnasia.[21] Indeed, in the circumstances the two might be regarded as two aspects of a relationship between an *anēr* and a *pais*. Much of the language is the same. Whether Cyrnus' lack of *sōphrosunē* ("self-control," "prudence") and his "betrayal" of Theognis were concerned primarily with the erotic or the political is frequently unclear. It may have been unclear at the time. I cite here a few lines, out of many possible: 101ff. "Let no one persuade you to *philein* a *kakos* man. What is the benefit of having a *deilos* man as your *philos?*"[22] 323–28: "Never destroy a *philos anēr* on a small *prophasis*, Cyrnus, out of belief in a harsh slander. If anyone were to be angry at all the misdeeds of his *philoi*, they would never become linked or friends to one another." The poet sums up by reminding Cyrnus that to err is human.

At some point in the history of the text, "Theognis" was divided into two books. The first—and longer—book contains for the most part those lines which are not explicitly erotic. The second part is more explicit: 1337–40: "I no longer love (*eran*) a *pais*, but have kicked away my harsh pains, and have gladly escaped grievous toils, and have been freed from yearning by well-garlanded Cytherea; but for you, O *pais*, there is no *charis* from me." 1341–44 (possibly by Euenus): "Woe's me! I love a soft-skinned *pais*, who tattles about me to all his [or 'my'] *philoi*, though I do not want him to. I shall put up with not having been able to keep the matter quiet . . . for it is no *aeikelios* ['unseemly' or 'lacking in good looks'] *pais* to whom, as everyone now knows, I am enthralled." There is no doubt about the last two quotations. *Eran* settles the matter. But *eran* is a species of *philein*, which is readily available in place of the more explicit word. Some Theognid poems show great sophistication in hinting at the nature of a relationship. Lines 237–54 are a good example.[23]

Taken as a whole, the vocabulary and situation of "Theognis" and "Lysias" are similar, or variants on the same theme. In the poems cited, "Theognis" seems to have been unfaithful. Cyrnus discovered the truth and apparently took some action which "Theognis" thought excessive. In 1341–44 it is the *pais* that is "telling," and the *anēr* who finds appropriate thoughts to console himself. We may note *prophasis* (323 and *Phaedrus* 234a8) for the pretext on which the lover breaks off a relationship from which passion has departed.

The values here illustrated are those of the most powerful citizens. They are not merely conducive to civil strife. They commend it under certain circumstances. All should be concerned about this, for the personal enmities of the governing group affect the well-being of all the inhabitants of a polis. Looked at in the appropriate light, the behavior of the lover is shown to be hazardous to public safety.

But in that case, why does Plato, much of whose philosophical energies were expended on advancing the claims of the cooperative excellences against those of the competitive excellences, reject with such vehemence the views of "Lysias"? Surely taking the advice of the nonlover, of whom words from the *philos-* root can now be used, would increase the amount of *philia* and diminish the amount of strife in any city.

Even after analysis, the speech ascribed to Lysias is problematic. What is more, it always was problematic to some extent. Given the manner in which authors' works were "published" in ancient Greece, even the first readers of Plato's *Phaedrus* might well have had difficulty in establishing whether Lysias was or was not the author of the speech. But they would not have been faced with all our problems, for they would have immediately been aware that the historical Lysias, a person rather than a number of written documents, possessed more than one characteristic. In consequence, they might have perceived—in some cases, shared—a certain ambivalence in Plato's motives for including the speech at this point in this dialogue, *and ascribing it to Lysias.* The aristocrat Plato, who had rejected the bloodthirsty behavior of the Thirty, might have other reasons of his own for disliking the Lysiases of Athens.

In fact, the speech of Lysias and the first speech of Socrates, with its palinode, are there to be rejected. Few editors and critics would disagree. But they do not ask on what grounds Plato holds that the speeches, and especially the first, should be rejected. Those who have discussed the matter simply assume that any reasons they have for rejecting the views of the nonlover are also Plato's reasons, even if this involves mistranslating the Greek. Nor do editors in general acknowledge that, if due attention is paid to the central importance of *philia* in Greek life, at the end of the nonlover's speech the nonlover is in a stronger position than the lover. The nonlover has not refuted himself out of his own mouth.

Nor is the position unfamiliar today. There is nothing incomprehensible about the judgments passed by "Lysias," whether or not all would agree with them, now or in Plato's day. Again, it is neither absurd nor self-contradictory to hold that a sexualized friendship—to use the phrase to denote what "Lysias" denoted by "nonlove"—is preferable to an exploitative sexual relationship, or at least that a sexualized friendship is more likely to endure as a stable relationship after sexual desire has cooled; and this is what "Lysias" claimed.

It is prima facie strange then that Hackforth rates "Lysias'" nonlover so low as to rank even behind the lover, as the latter is portrayed here. The reason is perhaps in part that "Lysias" characterizes as "nonlove" the *philia-* relationship that had such practical importance in Greek. Had he written "not *erōs* but *philia*" as an initial definition of the nonlover's motivation, his "message" would have been little changed. *Philein* readily expresses sexual desire, as we have seen, but does not suggest the uncontrollable passion that is *erōs*. Hackforth and some other commentators miss, I think, the central importance of *philia* in Greek life, and the resemblance of the goal of the marriage contract to what Lysias' nonlover is proposing as the goal for the relationship of *erastēs* and *erōmenos*.

But this is not the only problem. From the point of view of the citizen, as of the metic, *philiai* in alliances of mutual assistance were of the utmost importance. Having *philoi* might make all the difference between life and death. Nor was the extreme situation, the outbreak of civil war (*stasis*), a question of merely academic interest and importance. Thucydides (3.82) testifies that *stasis* was endemic in Greece during the Peloponnesian War; and the Athenians themselves had suffered two violent spasms of *stasis* in 411 B.C. and 404 B.C. The speech of the nonlover is concerned with the relationships of individuals, as suits the genre, but the passage from the quarrels of individuals and their *philoi* to general *stasis*, already understood by "Theognis" and Herodotus much earlier, could hardly have been missed by the mature Plato. Yet Plato, through Socrates, rejects the speech of Lysias' "nonlover," whose recommendations would be more likely to produce lasting *philiai*.

But perhaps more can be said. It should not be forgotten that Plato was descended in both the paternal and maternal line from the old Athenian aristocracy, while Lysias was "in trade" and could be representative of the mercantile values of the metic.[24] This would not endear Lysias' views to the *kaloi kagathoi*, or to any who embraced their values; but whatever else may be unclear in the *Phaedrus*, it is surely apparent that Plato is not commending the values of "Lysias" to his readers.

I suggest that, in the aftermath of the rule of the Thirty, some such criticism of the values of the gymnasia and of the behavior of the *kaloi kagathoi* was in fact in circulation and that Plato was aware of it.[25] Plato could not deny the force of the argument, but offers a two-stage reply. The first stage is to ascribe the argument to a metic, an alien who could not appreciate the behavior of Athenians, a thrifty bourgeois who could not appreciate the lavish *megaloprepeia* of the aristocrat. But Plato could not leave the matter there, for the arguments of "Lysias" strike home. Later in the dialogue he reinterprets the "madness" of the *erastēs*. He renders it not merely harmless to the *erōmenos* but the source of the blessings of philosophy. The gifts received by the youth are so great as to be termed divine (256e3ff.); "whereas the acquaintance (*oikeiotēs*) of the nonlover, which is diluted with a merely mortal good sense (*sōphrosunē thnētē*), dispensing miserly benefits of a mortal kind, engenders in the soul which is the object of its attachment a meanness (*aneleutheria*) which is praised by the majority as a virtue, and so will cause it to wallow mindlessly around and under the earth for nine thousand years."[26]

Plato is bringing all his big guns, social and eschatological, to bear upon the nonlover's position. The young *kaloi kagathoi* whom he was trying to persuade of the excellence of philosophy liked to think of their actions, whether in the gymnasia or elsewhere, as manifesting *megaloprepeia, eleutheriotēs,* and similar qualities characteristically favored by the members of leisured groups. In Athens, these qualities were in part shown by the giving of lavish gifts by *erastai* to *erōmenoi* with whom they were "in love." Anyone who wishes to persuade another of the choiceworthiness of an action or a way of life must necessarily begin from premises which the other is willing to accept, and then demonstrate that acceptance has consequences which the other had not previously realized. Plato, himself an aristocrat, favored the general connotations of *megaloprepeia* and *eleutheriotēs,* but not the interpretations of the behavior appropriate for the *megaloprepēs* then current in the gymnasia. Consequently, he offers a new account of *erōs,* madness and the gifts which the philosophical *erastēs* will give to his *erōmenos,* an account which, in Plato's view, will escape all the dangers of the former one.

The problem that has bedeviled most interpretations of the "speech of Lysias" arises from the assumption that, Plato being a moral philosopher, his criticism of the nonlover must be made on moral grounds, in some sense of "moral" instantly comprehensible to the modern reader. In consequence, "Lysias" must be not only advocating the sexual mores of the Athenian gymnasia but canvassing the claims of a particularly cynical version not only of the relationships of the gymnasia but of the whole of human life. In fact, as we have seen, "Lysias'" goal was to promote civic harmony and to advocate the kind of behavior that would be likely to sustain long-term sexual and other relationships of any kind. In the circumstances, the treatment meted out to "Lysias" seems a trifle hard.

NOTES

1. I follow the practice of Sir Kenneth Dover in *Greek Homosexuality* (Cambridge, Mass.: Harvard University Press, 1978) in retaining the Greek words *erastēs* and *erōmenos.* It will be apparent to any reader that this article is deeply indebted to Dover's work.

2. *The Collected Dialogues of Plato Including the Letters,* edited by Edith Hamilton and Huntington Cairns. Bollingen Series 71 (Princeton: Princeton University Press, 1961), 475.

3. R. Hackworth, *Plato: Phaedrus* (Cambridge: Cambridge University Press, 1952), 27.

4. It may appear fanciful to link this with Socrates' claim that he would "walk to Megara and back" with the inducement of hearing Lysias' speech. But Socrates had not left Athens along with the democrats during the rule of the Thirty, and this fact evidently increased suspicion of Socrates, however courageous his

behavior in opposing the Thirty may have been (*Apology* 32c4–d8, etc.). Plato rarely misses an opportunity—in fact, he often creates them—to try to rehabilitate Socrates. (I propose to discuss this topic on another occasion.)

5. He could of course compose an epideictic speech, like the one Plato attributes to him in the *Phaedrus,* either to be delivered *in propria persona* or as a commission.

6. As has often been noted, there is no possible dramatic date for the *Phaedrus.* See, for example, Dover, *Lysias and the Corpus Lysiacum,* (Berkeley and Los Angeles: University of California Press, 1968) and C. J. Rowe, *Plato's Phaedrus* (Warminster: Aris and Phillips, 1986).

7. In my translations of the speech of the nonlover I have tried to express the frequently colorless expressions and vaguenesses of the original. Plato may be trying to represent the diction of someone not in the throes of passion; the modern reader may interpret *ta pragmata* and "mutual advantage" in terms of the financial situation of the nonlover and conclude that some kind of financial arrangement is being proposed. As we shall see, this is not the correct interpretation.

8. Presumably because while the passion is at its height no one can try to control the lover by reasoning with him. Note again the vagueness of *toiouton pragma* and *toiautēn sumphoran.*

9. The meaning of *beltistos* here requires some explanation. In what sense is the "best lover" best? A frequent use of *agathos* and similar words is to commend social prominence, prosperity, and good family. This sense would be appropriate to Lysias' argument, and well contrast with *epitēdeiotatos,* "most suited" (to your social position, character, and temperament).

10. In Plato's *Charmides* 155aff. the youth Charmides is exercising in another part of the gymnasium. Socrates wishes to talk to him, and asks Critias, his guardian and cousin, to ask Charmides to join them. Charmides is said to be now old enough to do so, at all events in the presence of a close relative. Critias assents, but changes the message, and asks Charmides to come to be examined by a doctor. (Charmides had been complaining of headaches.) As a member of the Thirty in later life, Charmides, like Critias, showed himself to be a greedy and bloodthirsty tyrant; but at the dramatic date of the *Charmides* he was a very respectable youth of a very good family. Had he received a peremptory summons to join a group of older admirers and would-be lovers, delivered while he was exercising with his contemporaries and peers, there would have been comment from them immediately and from those to whom they gossiped later. A summons to see a doctor or a trainer, however, would be quite proper.

11. *Dialegesthai* is the ordinary Greek word to denote conversation. There is no allusion to Socrates in particular.

12. The train of thought is not immediately clear, and I have found none of the comments of the editors convincing. Hackforth (29, n. 1) supposes that "the non-lover counts it to his own advantage that the boy should be admired by others and so kept in a good humour." This is still not very clear. Dover (not commenting on this passage) mentions hero worship as a possible motive for the behavior of an *erōmenos*. This would account for youths clustering round, for example, a famous general, but not for several generals clustering around the same

handsome youth out of motives which the nonlover would regard as beneficial to himself.

13. Hackforth renders this phrase by "your general personality," Rowe by "the other aspects of his personality." Whether the genitive plural is masculine or neuter is unclear. Possibly Plato intended the lack of clarity, since in the Greek situation both make sense and reinforce each other. A prospective *philos* would concern himself both with the other members of the family and with the family's material situation. (I doubt whether Hackforth is right to treat the phrase as virtually synonymous with *ton tropon*. The phrase admittedly might be a hendiadys, but the ambiguity suggested here brings out more of the situation of Greek *philoi*.)

14. This is clarified by the passages of "Theognis" discussed below.

15. Hackforth claims that Lysias wishes to reduce all relationships to the calculation of personal advantage interpreted in the most cynical manner possible, so that he is utterly unable to explain the love of parents for children. Lysias, in fact, is concerned to make proposals about one kind of relationship only. He takes it for granted that the love of parents for children exists and uses this fact to argue against the lover's claims.

16. Eumaeus the swineherd is rebuked by Antinous for inviting a beggar (the disguised Odysseus) to the suitors' feast; and Eumaeus' reply indicates that he shares Antinous' values in this respect (*Odyssey* 17, 374–391, especially 387).

17. For further discussion, see A. W. H. Adkins, "'Friendship' and 'Self-Sufficiency' in Homer and Aristotle," *Classical Quarterly* 13 (1963): 30–45.

18. All Greek *philia* is reciprocal. See ibid.

19. "Well-being" always included the possession of material goods (at the level appropriate to the families concerned) and in political families would also include political advantage. In some cities, if the family searching for a spouse belonged to the ruling aristocracy, membership of that aristocracy would be assumed to be a necessary qualification for that spouse to possess. The *Theognidea* furnishes vivid and graphic indications of what might happen in a polis when some members of its ruling aristocracy abandoned the criterion of birth when choosing spouses.

20. For an incident in which actual fighting for friends against enemies was necessary, see Demosthenes, *Against Euergus*.

21. Pausanias' speech in Plato's *Symposium* (esp. 182aff.) suggests that the mores may have differed from polis to polis; but the present generalization will suffice here.

22. Here evidently *kakos* and *deilos* are used to decry the group opposed to the old aristocrats of Megara. For discussion and additional context, see, for example, Arthur W. H. Adkins, *Merit and Responsibility: A Study in Greek Values* (Oxford: Clarendon Press, 1960, and Chicago: University of Chicago Press, 1975).

23. This poem is discussed in Arthur W. H. Adkins, *Poetic Craft in the Early Greek Elegists*, (Chicago: University of Chicago Press, 1985), 142–53. The poet does not state bluntly that Theognis is Cyrnus' lover and that Cyrnus has betrayed him, but there are strong hints.

24. This may well also be the motive, or one of the motives, for Plato's intro-

duction of Cephalus, Lysias' father, and his views on money and justice, into the first book of the *Republic;* but the question is too large to discuss here.

25. The existence of the criticism is not essential to my case; but Plato seems to me not the kind of philosopher who delights in setting up straw persons for the sake of knocking them down.

26. The words in quotation marks are from the translation of C. J. Rowe, *Plato: Phaedrus* (Warminster: Aris and Phillips, 1986). "Nine thousand years" refers to the lot of the *psuchē* in the eschatological myth just related by Socrates.

A Toast to Arthur Adkins

David Grene

THERE IS NO NEED, it seems to me, to dwell on the contribution Arthur
has made to classical scholarship. No need, when one looks at the great
size of the audience that has come to honor him today. There can be very
few classicists in the United States, and even in the English-speaking
world, who would command so much attention and approval among
those of his own profession. *Merit and Responsibility* is certainly one of
the very significant books dealing with social and moral issues in the classical world, issues that reach out of that classical world to every culture
since that day to now. Equally certainly, the commentary on the Elegiac
poets is one of the great philological achievements of modern classical
scholarship. So, as I said, it would only be an impertinence in me to talk
further of Arthur's contribution to scholarship in writing.

What I much prefer is to give you all an idea of what I have known
Arthur to do in regard to students and a little of how generously and
warm-heartedly he has helped me in my own work. Arthur has never
spared himself in teaching the students who are formally in Classics. But
in addition, out of his good will and belief in his subject and its future, he
has helped many of his students in Social Thought. He has frequently
borne a major share in reading their theses. I can think of three such
within the last six or seven years. Not only has he been willing to super-
intend their written papers, done for regular classes of his, but he has
taken them in with his own students in Classics into his private reading
group, studying one author or another of special interest to them or him.
I know of no other disinterested means so effective in enhancing the excitement and joy which should inhere in the study of classics than the plain

Professor Grene proposed this toast at a banquet for Arthur Adkins on the evening of
April 8, 1994.—Editors.

evidence of the same sort of excitement and joy in their teachers—and there is no evidence for this better than, on top of all the work that it is *necessary* for someone in Arthur's position to do, that he is willing to take on this extra teaching.

For my own part he has very often been the final authority in delicate matters of translation and interpretation. Let me give you a single example (and luckily in this audience I do not have to *explain* too much about the quoted passage). In the piece about the birth of Cyrus in Herodotus 1.111 the historian describes how the shepherd who has been summoned by Harpagus to take the baby Cyrus away and destroy him returns to his home with the child. Then follows "His own wife had been in labor all that day and during this time (*tote kōs kata daimona tiktei*) had given birth." Now the question is how to render *kata daimona*. Some of the translations give: "As Providence ordained" or "As Fate decreed." I very much disliked the shopworn vagueness of that sort of expression for the elusive daimōn, but I thought that "as God would have it," which is how I wanted to render it, might be to overtranslate. So I called Arthur up and asked him did he think that Herodotus would have permitted himself such a blatant expression of meaning as I wanted. He hesitated for a moment— remember I had just directed his attention to the passage and he had no other preparation for my question, save that Arthur very rarely forgets any passage he has ever read with attention and never without the capacity to enter it in his total interpretation of his author. He eventually said: "No, I think you are safe in that translation with *Herodotus;* but it helps that he adds that *kōs,* 'somehow or other.' He is instinctively drawing attention to the hesitancy he experiences about the birth and the moment of it 'according to God's will.'" So my translation contains "as God would *some-how* have it." I was interested to note that the other two translations I happened to consult had also ignored the *kōs,* as I initially had done. It is the kind of inner sense of an author's meaning, grasped in a single phrase, that makes Arthur invaluable as critic or helper.

He read the whole translation of the *Oresteia* done by Wendy Doniger and myself with minute care, and his criticisms have nearly always won out with us. Again, such generosity of time and attention are very rarely to be had, rendered simply as help to another's work.

If one is a teacher of classics, a not quite ordinary position, I think, in the modern world—at any rate one that frequently carries a sort of bewildered recognition in the minds of even educated men and women— I find one acquires a somewhat unnatural, if not morbid, interest in one's fellow professionals. Are they admirable or the reverse? Do I think they cheer me up by being what they are in their job—when I am in that job as well? I have great reason for admiring Arthur as teacher and scholar—but also as man. The courage and tenacity of those long years of fighting illness, and winning against it, as the teaching and writing prove, are beyond praise or indeed emulation. But they are not beyond intense respect and admiration and that I am quite sure not only I but you accord him—

Arthur Adkins

A BIBLIOGRAPHY OF THE PUBLISHED WRITINGS OF ARTHUR W. H. ADKINS

BOOKS

Merit and Responsibility: A Study in Greek Values. Oxford: Clarendon Press, 1960; Chicago: University of Chicago Press, Midway Reprint, 1975.

La Morale dei Greci da Omero ad Aristotele. Italian translation of *Merit and Responsibility* by Riccardo Ambrosini with the assistance of Armando Plebe. With an introduction by Armando Plebe. Biblioteca di Cultura Moderna. Bari: Casa Editrice Gius. Laterza & Figli, 1964. Reprinted with a new introduction by Armando Plebe. Biblioteca Universale Laterza. Rome: Gius. Laterza & Figli Spa, 1987.

From the Many to the One: A Study of Personality and Views of Human Nature in the Context of Ancient Greek Society, Values, and Beliefs. London: Constable; Ithaca: Cornell University Press, 1970.

Moral Values and Political Behaviour in Ancient Greece. London: Chatto and Windus; Toronto: Clarke, Irwin, 1972.

Poetic Craft in the Early Greek Elegists. Chicago: University of Chicago Press, 1985.

The Greek Polis, edited with Peter White. Vol. 1 of *University of Chicago Readings in Western Civilization,* edited by John W. Boyer and Julius Kirshner. Chicago: University of Chicago Press, 1986.

Human Virtue and Human Excellence: Papers arising from an NEH Summer Seminar on Ancient Greek Values and Modern Values, edited with Joan Kalk and Craig Ihara. New York: Peter Lang, 1991.

ARTICLES

"'Honour' and 'Punishment' in the Homeric Poems." *Bulletin of the Institute of Classical Studies* 7 (1960): 23–32.

"Heidegger and Language." *Philosophy* 37 (1962): 229–37.

"'Friendship' and 'Self-Sufficiency' in the Homeric Poems and in Aristotle." *Classical Quarterly* 13 (1963): 30–45.

"Aristotle and the Best Kind of Tragedy." *Classical Quarterly* 16 (1966): 78–102.

"Basic Greek Values in Euripides' *Hecuba* and *Hercules Furens*." *Classical Quarterly* 16 (1966)193–219

"Greek Religion." In *Historia Religionum: Handbook for the History of Religions,* edited by C. Jouco Bleeker and Geo Widengren, 1: 377–441. Leiden: Brill, 1969.

"*Euchoma, Euchōlē,* and *Euchos* in Homer." *Classical Quarterly* 19 (1969): 20–33.

"Classical Studies: Has the past a Future?" *Didaskalos* 3 (1969): 18–35.

"Threatening, Abusing, and Feeling Angry in the Homeric Poems." *Journal of Hellenic Studies* 89 (1969): 7–21.

"The Use of Tape-Recorded Material in Teaching the Classics: A Report on One Method." *Didaskalos* 3 (1970): 227–39.

"Clouds, Mysteries, Socrates, and Plato." *Antichthon* 4 (1970): 13–24.

"Homeric Values and Homeric Society." *Journal of Hellenic Studies* 91 (1971): 1–14.

"Truth, *Kosmos,* and Aretē in the Homeric Poems." *Classical Quarterly* 22 (1972): 5–18.

"The Ghost of Classics Yet to Come." *Didaskalos* 4 (1972): 3–17.

"Homeric Gods and Values of Homeric Society." *Journal of Hellenic Studies* 92 (1972): 1–19.

"*Aretē, Technē,* Democracy, and Sophists: *Protagoras* 316B–328D." *Journal of Hellenic Studies* 93 (1973): 3–12.

"Meaning, Using, Translating, and Editing." *Greece and Rome* 21 (1974): 37–50.

"Art, Beliefs, and Values in the Later Books of the *Illiad*." *Classical Philogy* 70 (1975): 239–54.

"Merit, Responsibility, and Thucydides." *Classical Quarterly* 25 (1975): 209–220.

"The *Aretē* of Nicias: *Thucydides* 7.86." *Greek, Roman, and Byzantine Studies* 16 (1975): 379–92.

"Paralysis and *Akrasia* in Eth. Nic. 1102bl6 ff." *American Journal of Philogy* 97 (1976): 62–64.

"*Polupragmosunē* and 'Minding One's Own Business': A Study in Greek Social and Political Values." *Classical Philology* 71 (1976): 301–27.

"Callinus 1 and Tyrtaeus 10 as Poetry." *Harvard Studies in Classical Philology* 81 (1977): 59–77.

"Lucretius I, 136 ff., and the Problems of Writing *Versus Latini*." *Phoenix* 31 (1977): 145–58.

"*Theoria* versus *Praxis* in the *Nicomachean Ethics* and *Republic*." *Classical Philology* 73 (1978): 297–313.

"Laws versus Claims in Early Greek Religious Ethics." *History of Religions* 21 (1982): 222–39.

"Values, Goals, and Emotions in the *Iliad*." *Classical Philology* 77 (1982): 292–326.

"Divine and Human Values in Aeschylus' *Seven against Thebes*." *Antike und Abendland* 28 (1982): 32–68.

"Orality and Philosophy." In *Language and Thought in Early Greek Philosophy*, edited by Keven Robb, 207–27. The Monist Library of Philosophy. LaSalle, Illinois: Hegeler Institute, 1983.

"Form and Content in Gorgias' *Helen* and *Palamedes*: Rhetoric, Philosophy, Inconsistency, and Invalid Argument in Some Greek Thinkers." In *Essays in Ancient Greek Philosophy*, edited by John P. Anton and Anthony Preus, 2: 107–28. Albany: State University of New York Press, 1983.

"The Connection between Aristotle's *Ethics* and *Politics*." *Political Theory* 12 (1984): 29–49.

"Cosmogony and Order in Ancient Greece." In *Cosmogony and Ethical Order: New Studies in Comparative Ethics*, edited by Robin W. Lovin and Frank E. Reynolds, 39–66. Chicago: University of Chicago Press, 1985.

"Ethics and the Breakdown of Cosmogony in Ancient Greece." Ibid., 279–309.

"Gagarin and the 'Morality' of Homer." *Classical Philology* 82 (1987): 311–22. (A reply to Michael Gagarin, "Morality in Homer," which appeared in the same issue.)

"*Theoria* versus *Praxis* in the *Nicomachean Ethics* and the *Republic*." In *Schriften zur aristotelischen Ethik*, edited by Christian Mueller-Goldingen, 427–43. Olms Studien, vol. 7. Hildesheim: Olms, 1988. (Appeared originally in *Classical Philosophy* 73.)

"Human Nature in the Philosophical Ethics of Ancient Greece and Today." In *The Proceedings of an International Conference: As Humanidades Greco-Latinas e a Civilzação do Universal*, 337–69. Coimbra: Instituto de Estudos Clássicos, 1988.

"Plato." In *Ethics in the History of Western Philosophy*, edited by Robert J. Cavalier, James Gouinlock, and James P. Sterba, 1–31. New York: St Martin's Press, 1989.

"Greek Religion." In *The New Encyclopaedia Britannica*, 15th ed., 784–91, 801–2. Chicago: Encyclopaedia Britannica, Inc., 1990. (A revision of the article published in *Historia Religionum*.)

"Myth, Philosophy, and Religion in Ancient Greece." In *Myth and Philosophy*, edited by Frank E. Reynolds and David Tracy, 95–130. Albany: State University of New York Press, 1990.

"The Connection between Aristotle's *Ethics* and *Politics*." In *A Companion to Aristotle's Politics*, edited by David Keyt and Fred D. Miller, Jr., 75–93. Oxford: Blackwell, 1991. (An adaptation of the paper published in *Political Theory* 12 [1984].)

"The Sage of New Lanark and the Sage of Stagira: Ignorance and Culpability in Aristotle and Robert Owen." In *Law and Philosophy: The Practice of Theory: Essays in Honor of George Anastaplo*, edited by John A. Murley, Robert L. Stone, and William T. Braithwaite, 1: 164–83. Athens, Ohio: Ohio University Press, 1992.

"The Homeric World." In *The Self and the Political Order: Readings in Social and Political Theory*, edited by Tracy B. Strong, 25–46. New York: New York University Press 1992. (An abridgment of the second chapter of *From the Many to the One* [1970].)

"Homeric Ethics." In *A New Companion to Homer*, edited by Ian Morris and Barry Powell. Leiden: Brill, forthcoming.

REVIEW ARTICLES

Greek Popular Morality in the Time of Plato and Aristotle, by K. J. Dover. *Classical Philology* 73 (1978): 143–58.

Reason and the Human Good in Aristotle, by J. Cooper. *Ethics* 88 (1978): 266–71.

The Greek Concept of Justice from Its Shadow in Homer to Its Substance in Plato, by E. A. Havelock. *Classical Philology* 75 (1980): 256–68.

Mind and Madness in Ancient Greece: The Classical Roots of Modern Psychiatry, by Bennett Simon. *Ethics* 91 (1981): 491–98.

BOOK REVIEWS

Moral Values in the Ancient World, by John Ferguson. *Classical Review* 10 (1960): 50–52.

La figura di Ettore è l'etica dell' Iliade, by L. Quaglia. *Journal of Hellenic Studies* 81 (1961): 159

Sprachliche Deutung als Triebkraft platonischen und sokratischen Philosophierens, by C. J. Classen. *Journal of Hellenic Studies* 81 (1961): 187–88.

Order and History, by E. Voegelin, vols. 2–3. *Journal of Hellenic Studies* 81 (1961): 192–93.

Problems of Historical Psychology, by Zevedei Barbu. *Classical Review* 12 (1962): 300–301.

Hubris: A Study of Pride, by Robert Payne. *Classical Review* 12 (1962): 323.

Anthropology and the Classics, by Clyde Kluckhohn. *Gnomon* (1962): 300–302.

Göttliche und menschliche Motivation im homerischen Epos, by A. Lesky. *Journal of Hellenic Studies* 84 (1964): 159–60.

Les origines de la pensée grecque, by Jean-Pierre Vernant. *Classical Review* 14 (1964): 65–66.

Popular Ethics in Ancient Greece, by Lionel Pearson. *Classical Review* 14 (1964): 70–72

Hauptrichtungen des griechieschen Denkens, by Fritz Wehrli. *Ghomon* (1965): 529–32.

Plato and the Individual, by Robert William Hall. *Classical Review* 16 (1966): 28–31.

Arete bei Platon und Aristoteles, by Hans Joachim Krämer. *Classical Review* 16 (1966): 31–34.

Ananke: Untersuchungen zur Geschichte des Wortgebrauchs, by Heinz Schreckenberg. *Classical Review* 16 (1966): 68–70.

Myths of the Greeks and Romans, by Michael Grant. *Classical Review* 16 (1966): 78–79.

Kikeron kai Platonike Ethike, by Knostantinos Ch. Grollios. *Classical Review* 16 (1966): 119.

Prometheus—Archetypa I Image of Human Existence, by C. Kerény. *Classical Review* 16 (1966): 122–23.

Religions du salut. Annales du Centre d'Étude des Religions, vol. 2. *Classical Review* 16 (1966): 123.

Der religiöse Allbegriff des Aischylos, by Wolfgang Kiefner. *Gnomon* (1968): 610–12.

Sōphrosynē, Self-Knowledge and Self-Restraint in Greek Literature, by Helen North. *Gnomon* (1968) 712–13.

Death, Fate, and the Gods: The Development of a Religious Idea in Greek Popular Belief and in Homer, by B. C. Dietrich. *Classical Review* 18 (1968): 194–97.

Seers, Shrines, and Sirens: The Greek Religious Revolution in the Sixth Century B.C., by John Pollard. *Classical Review* 18 (1968): 197–98.

Some Traces of the Pre-Olympian World in Greek Literature and Myth, by E. A. S. Butterworth. *Classical Review* 18 (1968): 198–200.

Survival of Some Tribal Ideas in Classical Greek, by Borivoj Borecký. *Classical Review* 18 (1968): 321–22.

The Clashing Rocks: Early Greek Religion and Culture and the Origins of Drama, by Jack Lindsay. *Classical Review* 18 (1968): 344–45.

L'éternel féminin dans la religion méditerranéenne, by Uberto Pestalozza. *Classical Review* 18 (1968): 357.

Enter Plato: Classical Greece and the Origins of Social Theory, by Alvin W. Gouldner. *Philosophical Quarterly* 18, 73 (1968): 360–61.

Mythe et pensée chez les Grecs: études de psychologie historique, by Jean-Pierre Vernant. *Classical Review* 21 (1971): 80–82.

Dionysus, Myth, and Cult, by Walter F. Otto. *Classical Review* 21 (1971): 147–48.

Syngeneia: la parenté de l'homme avec Dieu d'Homère à la patristique, by Édouard des Places. *Classical Review* 21 (1971): 148–49.

Les maîtres de la vérité dans la Grèce archaïque, by Marcel Detienne. *Classical Review* 21 (1971): 220–22.

The Oracles of Zeus, by H. W. Parke. *Classical Review* 21 (1971): 235–37.

La Religion des Grecs, by Roland Crahay. *Classical Review* 21 (1971): 238–39.

Megaloprepia bei Platon, by Rudolf Stein. *Classical Review* 21 (1971): 290.

Der Neid in der griechischen Philosophie, by Ernst Milobenski. *Classical Review* 21 (1971): 293–94.

Ideales de la Formación Griega, by José S. Lasso de la Vega. *Classical Review* 21 (1971): 294.

Sophia und Kosmos: Untersuchungen zur Frügeschichte von sophos und sophia, by Burkhard Gladigow. *Classical Review* 21 (1971): 391–93.

Ancient Views on the Nature of Life, by Hans Regnéll. *Classical Review* 21 (1971): 403–5.

Saggio sul misticismo greco, by Dario Sabbatucci. *Classical Review* 21 (1971): 445–46.

The Socratic Paradoxes and the Greek Mind, by Michael J. O'Brien. *Philosophical Quarterly* 21, 82 (1971): 74.

A History of Greek Philosophy, vol. 3: *The Fifth Century Enlightenment*, by W.K.C. Guthrie. *Philosophical Quarterly* 22, 89 (1972): 357–58.

Greek Science after Aristotle, by G. E. R. Lloyd. *Journal of European Studies* 3 (1973): 389.

The Ancient Concept of Progress and Other Essays on Greek Literature and Belief, by E. R. Dodds. *Journal of Hellenic Studies* 95 (1975): 221–22.

The Justice of Zeus, by H. Lloyd-Jones. *Journal of Hellenic Studies* 95 (1975): 229–30.

Persephone: Three Essays on Religion and Thought in Magna Graecia, by Günther Zuntz. *Classical Review* 25 (1975): 239–41.

Intellectual Experiments of the Greek Enlightenment, by Friedrich Solmsen. *Phoenix* 31 (1977): 262–65.

Zeus and Hera: Archetypal Images of Father, Husband, and Wife, by C. Kerényi. *Classical Review* 28 (1978): 287–89.

Plato and Greek Painting, by Eva C. Keuls. *Phoenix* 35 (1981): 289–91.

The Presocratic Philosophers, by Jonathan Barnes, 2 vols. *Classical Philology* 78 (1983): 68–70.

Morality and the Inner Life: A Study in Plato's Gorgias, by Ilham Dilman. *Ethics* 93 (1983): 406–8.

From Myth to Icon: Reflections of Greek Ethical Doctrine in Literautre and Art, by Helen F. North. *Ancient Philosophy* 4 (1984): 249–51.

Isis among the Greeks and Romans, by Friedrich Solmsen. *History of Religions* 23 (1984): 385–87.

The Theory of Will in Classical Antiquity, by Albrecht Dihle. *Classical Philology* 80 (1985): 364–70.

Aristotle's Theory of Moral Insight, by Troels Engberg-Pedersen. *Journal of the History of Philosophy* 23 (1985): 581–83.

Plato, Prehistorian: 10,000 to 5,000 B.C. in Myth and Archaeology, by Mary Settegast. *Ancient Philosophy* 12 (1992): 185–86.

Ethics with Aristotle, by Sarah Broadie. *Classical Philology* 88 (1993): 349–53.

AIDOS: The Psychology and Ethics of Honour and Shame in Ancient Greek Literature, by Douglas L. Cairns. *Ethics* 105 (1994): 181–83.

Hybris: A Study in the Values of Honour and Shame in Ancient Greece, by N.R.E. Fisher; *Shame and Necessity*, by Bernard Williams; *AIDOS: The Psychology and Ethics of Honour and Shame in Ancient Greek Literature*, by Douglas L. Cairns. *Classical Journal* 90 (1995): 451–55.

NOTES ON CONTRIBUTORS

ARTHUR W. H. ADKINS was Edward Olson Professor of Classical Languages and Literatures, New Testament and Early Christian Literature, the Ancient Mediterranean World, Philosophy, University of Chicago.

WENDY DONIGER is Mircea Eliade Professor of the History of Religions, University of Chicago.

CHARLES GRAY is Professor of History and Lecturer in Law, University of Chicago.

DAVID GRENE is Professor Emeritus in the Committee on Social Thought, University of Chicago.

ROBERT B. LOUDEN is Professor of Philosophy, University of Southern Maine.

STEPHANIE NELSON is Lecturer in Core Curriculum, Boston University.

MARTHA NUSSBAUM is Professor of Law, Literature, and Ethics, University of Chicago Law School.

RICHARD POSNER is Chief Judge, United States Court of Appeals for the Seventh Circuit, and Senior Lecturer, University of Chicago Law School.

PAUL SCHOLLMEIER is Associate Professor of Philosophy, University of Nevada, Las Vegas.

CANDACE VOGLER is Assistant Professor of Philosophy, University of Chicago.

JAMES BOYD WHITE is L. Hart Wright Professor of Law, Professor of English, and Adjunct Professor of Classical Studies, University of Michigan.

Bernard Williams is Monroe Deutsch Professor of Philosophy, University of California, Berkeley.

Lee Yearley is Walter Y. Evans-Wentz Professor of Religious Studies, Stanford University.

INDEX

Walcot, Peter, 31 nn. 3, 5, 6
Waltz, Pierre, 32 n.12
Watson, William, 62 n.2
West, M. L., 17, 27, 31 n.3, 32 n.9, 34 n.22, 35 n.33, 36 n.37, 38
White, James Boyd, 4
Wild Duck, The (Ibsen), 49, 59
Williams, Bernard, 3, 11, 88 n.16, 89 n.19, 158 nn. 2, 5
Winkler, John J., 10, 174, 175, 183, 211 n.77
Wittgenstein, Ludwig, 46–47, 87 n.9, 129 n.4
women: Aristotle on inequality of, 203; in Athens, 203; female domination in warlike societies, 217 n.124; female-female homosexuality, 175–76, 203, 208 n.44; misogyny and Greek attitude toward homosexuality, 203; Pandora, 26, 32 n.13, 38; Plato on educating, 203; as passive, 176, 192, 197, 198; prostitution, 176, 177, 187, 227; Sappho, 174, 175; Socrates engaging in philosophical questioning, 210 n.66; in Sparta, 203. *See also* marriage
Women of Trachis, The (Sophocles), 50–52; Deianeira, 50–51, 54; Heracles, 50, 51; Hyllus, 51, 60; necessity in, 51; *Oedipus Tyrannus* and *Philoctetes* compared with, 50
Works and Days (Hesiod), 17–42; the Erides, 17, 26; as a farmer's handbook, 17, 31 n.6; on farming, 18–21, 36–37; Hesiod's case with Perses, 23, 25, 26, 27, 29, 30, 34 n.24, 41; introductory myth, 26; judicial sense of *dikē* in, 22–24, 33 n.20, 34 n.21, 37; on justice and farming, 25–27, 29–30; on justice as balance, 21–22, 29, 38; justice's positive side in, 27–31; key linking words in, 23; on lucky and unlucky days, 24, 34 n.22; myth in, 5–6, 42; as *sui generis*, 25–26; *Theogony* compared with, 17; topics discussed in, 17; on what it feels like to farm, 18–19, 36–37; as a Zeus poem, 31 n.5

Xenophon: on Achilles and Patroclus in Homer, 209 n.54; on arranged marriage, 233; on homosexual desire, 207 n.35, 211 n.74; Socrates view on homosexuality represented by, 181, 182; as source of information on Socrates, 180

Yearley, Lee, 3, 11

Zeus: and the five Ages of Man, 39–40; Hesiod on justice as the will of, 26–27; Hesiod on morality as the will of, 8, 30; making human life hard, 26–27, 38–39; necessity in acts of, 51; and Pandora, 26, 38; on passionate longing, 188; *Works and Days* as a Zeus poem, 31 n.5